Life, Death, and Entertainment in the Roman Empire

Life, Death, and Entertainment in the Roman Empire

D.S. Potter and D.J. Mattingly

Ann Arbor

THE UNIVERSITY OF MICHIGAN PRESS

Published in the United States of America by
The University of Michigan Press
Manufactured in the United States of America
⊗ Printed on acid-free paper

2002 2001 2000 4 3

A CIP catalog record for this book is available from the British Library.

Library of Congress Cataloging-in-Publication Data

Life, death, and entertainment in the Roman Empire / D. S. Potter and D. J. Mattingly.
p. cm.
ISBN 0-472-10924-3 (acid-free paper)
ISBN 0-472-08568-9 (pbk. : acid-free paper)
1. Rome—Civilization. 2. Rome—History—Empire, 30 B.C.—476 A.D.
I. Potter, D. S. (David Stone), 1957– II. Mattingly, D. J.
DG272 .L54 1998
937'.06—dc21 98-40201
CIP

Preface

The current volume is the product of two phenomena. One is the growth of interest in all aspects of the Roman world among nonclassicists, especially as manifested by the large numbers of nonclassicists who chose to take courses on classical civilization. The other is the United States Supreme Court decision in the so-called Kinko's case, which vastly complicated the production of large photocopied "course packs" that have been used to place a wide variety of readings before such audiences in U.S. universities. The great value of the course pack was that it enabled instructors to place up-to-date work before their students, allowing them to discuss the subject in conformity with the current state of their discipline. But for legal reasons, it now behooves members of the academy to seek alternative formats. This book and its projected companion volume, *Bondage and Domination in the Roman Empire,* offer possible models for that presentation.

In the course of the last several decades, classicists have tried to make their material accessible to all who are interested in it through volumes of translated sources and a variety of monographs, increasingly specialized, on specific aspects of ancient social history. With the advent of software that has made the use of electronic media far more flexible for classroom use, the production of yet another "source book" in print format seems to us to be redundant. Our experience of teaching broad survey courses in Roman social history has shown the need for materials that set translated sources in a wider context and that cover a wider range of topics and approaches than the traditional single-authored monograph. Meeting this need was one of the greatest merits of the course pack and forms the rationale behind this book. With its mixture of teaching tools, the present volume is intended to offer a reasonably coherent, though still diverse, range of approaches.

The structure of this volume, and a companion volume, has evolved out of the experience of teaching a particular course in classical civilization at the University of Michigan, and hence many of the authors have a Michigan connection. But the books are not intended to represent a prescriptive Michigan view of the subject—indeed, there is great diversity of opinion among those authors with connections to the University of Michigan—and it is hoped that the collection will prove of great value to teachers of Roman social history and classical civilization at many different levels and institutions. Through the combination of specially commissioned essays and established "classics" (which will appear in the companion volume rather than in this one), it is hoped that the books also provide viable models for how to fill the gap that the course-pack crisis has left behind.

We would like to thank Jill Wilson, the copy editor for this volume, for her fine work on the manuscript.

Contents

Figures

A Note on Papyrological and Epigraphic Sources

Information about the Roman world derives from many kinds of evidence. Each form of evidence, be it archaeological, from the manuscript tradition, papyri, or inscriptions also has its own rules of presentation and publication. We hope that references to archaeological and literary works in the text and the notes are easy to follow up as they are. The same cannot always be said in the case of inscriptions and papyri for which somewhat specialized conventions have developed.

Papyri

The Romans and those who lived in the Roman provinces surrounding the ancient Mediterranean used rolls of papyrus and individual sheets cut from the rolls as a common writing material. The papyrus plant grew principally in the Nile delta of Egypt, and Egypt was the main center for the making of this ancient equivalent to paper. The documents written on papyrus that survived to modern times have been unearthed mainly in Egypt and in other desert areas of the eastern Mediterranean; papyri have also survived in more humid climates when carbonized through exposure to fire, such as in the ancient town of Herculaneum in the Bay of Naples, buried during the eruption of Vesuvius in A.D. 79. There were other materials that frequently received writing, such as pieces of broken pottery called "ostraca," wooden and waxed tablets, strips of metal, and sheets of leather, the finest of which was "vellum." With an ever increasing intensity since the end of the nineteenth century, papyrologists have been studying these examples of ancient writing, not only deciphering and explaining what was written several millennia ago but also clarifying the ancient context that produced the text, whether private letter, tax receipt, government circular, or list. These documents open up a direct and immediate contact with the ancient world, as we read messages certainly intended for other eyes than our own.

By 1998 nearly 40,000 such documents have been deciphered and published; most of the volumes edited in the United States and England include English translations of texts that have much to tell about life in the Roman world. The titles of papyrus volumes are routinely referred to in abbreviated form, as with the sources for the letters exchanged among Aline, Apollonios, Eudaimonis (and others in their circle) that are translated in the chapter on the Roman family. Abbreviations for papyrological collections are identified, together with full publication data that often give a hint as to the volume's contents, in J.F. Oates, R.S. Bagnall, W.H. Willis, and K.A. Worp, *Checklist of Editions of Greek and Latin Papyri, Ostraca, and Tablets*, 4th edition (Atlanta 1992) (= *BASP* Supplement 7). New papyri continue to be unearthed and those already in library collections are constantly being published: an up-to-date version of the *Checklist of Editions* is maintained on the WWW by Duke University (http://odyssey.lib.duke.edu:80/papyrus/), a site that also provides information about the papyrus collection at Duke, as well as access to similar sources of information on papyri to be found on the WWW. The Kelsey Museum of Archaeology, University of Michigan, frequently features in its on-line exhibitions materials from Roman Egypt (http://www.umich.edu/~kelseydb/Exhibits.html#current).

The *Checklist of Editions* contains nine different sections in which abbreviations of various kinds are explained: the first section deals with papyri; the second, ostraca and tablets; and the third, corpora (or specialized collections). The abbreviation for most volumes containing papyri begins with "P.," followed by either the place in the United States or Europe where the papyri are housed, the site in Egypt, or elsewhere in the Near East, where the papyri were found, or the name of the ancient person who figures most prominently in the papers. Thus, *P.Giss.* refers to papyri housed in Giessen, Germany, and *P.Brem.* refers to papyri housed in Bremen, also in Germany; in both volumes commentary and translations are in German. Interesting series with commentary and translations in English are: *Michigan Papyri* (= *P.Mich.*), currently totaling eighteen volumes; the *Oxyrhynchus Papyri* (= *P.Oxy.*), named after the town in Egypt where they were unearthed and currently totaling sixty-four volumes; the (Greek) Documents from the Bar Kochba period in the Cave of Letters (= *P.Babatha*) are named for Babatha, a Jewess who fled with her papers to a cave near the Dead Sea as the revolt drew to its bloody finale. Ostraca and tablets are named according to the same principles, although their abbreviations begin with "O." and "T.," respectively; for the collection of wooden tablets found near Hadrian's Wall in the north of England, see the two volumes *Vindolanda Writing Tablets* (= *T.Vindol.*). A volume of papyri on a common theme and drawn from many collections is often called a "Corpus" and the abbreviation, for the most part, begins with "C."; thus, *CPJ* = *Corpus Papyrorum Judaicarum,* a three-volume series pertaining to the Jews living in Hellenistic and Roman Egypt, with commentary and translations in English. Those who would like to learn more about papyri may want to begin with R. Bagnall, *Reading Papyri, Writing Ancient History* (London, 1995).

Inscriptions

Several hundred thousand inscriptions on stone or bronze have survived from all parts of the classical world and all periods from the invention of the alphabet in the eighth century B.C. onward. The ubiquity of the habit of inscription makes epigraphy, as the study of inscriptions is called, an extraordinarily valuable tool for the study of the classical world. Inscriptions preserve texts as varied as epitaphs on tombstones, rules for associations, texts of laws, decrees in honor of individuals, dedications of buildings, milestones, dedications to the gods, expressions of pride, of sorrow, of love. They reveal to us forms of Greek and Latin that we would otherwise have lost and the lives of people from all parts of the ancient world.

While the value of this evidence was recognized well before the beginning of the nineteenth century, it was in the course of the last century that institutional support for the systematic cataloguing of these inscriptions came into being. The principal nineteenth century projects, cataloguing Greek inscriptions from Greece in the series *Inscriptiones Graecae* (*Inscriptions of Greece,* abbreviated *IG*) and Latin inscriptions from all over the Roman Empire (the *Corpus Inscriptionum Latinarum,* the *Corpus of Latin Inscriptions* or *CIL*) have never been completed nor can they be as the constant discovery of texts means that any comprehensive effort is dated by the time that it can be printed. They are organized by location, and for each location the inscriptions are divided by type.

In the late nineteenth and early twentieth centuries four large collections, offering samples of Greek and Latin inscriptions were assembled (all of them still very useful and equipped with excellent notes). These are W. Dittenberger's *Orientis Graeci Inscriptiones Selectae* 1–2 (*Select Inscriptions of the Greek East* or *OGIS*) and his *Sylloge Inscriptionum Graecarum* i–iv³ (*Collection of Greek Inscriptions* or *SIG*³), R. Cagnat's *Inscriptiones Graecae ad Res Romanas Pertinentes* (*Greek Inscriptions Relating to Roman History* or *IGR*) and H. Dessau's *Inscriptiones Latinae Selectae* i–iii (*Selected Latin Inscriptions* or *ILS*). These collections are valuable not only because they make particularly interesting texts readily available but also because of the brief but extremely intelligent annotation that accompanies each text. There are three annual reviews of epigraphic publication, the *Bulletin épigraphique* (*BE*), *Supplementum Epigraphicum Graecum* (*SEG*) both for Greek inscriptions and *L'Anné épigraphique* (*AE*) for Latin inscriptions.

In addition to the larger collections, there are numerous collections of inscriptions by topic, date, or location, varying enormously in size and shape. L. Robert, *Les gladiateurs dans l'orient grec* (*Gladiators in the Greek East*) and L. Moretti, *Iscrizioni agonistiche greche* (*Greek Agonistic Inscriptions*) are, for instance invaluable resources for the study of Greek and Roman public entertainment both because of their presentation of the texts and the excellent discussions of each text in the commentaries that they offer; V. Ehrenberg and A.H.M. Jones, *Documents Illustrating the Reigns of Augustus and Tiberius* (E&J) while invaluable for the range of documents, offers no commentary at all. Those who would like a more extensive, though manageable, introduction to the use of inscriptions for Roman history may want to refer to L. Keppie, *Understanding Roman Inscriptions* (Baltimore, 1991).

Introduction

David S. Potter

The Roman empire was the product of violence. In the early fourth century B.C., the citizens of Rome recovered from a humiliating encounter with a Gallic war band—which had captured their city and compelled them to pay a large ransom—to initiate a period of aggression that concluded with the conquest of the Italian peninsula. Italy, at that time, was a unity only in the eyes of outsiders. The word *Italia* is Greek, and the region that it described was divided by geography, custom, and language into numerous, diverse communities. By the end of the fourth century, while linguistic and cultural divisions remained, the Roman state, claiming divine approbation for its actions, had reduced most of the geographic region to dependency on itself. Peoples who had been defeated in battle had been compelled to surrender territory and to join a system of alliances that the Romans had devised to ensure both their own security and their ability to mobilize overwhelming force against any foe.

In the course of the third century B.C., Rome completed the conquest of Italy and then engaged in two great wars with Carthage, the Phoenician settlement in North Africa that had, for centuries, controlled the sea lanes of the western Mediterranean and contended with the Greek states of Sicily for the domination of that island. The first of these wars was fought primarily in Sicily and on the surrounding waters, as Rome created, virtually overnight, a naval capacity that was as impressive as the force that it controlled on land. The second war with Carthage was fought in Italy itself, as Hannibal the Carthaginian sought to undo the Roman system of alliances. When Hannibal's efforts were met with stalemate despite massive victories in the field, the main theaters of operation were transferred to Spain, which Hannibal's family had developed as a base to support operations in Italy, and then in North

Africa itself. By 200 B.C., the Roman state was in control of the former Carthaginian lands in Sicily (as well as those territories of the formerly independent Greek states on the island), Sardinia, Corsica, and Spain. Carthage lost its hegemonic position on the coast of North Africa, being now hemmed in by a powerful Numidian state that was largely the product of Roman policy. It was also in 200 B.C. that Rome turned its attention to the east. Despite centuries of cultural contact, Rome had shown little interest in the eastern Mediterranean, and its first moves onto the east coast of the Adriatic had been prompted by Italian concerns. Now, however, as Philip V of Macedon had allied himself with Hannibal in Rome's darkest hours and then completed a treaty with Rome just before the final campaigns to humble Carthage, Rome had other interests. Philip was defeated by 197 B.C., and Rome became a major player in the politics of the eastern Mediterranean.

The second century B.C. witnessed Rome's acquisition of unparalleled hegemonic power in the eastern Mediterranean. Only choosing to establish direct control after experiments of indirect domination had failed, Rome had reduced the kingdoms of the Hellenistic world, the amalgam of states that had sprung up after the death of Alexander the Great in 323 B.C., to effective subordination. Peace was not thereby forthcoming. The acquisition of empire led to class conflict in Italy, and large portions of the population became alienated from the government of the Roman state, dominated as it was by a small class of office-holding nobles.

The Mediterranean world of the first century B.C. was awash with blood, enduring conflicts whose fury and attendant devastation knew no parallel in its past history. One result was the acquisition of vast new territories, with virtually all of the Mediterranean rim, those portions of Europe south of the Rhine and Danube Rivers along with those portions of the Near East west of the Euphrates River and the eastern rim of the Anatolian plateau, coming under direct Roman rule. As these conquests were being completed, the empire also acquired a new government, with power passing from the quasi-democratic institutions that had supported the office-holding oligarchy to a single man. First Sulla (81–78 B.C.), then Caesar (49–44 B.C.), and finally, after years of civil war, Caesar's grandnephew and heir, the emperor Augustus (31 B.C.–A.D. 14), emerged triumphant. The great accomplishment of Augustus was the creation of a monarchy that, despite periods of instability, brought a remarkably coherent administration to the region that had been acquired under the Republic and in the course of his long reign.

The last ruler in the administrative, though not biological, line begun by Augustus did not perish until 1452 A.D., in the capture of Constantinople (thereafter Istanbul) by the Turks, and it is arguable that the last heir of Rome's direct political legacy ceased to exercise those functions in 1806 A.D., when Napoleon compelled the king of Austria to lay aside the title of Holy Roman emperor. Although monarchy may appear a silly, or outmoded, form of administration to modern eyes, it is the oldest form of government among the developed states of the earth, and until this century, it was the most widespread.

What, then, was this system of Roman government? In the period covered by this volume, the central institutions of the Roman state were the palace, the army, the population of the city of Rome, and the administrative aristocracy, defined by the senatorial and equestrian orders. Senators were those aristocrats of sufficient means (defined under Augustus as property valued at 1,200,000 sesterces—henceforth HS, the standard Roman abbreviation for the coin that was the basic unit of exchange—or roughly twelve hundred times the average income of a day laborer) who held the traditional Republican offices that offered access to military and other provincial offices. Equestrians possessed property (again under the Augustan dispensation) of 800,000 HS and, if they chose to, could serve in the palace bureaucracy, the army, or offices connected with the central administration.

The palace very rapidly became an enormous institution. Augustus inherited vast resources from Caesar, and he supplemented them through the acquisition of even greater estates during the civil wars and, after that, through legacies received from other aristocrats. The emperor's personal holdings in the provinces required their own bureaucracy, consisting primarily of the emperor's slaves, freedmen (ex-slaves), and equestrians. His personal treasury, or *fiscus*, likewise required administrators, and its resources were required not only to pay those administrators but also to fund the emperor's luxuries, to provide gifts (to communities and individuals) that were regarded as the obligation of any important person, and, from time to time, to supplement the resources of the state treasury. The emperor also required a substantial office staff to handle the enormous range of communication that he received. The officials of this staff, whether of slave or free birth, came rapidly to attain a status that put them on a par with the most important members of the administrative aristocracy. Furthermore, the emperor had to have his own army, in the form of the Praetorian Guard, albeit in this case an army funded by the state treasury.

The emperor was both an aristocratic magnate in his own right (easily the richest person in the Mediterranean world) and the chief administrative official of the state. The overwhelming majority of Rome's soldiers served directly under the command of officials who were his technical subordinates (a point made plain by the fact that their victories were held to reflect his relationship with the gods), and he possessed the authority to issue binding orders in every part of the empire. In Rome, he possessed powers, descended from those of Republican magistrates, that enabled him to dictate, if he should choose, the actions of other magistrates. But he was not all-powerful. He was bound by social convention to treat others with respect, and breakdowns in his relationship with either the administrative aristocracy or members of the palace staff were often fatal.

The Roman administrative aristocracy was extraordinarily open. Within a century of the victory of Augustus, the aristocracy that had dominated the Republic for centuries, ensuring its own continuation through a wide variety of family-planning strategies, had virtually disappeared. Membership of the ruling class subsequently extended to the aristocracy of Italy and then to that of the provinces. Galba (A.D. 68–69) was the last descendent in the male line of a family that had won numerous consulships under the Republic.

The administrative aristocracy's openness to outsiders sets the Roman empire apart from the imperialist endeavors of later European history. No Indian raja could have aspired to become viceroy of India, and no tribal leader could aspire to a seat in the British Parliament or the German Reichstag, but Lusius Quietus, a tribal chieftain from North Africa could, with success, aim at the consulship. A descendant of North African provincial aristocrats, Septimius Severus, could (and did) become emperor (A.D. 193–211). The class whose style of self-definition is the subject of Professor Gleason's chapter in this book was a truly pan-Mediterranean group, bound together by an amalgam of shared cultural assumptions. This class separated itself, both culturally and economically, from the great mass of peasants on whose backs its fortunes were supported.

Romanization is a very complicated phenomenon. The people of the empire participated in "Romanness" in very different ways. Latin was still an unusual language in many parts of the empire in the third century A.D.; native languages were still to be heard everywhere, and Roman governors were expected to hold court in Punic and Aramaic as well as Latin and Greek (*Digest* 45.1.1.6). The fact that the upper class was largely bilingual in Greek and Latin is likewise of great importance, as is the fact that the standard of their linguistic perfection was measured against books written centuries earlier rather than the language of the streets. It would be as if we would now expect our leaders to speak with the language of the King James version of the Bible when addressing us. You could tell an aristocrat as soon as he opened his mouth, even if he were swimming naked next to you in a bath. The linguistic attainments of the aristocracy facilitated the creation of a common, urban, cultural idiom that existed in stark contrast to that in the countryside or streets and that was, to varying degrees, resented by many who could not participate to the fullest degree.

No urban population was nearly so potent as that of Rome. Rome was an enormous city, with a population of around a million people, whose demands distorted the economic pattern of the entire Mediterranean world. As a group, the inhabitants of Rome could exercise great influence simply by virtue of the physical proximity of the emperor. The emperor was expected to ensure that the inhabitants of the capitol were fed and entertained. If he failed in this task, they could (and occasionally did) riot. The emperor's personal army, the Praetorian Guard, was not in Rome to act as a police force. It was there to provide him with a preponderance of deadly force in an emergency.

It is commonly assumed that the Roman food-supply system was only or primarily concerned with the shipment of cereals to Rome for free distribution. The evidence presented by Aldrete and Mattingly in their contribution to this book suggests that the system was more broadly based on a range of foodstuffs, some subject to free distribution, others, perhaps, to price-fixing agreements. And in the end, it was not limited to Rome itself. The control of food marked the emperor in the eyes of his subjects. As one fourth-century historian put it, he could bring grain from diverse places to those in need (Ammanus Marcellinus *History of Rome* 14. 7.5), and those who sought his favor might do so through offers of food to support his legions on the march. Public munificence in the cities of the Mediterranean world was not only a matter of games and amusements; it was also a matter of eating. Public sacrifices were often accompanied by public feasts well before the emergence of the Roman monarchy, and all cities that could do so had some mechanism for regulating the supply of foodstuffs. But the size and scale of these operations changed under the emperors.

The impact of Rome on the development of local economies cannot be quantified, but it is nonetheless perfectly obvious. For instance, North Africa attained unprecedented capacity to produce agricultural surplus for export, and in Southern Spain similar developments are obvious. The economy that evolved in the centuries after Augustus may have its closest parallels in the mercantilist world of preindustrial Europe, where agricultural surplus was transformed into new wealth through an enhanced capacity to export it. And as was often the case in preindustrial Europe, it seems likely that money made in trade might form the basis of a fortune in landed property. Aristocrats were supposed to be seen to be rich but were not supposed to be seen as making money.

The administrative apparatus of the Roman state was, for much of the period covered in this volume, remarkably small. Rome's success in governing its empire stemmed from its ability to mobilize local government to fulfill its basic needs. Of these needs, the most important was the provision of tax revenue to the state treasury. Taxes were of many sorts, reflecting the diverse needs of the state. Collected either in cash or produce, the flow of revenue could be diverted to a wide variety of uses, and although we cannot be completely certain of this, it is likely that much of what was collected did not travel very far from its point of origin. Although there were grain fleets carting food to Rome, there were no complementary treasure fleets bearing hoards of gold and silver.

One of the great gaps in our knowledge of the Roman empire is precisely where all the tax revenue really went and how much there actually was. On the basis of analysis of income and expenditure, it is possible to estimate the imperial budget at around 1,000,000,000 HS a year, somewhat over half of it taken up by the army (a relatively small proportion by the standards of premodern states), and another quarter by the supply of Rome. Salaries of provincial officials were presumably moved through provincial banks. Coins to pay the army came from imperial mints in the provinces. The actual amount of coin that was needed is impossible to determine with precision, because Roman soldiers received a portion of their salary in produce and were subject to large deductions for the purchase of their equipment. Transactions based on reductions in pay do not require coins. Provinces that had large armies and paid the bulk of their taxes in coin (e.g., Pannonia in the Balkans or Syria in the east) would probably not see much of that money leave the province. Coin did not travel great distances in the Roman empire, though bullion from mines controlled by the emperor might, to be minted into coin where and as it was needed. The picture that is beginning to emerge is of an empire consisting of a number of discrete economic zones linked by the fact of imperial administration and in some, but not all, cases by the needs of large urban areas for agricultural surplus.

In the premodern and modern worlds, European colonization had a distinctively religious component. The conquerors brought their religion with them and encouraged the conquered to participate in it, sometimes with a great deal of violence. One of the crucial points connected with the religious system of the city of Rome is that it stayed at Rome. The intricate series of rituals that characterized the religion of the capitol city or most any other religion were not readily transferable. The most obvious counterexample to this statement proves the rule. Judaism did spread far from its geographical roots in Palestine, but Judaism came to be based on scripture, a way of life prescribed in a book. The Roman state offered no books of scripture.

The Romans did not impose a system of worship on their subjects. The religious practices of the Roman people were similar to those of most people in the Mediterranean world in that they were based on a highly proactive view of the gods, whose presumed interest in the details of human existence was staggering. But there were no common set texts, and it was recognized that all places had their own ways of communicating with divinities. The divine club was not exclusive. New members could be admitted, new gods could come to Rome, and Roman gods could be exported with Romans to the provinces. Unless a specific practice (e.g., human sacrifice) was felt to be particularly abhorrent, the Romans did not insist on the abolition of indigenous practice. In those cases where it did ban a practice, the Roman state did not insist on the exclusive worship of the Roman pantheon.

Religious intolerance, when it appeared, was a function of public safety. The Roman obsession with ritual performance is a feature of a system intended to safeguard the state from random divine action. As long as the proper forms were maintained, the gods appear to have been bound by an implicit agreement to ensure Roman success. Failure to respect the will of the gods led to catastrophe, and this is one context for the sporadic persecution of the Christian church, an activity that, paradoxically, appears to have strengthened the Christian sense of communal identity. The concept of "witnessing" to the truth of Christ's revelation through the endurance of torture, prison, and death appears very early in Christian dogma (the word *martys* in Greek means "a witness"). It is plainly established by the time that Luke wrote his account of Stephen, the "protomartyr," in (probably) the nineties A.D. (*Acts* 7.29–60), even without using the word *martys* in that sense; while at roughly the same period, Clement of Rome did use the word of Peter and Paul, who had met their end under Nero (54–68 A.D.) (*Letter to the Corinthians* 5.4–5). Conduct that was rebarbative to the imperial authorities would appear self-evident in a cult celebrating the divinity of a person who had been executed by order of an imperial official. But that was not all. You could call whoever you wanted to a god, and that might simply be regarded as being a little (or a lot) strange. But to do so while denying that the gods of the state should receive worship raised the very obvious question as to whether your very presence in a community did not constitute, in and of itself, an affront to the gods. Opinions remained mixed on this subject up until the fourth century A.D., when the conversion of Constantine to Christianity marked the beginning of a new age in the intellectual history of the West.

The Christian concept of "witnessing" is not, however, to be explained simply within the church. As it developed, the concept was intimately related to the style with which justice was administered in the empire. As a result of the coincidental preservation of many accounts of martyrdom, we are able to study this phenomenon as an act of government as well as of faith.

One aspect of Roman imperial government, as we have seen, was the co-optation of the highest provincial aristocracy. Another was the monopolization of extreme force by the agents of the central government. The tax collector who was afraid of his reception in some upland villages might ask the governor for a few soldiers to help him make his point (Pliny *Letters* 10. 27). The governor was himself in constant motion, traveling from district to district within his province to hold court. His annual appearance brought the reality of Roman power before the eyes of Rome's subjects with especial force. Trials were public events, and the torture of defendants in criminal cases was routine and did not take place in a dungeon, removed from public view. Rather it was a public event, for all to see, hear, and smell. Governors were frightening people. One of the worst things that you could do to a local rival was to have him investigated, since that could result in torture or worse. The penalties that the governor could inflict were horrific: crucifixion, while not a Roman invention, is one of the most lasting images of Roman power in the Western world. Prior to the affixing of an individual to a cross, that person would be subject to a harsh flogging, either with rods or whips (of which there were a wide variety, the most fearsome being the *plumbum,* or whip with lead weights). If crucifixion were not the sentence, it might be exposure to the beasts in the arena (often accompanied by a variety of tortures) or burning at the stake. A wealthy person might get off with simple decapitation. What these penalties have in common (aside from being intensely painful) is that they were all carried out in public, acts of social vengeance against a person who had offended societal norms. In this sense it is perhaps not surprising to find them in the context of public entertainment. Roman public entertainments were celebrations of the social order and the shared culture of the elite, offered for the delectation of the masses. The celebration of common culture could be through positive assertion, the display of famous athletes, theatrical performers, gladiators, or charioteers. Or it could be negative, involving the taking of vengeance on those who offended.

The power of the state was thus brought home through exemplary action. It was the Roman state that made it possible for people in Syria to enjoy entertainments that had their origin in Greece or Italy, for people in Turkey to watch contests between humans and wild animals. No provincial display could ever match the glamour of one at Rome, but they could offer all a taste of the splendor of the capitol. Rome could not possibly govern its empire without resort to spectacles of this sort.

It was control of the Mediterranean that enabled Rome to communicate with its subjects, the openness of the upper class to provincials that enabled Rome, alone of the preindustrial empires in this region, to avoid the construction of local dynasties through the regular circulation of governors and to create a competitive atmosphere between cities and within cities, for which the governor was the referee. The central government conditioned tastes and then controlled access to the rewards that it had made most desirable. But this was not the whole story. There was always the army, garrisons linked by a system of roads that could not be closed for long periods of time by the weather.

Roman roads were the marvel of preindustrial Europe. Marked every mile with a statement of imperial domination in the form of a milestone, they were symbolic of the imperial presence. But any student of the military history of premodern Europe sees another aspect as well. The movement of large numbers of troops over dirt roads rapidly destroys the road, especially when undertaken in the rain. Napoleonic campaigns could literally bog down in knee-deep mud. The internal movement of the legions was not subject to such constraints as long as they stayed on the roads that had been constructed for their movement.

In 1776, Edward Gibbon described the Roman army as the institution that had created the empire, and the one institution that could destroy it. His perception was correct. The army was the ultimate instrument of violence, the power behind the facade of civil government. Rome's subjects would never forget that its army was there, even as it transformed itself from a symbol of conquest to one of protection. One purpose of the army was to conquer new territories; the other was to defend civilization from the forces of barbarism that pressed on the boundaries of the empire. Idealized pictures of the empire had it bounded by rivers and the ocean or, in the second and third centuries, as an armed camp. Complaints that the army was rarely used for offensive purposes after the reign of Augustus could be countered by the argument that all the world worth conquering was already under Roman control. But whether it served to protect or conquer, the army remained an institution separate from civilian life. In Augustus' day we find that the soldiers or veterans were, possibly for the first time, recognized as a special group within the citizen body. They were professionals who would never return to the life of the average civilian, even when they retired with bounties, again institutionalized by Augustus, that would make any man who survived a twenty-five-year tour of duty wealthy by the standards of the normal person.

Military service was for young men; its institutions were intended to enhance their aggressiveness. The army of the Republic appears to have been dominated by a doctrine that demanded decisive battle. Soldiers were trained to maintain their cohesion on long hot afternoons under conditions of great personal danger, following officers drawn from the upper classes who were expected to lead from the front. Pity was not a virtue: when the enemy turned in flight, it was time to strike him down; when a city was captured, it was not unknown for Roman generals to order their men to kill every living thing within it. After Augustus, as the mission of the army changed, it acquired greater capacity for other sorts of conflict, for "dirty wars" on the frontier, wars of attrition against barbarians, or brutal operations to suppress a revolt.

Killing was a very personal thing. Missile weapons might injure an enemy and sometimes killed one, but the main burden of destruction fell on the individual soldier in hand-to-hand combat. It was his job to drive his sword into the body of his foe, watch him die, and proceed, very likely covered in his enemy's blood, to kill another. The extremely personal, physical nature of killing demanded intense training, and the young men who were brought into this environment were taught that their ultimate duty was to their comrades, cut off from long-term relationships with women, and, to some degree, dehumanized.

It appears to have been a commonplace that untrained men should not be led into battle. Training exercises were calculated to transform a young man into precisely the kind of killer that the nature of combat demanded, and we are told that in the civil war of 43 B.C., newly recruited legions stood aside and watched as three veteran legions fought it out (Appian *Civil Wars* 3.68). The new troops obviously had no chance against such men, and their officers evidently knew it. Another truism was that the Roman army in battle resembled the Roman army on training exercises, with blood added. Roman soldiers liked to attack, and at times their generals would have trouble restraining them. Even Caesar, whose army was possibly the best in Roman history, lost control on two occasions, with his troops either launching an attack before he ordered it or failing to halt one when they ought to have. It appears to be the case in the modern age that something less than 50 percent of the troops engaged in combat actually take offensive action. The stress on discipline and intense training in hand-to-hand combat in the Roman army may reflect an effort to correct a similar situation.

Discipline was harsh, flogging a routine camp punishment. Other penalties, left up to the creativity of a commanding officer, involved standing for long hours, a diet of inferior food, or the requirement to encamp in dangerous areas. Penalties could be either individual or collective, and the most severe involved direct participation by the soldiers themselves. A unit guilty of gross dereliction of duty could be decimated, lots being drawn so that every tenth man was subject to a death penalty, inflicted by the members of the unit who had escaped his fate. The sentence was carried out by clubbing the unfortunates to death, and our evidence shows that this penalty, attested in accounts of the Republic, was in use after Augustus (Suetonius *Life of Augustus* 24; Tacitus *Annals* 3.21).

There was an odd democracy to punishment. In A.D. 14, after a mutiny by the legions in Dalmatia had fallen apart in the wake of an eclipse of the moon, which soldiers had taken as an omen of the ultimate failure of their endeavors, those who had been most active in the revolt were killed either by their officers and members of the general's personal guard or by their comrades (Tacitus *Annals* 1.30). In the same year, after a revolt by the Rhine garrison had been suppressed, "the legions stood in the meeting with their swords drawn, and when each accused was brought before the tribunal; if they called out that he was guilty, he was killed immediately, and the soldiers were pleased by the deaths, as if they were themselves absolved of guilt" (Tacitus *Annals* 1.44). At another site, the general in command sent the men who were loyal to attack those who were not. No officer, we are told, stepped in to stop the slaughter until the troops had exhausted themselves (Tacitus *Annals* 1.49). In the civilian world similar attitudes seem to have prevailed, as publicity was an essential feature of a trial, and the crowds that had assembled to watch a trial would shout out their feelings about the case. The difference here was that members of the crowd would then sit back and watch rather than involve themselves in the actual infliction of damage.

Prior to the end of the second century, soldiers were not permitted to marry while on service. The issue has often been taken as a peculiarity in Roman law, especially as soldiers had many privileges not enjoyed by civilians. Moreover, it was inevitable that soldiers would form relationships and produce children, leading to a number of legal anomalies. Why did the ban endure if it could not prevent the formation of affectionate liaisons; if it created a class of people with an unusual legal status, causing emperors to bend other laws in order to accommodate the children and partners of soldiers; and if complaints had begun to surface a generation after the legions had acquired relatively fixed quarters? The answer may lie in the language of the historian who tells us that the ban was lifted, for he says that marriage was thought to be among practices that were "alien to military discipline and prompt readiness for action" (Herodian *Roman History* 3.8.5). The emperor who lifted the ban, Septimius Severus (193–211), depended on the army to hold the throne that he had claimed in civil war, and thus he gave in to the pressure that had been building. Soldiers were meant to be devoted first and foremost to their comrades; attachment to others divided loyalties and made soldiers more difficult to move about, since they would either want to bring their families with them or create difficulties if they thought that they were leaving them in danger (transfer far from the home camp was a penalty for rebellion in the fourth century and caused great unhappiness in the third). Augustus and his successors down to Severus clearly thought that, whatever the difficulties, it was better to try and keep soldiers focused on life in camp and cut off from life outside of it.

The ban on marriage was thus intended to maintain separation between the army and the surrounding population. Even where the army was quartered in or near cities, as in the eastern provinces, or when cities developed around camps, as in the west, the army remained detached from ordinary civilian life. It was, as some modern scholars would have it, a "total institution," with its own rules; the legions were societies with their own habits. Women who dealt with soldiers could not do so on an equal footing, and we may well be entitled to imagine a class of camp prostitutes, possibly servicing the legions at the ratio of 1:48 that we find in British India, where a similar separation of the occupying European army obtained. The pent-up sexual energy of the military may well have been a serious problem: one Jewish text suggests that if a woman were captured by brigands, it was not a necessary assumption that she had been raped; it was if she had been seized by soldiers. And the problem did not involve only women. While, as Gleason shows, Roman aristocratic society was deeply ambivalent on the subject of same-sex intercourse, Roman military society may have been rather less so. As long as soldiers were not passive partners, a blind eye may well have been turned to their depredations on the boys of the provinces. In one case we know that the commander of a detachment that turned up in a district near the mouth of the Rhine demanded young men for his pleasures (Tacitus *Histories* 4.14). Tacitus, who tells this story, records the event with disapproval, but it is not likely to have been the first or last time that it happened. The inherent inequality of sexual relationships between soldiers and provincials was paralleled in other ways. Soldiers could be billeted in the houses of civilians (something that civilian communities dreaded), and they could force civilians to carry their burdens for them on the march. The New Testament parable urging the faithful to "go the second mile" is based on the fact of forced transport. The threat of military occupation that hung over the heads of provincials was thus not simply that soldiers would show up in their town but rather more that they would show up in their houses, taking whatever it was that they desired.

The great paradox in Roman domination is the dichotomy between assimilation and force. Acquiescence in Roman rule brought real benefits, and the regime was open to its subjects in ways that are unparalleled in other imperial societies of European history. Refusal to abide by the social contract implied by the imperial regime was met with extraordinary brutality, and the army was the ultimate arbiter of internal order. Rome reshaped the Mediterranean world, unifying regions that were never before, or since, so closely linked. It poured forth a constant and coherent ideology of power, and the fact of the emperor's existence was plain wherever a person turned. Time was measured according to his years in power; the face of a Roman emperor was in a person's hands whenever he or she engaged in a monetary transaction; he was commemorated at any public gathering and in the center of every town. Whatever their ultimate ethnic origin, the inhabitants of the empire were bathed in the shared culture of Romanness. Rome governed through institutions that concentrated attention on the agents of the central authority, the ultimate referees in internal disputes. It did so with a relatively small army, but with an army nonetheless. Rome offered security in return for obedience. When it failed to provide that security, and it did, the seeds of the dissolution of the empire were sown next to those sprouting from a population that had reached the limits of ecological possibility.

The Present Contribution

The story of Roman domination can be examined from a wide variety of perspectives. In the first part of this volume we have chosen to deal with issues connected with the ordering of the basic human experience: life, death, childhood, marriage, and the social construction of the model person and/or family. In the second and third parts of the book, the contributions are concerned more with the ordering of the world of the public person—with the nature of religious belief, the impact of empire on the economy of the Mediterranean world, the structures of entertainment and leisure activities.

The essays in this book are concerned with life in only a brief period of the history of the Roman monarchy, even though they are concerned with a period of some three hundred years, and though the demographic conditions described by Bruce Frier obtained in Europe until the industrial revolution and in other parts of the world somewhat longer, before the medical revolution of nineteenth-century Europe began to have a substantial impact. The reason for this limitation (aside from practical concerns) stems from the fact that the Roman world was itself subject to profound intellectual and administrative changes in the course of the fourth century A.D. Efforts to chronicle those changes would have resulted in an unmanageable volume.

Frier's analysis of the demography of the Roman empire raises a series of profound questions to which the other essays in this volume contribute a variety of answers. Chief among these issues is the way that people functioned in the face of the harsh realities of their existence. While in the Roman empire average life expectancy, the demographer's basic measure of a society's welfare, may have hovered at levels that were comparable with those of the Neolithic period, no one would confuse the Roman Mediterranean world with that of the late Stone Age. Greg Aldrete and David Mattingly show how the economic patterns of this world were transformed by the fact of Rome (more on this anon), while David Potter's discussion of the religion of Rome illustrates a system of thought that human beings felt gave them some control over the uncontrollable. The extraordinary expenditure on public entertainment that is the subject of the last two essays in this book reveals another way in which the inhabitants of the Roman world were drawn together through the pursuit of pleasure. The period covered by those two essays saw the emergence of a shared environment of pleasure that was supported by the fabric of urban life and the Roman government. Maud Gleason's contribution examines the psychology of the aristocratic society that dominated this urban society, demonstrating a cultural fascination with the external person, a cultural emphasis on the point that people were what they did, public benefaction being one critical way for a man to prove his worth. At the same time, people worried that what you saw was not what was really there, that the external facade might conceal some deep internal failing, that there was not a perfect unity between the public and private person.

Ann Hanson looks behind the numbers that Bruce Frier has now made central to the study of Roman social and economic history. What was it like for a woman to live with the expectation that half of her children might die before they learned to walk? What impact did the patriarchal structure of Roman family life have on social relations within the household? What was it like to be a child? What impact did low life expectancy have on the development of personal bonds within the family? There are no simple answers here, and we are constantly reminded that our evidence must come from various sources, the documentary record as well as the literary, and from different levels of society. The Egyptian girl who married in her late teens to a man a few years older than herself would have a very different experience of marriage than the wealthy Roman girl who was joined at the age of twelve to a gentleman old enough to be her father.

The experience of childhood was clearly a very important one. Hanson shows that there was a clear concept of childhood as a phase of development in the Roman world. Likewise, she shows a wide range of deep emotional attachment between family members of all ages. In a society where divorce was a relatively simple operation, a successful marriage had to be an emotionally fulfilling one. But it was rarely a long one by modern standards, as the harsh realities of the demographic regime would mean that a successful marriage would end when one or the other partner was still in his or her thirties. Hence Professor Hanson concludes that "the flexibility inherent in Roman notions of family fostered a sense of continuity that not only extended from one generation to the next but united family members with the spirits of their ancestors, as the living celebrated festivals of remembrance for the dead and the dead awaited the living in the family tomb."

Another question raised by Bruce Frier is the impact of the long imperial peace on the overall health of the population. From a demographic perspective, the peace brought by Rome may have allowed the overall population of the geographic region encompassed by the empire to reach the limit of the "carrying capacity" of the land—that is to say, the inherent, if hard to define, ecological limit of the population. A population reaching the limit of the land's carrying capacity tends to be unhealthy, the great majority of people living close to or at the subsistence level. This population level, compounded by the much greater ease of movement around the Mediterranean world, would make the population more susceptible to disease. The seeds of the fall of the Roman empire thus lay in its very success—not because of some internal moral rot that stemmed from the political system as Edward Gibbon suggested in his powerful and still important *Decline and Fall of the Roman Empire,* but rather because it could not analyze and control the factors that were basic to its health.

PART ONE

Social Structures and Demography

CHAPTER ONE

The Roman Family

Ann E. Hanson

Familia and *Family*

Although the Roman word *familia* is the antecedent of our English word *family* and although both words can be used to refer to father, mother, and children, living together in a single household, various circumstances contribute to the fact that the notions we attach to the word *family* as the twenty-first century begins share few features in common with the Roman familia—whether we look to the privacy and closeness the modern home can afford the nuclear family, to the relatively egalitarian status of both parents in the family's legal and economic dealings, or to modern mortality functions that have drastically lowered infant and early-childhood deaths and have significantly extended the average life span among adults.[1] The Roman household often embraced not only parents, children, and other relatives in the male

The following essay has no pretensions to originality, and I hope only to provide a clear, but brief, summary of those aspects of the Roman family that seem to me particularly important. Footnotes offer suggestions for further reading, and most studies mentioned are in English; a modern work is normally mentioned only once, although many will prove useful for a number of the topics considered here. I have made my own translations for passages quoted in the text. The footnotes often refer to other English translations from ancient writers and documents, cited by number from two useful collections: N. Lewis and M. Reinhold, eds., *Roman Civilization,* vols. 1 (*Republic and Augustan Age*) and 2 (*Empire*) (New York, 1990), cited as L-R I and L-R II; and Lefkowitz and Fant 1992, cited as L-F.

1. A good overview of the Roman family is in Saller 1994, 71–101; useful for retrieving ancient sources is Fayer 1994; a collection of passages from ancient authors in English translation is in Gardner and Wiedemann 1991; cf. also the energetic discussion in Veyne 1987. Bradley 1991 fleshes out the minor figures of the *familia;* for the most visible families see Corbier 1991.

Fig. 1. The necropolis of Isola Sacra on one of the roads leading out of Ostia. Those buried in the necropolis were once residents of Ostia, as was typical of such "cities of the dead." The tombs provide a focal point for commemoration of the departed. They are modeled on the houses of the living and recall the status of the families—in this case largely working-class people, a number of whom advertise their professions in reliefs and inscriptions affixed to the tombs. (Photo and reconstruction courtesy of Dr. B. Harvey.)

line of descent but slaves and freed or free dependents that were not kin at all. Family members with blood ties sometimes lived together in a multigenerational household, yet it was also common for a grown son to establish an independent domicile for his wife and children. Household configuration knew many other forms as well. In death, however, the familia of kin and nonrelated dependents recongregated to share space forever in the family's tomb. Legal status, economic wealth and political class, age, and gender determined one's position within the power structure of the hierarchically ordered Roman household. The typical house-tombs of the Principate that line major roads leading from urban areas often bear the names and portrait busts of prominent family members on their austere, outer facades. The lavish decorations on the interior likewise focus on those who were dominant family members in life; those who played subservient roles were allotted less space also in death, and dependents, freedmen, and slaves were relegated to a niche in the wall for an ash urn and a small memorial plaque to cover it. Racial origins and level of education might influence the manner and intensity with which a member of the familia participated in its affairs and activities, with the slaves, the freed, and the women being particularly valued for their acquired skills.

The word *familia* might also be used to refer to the principal residence of the Roman family, its *domus,* or to the family's subsidiary properties (scattered over wide areas in the case of the wealthy), to the slaves who staffed the properties and labored in the family's fields, and even to the animals and movable possessions in the various residences.

The Roman Name

The oldest living male—the *paterfamilias*—was legally empowered with the right of life and death over all members of the familia; he controlled familial wealth and property, not only for minors, females, and slaves, but for adult sons and daughters as well, unless specific steps of manumission were taken to remove the father's authority from his sons or unless his authority over a married daughter was transferred to her husband and his authority over slaves was transferred to a new master or to freedom through manumission. After the early Republic, the name of every member of the household except the wife, *materfamilias,* reflected the name of the paterfamilias—a name that consisted of three elements, the *tria nomina*.[2] The first element in the Roman man's name was the *praenomen,* with a group of some seventeen praenominal names accounting for 99 percent of male Romans during the Republic. *Aulus* (Aul.), *Gaius* (C.), *Gnaeus* (Cn.), *Decimus* (D.), *Tiberius* (Ti.), *Titus* (T.), *Lucius* (L.), *Marcus* (M.), *Publius* (P.), *Quintus* (Q.), and *Sextus* (Sex.) were the most common. So insignificant a part of the name was the praenomen that it was usually abbreviated and was seldom used alone outside the confines of the family, because it failed to distinguish a man from the many others with the same praenomen. Of course, within the family, both a father and the eldest son often bore the same praenomen, but it would be intoned differently, depending on who was speaking to whom. Surely, the wife would make it clear by her tone of voice whether she meant her husband Marcus or her growing boy Marcus. The few very distinctive praenomina employed only in certain aristocratic families, such as *Appius* in the Claudian family or *Kaeso* in the Quinctian family, did serve to distinguish those who bore them in the world outside the family. The second element was the gentilitial, or clan, name, the *nomen*—such as *Julius, Claudius, Cornelius, Aemilius, Sempronius, Domitius,* and *Fabius*—and it was borne by all male children in the patrilineal line of descent. It was the *nomen* that distinguished a man from his fellows. With increasing frequency in the later Republic and in the Empire, however, a *cognomen* was added to distinguish branches within the larger clan, or *gens;* examples are *Caesar, Pulcher, Scipio, Paullus, Gracchus, Ahenobarbus,* and *Maximus.* Many cognomina give the impression of having been the nicknames of particular men before they were employed as formal names by descendants: examples are *Pulcher,* "Handsome"; *Ahenobarbus,* "Bronze Beard"; *Maximus,* "Greatest"; *Cicero,* "Chickpea"; *Verrucosus,* "Warty"; *Strabo,* "Squint-eyed"; *Scapula,* "Shoulder Bone." In 183 B.C., one of the two consuls (the chief executive magistrates of the Republic) was named M. Claudius Marcellus; this Marcellus was the son of an M. Claudius Marcellus and the grandson of an M. Claudius Marcellus; he, in turn, fathered an M. Claudius Marcellus; and men bearing this same name appear generation after generation among the lists of the chief magistrates at Rome

2. Still useful is the clear and concise account of Roman nomenclature in Egbert 1896, 82–113; the last hundred years have, however, brought refinements in matters of detail (see, e.g., Salway 1994).

for the next two hundred years.[3] A second son born into the family was also Claudius Marcellus, but he received a different praenomen, such as *Gaius,* if a brother named Marcus were living. During the late Republic and the early Empire it became increasingly fashionable for men to bear additional nomina and cognomina to commemorate other illustrious family members, especially members of the mother's family, since the traditional naming patterns gave no reflection of matrilineal descent. So flexible were naming patterns that the official name of one of the consuls of A.D. 169 was composed of fourteen nomina and twenty cognomina. The family controlled naming patterns, and the *gens Claudia* stopped employing Lucius as a praenomen after the disgrace of a certain Lucius Claudius, while the *gens Antonia* forbade the use of the praenomen Marcus after Marc Antony, disgraced by his liaison with Cleopatra VII, the last Ptolemaic monarch of Egypt, was defeated and died at the hands of Augustus.

Throughout her life a daughter bore the feminine form of the nomen of her paterfamilias, closely identifying her with the family of her birth: Julia's name forever proclaimed her "daughter of Julius," and such names as *Claudia, Cornelia, Aemilia, Sempronia, Domitia,* and *Fabia* pointed back to a woman's natal family after her marriage. This name distinguished a woman in public contexts, although if she were appearing in the company of one or more sisters or with her paternal female cousins, all of whom had the same name, "wife of Julius" or "daughter of Pulcher" could be appended to her name to give her separate identity. Within the family, order of birth seems to have supplied a handy means for distinguishing among the like-named daughters—for example, "Julia the Elder," *Iulia maior,* and "Julia the Younger," *Iulia minor.* Some families simply counted the daughters of a single generation—for example, "Claudia the First," *Claudia prima;* "Claudia the Second," *Claudia secunda;* "Claudia the Third," *Claudia tertia;* "Claudia the Fourth," *Claudia quarta.* Fashions changed in the names of women also, and in the late Republic and Empire cognomina were attached to their names as well. Not only did girls bear a female form of their father's

3. Elite Roman family members who held Roman magistracies over generations during the Republic can be traced in Thomas R. S. Broughton, *Magistrates of the Roman Republic,* vols. 1–2 (Cleveland, 1952) and 3 (Atlanta, 1986); cf. also Hopkins 1983, 31–119 (chap. 2, "Political Succession in the Late Republic, 249–50 B.C.").

name just as boys bore the masculine form, but generic terms for "son" and "daughter"—*filius, filia* and *natus, nata*—also implied an equality of sorts among siblings to a degree that was avoided in the Greek-speaking east, where quite different words were used for "girl-child" and "boy-child." In instances of intestate succession Roman siblings were also treated equally.

Slaves were their master's property.[4] They had but a single name, followed by the name of their master, *dominus,* or paterfamilias—for example, "Helenus, slave of M. Claudius Marcellus." Transfer to another master, either by purchase or inheritance, changed the slave's name to, for example, "Helenus, slave of M. Fulvius Nobilior." Upon manumission, however, the male slave Helenus not only became a freedman, *libertus,* but was usually absorbed into the ranks of Roman citizens through the patronage of his former master and the master's family. Not only did manumission bring the former slave freedom, but the manumitted slave also assumed the Roman *tria nomina* (taking the praenomen and nomen of his former master), so that he became, in this instance, M. Claudius Helenus. Helenus' male descendants were born free men and citizens of Rome, yet they continued to be bound by name and other ties of obligation to the Roman family from which their ancestor Helenus had been manumitted. Although they were never blood kin, freedmen dependents were partners in worshiping the ancestral gods of the family that manumitted them. Roman citizenship, along with Roman institutions, was spread during the Republic largely through manumission of slaves and through grants of citizenship to wealthy and privileged individuals in the provinces. The pace of such extensions quickened under Julius Caesar and the emperor Claudius, as entire regions gained citizenship at one moment.[5] In A.D. 212 the emperor Caracalla granted Roman citizenship to all provincials, and these populations assumed his official praenomen and nomen, *Marcus Aurelius,* or *Aurelia;* the new Roman citizens, drawn from the many geographical regions and ethnic backgrounds of the Empire, retained as a

4. A general survey is in Bradley 1994; for an attempt to recover the slave's point of view see Hopkins 1993. Cf. L-R I, nos. 94–95; II, nos. 24, 50. For inscriptions recording senatorial and equestrian careers see L-R II, nos. 13–14; for freedmen and slaves see L-R II, nos. 48–49.

5. For documents relating to the extension of Roman citizenship see L-R I, nos. 150–51; II, nos. 15, 106.

cognomen the name by which they were previously known. In late antiquity the nomen *Aurelius* came to designate those of lesser socio-economic standing within the empire, while the elite used the nomen *Flavius*.

The eldest living male member of an aristocratic Roman family was likely to have held political magistracies and military commands, to have become an important senator, and to have inherited vast landed properties he aimed to increase, or at least not lose; such a man also was the emperor, beginning with Augustus, the grandnephew of Julius Caesar. The names a Roman man bore were shared with his father and male ancestors, as well as with his own sons and male descendants; like the family's political fortunes, economic prosperity, and religious obligations, his name was his only for a lifetime, and he must pass it on enhanced, or at least not diminished, to the next generation. Individual family members lived and died, but the name was a constant and tangible symbol of the family's continuity over generations—the goal of the Roman familia. According to the second-century B.C. historian Polybius, the funeral of an illustrious man allowed the family to celebrate not only this man's great deeds through a public funeral speech (delivered by his son, if he had one living) but also the greatness of the family's ancestors, by having the family's young men don masks, *imagines*, resembling the deceased ancestors of previous generations and assume the formal dress and symbols of office that the ancestors achieved in their lifetimes.[6] The paterfamilias without a son preferred to adopt, rather than to allow the family to disappear. The adopted son usually took on the name of his adoptive family, so that after the childless C. Julius Caesar adopted in his will his nineteen-year-old grandnephew C. Octavius, his sister's grandson, the young man became C. Julius Caesar Octavianus. Only his second cognomen recalled the name of his natal family, but through his new name he became heir not only to his uncle's property but also to the political following his uncle had built through a lifetime of ordinary and extraordinary magistracies and military commands in Spain and Gaul. After 27 B.C., C. Julius Caesar Octavianus had himself called by the cognomen *Augustus*, in order to shed

6. Polybius *Histories* 6.53.1–54.2 (= L-R I, no. 182 and cf. also no. 181); for funeral eulogies of women see L-F, nos. 39–41, 43, 45, 47, 49–50, 168 (and cf. no. 53), 239, 363–68; L-R I, no. 183.

the brutal and revolutionary past by which he rose to supreme power.[7] Roman naming patterns underscored descent in the male line and the legally preferred patterns of inheritance that passed property and assets from father to son.[8] Kinship terms within the family carefully maintained such distinctions, with names for relatives on the father's side of the family being different from those for relatives on the mother's side: to his children the father's brother was *patruus;* his sister, *amita;* paternal cousins were *fratres patrueles.* Inheritance did not normally pass through the female line, and different names for "uncle," "aunt," and "cousin" distinguished mother's family: her brother was *avunculus* to her children; her sister, *matertera;* maternal cousins were *consobrini.* The children of a marriage belonged, without exception, to their father's family.

Family Members

The Roman Father *(Paterfamilias)*

The sweeping powers of the paterfamilias, his *patria potestas,* embraced the members of his familia during his lifetime.[9] They were a distinctive feature of Roman social organization, unparalleled elsewhere, and present a paradigm of overarching patriarchy. Early Roman legends tell of the just but terrible retributions carried out by patresfamilias against their own children, as a man's duty to city-state and clan outweighed the appeals to a father's clemency. The man who expelled the last of the Etruscan monarchs (the Tarquins), Lucius Junius Brutus, ordered the execution of his sons, Titus and Tiberius, after proof of their implication in a plot to restore the monarchy came to his attention as he was serv-

7. Essential for the sweeping social changes in the latter half of the first century B.C. leading to the Principate is Syme 1939; for "family values" in the Age of Augustus see Galinsky 1996, 128–40. Cf. L-R I, nos. 194–96, 204–206; L-R II, nos. 95–100; L-F, nos. 120–28.

8. For Roman priorities in inheritance see Champlin 1991; Saller 1991. For documents pertaining to death and burial see L-R II, nos. 52–54.

9. The important study of Roman marriage and the roles of the spouses is Treggiari 1991; see also Dixon 1992. Bauman 1992 traces the lives and strategies of elite women, and Gardner 1993 looks to legal rights and responsibilities of citizens.

ing as one of the first two consuls of the Republic. Some sixty years after the expulsion of the Tarquins, one of the ten commissioners appointed to codify Rome's laws, Appius Claudius, became infatuated with the girl Verginia, betrothed to the tribune Icilius. To gain possession of Verginia, Appius suborned a man to claim that she was his slave and not a freeborn woman, and during proceedings to determine her status, her own father, the brave soldier Verginius, drew a knife and killed his daughter to preserve her honor intact.[10] Demographic variables affecting the Roman populations, however, make it highly unlikely that large numbers of patresfamilias lived long enough to exercise the powers the law allowed them over grown children in their daily lives. Life expectancy at birth was low, probably about twenty-five years, and about half the babies born died before reaching their fifth birthday. What was it like for the tiny child to watch nearly half his playmates die or to lose a parent or a beloved nurse—for this was the common experience. Those who survived to their tenth birthday represented just under half of all babies born ten years before, but of that group who made it to ten years of age, nearly half survived to reach age fifty, and about a third survived to age sixty. Expressed in different terms, less than 20 percent of the population celebrated a sixtieth birthday. This, in turn, had greater effect on grandfathers than on grandmothers, because most men entered a first marriage between the ages of twenty-five and thirty, while most women were marrying in their mid- to late teens, and the babies began to come soon after marriage.[11] Grandmothers were younger than grandfathers, and a three-generational family headed by a paternal grandfather lay outside the experience of most Romans. Rather, potential grandfathers were either already dead or dying about the time their sons were entering their first marriage, and Roman children were likely to be without a paternal grandfather: many even lacked a father. A third of Roman children probably lost their fathers before reaching puberty, and as many as two-thirds were fatherless by the time they reached age twenty-five. Demographics alone suggest that legends about the all-powerful patresfamilias who

---

10. Both stories are in Livy's *History of Rome (Ab urbe condita)*, one at 2.3.1–5.8 and the other at 3.44.1–48.9. For other stories with moral implications from early Roman history see L-R I, no. 8; L-F, nos. 165–66.

11. Shaw 1987.

interfered in their adult children's lives rested on the examples of a very few.[12]

Roman law sanctioned the supreme authority of the paterfamilias over his familia. Social custom and the political system likewise gave highest respect to maleness and longevity. The Roman senator was also called "father," *pater,* and seniority determined the order of speaking within the senate—normally the right of the eldest surviving ex-consular senator, or *princeps Senatus.* He could, of course, yield his right of speaking first to others and occasionally did so; during the Empire, the emperor sometimes preempted the right to speak first, but otherwise the rule of seniority continued to prevail. Although Roman women were also citizens, their gender prevented them from office holding and from any direct or responsible participation in political and military affairs. The image of an authoritarian and all-powerful father extended to other sociopolitical relationships: the wealthy and aristocratic paterfamilias was also a patron *(patronus)* to his dependents *(clientes),* to whom he offered protection in exchange for their support as soldiers when he or his sons led armies of Rome out to fight the enemy or to govern in a province and for their support as voters in the citizen assemblies of the Republic. A man's importance was judged by the numbers of those who visited his home to pay their respects and followed in his retinue whenever he appeared in public. As owner of properties, he was also absolute master, *dominus,* to his slaves. The activities of these powerful men dominated the history of Rome, as what was initially a small city-state on the Tiber (much like neighboring cities in Latium and northern Campania) gradually incorporated through conquest the entire Mediterranean basin and welded much of western Europe into an empire, which, at its greatest extent in the second century A.D., spanned from England to the Euphrates, from the Rhine to the deserts of North Africa. The civil wars of the first century B.C. brought redistributions of wealth and political power, as well as increased social mobility to groups outside the aristocracy of the city of Rome; government changed from a narrow oligarchy to a monarchy (called "the Principate" in the first two centuries of the Empire, and "the Dominate" thereafter, when Republican trappings were largely

12. For a general overview of Roman mortality functions see Parkin 1992; for implications to be drawn from Roman demographics, Saller 1994, passim. Demographic evidence is abundant and fairly reliable for the Roman province of Egypt during the Principate; see Bagnall and Frier 1994.

dispensed with). The emperors of the Principate, especially those judged the more successful by their contemporaries, adhered to many of the same patterns of behavior that prevailed among the patresfamilias of the Republic. Men without sons to inherit adopted suitable replacements; they married their daughters off to cement political alliances; they protected their dependents; they oversaw diverse family assets; they suppressed foreign enemies with considerable vigor and, after conquest, took up the task of organizing foreign areas into provinces whose resources contributed to the profit of Rome. Conducting wars of conquest, policing the Mediterranean basin and the frontiers of the hinterlands, and establishing the rule of law, the habits of peace, and the amenities of urban living were tasks elite Roman males shouldered for centuries. Idealized stereotypes for aristocratic male conduct looked to excellence in public deeds (*res gestae,* "the things they did"); to seriousness of purpose *(gravitas);* to manliness and courage *(virtus)* at home and abroad; to clemency and protection for weaker dependents (*clementia* and *iustitia*); to the fulfilling of obligations to family, Rome, and the gods *(pietas).* Although the legal system permitted the paterfamilias vast powers in the various spheres in which he operated, social customs did not encourage him to unleash against wife and children the same severity and savagery he displayed toward cowardly troops who proved unfaithful in battle, toward insidious foreign enemies who violated the terms of a treaty, toward friends at home who played him false, toward recalcitrant slaves who flaunted their master's will.

An influential and popular comic playwright, T. Maccius Plautus, stands at the beginning of Latin literature in much the same way as Shakespeare does for English literature, producing his plays during and after the Second Punic War against the Carthaginian Hannibal (218–201 B.C.).[13] A major motif in many Plautine comedies is the duping of the paterfamilias by his clever slave, usually to help the son of the family carry on a liaison with his ladylove. Although the object of the son's affections is at first thought to be a woman unsuitable for the young man to marry, the intricacies of the plot frequently prove the girl freeborn after all and therefore an eligible bride. As the drama wends

13. For a readable translation of Plautus' surviving plays see David R. Slavitt and Palmer Bovie, eds., *Plautus: The Comedies,* vols. 1–4 (Baltimore and London, 1995); my favorite is "Two Sisters Named Bacchis" *(Bacchides).* For Plautus' humor see Segal 1968; for audience criticism, Slater 1985.

its way toward such happy conclusions, the paterfamilias complains about the lack of serious behavior displayed by his son, but he usually forgives the young man in the end; he is seldom willing to extend his indulgence to the clever slave, who is promised a beating or even crucifixion. Thus, in Plautus' play *Ghost (Mostellaria)* the son's friend Callidamates pleads the case of young Philolaches before his stern father, Theopropides.

Callidamates: You realize that I was your son's confidant in everything. He came to me, because he was ashamed to appear before you, because he knows you know what he did. Now, please, forgive his stupidity, his youthfulness. He is your son. You know that young men his age like to play around. Everything he did, he did together with me. It's quite my fault. His debts, both principal and interest, and the money he spent on his girlfriend—I'll pay it all back, honestly I will, and it won't cost you a cent.

Theopropides: He could not have found a better advocate than you. I'm not so mad at him, nor am I very angry. Why, now that I am back home, let him drink and do what he wants, so long as he is ashamed for having wasted all that money. That's enough for me

Callidamates: Oh, he is very sorry.

Tranio (the clever slave): Now that you're feeling indulgent, what happens to me?

Theopropides: You're going to die hanging [on a cross], with a beating.

Tranio: Even if I'm sorry?

Theopropides: As I live and breathe, I'll do you in, by Hercules.

Callidamates: But sir, make your indulgence for all. Forgive Tranio, please, for my sake.

Theopropides: I'd rather you ask me anything else than that I not punish that criminal for all his criminal deeds.

Callidamates: Please, release him too.

Theopropides (after Tranio has made an inappropriate gesture): Do you see how he remains a total scoundrel?

Callidamates: Be quiet, Tranio, if you're smart.

Theopropides: You too stop begging me, and I'll silence Tranio with a proper beating.

Tranio: There's no need for that, sir.
Callidamates: Just let me persuade you, sir.
Theopropides: No, I don't want you to beg.
Callidamates: Please!
Theopropides: No, I tell you—stop begging.
Callidamates: Give up and grant only this one little thing, for my sake.
Tranio: Why so serious, sir? As though tomorrow I won't deserve another beating because I've done something else. Why then you can beat me up properly for both offenses—this one and that.
Callidamates: Please let me persuade you.
Theopropides (to Tranio): Okay, okay. Go away without your punishment—but he's the one to be grateful to.[14]

The butt of Plautus' jokes was often the paterfamilias, but the father's obvious discomfort in his dramatic surroundings aroused laughter, not anxiety, in Plautus' audience, and the plays that permitted a perilous moment of triumph to the clever slave over his *dominus* or to the intelligent wife over her dullard husband were revived for generations after Plautus' lifetime.

The Roman Mother *(Materfamilias)*

Most Roman women entered a first marriage at ages some five, ten, or more years earlier than did a man, with virtually all women married by their early twenties.[15] If marrying for the first time, brides from elite and propertied families were sometimes as young as ten to thirteen years. The marriage was arranged by the girl's father, in consultation with her mother, and negotiations took place with the prospective groom or his elder male kin. Mothers were particularly likely to suggest a marriage with someone from their own family, and although the

14. Plautus *Mostellaria* 1153–80.

15. In addition to Treggiari 1991, see the overall survey of Roman women from the Republic to the late Empire, with copious bibliography and elegant illustrations, in Fantham, Foley, Kampen, Pomeroy, and Shapiro 1994, 207–394; see also Dixon 1988; Gardner 1986. For women in Roman religion see Scheid 1992. For documents illustrating the status of Roman women see L-R I, no. 191; L-R II, nos. 91–94; L-F, nos. 107–59, 174.

children of fathers' brothers did not often marry their paternal cousins in aristocratic families, cousin-marriages with mothers' kin were very common. Political and economic considerations dominated what represented not only the creation of a new family but also a very public merging of two established families and their interests. The groom, considerably older than his bride, was expected, for example, to help in launching the political careers of his wife's brothers, likely to be nearly a half generation or so younger than he, so that a sister's successful marriage could well be an important asset for her brothers. Evidence for marriage patterns among the lower classes is sparse. Even so, craftsmen seem to have married daughters of fellow craftsmen, and although Roman soldiers were forbidden to marry during their active service until the ban was lifted by the emperor Septimius Severus in A.D. 197, soldiers did form less formal liaisons, often with daughters of veterans or of fellow soldiers, converting this to a legal Roman marriage upon discharge. Respect, affection, and conjugal love were expected to develop during the course of a shared life and the birth of common children, but these were seldom preconditions for a marriage. Certain marriage ceremonies formally transferred a girl from the control and jurisdiction *(manus)* of her father to that of her husband, and as a result she became a member of his family, losing her right to inherit from members of her natal family and worshiping the household gods of her husband's family, not those of her own. By the end of the Republic, however, the majority of women remained instead under the jurisdiction of their fathers as long as the fathers lived, eschewing the marriage formulae that transferred a woman from the control of the paterfamilias of her family to that of her husband and the power structures operative within his familia. By remaining a member of her natal family, she retained a legal, economic, and religious position in the household whose name she shared throughout her lifetime. The dowry the girl brought with her to her marriage was intended for her own maintenance, although if she had left her father's jurisdiction, it did become her husband's possession; her family expected to recover the dowry should the marriage terminate through either death or divorce, unless it had passed to her children in the event of her death. When her bridegroom was yet under the jurisdiction of his paterfamilias, her dowry was an important item in the resources available to the young household, providing the couple with a measure of financial security and even luxuries they might otherwise lack. Throughout the Republic an adult woman had to be represented by a male guardian when conducting legal business; she could neither buy nor sell property, nor could she incur debts in her own name. Under the first emperor Augustus, laws were enacted by which motherhood brought a woman release from some restrictions, including the requirement that a guardian conduct transactions in her behalf, if the agreements were to be legally binding on the parties. To qualify, freeborn women had to have birthed three live children, freedwomen four children. In subsequent centuries, financially capable matresfamilias become more and more visible as managers of their own estates and other properties.

The purpose of marriage was the birth of legitimate children, especially males, to carry the father's family into a next generation, and infertility often persuaded a husband to discard one wife for another. A regime of "natural fertility" prevailed at most levels in society, and the majority of women gave birth throughout the entire extent of their fertile lives.[16] The high death rate among infants and small children required the average Roman woman to give birth to between five and six live babies merely to leave behind at her death replacements for herself and her husband. The Greek physicians who doctored the Roman upper classes report about contraceptive medicaments and procedures, as well as methods to induce abortion, although the doctor Soranus adds that he prescribed these only when the life of the mother was endangered because she was either too young for a successful pregnancy or otherwise in ill health and physically exhausted, assuring his readers he would never aid a woman seeking to hide the fruit of illicit sex or wanting to avoid damage to her youthful beauty.[17] Limiting fertility, with its attendant risks of sterility, was likely to have been of greater interest to prostitutes and women of the demimonde than it was to the legitimate wife, and it is unclear to what extent effective knowledge of any techniques besides abstinence penetrated other Roman social communities. The materfamilias, younger than the paterfamilias when the babies were born, was more likely than her husband to remain a conspicuous presence in the lives of her children, partici-

16. Important is Frier 1994.

17. Soranus *Gynecology* 1.60–64. For a readable English translation see Owsei Temkin, ed., *Soranus' Gynecology* (Baltimore, 1957); useful notes and extensive bibliography are in *Soranos d'Éphèse: Maladies des Femmes,* vols. 1–3 (Paris, 1988–94), with volume 4 forthcoming. See also Hanson and Green 1994 and Gourevitch 1984.

pating fully, as noted earlier, in arranging their marriages. Bloodlines and important ancestors were qualities elite parents sought in prospective spouses for their children; wealth and attractiveness were desirable, as was chastity for the bride in a first marriage. High rates of maternal death widowed many men, and the age difference between partners often left wives of childbearing age as widows. Women marrying for a second or third time sometimes enjoyed greater control over choice of a spouse, and others refused remarriage outright. If Roman society had no place for the "old maid"—she is almost never encountered—it did find a place for the woman who chose not to remarry. The *univira*, "a woman of one husband," was treated with respect, and many examples are known. There is little sign that considerations of political power and economic prestige were ever absent from marriage alliances. When the historian Tacitus pictures the beautiful and ambitious Poppaea Sabina pressing the young emperor Nero to divorce his stepsister and childless wife, Octavia, to contract a marriage with her, he makes Poppaea put greatest emphasis on her excellent bloodlines—her grandfathers had celebrated triumphal victories over the enemies of Rome—and her proven ability to bear children to her previous husband; Poppaea mentions her good looks and her obvious intelligence merely as added attractions.[18]

From the first century B.C. onward divorce became more frequent, as often reflecting shifting political alliances within a family as it did personal incompatibilities. The children of a dissolved union, including the child still in its mother's womb, belonged to the father and his family. The former wife was required by law to announce her pregnancy to her husband if he was living and to his family if he was deceased. The former in-laws retained the right to verify the diagnosis of pregnancy, to monitor each of its advancing stages, and either to attend the birthing in person or to send their representatives—five women of free status, but no more than ten, plus two midwives and six female slaves—so that the interests of the two families, the mother's and the father's, would each be represented at the birth. Further, the law specified that the newborn had to be shown to the interested parties or their representatives. If they wished, they could inspect the child while it was still attached to its mother via umbilical cord and placenta, for

18. Tacitus *Annals* 14.1; for more about Poppaea Sabina see Tacitus *Annals* 13.45–46, 14.59–64 (the divorce and exile of Octavia); 15.23 (birth of Nero's daughter); 16. 6 (Poppaea's death).

these attachments guaranteed that the child was hers and was legitimate in the female line. The procedure looked to protect not only the right of the child to inherit from his father and become his heir, despite the divorce of his parents or his father's death, but also the interests of the deceased father's family and his other heirs, lest an unscrupulous former daughter-in-law foist a suppositious child, slipped into the delivery room in a basket, into their midst.[19]

Roman infants were subject to postnatal inspection by a midwife, who looked the baby over for physical defects; then she placed it on the ground. Only the paterfamilias had the right to raise up the child, and this gesture was a sign that the infant was now accepted as a member of the paterfamilias' family. He seems not to have raised up the severely deformed neonate or the monster.[20]

The Roman wife was to live in concord and harmony *(concordia)* with her husband and to bear children whose likeness to their father proclaimed her fidelity; the inscriptions on tombs of Roman women reiterated these prime virtues again and again. At the same time, women were seldom the only, or even the primary, caregivers for young children or for the men of the family who fell ill, and the modern stereotype of woman as nurturer was not invoked for the materfamilias.[21] Rather, her industriousness found her spinning with her slaves at daybreak, and her intelligence and self-restraint enabled her to supervise the economic activities that made her household as autonomous and self-sufficient as possible. She was the just and stern arbiter of family matters, for often she was forced to oversee family property in her husband's many absences on public business; wives of Roman administrators and generals almost never accompanied their husbands to the provinces but instead watched over family interests in Rome. She was *matrona* in religious ceremonies entrusted to the married women of Rome and *matrona* to the family's dependents; she was mistress, *domina,* to its slaves. Her virtues and her unswerving seriousness of purpose *(gravitas)* were modeled on those of her husband in his conduct of public business. The younger Pliny included the following praises for Trajan's wife Plotina in the course of his very long speech praising the emperor Trajan (d. A.D. 118).

19. For discussion see Hanson 1994a; see also Gardner 1984, 132–33, and Rowlandson forthcoming, especially chapter 6.

20. Hanson 1994b.

21. This point is well made for both Greece and Rome by King 1991.

> A wife taken on without proper thought, or one patiently retained, has brought much dishonor to many illustrious husbands, and scandal in the family has often destroyed famous men, with the result that they are not thought to be excellent citizens, because they were deficient as husbands. But your wife brings you honor and glory. What is more pious, what is more old-fashioned than her? Why, even if we had to choose a wife for the chief priest *(pontifex maximus)*, would we not choose her, or someone just like her (if, in fact, there is such a one)? She wants nothing for herself from your good fortune, but only to bring you joy. How faithfully she reveres not your temporal power, but you yourself. Both of you in turn are as you once were, and good fortune has added nothing to you, except what you already possessed at the outset. How well you both bear your good fortune. How modest she is in her appearance and behavior, how few accompany her as she goes about, how like a normal citizen she walks. It is a husband's responsibility to instill these qualities in his wife, and it is sufficient for a wife to follow his glory. When she sees that no fears, no ambitions accompany you, does she not follow quietly behind, treading in her husband's footsteps, to the extent that a woman can? This suits her, even when you are carrying out a variety of your duties . . . .[22]

Roman Children: A Boy *(Filiusfamilias)* and a Girl *(Filiafamilias)*

Roman infants were thought to be soft and pliable in body and mind, and the baby's earliest years were devoted to shaping first its physical nature and then its intellect.[23] Within hours of its birth the child was wrapped in swaddling clothes and often turned over to the care of a wet nurse *(nutrix)* for a year or two. The doctor Soranus criticized Roman mothers for carelessly allowing children to walk on hard surfaces before their legs were firm enough to carry them without bowing

22. Pliny *Panegyric* 83.4–5; for an English translation of other portions of this long speech in praise of Trajan see L-R II, no. 7.

23. For general discussion of infants and children see Wiedemann 1989; for daughters of important men, Hallett 1984; for children of lower-class families, Rawson 1986 and Weaver 1991. For the baby as unformed and in need of molding see Gourevitch 1995. For documents on children and their parents see L-F, nos. 249–66.

Fig. 2. Wood, bone, and terracotta objects that served as children's toys. The education of Roman children focused on preparing the child for life as an adult. Children's toys such as these found at Karanis in Egypt enabled a child to play at being a "grown-up." Note the miniature writing desks for a scribe and the small comb, possibly a carding comb. (Courtesy of the Kelsey Museum.)

outward, and he thought the best wet nurse to be a native speaker of Greek, so that the nursling could imbibe that language along with its milk. Although some mothers nursed and cared for their infants themselves, there is little evidence that physical bonding between infant and mother or father was considered important, and babies at all social levels were frequently given over to the care of child-minders, both men and women, slave and free. High mortality rates among Romans of all ages orphaned many children at young ages, while divorce and remarriage broke up one family unit and reconstituted another.

In such a milieu, forming the child's body and mind was a communal task that concerned many members of the familia at various times, rather than being simply a duty of the parents alone. Greek doctors at Rome, such as Soranus and Galen, described for their elite patrons the characteristics that marked the best midwives and wet nurses to care for their children, and the child-minders, often drawn from the family's dependents, were a necessity when parents were unable to care for a child. These people provided a stable presence for all children and especially for orphans. Grave inscriptions testify to continuing ties based on communal experiences in babyhood, and sharing the same wet nurse made children, even those of different status, into "milk-fellows" *(collactanei)* and created a special bond between them that lasted throughout their lifetimes. Saint Augustine, however, claimed that enforced sharing of a single nurse's milk also had roused in him his first feelings of jealousy and hatred, as he watched the other infant sucking at the breasts that were his. The emperors Caligula (d. A.D. 41) and Nero (d. A.D. 68) remained particularly close throughout their short lives to those who had cared for them as infants and children; both had been orphaned by the deaths of their fathers at a very young age, and Nero's mother was also for a time in exile. Nero advanced the careers of several of his male caretakers, and as freedmen they rose to considerable positions of imperial authority; after his suicide, it was Nero's former wet nurses that were concerned to deposit his corpse in the family tomb. By contrast, Nero was apparently unaware that his mother, Agrippina the Younger, was a capable swimmer, since one of his plots to rid himself of her involved drowning her in a collapsible boat—a plot she foiled by swimming to shore. Nero had grown up in the household of his paternal aunt, and Roman gossip held that his early education had been neglected, that his child-minders in the formative years were a dancer and a barber. The proof came from the fact that when he became emperor at the age of seventeen, he was the first in the Julio-Claudian family to lack the rhetorical skills to compose a funeral oration for his predecessor and adoptive father, Claudius, and was forced to recite a speech written by another.[24]

Those who attended the child on a daily basis did provide a locus for the young child's affections, as it learned to make its desires known. The Latin language effectively lacks words for "yes" and "no," and the two-year-old cried out instead, *Volo, volo, volo!* [I want, I want, I want it!] and *Nolo, nolo, nolo!* [I don't want, I don't, I don't!]. Relatives and friends often discussed with a parent how best to raise a child so as to form it into a suitable adult. Older boys accompanied their fathers,

24. For childhood memories and stories see Augustine *Confessions* 1.7; Suetonius *Life of Caligula* 8–11 and Philo Judaeus *Embassy to Gaius* 166–78 and 203–206 (Caligula's attachment to his servant Helicon); Suetonius *Life of Nero* 6–8 and Tacitus *Annals* 13.3 (Nero's education) and 14.2–13 (the collapsible boat and the death of Agrippina by stabbing). For Nero's burial see Suetonius *Life of Nero* 50.

uncles, and grown cousins as they carried out their public duties at home and abroad, gaining firsthand experience about how a Roman statesman and general must conduct himself. Older girls were shaped by observing their mothers and other female relatives of their father's household. M. Porcius Cato the Elder (consul in 195 B.C., censor in 185 B.C.) was noted for his ferocity as a pleader in the law courts, his zealousness in attacks on political rivals, and his strictness with the soldiers under his command in the field. His biographer Plutarch quoted him as saying, however, that the man who hit his wife or child was laying hands on the holiest of things, and that he cared more about being a good husband than a great senator. Only urgent public business prevented Cato from being present when his wife bathed and wrapped his tiny son in swaddling clothes. His wife nursed the baby herself and also gave suck to slave infants of the household, in order to instill in them brotherly affections for her son. Cato taught the boy to read, since he thought it wrong for him to be scolded by a slave or have a slave pinch his ears when he was slow to learn. He also tutored him in more advanced studies and the law, and he hardened the child's body with athletic activities—riding horseback, throwing the javelin, and swimming in the chilly and swirling flows of the Tiber.[25]

Because the infant was a member of his father's household once the paterfamilias had raised up the baby from the ground, the father and his family exhibited great care in protecting the child left fatherless while still underage—boys up to fourteen years of age and girls up to twelve. The earliest codification of Roman law, the Twelve Tables, affirmed a father's right to divide his estate among his designated heirs through a will and to name guardians *(tutores)* to protect the property that came to his minor children after his death. Thus, both the state and the father's family combined to protect the orphaned child once its legitimacy was established. In the absence of a will, the father's male heirs—most often his brothers or paternal uncles—assumed the duty, although during the empire jurists thought it best when the relatives also made a deposit to guarantee the safeguarding of a child's inheritance and when they were asked to make periodic reports on the child's estate. Wives and other women could inherit but could not serve as guardians for minor children; in the absence of a male family member,

25. Plutarch *Life of M. Porcius Cato* 20.3–6 (= L-R I, no. 186). For Cato's public face as a politician at Rome see L-R I, no. 159; as a gentleman farmer, L-R I, no. 166.

the state arranged for the appointment of a guardian. The motherless infant, however, might soon be presented with a stepmother *(noverca)*, and her wicked reputation for craftily diverting the father's attention away from his children of the previous marriage in the direction of the new children she bore him was legendary. A mother's absence was deeply felt by her children, and although neither the state nor the father's family was required to make up the child's emotional loss, paternal grandmothers and aunts might come to stand in a mother's place.

According to Soranus, after the wet nurse had finished her task of molding the infant's body, the young child was turned over to elementary teachers *(magistri)* and other supervisors *(paedagogi)*; many of these were men, family dependents or slaves. Some parents prided themselves on educating and training their children themselves, but their boasts suggest that this was the exception rather than the rule. Elite and other wealthy families provided private tutors in the home for their children, and group instruction was usually available in most urban centers, less so in villages and in the countryside. Early education for Roman children was never an organized enterprise, but the ability to read and write was expected among members of the upper classes, especially males, and literacy was useful at all socioeconomic levels, since literate persons did not need to search for someone reliable and trustworthy to read and sign their documents.[26] The following imaginary conversation derives from a late antique, bilingual Greek/Latin schoolbook, and it describes the young boy's experiences as he gets up and goes to school. In particular, the conversation socializes the Roman child to speak with adults and to give orders to slaves, and through copious use of synonyms (not all of which are repeated below), it expands his vocabulary in the target language.[27]

> Then I waked my slave; I said to him, "Get up, boy. See if it is now light. Open the door and the window!" And he did so. Then I said to him, "Give me my cloak and my shirt."
>
> "Here."

26. For Roman education see Stanley F. Bonner, *Education in Ancient Rome* (Berkeley and Los Angeles, 1977); for how children learned to write, Cribiore 1996; for literacy in the Roman world, Harris 1989; for strategies available to the illiterate in what was essentially a literate society, Hanson 1991.

27. Dionisotti 1982, 97–101.

I take also other things. Then I leave my bed, I put on my belt and I set my shirt around my neck; I dress myself, as suits the son of the family, a wellborn man. I ask for my shoes to put them on. Water is given me for my face, and I wash. I rinse out my mouth and dry with a clean cloth. "Give me the drying towel. Bring fresh water to your master, my brother, so that he also may go out with me in public, to school." And I give my commands in order . . . .

Now all dressed, we pray to all the gods and ask for a good outcome to the whole day. After this, I go from my house in public, to the classroom, to the bridge, to the neighborhood, to the forum, with the slave who carries my book bag, or with my pedagogue, or with a fellow pupil. If anyone I know or a friend comes up to me, I greet him by his name. He greets me in return with my name: "Hello, sir. May all be well for you." Then I return to my father's house; I go to greet my relatives, my father and mother, my grandpa and grandma, my brother and sister, and all my relatives, my nurse and caretaker, the steward, all the freedmen, and the doorkeeper, the housekeeper, the neighbors, all my friends. . . .

I went into school and I said, "Greetings, teacher; greetings, instructor," and he greeted me in return. He gives me a manual and orders me to read five pages in his presence. I read accurately and well. Then I gave the manual to another. Next I went to the assistant teacher. I greet him and my fellow pupils, and they greeted me in return. Then I sat in my place on a bench, or chair, or step, or stool, or large chair. While I am sitting down, the slave who carries my school box hands me my little tablets and my writing case, my straightedge, my tablet, and my lupines [for counting]. I subtract, I do math, I compute, I count and I shall count, I add and I subtract, I multiply, I divide. . . . I cross out and I write an addition above the line, and I write and show it to my teacher. He praised me because I wrote well. I reread what I wrote word by word. I recite. I recited before you. Lies, I do not lie.

"If you speak truly," my pedagogue said to me, "let us go home so that we can go to the Greek and the Latin teacher." Then we are dismissed for sports, for Latin and Greek studies. We entered the school of the Greek teacher and the lecture room of the Latin teacher. I learn my texts thoroughly. If I am ready, I hand them in immediately. If not, I read them again. . . . I took the text, verses,

> notes. The unknown book is explained to me, or the unknown passage. Explication is offered. I take my place, and others together with me read extemporaneously; the rest repeat it accurately. The younger boys practice interpretation and syllables, declensions, a lot of grammar, speech, all in front of the assistant teacher. . . . The older boys go to the teacher; they read a text about the *Iliad*, another about the *Odyssey*.[28] They take up a theme, a hortatory speech, a debate, history, comedy, narratives, every kind of oration, causes of the Trojan War . . . .

Older children received training for adult responsibilities from parents, relatives, and friends of the family. The *filiusfamilias* might be given additional schooling with advanced teachers, *grammatici* and *rhetores*, in Rome; sons were also sent abroad to study with experts in the older educational centers of the eastern Mediterranean—Athens, Alexandria, and the cities of Asia Minor.[29] The *filiafamilias* more often remained closer to the family's home, learning the skills she would need when she left her family as wife, representative and symbol of the ties her family was now forging with her husband's family. The first emperor Augustus, the former Octavian, used the women of his family to cement political alliances, as he went about consolidating his hold on the government of Rome; he married his widowed sister Octavia to Marc Antony to bolster their fragile political alliance.[30] Augustus' only surviving child, a daughter, was born from his second wife, Scribonia: Julia was first married in her early teens to a very young groom, M. Claudius Marcellus, son of Octavia and her first husband; after Marcellus' death, Augustus married Julia to his best friend M. Vipsanius Agrippa, even though at the time Agrippa was married to one of Octavia's daughters, named Marcella, and had children with her. Julia's marriage to Agrippa produced five children, three boys and two girls; after Agrippa's death Augustus married Julia to a stepson he

28. Roman education beyond the lowest levels included instruction in Greek as well as Latin, and the first serious reading was in the epics of Homer.

29. For advanced education among *grammatici* and *rhetores* see Kaster 1988. For documents relating to advanced education see L-R II, nos. 55–62. Poems by Roman women, no matter the subject, underscore the fine education the women had received; see L-F, nos. 24–26.

30. For Augustus' private life see Suetonius *Life of Augustus* 61–96. For a family tree of the Julio-Claudians and discussion see Corbier 1995, 178–93.

acquired through his third marriage, Ti. Claudius Nero, who also was forced to divorce his current wife, Vipsania, Agrippa's daughter. Augustus had his daughter and granddaughters taught spinning and weaving, and he discouraged even respectable young men from approaching them. Because he lacked sons of his own, he adopted Julia's eldest two sons as his own; he taught the young Gaius and Lucius, as they were called after their adoption into the Julian gens, reading and swimming and spent considerable time in their company. As his designated successors, the boys were given considerable political and military responsibilities at home and in the provinces, with their grandfather's friends dispatched with them to watch and supervise. Although Augustus was sickly from his youth, he survived to age seventy-eight and outlived those he had early designated as his successors, including his grandsons from the marriage of Julia and Agrippa. He was finally succeeded in A.D. 14 by Julia's third husband, who also had been adopted as Augustus' son, in the emperor's last years. By that time, however, Augustus had banished Julia herself for immoral behavior, and she went into exile, with her mother, Scribonia, accompanying her; Julia's own daughter, another Julia, was also exiled for misconduct similar to that of her mother.

Generalities and Specific Examples

The Nature of the Evidence about Roman Families

Our evidence is fullest for the elite families who controlled the destinies of the Roman Republic and, during the Empire, either ruled as the imperial family, or stood in close proximity to it, as governors and generals in the provinces and senators and advisers within the City, or *Urbs*—for Romans called Rome "The City." The historians and writers of literary and subliterary texts were almost invariably males. They seldom afford a concentrated or sustained look at the Roman family or at Roman family life, and when they do, they present an elite, male point of view and emphasize the deeds of the men, for the paterfamilias was held to be responsible for every aspect of the lives of the women, children, and slaves dependent on him. Only occasionally do Roman writers report about wives, children, dependents, and slaves, and these latter have little opportunity to speak for themselves. Inscriptions and other documents sometimes give them a voice, but this kind of evidence tends to overemphasize some aspects of family life at the expense of others: the myriad funerary inscriptions tell much about Roman habits of commemorating the dead, about the empire-wide variations in sentiments expressed, and about which items of biographical information were recorded on tombs. Those who died in their teens and twenties were particularly likely to have living kin or relatives by marriage whose grief impelled them to erect a monument and to have suitable sentiments carved on it. We also know much about the legal codes under which Roman citizens lived and the interpretation jurists made of these rules, but it is often difficult to separate what was the experience of most or many Romans from what represented unusual or bizarre circumstances. Further, inscriptions represent chance finds, and conflicting interpretations of individual texts by modern scholars often raise more problems than are solved.

Concentration on the Roman family is a relatively recent scholarly endeavor, after centuries of concern with Roman politics and wars of conquest, with the legal codes for Roman citizens and the regulations for provincials, with the gradual homogenization of the Empire's urban centers ringing the coastal lands of the Mediterranean basin and following the rivers upstream as these flowed into the hinterland. The first generations of social historians in the twentieth century interpreted Roman reticence to express affections for family members in ways that are familiar to us as signs of coldness, aloofness, and distancing. For example, the papers of a tax collector named Nemesion in the Roman province of Egypt under Julio-Claudian emperors include only one letter to Nemesion from a woman, most probably written by the woman herself; although it can be deduced from the contents of the letter that Thermouthis was somehow a member of Nemesion's immediate family, since she is managing the family's financial and agricultural affairs in his absence on business, nothing she says clarifies her relationship to him (fig. 3). Thermouthis' name also appears in one of her husband's accounts as the person responsible for paying laborers who were digging out irrigation canals. We learn that she is Nemesion's wife from the fact that a tax receipt, made out to Nemesion's sons years later, says that the name of the boys' mother is Thermouthis. What this letter does show is that Thermouthis is as shrewd and careful in business as is her husband, and although a less accomplished letter writer than he, she can nonetheless write it with her own hand. Their common ways of behaving and their shared goals, as well

Fig. 3. Thermouthis' letter to her husband Nemesion. The text reads: "Thermouthis to Nemesion, greetings. I want you to know that Lucius has come. With regard to his thick tunic that you have in the metropolis, if you come down, bring it back with you. He has the hood to it here. I already gave it to him on his word alone, so he might have it until your arrival. And with regard to the wages of the shepherds, he said, 'I am sending a soldier . . . right away, so that he may seize whatever remains of the shepherds' belongings.' Our mattress he has not given me—'Bring my old one,' he says. And with regard to the shovel, he says that you asked them three staters for the shovel. Farewell. Year 5 of Nero, Epeiph 13. [A.D. 7 July 59]" Thermouthis' letter was written in awkward Greek letters by an unpracticed hand; its writer was not in the habit of using pen and ink frequently, and the spelling and grammar are also uncertain, even by ordinary standards of the day. (P. Cornell Inv. I 11 [ZPE 22] 1976; courtesy of the Rare Books Collection, Graduate Library of the University of Michigan.)

as their common children, perhaps provided the couple with a basis for marital harmony.[31]

More careful reading of the various messages available in the ancient evidence is now resulting in more nuanced views of the ways in which Romans and Roman provincials expressed concern for fellow family members, and conclusions are now tempered by a better understanding of the demographic realities that prevailed in the Roman world. The young child's experiences in its first five years were likely to include the death of nearly half the child's little playmates and young siblings, the death of the child's grandparents (if they were not dead already before the child's birth), and even the death of a parent or a beloved and trusted caretaker. Life was as precarious as it was precious, and those who were the survivors found themselves ever in the midst of death and dying, for people of all ages perished at a rate no longer known in the modern democracies of the Western world. The dominant feature of Roman family life was its flexibility and versatility in the face of these harsh mortality functions, for the semblance of a family often took the place of the nuclear family of our experience. Continuity of the family over generations was the goal. We assess affective feelings among Roman families from the evidence that chance has preserved for us, well aware that their methods for expressing affection toward family members are not necessarily equivalent to our own. Romans' concerns show clear in the father's will that appoints guardians for his minor children in the event of his death, in the mother's efforts to assure that good marriages are arranged for her children. Grave monuments celebrate long-lasting and harmonious marriages, honor a spouse who dies first as one who "well deserves" the monument and its praise, and remember a host of individuals who played important roles in a child's early life. A brief look at the families of Cicero and of Pliny the Younger, two prolific writers of letters that have survived for us, may bolster some of the generalizations that are presented in this essay.[32]

The statesman and orator M. Tullius Cicero was born in 106 B.C. to an important family of equestrian status in the hill town of Arpinum, seventy miles east of Rome, on his grandfather's country estate. We know

---

31. For more about Thermouthis and her husband, Nemesion, see chapter 6 in Rowlandson forthcoming.

32. For other letters from Cicero's correspondence in English translation see L-R I, nos. 108, 113, 145; see also excerpts about the aristocratic Clodia and her misdeeds in Cicero's speech in behalf of M. Caelius Rufus in L-F, no. 71.

for certain that grandfather, father, and son also bore the same name that Cicero himself passed on to his only son; Cicero's grandfather died shortly after he was born, while his own father survived until he was in his late thirties. Cicero's brother, Quintus, was several years younger than he. When the boys were approaching their teenage years, the family bought a house in Rome; they were given the best education available in the City, and they also studied in Greece and Asia Minor. Cicero tells little about his own parents, although his mother, Helvia, was parsimonious and strict, while his father was sickly, devoted to literary studies, and more content to live in Arpinum than in Rome. We do not know when Cicero married his first wife, Terentia, but she was both wealthy and of aristocratic Roman connections; she bore him a daughter, Tullia, not long after they were married and a son, Marcus, in 65 B.C. Cicero was never extraordinarily wealthy by elite Roman standards, but he eventually possessed a number of country residences, including a suburban villa at Tusculum, in addition to a house on the Palatine Hill in Rome.[33]

About 69 B.C. Cicero arranged the marriage of his younger brother, Quintus, to Pomponia, sister of his childhood friend T. Pomponius Atticus; Pomponia was older than Quintus by several years. The couple had a son, also named Q. Tullius Cicero. For over twenty-five years Cicero and Atticus worked continually on their respective siblings to keep this marriage intact—and the many letters that passed between the two friends speak of considerable frictions between a difficult wife and an insensitive husband that they were nonetheless able to smooth over, until the cumulative weight of ill will between the couple finally led them to divorce in 44 B.C. As paternal and maternal uncles to the younger Quintus, the two friends also worried about their nephew's development, trying to insert their own sensible influences as a means to counteract the volatility of his parents and to shape him into the adult they longed to see.

Around the time Cicero's son was born, Tullia was thought old enough to be betrothed to a young nobleman, C. Calpurnius Piso Frugi, and the wedding probably took place some years later. Piso

33. Good maps of ancient Rome and photos of the remains of the interior of private houses on the Palatine Hill roughly contemporary with the lifetime of Cicero are in Coarelli 1975, 135–61; the emperor Augustus also had a house on the back side of the Palatine, while his Julio-Claudian successors built on the face overlooking the Roman Forum. What made the Palatine highly desirable as a residential area was its proximity to the Forum.

died about 57 B.C., and about a year after his death Tullia married another young nobleman, Furius Crassipes. That marriage dissolved after two or three years, and she and her mother arranged a subsequent marriage to P. Cornelius Dolabella (consul in 44 B.C.), with whom she had two sons, neither surviving infancy. Tullia and Dollabella also divorced, and not long after the death of the second child, Tullia herself died (45 B.C.); Cicero's grief was inconsolable and he lamented the loss of his daughter for the remaining two years of his life. Some time not long before Tullia's death and after nearly thirty years of marriage, Cicero divorced Terentia; in letters to his friend Atticus, he alluded to, but never fully explained, Terentia's dishonesty and underhandedness in her dealings with him. Returning Terentia's dowry created considerable financial hardship for Cicero. Although he was now about sixty years old, Cicero looked for a new wife and soon settled on a very young woman named Publilia, whose considerable fortune Cicero was holding in trust in accordance with the terms of her father's will. The couple was soon divorced, and again Cicero faced the return of a wife's dowry.

Cicero lived through tumultuous times, when Rome was convulsed in civil wars. He knew great political successes, becoming consul in 63 B.C. although no other member of his family had ever achieved the office; he knew exile and was murdered in the proscriptions that followed in the wake of Caesar's death and the struggles for supreme power that ensued thereafter between Caesar's heir, the young Octavian, and the factions of Caesar's friend and protégé Marc Antony. When Cicero governed the province of Cilicia in Asia Minor (51–50 B.C.), his son and nephew accompanied him, as did his brother, a man with greater military experience than Cicero himself. Some eight hundred letters written by Cicero survive, over half of which were written to Atticus; twenty-seven were written to his younger brother, Quintus, but some of these are very long, full of advice about how Quintus should conduct his public and private life. We have all of this or most of it as a result of the devoted labor of one other member of the household. Cicero freed his slave and secretary Tiro in 53 B.C. Tiro lived for nearly forty years after Cicero's death in 43 B.C., collecting his letters, arranging for their publication, and composing a biography of his former master.

C. Plinius Caecilius Secundus ("Pliny the Younger") was born about A.D. 61 to an important family of equestrian status at Comum on Lake

Como in the Cisalpine region of northern Italy. His father died before he was fourteen years old, and his estate was guarded for him by a *tutor* his father, Caecilius Secundus, had named in his will. His maternal uncle, C. Plinius Secundus, adopted his nephew in his will, and so the adoption became effective only after his uncle's death during the eruption of Vesuvius in A.D. 79 that buried the towns of Pompeii and Herculaneum. Following the fashion of his own time, the younger Pliny retained his natal nomen *Caecilius* after he assumed the name of his uncle. His education began at Comum, where he studied with a *grammaticus,* but for his advanced oratorical studies he went to Rome, where he was the pupil of Quintilian, appointed to the chair of rhetoric at Rome by the emperor Vespasian (d. A.D. 78). Little is known about Pliny's first marriages, although his second wife, from an aristocratic and wealthy family at Rome, seems to have died. His third wife, Calpurnia, like Pliny himself, was from a wealthy family of Comum, and she was considerably younger than her husband. The girl's parents were dead when the marriage was arranged, and she was being raised by her paternal aunt Calpurnia Hispulla, who was living in the household of her own father, L. Calpurnius Fabatus. By this time Aunt Calpurnia was Fabatus' only surviving child. Pliny had a distinguished career in the senate at Rome, becoming consul in A.D. 100, during which time he delivered the speech in praise of the emperor Trajan quoted earlier in this chapter. Trajan also sent Pliny to govern Bithynia as the emperor's legate, and some eighty letters that passed between the emperor and his legate survive from Pliny's days in the province. Pliny's letters to his young wife Calpurnia show him as a devoted husband, well aware of the pleasures of family life and the charms of his young bride. His letters to the girl's aunt and grandfather that speak of the couple's life together are perhaps even more revealing, and translations of four follow. The order of the letters is that which Pliny himself assigned to them.[34]

34. Pliny *Letters* 4.1, 4.19 (= L-F, no. 243), 8.10 (= L-F, no. 247), 8.11. Other letters to Calpurnius Fabatus, mostly dealing with public affairs and business, are 5.11, 6.12, 6.30, 7.11, 7.16, 7.23, 7.32; there are no other letters to Hispulla but several to his wife Calpurnia—6.4 (= L-F, no. 244), 6.7 (= L-F, no. 245), 7.5 (= L-F, no. 246). For a letter describing Pliny's seaside villa see 2.17 (= L-R II, no. 44); for the way Pliny spent his day, 9.36 (= L-R II, no. 45); for his philanthropy, 4.13 and *CIL* V 5262 (= L-R II, no. 71); for letters about women friends of the family, 3.16, 7.19 (= L-F, nos. 170, 172).

C. Plinius to Fabatus, his grandfather-in-law *(prosocer)*, greetings.

You have wanted to see your granddaughter and me for a long time. This wish of yours is very pleasing to both of us, I assure you, because we both want to see you and intend not to delay the pleasure any longer. Our baggage is ready for the trip and we shall hasten to you as fast as the journey permits. We intend to stop only once in Tuscany—not to see our estate and personal property, because we could do that another time, but to carry out a necessary obligation. Near my estate is a town called Tifernum-on-Tiber, which made me its *patronus* when I was still just a boy, with more eager anticipation and perhaps with less good judgment. They celebrate my arrival, feel sorry when I leave, and rejoice at my advancing career. In order that I pay back their good favor (for it is not good to have others outdo you with their good will) I built a temple there at my own expense. It would be impious of me to postpone its dedication, since it is now finished. We will therefore be in the town for dedication day, and I have decided to celebrate this with a public feast. We may be able to leave on the following day, but we shall certainly rush on our trip all the more. I hope we find you and your daughter in good health, for I know you will be happy when you see us safely arrived. Farewell.

C. Plinius to his Calpurnia Hispulla, greetings.

You are an example of faithfulness. You loved your dear departed brother with a special affection that he reciprocated and you love his daughter as your own, not only as an aunt *(amita)*—you even supply her with the affection of her lost father. So I have no doubt that you will be overjoyed when you hear that she has turned out to be worthy of her father, worthy of you, and worthy of her grandfather *(avus)*. She is very clever and extremely thrifty; she loves me, which is an indication of her purity. Her love for me leads her to the study of literature—she picks up my compositions, reads them, and even learns them by heart. She is as concerned for me when I start a new court case as she is happy for me when it is over. She sends people to the court who tell her how the case is going, what applause I get, and what the end is. When I recite my work, she sits nearby, discreetly behind a curtain, and eagerly listens as people praise me. She sings the verses I write and accompanies herself on the lyre. She has no teacher but Love—the very best. From this evidence I think it most certain that the harmony between us will be only greater in all our days to come. For she loves neither my youth nor my body, for these are gradually declining and growing old, but my glory. The reason is that she was brought up by your hand and formed by your instruction. In living with you she saw nothing except what was moral and honorable, and learned to love me from what you told her about me. For you honored my mother as if she were your own child and you shaped me from the time I was a little child, praising me and forecasting that I would be the man my wife thinks I now am. So, we both thank you very much—I, because you gave her to me, and she, because you gave me to her, as though you chose us for one another. Farewell.

C. Plinius to Fabatus, his grandfather-in-law, greetings.
I know how much you want to see a great-grandchild from us, and therefore you will be all the more sad to learn that she has had a miscarriage. Due to her inexperience, she did not realize she was pregnant; she did not take proper care of herself and did things she should not have done. She has learned a very serious lesson and almost died as a result. So, even though it is hard for you at your age to accept the fact that a prospective child has been lost, nonetheless, you need to thank the gods because although they denied you a great-grandchild *(pronepotes)* for the moment, they saved your granddaughter *(neptes).* They will certainly give babies, since, despite what has happened, we now know that she is capable of conceiving a child. I encourage and advise you with the same thoughts I use for myself. You cannot want great-grandchildren any more than I want children. The path to public offices will be easy for them, since they are your offspring and mine, with our well-known names and a family-tree that goes back for generations. I hope we see them born and that it changes our present sadness into joy. Farewell.

C. Plinius to his Hispulla, greetings.
I think you love your brother's daughter even more than a mother might, and so I must tell you my latest news before the other things, in order that the happiness you will feel will not give

way to anxiety. Although I am still afraid that after your joy you will relapse into fears and even as you rejoice that she is out of danger, you will at the same time be horrified at how endangered she was. She is now in good spirits and restored to her old self and to me; she recovers as rapidly as she was once in danger. She was frightfully ill—may I say this without ill omen—but it wasn't her fault, so much as her youthful foolishness. As a result there was a miscarriage and a sad experience for her inexperienced womb. Even though you can take no consolation for the loss of your brother from either a little nephew *(nepotes)* or niece *(neptes)*, just remember that your desire has only been postponed rather than denied. You see she herself is safe and it is from her that the child will come. Please make excuses to your father for this accident, for he is more likely to indulge you, for you are a woman. Farewell.

Sadly, Pliny and Calpurnia do not seem to have ever had children after her miscarriage.

Family Life in the Provinces at the Middle Ranks of Imperial Society

In order to hear wives and mothers speaking their concerns in their own voices, it is necessary to turn to the dry sands of the Roman province of Egypt, for women's letters have been preserved there in a quantity equaled nowhere else in the ancient Mediterranean world.[35] The families represented are neither prodigiously wealthy nor abjectly poor; some have considerable property, while others have only a small bit of land. Nonetheless, their property was sufficient for the family to acquire and preserve documents that safeguarded the family's possessions, and it is these written documents and the private letters family members sent to one another when separated that provide a particularly close look at family life in the middle levels of imperial society. For

35. For texts about the family in Roman Egypt in English translation see Rowlandson forthcoming; White 1986; A.S. Hunt and C.C. Edgar, eds., *Select Papyri,* vol. 1 (Cambridge, 1932), cited as *Sel.pap.* I. See also Pomeroy 1988. The population of Roman Egypt continued the age-old practice of mummifying the body for burial, placing a portrait of the deceased, made in life, over the face. Elegant and copious reproductions of the mummy portraits are in Doxiadis 1995.

example, an archive of over two hundred papyri, written in Greek, once belonged to the family of Apollonios, governor of a small area in Middle Egypt and owner of estates in neighboring districts to the north; the family papers are dated between A.D. 113 and 120 and were found by clandestine diggers in Hermopolis, either in the family's residence in the town or in their suburban villa, since the family owned more than a single residence. Although not Roman citizens, the family belonged to the upper strata of provincial society. The women of the family, Apollonios' wife, Aline, and his mother, Eudaimonis, supervised the family's weaving, together with servants and slaves. These women were also able to read and write to some degree, and although they employed scribes to write the body of their letters, they usually penned closing greetings in their own hands, and they sometimes inserted interlinear messages as well, as they reread a letter before its dispatch. The eldest daughter of Apollonios and Aline, Heraidous, was perhaps their first child to survive infancy, and she lived with her grandmother Eudaimonis in Hermopolis, being schooled there with a private tutor. Apollonios himself rose to the highest Roman bureaucratic office available to Greco-Egyptians during the Roman Principate, becoming *strategos* of the Apollonopolite (Heptakomias) nome by 12 June 114; he was still serving some five or more years later. Apparently he brought many of his public documents back home with him after his term of duty. These papers and letters of his provide much information about the management of government affairs, but it is the letters written by his wife and mother that offer a closer look at the family. Apollonios had the misfortune to be in office when the Jewish revolt that began in Cyrene spread to Egypt on its way eastward to Mesopotamia and northward to Cyprus; as a result of the revolt, Jewish settlements in Egypt were largely destroyed and the Jewish population was killed or scattered. Within Egypt the uprising began in Alexandria and advanced southward into the countryside and to Hermopolis in Middle Egypt. Although a civilian official, Apollonios was nonetheless called on to take part in the fighting in various areas, even campaigning as far north as Memphis, not far from modern Cairo. By late fall of 117 Apollonios had twice written to the prefect of Egypt, requesting a leave of sixty days so that he could attend to his private affairs and restore to working order his estates in and around Hermopolis—these had suffered, he claimed, because of his absence "and also because of the attack of the impious Jews." Aline was not infrequently with her husband during his tour of duty as *strategos,* and although she was separated from Heraidous, other, unnamed children accompanied her and Apollonios.

The letters, some of which follow, were written on sheets of papyrus, then folded and addressed for dispatch. Since they are nearly 1,900 years old, parts of the papyrus sheets may have broken off or the ink may have become faded.[36]

Eudaimonis to Apollonios, 30 June 115 (?).

. . . at any rate, if the gods are willing, and especially the unconquerable Hermes, may they not defeat you. As far as the rest is concerned, may you be well for my sake with all of your people. Heraidous salutes you, your daughter whom the evil eye may not touch. Epeiph 6.

(Address on the back.) To Apollonios.

Aline to Apollonios,[37] early September 115 (?).

Aline to Apollonios her brother, many greetings. I am very worried about you, because of events that are said to be taking

36. Volumes of papyri are cited in abbreviated form—see the list of abbreviations and full bibliography for the volumes in the *Checklist of Editions* (cited above, p. xii). The letters from the archive of Apollonios translated here are *P.Giss.* 24 = *WChr.* 15 = *CPJ* II 437 (+ *BL* VII 59); *P.Giss.* 10 = *CPJ* II 436; *P.Brem.* 63 = *CPJ* II 442; *P.Giss.* 78; *P.Flor.* III 332 = *Sel.pap.* I 114 (+ *BL* VII 54); *P.Giss.* 21 (+ *BL* V 34); *P.Giss.* 23; *P.Giss.* 77 (+ *BL* III 68); *P.Giss.* 80 = *Sel.pap.* I 116 = L-F, no. 215; *P.Giss.* 85 (+ *BL* III 68) = L-F, no. 216. For other texts from the archive of Apollonios with English translation see *CPJ* II 436–44 and *Sel.pap.* I 115 and II 298, 354, 423. Also part of the archive are *P.Brem.* 1–82 and *SB* X 10277–78; *P.Giss.* 3–27, 41–47, and 58–93; *P.Flor.* III 326–34; *P.Alex.Giss.* 14–61 = *SB* X 10639–53. Discussion of the archive is in *CPJ* II, pp. 225–27.

37. While it is certain that Apollonios is Aline's husband, early papyrologists and ancient historians supposed that they were also brother and sister, since close-kin marriages were not uncommon in Roman Egypt. Although Eudaimonis calls Aline her daughter in letters to Aline alone, she never does so in letters she sends jointly to Apollonios and Aline, suggesting that she uses the term "daughter" as a gesture of affection for Aline, not because she is her birth mother. Thus, when Aline calls Apollonios her "brother," she, too, is more likely broadening the emotional ties that bind her to her husband; Aline also calls Tetes "mother," even though the woman seems to be a servant in the household.

place and because you left me suddenly. Neither drink nor food do I approach with pleasure, but staying awake night and day, I have this single concern about your safety. Only my father's care raises me up, and on the first day of the new year—I swear by your safety—I would have stayed in bed without eating a bite, if my father had not come and forced me. Please, then, take care of yourself without mishap and do not endure danger alone without a guard, but, as the *strategos* here assigns the burdensome tasks to his officers, you too do the same thing. . . . my father . . . because the name of my brother was proposed . . . but god will . . . him. If, at any rate, brother, . . . from your affairs . . . write to me . . . to you . . . is coming up . . . of your safety. . . .
(Address on the back.) To Apollonios my brother.

Eudaimonis to Aline, 16 July 116 (?).

Eudaimonis to Aline her daughter, greetings. I pray first of all that you may be delivered of your child in due time and that you get an announcement that it's a boy. You sailed up river on the 29th and on the next day I was drawing down [the wool from the loom]. With difficulty I got the material from the dyer on 10 Epeiph. I am working together with your slave women to the best of my ability. I do not find women capable of working with us, for all of them are working for their own mistresses. Our people have walked around the entire town, offering higher wages. Your sister Souerous was delivered of her child. Teeus wrote me, praising you, so that, my lady, I know my commands remain in force. For, once she left all her own people, she set out to be with you. The little girl [Heraidous?] salutes you and is steadfast with her lessons for school. Know that I am not going to pay attention to god [Hermes?] until I am reunited with my son safe and sound. Why did you send me the 20 drachmas, when I am having a difficult time? Already I have before my eyes the notion that I shall be naked throughout the winter.
(2nd hand.) Farewell. 22 Epeiph.
(1st hand, written in the left margin.) The wife of Eudemos does not leave my side and I express my thanks to her.
(Address on the back, 3rd hand.) To Aline my daughter.

Aline to Tetes, undated.

Aline to Tetes her mother, greetings. You told me about the sale of the garments. Now please expedite also the remaining items. I have made certain that I finished drawing down [from the loom] your . . . —necessarily, in fact, as you know, also because of the . . . , until [the matter?] is finally [?] brought to a successful conclusion. When my little Heraidous wrote to her father, she did not send a greeting to me, and I do not know why.
(2nd hand.) I pray that you are well.
(Address on the back.) To Tetes my mother.

Eudaimonis to Apollonios, c. 30 September.

Eudaimonis to Apollonios her son, greetings. It does not escape you that two months ago today I journeyed to the unmanageable Diskas, since he was not waiting for your arrival. Well, he is seeking to attack me now in your absence with other friends of his also from the gymnasium, supposing that he can get hold of our affairs unjustly. I have already done my part, and I have neither bathed nor worshipped the gods, because I am so fearful about your unfinished business, if indeed it is still unsettled. Don't let it be unsettled any longer, lest I be dragged off to the law courts. Before all things I pray that you are well, together with all my little children and their mother. Keep writing to me about the health of you all, so that I might have a consolation for my journey. Farewell, my lord. Phaophi 3.

At your wedding the wife of Diskas my brother brought me 100 drachmas. Since now Nilos her son is about to marry, it is only fair that we also give a gift in return, even if there are unresolved claims against them.
(Address on the back.) To Apollonios her son.

Eudaimonis to Apollonios, c. 20 December.

Eudaimonis to Apollonios her son, greetings. I was quite overjoyed to hear that you are well and also your sister Soeris. From the day on which you sent me notice, I have been hunting for the Spartan-style garment, but only found a worn-out Pergamene one instead. You are not unaware that you gave us raw wool [?] for producing the white garment. (2nd hand.) And you made a mistake! (1st hand.) As a result, you are spending a pound and a

stater of weight. At any rate, you are to buy it and send it, so that speedily it may be dispatched onward. Please, stay at home so that you do not distress me . . . Salute your sister Aline. Soeris thanks you very much and she wrote me a letter about this. Little Heraidous salutes you and her mother.
(2nd hand.) Farewell, my child. Choiak 24.
(Address on the back.) To Apollonios *strategos* of the Apollonopolite nome.

Eudaimonis to Aline, undated.

Eudaimonis to Aline her daughter, many greetings. I have as the most compelling of all my prayers the one for your health and that of your brother Apollonios and of your [children] whom the evil eye may not touch. Next, thanks be to god that you . . . Souerous salutes you and also Heraidous. Farewell. . . .
(Written in the bottom margin.) But she (?) made. . . .
(Written in the left margin.) After you have sent them to me . . . a suit (?) for Heraidous. Pauni . . .
(Address on the back.) To Aline from Eudaimonis.

Teeus, to Aline, c. 19 November.

Teeus to Aline her mistress, greetings. First of all, Heraidous salutes you and I salute all your people. When they were here with us, ... of mine, when I am leaving . . . . Then I knew that you sent the tunic to me. I praised you very much before all the gods, because you clothed me. I hope it turns out, then, that I shall pray on your behalf under the lucky circumstance that you have given birth to a boy baby and . . . the women have been summoned by [?] . . . to Amounis. . . . Imagine that I am . . . and if you are going to give me something, . . . a little . . . , . . . instead of me and send me what you have. Farewell mistress, Hathyr 23.
(Address on the back.) Deliver to Aline.

Fragment of a letter about Heraidous, c. 13 December.

. . . . Heraidous salutes you and so does Hemou. . . [?] and Helene and Tinoutis and her papa and all in the house, and the mother of our very sweet Heraidous. The doves and the chickens which I am not accustomed to eat, send to . . . , the teacher of Heraidous. Helene, mother of Apollonios, has asked you to keep her son Hermaios under your hand. All the things I did not eat when I was visiting with you . . . send to the daughter's teacher so that he may put in much effort for her. I pray that you are well. Choiak 17.

Fragment of a letter from Hermaios to Apollonios, c. 30 August.

. . . . I [Hermaios] thank you alone [Apollonios] so very much in front of lord Hermes and I do not omit making obeisance on your behalf each day. The little Heraidous salutes you and [so does] your mother Helene. I, Hermaios, likewise salute you. I beg you to . . . to the administrator, so that he may furnish me with things suitable for school, such as a book for Heraidous to read. Farewell, my lord. Thoth 2.

Other Roman Families

Many Roman families are nearly lost from our view.[38] We know more about the cramped rooms and tiny apartments of the urban poor than we know about the men and women who inhabited them. Tenements *(insulae)* occupied an entire city block, their external walls extending almost to the street, their interior walls enclosing a courtyard of common space open to the sky. The inhabitants carried water from nearby fountains and cisterns; they dumped their chamber pots into open sewers out in the street; they kept charcoal braziers in their quarters for cooking, although the live coals created a constant danger of fire. Apartment buildings seldom rose beyond four or five stories, and the cheapest and smallest accommodations were on the top floor, after a long climb up increasingly rickety stairs or even a ladder. The ground floor was often occupied by shops, and shopkeepers slept in lofts above their shops, guarding their wares by night against incursions of thieves. Living space was always at a premium in the cities and large towns, and public spaces afforded some relief and sources of entertainment

38. The ruins of Ostia, the commercial port of Rome, preserve apartment buildings of various types. For plans and discussion of the inhabitants see Meiggs 1973; for a more general view from a wider selection of evidence, Joshel 1992. For documentary evidence on work see L-R II, nos. 24–28, 102, 116–17 (farming); for women's occupations, L-F, nos. 283–85 (farming), 389–94 (prostitution), 295–302 (work in the arena), 307–37 (craftswomen, artists, and laborers), 369–74 (medical practitioners).

from cramped domestic quarters. Much of Roman life was lived outdoors in the relatively dry and beneficent climate of the Mediterranean. The men and women who lived in the rooms and apartments did band together for festival occasions, and they formed burial associations, pooling their meager resources to provide for memorial banquets, commemorative plaques, and dedications to the gods. Agricultural labor occupied most peoples in Italy and throughout the Empire, but few of those who labored in the fields left anything of individual identity behind them. The poor of the countryside are thus almost totally hidden from our view, although it was commonly said that the life of a homebred slave *(verna)* in the city or town was more pleasant than the lot of the poor man in the country.

However poor, freedmen and freedwomen were Roman citizens, and they could form legitimate marriages that were recognized and respected in Roman law; if the couple's union antedated manumission and transfer to free status, the children born to them in slavery remained slaves, unless specific steps were taken by the parents to manumit them. Slaves were never able to form legitimate marriages of any kind, yet the breeding of slaves within the household increased as Roman conquests began to net the conquerors captives fit only for agricultural labors on their estates and not skilled and literate prisoners like those that had been captured in the earlier wars of conquest in the urbanized areas of Sicily and Greece. The earlier captives were suited by virtue of their previous lives to be a wanted addition to a sophisticated household. Education, when combined with shrewdness, brought privileges to slaves and even the opportunity of purchasing freedom for themselves and a fellow slave. Those with service skills were valued members of the household, and the titles they bore in life—such as *ornatrix,* "hairdresser"—continued to individualize their slots in the family tomb. Homebred slaves shared in the amenities of an aristocratic household, at times becoming childhood fellows with the master's sons and daughters and following the little ones into their important adult careers. Little served, however, to bind a slave family together, and its members were subject to separation through sale as well as individual manumissions. Slaves were property, the master's to dispose of as he chose; it was a matter of investment and return, and as long as the supply of slaves fit for agricultural work remained plentiful, there was little incentive to do other than work field hands until they died. Despite the inherent fragility of the slave family, a sense of kinship was sometimes strong enough for a family of urban slaves to unite in grief and erect a modest memorial for deceased kin.

Lifestyles and Patterns of Living

The House *(Domus)*

The layout of the aristocratic house reflected the highly public concerns of the paterfamilias: those rooms on the direct axis with the front entranceway were for public display, and access was permitted to all callers who passed through the entranceway and the scrutiny of the doorkeeper, or *ianitor*.[39] According to the architect Vitruvius, writing at the very end of the Republic and the early days of the Principate, men of rank, who had numerous obligations to their fellow citizens because of holding magistracies and military commands, required lofty entrance courts in regal style, followed by a spacious reception hall, or *atrium*. This large room was partly open to the sky through an opening *(impluvium)* in the center of the roof; the gods of the ancestors and the family were housed there in cabinet-like shrines, and the masks of ancestors, *imagines*, were on permanent display along the atrium's walls. Many of the family's ceremonies, both sociopolitical and religious, were held in the atrium, including funerals. The second room on the main axis, the *tablinum*, was given over to the public business of the household; family accounts and records *(tabulae)* were stored there, and the room's proportions were to reflect those of the atrium. The paterfamilias and materfamilias might preside over family business in the *tablinum*, receiving reports from stewards of the household and overseers of country estates, checking the household's store of raw materials, or arranging for the distribution of products from the family's urban and agricultural workers. Men of rank also needed additional interior space with gardens, as well as covered and open walkways *(peristyles)*; their dining rooms *(triclinia)* were appropriate for the various seasons of the year, with the one for inclement weather enclosed and protected but that for fair weather opening onto the adjacent interior courtyard. The grand house often included private bathing accom-

39. Vitruvius *Architecture* 6.1.1–8.10 deals with the layout of Roman houses at the beginning of the first century A.D. Many examples of house architecture are known from the towns buried by the eruption of Vesuvius in A.D. 79: see Wallace-Hadrill 1994; Deiss 1985. See also Clarke 1991; D'Arms 1970.

modations *(balnea)*, all in proportions commensurate with the family's dignity and fortunes. Although some of these refinements were considered Greek luxuries in their origin, they quickly became an integral part of the wealthy Roman house, and the interior central courtyard, in particular, continued to develop and expand as the focal point of the family's living quarters at the expense of the more formal atrium and *tablinum.* Grand houses also contained libraries, picture galleries, and meeting halls, finished off with an elegance similar to that in the great public buildings, since public councils as well as private law suits and hearings before arbitrators were often held in the houses of powerful men. The urban centers and seaside villas buried in the eruption of Vesuvius in A.D. 79 have preserved both modest quarters and elegant residences much as they were when the families lived in them. The seaside villa belonging to the family of Nero's second wife, Poppaea Sabina, proclaimed the elegant taste and abundant wealth of its owners through the coordination of its mosaic pavements, its painted walls, its stucco moldings and cornices, and the tendency for a suite of rooms in it to be decorated in similar style. A covered walkway faced toward the sea, and adjacent gardens boasted a large swimming pool.[40] Antique sculptures in marble and bronze were imported from conquered Sicily and Greece, and copies were made by local artists; these decorated the gardens and courtyards. When the emperor Hadrian (d. A.D. 138) built a magnificent villa at the base of the Alban Hills to the southeast of Rome, he created an estate composed of many separate buildings, often mimicking the layout and architecture of sites he encountered in his travels throughout the Empire.[41]

Vitruvius considered some parts of the house totally "private" and intended for the exclusive use of family members (including slaves and dependents) and specially invited guests. These were the sleeping rooms *(cubicula)*, dining rooms, baths, and the like. "No outsider has the right to enter these rooms without a specific invitation," he commented, and such rooms were usually not on the main axis of the entranceway. Bedrooms are conspicuous for their overall smallness and tiny windows, since keeping them cool during the long hot days and warm nights of summer was more important than keeping them warm in winter; there were other rooms, such as warm baths and a

40. Good reproductions of the villa and its wall decorations are in the German edition by de Franciscis (1975).

41. For the estate of Hadrian see Boatwright 1987, 134–60.

solarium with a southwestern exposure, to draw the thinner, winter sun. Many bedrooms of Herculaneum and Pompeii give the impression of not having been reserved for the exclusive use of a particular family member; these are sparsely furnished with bed, lamp, and cupboards and generally lack individuation. There were no separate quarters for the Roman wife and her female retinue, as there were in Greek houses, and Roman women not only dined together with their husbands at home but also accompanied them to the homes of friends.

Kitchens and other workrooms were not infrequently in detached buildings, where stewards, overseers, cooks, and slaves were the major presence. Cereals and breads formed the staples of the ancient diet, supplemented by fresh fruits and vegetables in season or dried versions in wintertime.[42] Edible nuts, olives, and grapes were grown throughout the Mediterranean, making sauces, oils, raisins, and wines plentiful. Difficulties in preserving meat and fish often meant that these were either consumed immediately or preserved in smoked, salted, or pickled forms; fowl provided not only meat in relatively small quantity but also eggs. A cookbook with recipes by Apicius—the copies we have in medieval manuscripts include recipes from other writers as well—were intended for the wealthy household, and it includes such items as stuffed dormice *(glires)*. The family's friends and dependents lived in their own establishments, visiting for festive meals and celebrations. A full complement of slaves dwelt with the family, quartered in small rooms at the edge of the domicile or in adjoining buildings. They were expected to move about the house via cramped passageways and narrow staircases, as inconspicuous as possible in their duties of service for the family.

As Roman interests expanded in the Italian peninsula during the Republic, local aristocrats in growing numbers transferred their family seat to Rome and cast their lot with the upper classes of the City. From the middle of the first century A.D. onward, leading provincial families were acquiring Roman citizenship in ever greater numbers, and while some quickly aped Roman elite behavior and aspired to Romanness,

42. Useful collections of essays are Wilkins, Harvey, and Dobson 1996 and Murray and Tecusan 1995. For a literal English translation of Apicius see Joseph Dommers Vehling, *Apicius: Cookery and Dining in Imperial Rome* (New York, 1977); for a version of Apicius adapted to the modern kitchen, Ilaria Gozzini Giacosa, *A Taste of Ancient Rome* (Chicago and London, 1992).

others retained within their households more traditional patterns from their homeland, even after transfer of the family's residence to Rome. Aristocratic women of Roman origins, as well as Italians and assimilated provincials, became increasingly visible in public in the later days of the Republic; women whose families preferred Greek patterns for female behavior, however, might still lead cloistered and separate lives in the women's quarters. The Greek physician Galen (d. ca. A.D. 213), who came from Pergamum in the eastern Mediterranean, encountered both Greek and Roman patterns of behavior among important women in the City.[43] On the one hand, as physician he had complete access to the wife of Justus and visited her day after day. She was wasting away from sleeplessness and a distaste for food, but from her pulse he diagnosed that she suffered from "lovesickness," for her heartbeat elevated merely at the mention of a famous dancer named Pylades. In the imperial palace, Galen discussed the sore throat and fever of the young crown prince Commodus with one of the emperor's relatives, Annia Faustina, who was concerned about the boy; at the same time, Galen was annoyed at the sassy way in which she teased him about his medical reputation and his pugnaciousness, and he considered her impertinent in her boldness. Galen no doubt told this story (in which he was the butt of the joke) to prove yet again how closely associated he was to the imperial family and to the emperor Marcus Aurelius (d. A.D. 180). On the other hand, in the household of an ex-consular senator, Flavius Boethus, from a provincial family of the Greek-speaking province of Syria Palestina, Galen was expected to learn about the wife's condition through discussion with the woman's husband and with her nurses, "the best in Rome," he adds. He prescribed treatments for the wife, with her nurses acting as intermediaries, and he saw the wife only once in person, on a chance occasion when she had fainted while at the baths and Galen happened to be nearby. Her nurses were shrieking with helplessness; Galen rushed forward, pushed them aside, and went about the business of trying to revive her. It was then and only then that he saw her face-to-face and touched her body; this experience gave him the clues he needed for discovering those therapies that would cure her

43. Galen *Prognosis* 6 (wife of Justus), 8 (wife of Boethus), 12 (Annia Faustina); *Prognosis* is Galen's "medical biography," and it vividly portrays elite behavior at Rome toward the end of the second century A.D. For English translation by Vivian Nutton see *Corpus Medicorum Graecorum* V 8.1 (Berlin, 1979).

and bring him in the end a fine present of four hundred pieces of gold from her husband.

Roman domestic architecture emphasized the public position and the obligations of the paterfamilias, as well as reflecting the wealth of the familia, its ties to the past, and its hopes for the future. It also emphasized the difference between rich and poor, and Vitruvius noted that free men of modest fortune did not need entrance courts, an atrium, or a *tablinum*, built in grand style, because such men were more apt to discharge their social obligations by going around to visit others, rather than by having others come to them.

The Romans referred to themselves as "a nation of wearers of the *toga" (gens togata)*. This full-length basic garment, which underwent many changes in the course of centuries (becoming ever more elaborate), was the distinctive Roman dress for men. The toga, in its many different forms and variations, proclaimed the status of the wearer; it was usually made of wool and draped on the body. The toga's bulkiness made it unsuitable for workers, who wore it only on holidays; and even members of the upper classes came increasingly to favor less unwieldy clothing, reserving their togas for formal occasions.[44] Prior to puberty, all children wore the *toga praetexta*, a toga similar to that worn by adult males but with a narrow purple border along one edge. While the boy assumed the man's toga at about twelve years of age, the girl did not wear the distinctive garb of the Roman matron until after her marriage—a tunic surmounted by a woolen stole (*stola*) and a mantle (*palla*) that veiled her head when she appeared in public.

Elite families usually possessed several residences, although a family's primary establishment was its house in Rome or in another urban center. Country villas near Rome, either in the Alban Hills to the east of the City or seaside in the Bay of Naples, provided Roman family members with a retreat from the City's heat in the unhealthy seasons of late summer and early autumn. The toga and all the responsibilities it symbolized could be left behind in Rome. Those who could afford to do so also maintained residences and staffs of domestic slaves on properties at greater distances from the City and in the provinces, in addition to the agricultural slaves that farmed their lands under the master's overseer. Such residences furnished family members and friends with their

44. Useful essays on clothing, footwear, hairstyles, and jewelry are in Sebesta and Bonfante 1994.

accustomed amenities as they journeyed in Italy and the provinces. For the less affluent, there were inns (*stabulum* or *hospitium*), with small guest rooms and space in which to quarter animals; some inns seem also to have functioned as brothels.

Public Buildings at Rome and in the Provincial City

Domestic architecture throughout the Empire often retained local features, because these were particularly suitable to the climate of the area. But Roman notions about public architecture and the layout of public space came to dominate not only Italy and the western provinces, as urban settlements were being built from the ground up on the model of Rome, but even the eastern provinces, where city life had long been a dominant feature.[45] A centrally located *forum* was given a paved surface and surrounded by a colonnade; permanent public buildings lined the forum's sides. In the apsed building *(basilica)*, local magistrates conducted public business and presided over law courts; a *curia* housed meetings of the local senate; a temple that celebrated the emperor, the imperial family, and the gods of Rome provided a focal point for public festivals. Specialized markets tried to provide continuous supplies of basic foods to the urban dwellers, and some were elaborate edifices, surrounded by covered walkways. Stone bridges crossed the rivers to facilitate trade, and aqueducts brought supplies of fresh water from higher ground to feed the fountains and the wide proliferation of public baths. Although Rome itself was slow to build a stone theater, with the first one dedicated only in 55 B.C., theaters for dramatic performances, amphitheaters for gladiatorial games, and circuses for horse racing *(hippodromes)* were being erected in cities and towns throughout the Empire through benefactions by the emperor and by wealthy local families, as these vied with one another in proclaiming their importance through the amenities they provided fellow citizens. Greek cities of the eastern Mediterranean possessed monumental public structures when Rome was little more than a country village, yet Roman patterns for public architecture spread here as well. Greek theaters were remodeled to accommodate changing tastes, with their lower courses covered

45. For public buildings see MacDonald 1982, 1986; for a descriptive catalog of the public buildings in Rome, Richardson 1992. For Roman town planning, see Perring 1991. For Rome and other ancient cities as a place in which to live and work see Stambaugh 1988. Cf. also L-R I, no. 208; II, nos. 16–17, 22, 134, 194.

with waterproof cement so as to add the staging of mock naval battles to their repertoires of dramatic performances. The lavishness of the public buildings in the major urban centers offered less affluent families of the cities and the urban poor both entertainment and pleasant surroundings in which to spend their leisure time. The excitements and amenities of the city and the town compensated in part for the crowded conditions in which less wealthy inhabitants were forced to dwell.

Although some Romans lived long and productive lives, the life of the average Roman was short when measured against modern experience. Habits of Roman families—their naming patterns, their identification with the family's domicile and the city in which the primary *domus* was located—created impressions of permanence that extended far beyond the brief lifetimes of specific individuals within the family. The flexibility inherent in Roman notions of family fostered a sense of continuity that not only extended from one generation to the next but united family members with the spirits of their ancestors, as the living celebrated festivals of remembrance for the dead and the dead awaited the living in the family tomb.

CHAPTER TWO

Elite Male Identity in the Roman Empire

Maud W. Gleason

To ask how an aristocratic male's gender identity was constructed in the Roman Empire is to assume that it was something fabricated by culture rather than automatically bestowed by nature. This is a proposition to which few gentlemen in any era would publicly assent. All forms of aristocratic socialization straddle the ambiguities suggested by the English word *breeding*. Is "good breeding" something inherited or acquired, a matter of good genes or good manners? The cultural reproduction of social superiority (male over female, aristocrat over commoner) is a project that presents a double face to the world, representing itself as natural and inevitable to outsiders, but stressing to insiders the importance of nurture and the vulnerability of the entire project to lapses of taste and self-control.

The literary remains of Roman civilization (that is, almost everything written except inscriptions and papyri) constitute a discourse confined to insiders. While functional literacy was a skill widely distributed in the nonaristocratic urban population (slaves and freedmen have left us contracts on papyri and epitaphs on stone), "literary" literacy was a privilege—indeed a sign—of upper-class status. Of what women read, we know little; of what they wrote, almost nothing survives. Public speaking, even more than literary writing, was the hallmark of the socially privileged male. A woman who spoke for herself in court earned a place in a catalogue of curiosities—and the nickname *Androgyne* ("Man-Woman") "because she exhibited a male spirit in the outward form of a woman" (Valerius Maximus *Memorable Deeds and Sayings* 8.3.1). To exhibit courage or excellence *(virtus)* was by definition to exhibit the qualities of a man *(vir)*.

For the purposes of this study it is perhaps fortunate that the literary production of the Roman empire was confined to aristocrats, for these gentlemen were greatly exercised about proper masculinity, and their writings bear traces of this preoccupation. The comments they directed to their peers about "gender correctness" (or the lack thereof) were part of the social performance of being a man and must be evaluated with some care as public pronouncements. Except for the private notebooks of Marcus Aurelius, no introspective writing survives from the high empire to give us insight into how a man might experience these matters subjectively.[1] From the second century A.D. the diaries of Aelius Aristides record the interventions of the healing god Asclepius in the convoluted course of a literary hypochondriac's career, but Aristides wrote to celebrate the god's providence and displays a complete lack of interest in the complexities of his own motivations. From the fifth century, we have Augustine's *Confessions,* which is like Aristides' diaries in that it celebrates the working out of divine providence in the course of an individual human life, but which is unlike Aristides' writings in that the battleground in the *Confessions* is not the human body but the human will. The intimacy of these reminiscences evokes a jolt of recognition in modern readers, but we must remember that Augustine was probably not the first Roman to steal fruit as a child and worry about it as an adult; the reason he was the first to write about such things is that only in the context of Christianity did such self-examination have any public meaning. Introspective writing in traditional pagan culture would have been a contradiction in terms, because literary education groomed men for public life. All writing was other-directed. A cultured person was not a private consumer of fine wines and Shakespeare reruns on public television, as in the United States; a cultured Roman was a public performer who spoke the language of the classics. Literary study aimed at the complete appropriation of classical models and the internalization of firmly traditional paradigms of self-presentation.

Just as there are no subjective documents, there are of course no media stereotypes we can turn to; there is no Marlboro Man to proclaim the cultural expectations of manhood in the Roman world. Statues, not billboards, dominated the urban landscape. Bronze and marble effigies, the commemorative statues of individual civic leaders, towered over every place of public assembly—the forum, the baths, the theater, and columned shopping arcades—just as their living originals dominated every public procession. These figures show certain common traits.

1. There is not much lyric poetry from this period.

Fig. 4. This statue of a priest from Aphrodisias in Caria (modern Turkey) projects the image of the dignified authority of a leading citizen accustomed to unquestioning respect. His role as father and husband is implicit, rather than explicit, in this image. (Courtesy of Professor R.R.R. Smith.)

Sometimes they wear the heavy crown of an imperial priesthood (fig. 4), sometimes the beard of a philosopher. Sometimes the hand that emerges from the folds of drapery carries a scroll, a token of the learned man. The stance is calm and solid, the body heavily clothed—the figures exhibit not the heroic nudity of the classical Greek athlete but the dignified authority of a leading citizen accustomed to unquestioning respect.

The Marlboro Man is, of course, a mythic figure, whose primal association with the great American outdoors is supposed to rub off on any man who smokes his brand of cigarettes. We simply do not know what mythic images of maleness appealed to ordinary Romans, although the tremendous popularity of successful chariot-racing drivers and gladiators offers a clue. But for educated Romans, as for the educated Greeks they ruled, their own history functioned as a mythology, providing an instructive array of paradigmatic male leaders. Alexander, Demosthenes, Cato, and Cicero—the great men of the past were invoked over and over again to inspire or excoriate their underachieving descendants. As we shall see in this chapter, impersonating these paradigmatic figures in public speaking contests was a major part of higher education for young aristocrats.

This higher education produced adults with strong opinions about appropriate deportment and deeply embedded expectations about gender roles. In the discourse these men conducted amongst themselves, in the prescriptive and censorious comments that they dropped in passing, we have a chance to discern what it meant to be a man. Where we find overlap between explicit moralizing pronouncements and the assumptions about gender embedded in more technical writings (e.g., medical, rhetorical, and physiognomical treatises), we may be fairly sure we have encountered beliefs that run deeper than public posturing.

To begin with the body: male and female bodies were considered not so much different in kind as in degree. Women's reproductive organs, after all, were the same as men's (uterus corresponding to scrotum, ovaries to testes, vagina to penis) but inverted, perhaps because of a deficit in natural heat during gestation, and therefore imperfect (fig. 5). The perfect body was male. Everybody knew that. Male flesh was warmer and drier than female flesh and better aerated by pores. This was important because disease was a matter of being clogged by one's own humors. We in the twentieth century tend to think of illness as caused by the intrusion of alien substances (be they toxic chemicals or infectious microorganisms) from the outside. The ancients, completely innocent of the germ theory of disease, worried about the body being poisoned by the imbalanced accumulation of the by-products of its own metabolism. Good pores favored the excretion of bad humors. Good flesh, that is, male flesh, thanks to its superior pores, would also be well aerated by pneuma, a sort of "vital spirit" that helped to keep it warm and dry. Pneuma was also a major ingredient in sperm. In the view of elite Greco-Roman doctors and the educated laymen who employed them to explain their illnesses as much as to treat them,

Fig. 5. This statue of an ideal woman, found at Pozzuoli, Italy, reveals many of the same characteristics representative of the ideal man: dignity, authority, and self-control. The figure of the *matrona* displays dignity rather than sexuality. (From the Francir Bartlett Donation, courtesy of the Museum of Fine Arts, Boston.)

women were clammy, Gollum-like creatures whose perpetual humidity was only somewhat relieved by regular menstruation.

For men, maintaining the ideal balance of their constitution was a challenge. First there was the question of what to eat. Wheat, the premium grain of the Mediterranean, warmed the flesh, while barley, in many regions the staple food of the poor, cooled it down. At the dining tables of the rich, an ethic of self-conscious frugality competed with the gross logic of overconsumption: excess is power. In this equation, the emperor could outdo everyone. Vitellius concocted a gigantic casserole he called "Shield of Minerva the Protectress," which provided graphic, edible symbolism of the extent of his power: "in it he mixed livers of parrot fish, pheasant and peacock brains, flamingo tongues, and the sperm of moray eels collected by captains and warships from the Parthian frontier to the Straits of Gibraltar" (Suetonius *Vitellius* 13). In an economy of scarcity, it is hard to say which packed more punch: the flamingo tongues on the banquet table or the heap of discarded carcasses in the trash. But not all wealthy men staged orgies. Drawing on the myths of a frugal Roman past and on the ethical precepts of Greek philosophy ("Nothing in excess"), some Roman aristocrats elaborated an ethic of self-control that stressed discipline and restraint. In their view, self-mastery, rather than self-indulgence, was the ultimate way to demonstrate one's entitlement to power over others. As to the effect of these dining choices on the body, everyone knew that a simple diet was healthier: "The penalty comes all too soon when you strip your bloated belly and haul a load of undigested peacock into the bath: sudden death and an intestate old age . . ." (Juv. *Satire* 1.142–44). A philosophically educated gentleman exacted from himself what poverty exacted from others. Note the irony of the following piece of graffiti from a latrine in the suburbs of Smyrna, which extols the excretory prowess of the rustic laborer in elegant Greek verses that he would of course be unable to read.

Well done, long-suffering tiller of the soil!
The stress of spadework and poverty is your lot in life.
Your meals are simple; you bed down in the woods;
You fill your bottomless tank with nothing but water.
You're sound, in good shape, and sit here only a few moments to lighten your belly.
You don't have to rub your lower back or slap your thighs,
But dump your load spontaneously.
The really wretched people are the rich, and those who hang around with them:
They prefer feasting to health.

(*Palatine Anthology* 9.644)

The philosopher Plutarch wrote a treatise on health precepts for cultivated men involved in public life. He observes that persons who have overloaded their digestive systems often do further damage by bowing to peer pressure to visit the baths, exercise, or even attend another drinking party. He recommends that a gentleman should maintain the balance of his constitution by watching himself closely for premonitory signs of "fullness" that indicate superfluous residue or polluted pneuma and taking precautions accordingly. One must be careful to do this, he says, without ostentation or the sort of holier-than-thou attitude that annoys one's peers. Asceticism ought to be discreet.

Upper-class people, on the advice of their doctors, worried about when to have sex. The pleasures of Aphrodite had an alarming way of leaving the body flaccid, metabolically weakened, and hence vulnerable to the toxic by-products of inefficient digestion. Besides, ejaculation produced a net loss of vital pneuma. Erotic overindulgence, in general, cooled one down, though baths, massage, and breathing exercises might prove restorative. Bathing itself required decisions: should a hot tub precede a cold plunge, or should it be the other way around? Public baths were a highly elaborated feature of urban life. The fanciest ones, endowed by emperors or provincial grandees, contained libraries, pleasure gardens, and lecture halls in addition to exercise grounds for wrestling and ball games, steam rooms, swimming pools, hot plunge tubs and sweat-scraping stations. Tendencies toward coed bathing were periodically restricted by imperial decree, but for men nudity was standard. Since the price of admission was fixed very low, the baths were one place where a gentleman would be expected to mingle with his social inferiors in the buff. Here the extent of one's paunch advertised the extent of one's wealth (or self-control). Here a man's physical carriage—posture, voice, and gesture—proclaimed his social status (as did his retinue of slaves, of course, and the style of salutation offered by friends and dependents).

Exercise was another means of regulating one's bodily constitution. But here again one had to make careful choices. Warfare was vigorous but irregular—not to mention dangerous—as a form of exercise. Indeed, military officers were increasingly recruited from outside the ranks of the upper classes. There was hunting on one's country estate, of course, but Galen readily concedes that hunting expeditions are both tedious and impractical for gentlemen with busy schedules (he promotes his own "small-ball workout" in a treatise of that name). To be a courtier or to assist a great magistrate all day is, in Galen's opinion, to be little better than a slave, since such people are too busy to care for their bodies. Health requires autonomy. This is not to say that Galen or anyone else advocated vigorous muscle-building exercise. Remember that in antiquity a gentleman had no desire to acquire the physique of a manual laborer (whereas today, a potbelly often indicates working-class status, while physical fitness is apt to be a sign of wealth and leisure). One medical advice book written for ancient Romans condemns athletic exercise outright, arguing that it renders the flesh dense, resistant, insensitive: "It is for this reason that athletes are generally more thickheaded than other people" (Oribasius 6.10.16). (For their part, athletic trainers were known to claim that intellectual conversation at dinner impaired nutrition and made the head "heavy.") Ball playing and shadowboxing (a Roman version of tai chi?) were thought to foster the ideal constitution. Oddly enough, vocal warm-ups were thought to do the same. Some physicians enthusiastically recommended vocal exercise as promoting aeration of the flesh through the dilation of the pores and the inspiration of pneuma. Since public speaking was, as we have said, the hallmark of the aristocratic male, interest in voice training was widespread in this sector of society, and many men were probably glad to hear that there was a scientific rationale for the exercises they would have practiced anyway. What the lower orders made of this habit we may infer from a comment by Plutarch, who recommends that his readers do vocal warm-ups, declaim, or read aloud, every single day.

> So neither a sea voyage nor a stay in a hotel should be an excuse for silence, not even if everybody laughs at you. For certainly it is no disgrace to exercise in a place where it is respectable to eat. But what really is shameful is to feel scared and self-conscious in front of sailors, muleteers, and innkeepers, who never laugh at travelers who work out by playing ball and shadowboxing, but only laugh at the man who uses his voice, even though in *his* exercises he teaches, questions, learns, and uses his memory. (Plutarch *Moral Essays* 130EF)

Clearly there was something embarrassing about revealing to outsiders the backstage preparation undergirding aristocratic male performance. Traveling could be stressful. Yet back at home, in a habitually deferential environment, aristocrats pursued their health regimens buttressed by the same sense of physical invulnerability that enveloped their wives, who bathed naked with complete composure in the presence of their slaves and social inferiors.

We have seen how much effort might go into maintaining a male constitution. It is now time to ask what it was that a man thought he was preventing by performing these routines. In the Roman world, sex differences were perceived to be matter of degree rather than kind. Since a man's gender identity was radically underdetermined by his anatomical sex, the ever present possibility of slipping into effeminacy awaited the lukewarm or the unwary. The specter of gender indeterminacy—even gender reversal—always lay in wait for potential deviants from the norms of correct deportment. What constituted correct deportment? "Absolutely every thing is significant," wrote Seneca, "if carefully observed. And it is possible to draw conclusions about someone's character from the most minute signs. A man who is sexually dissolute, for example, is revealed by his walk, by a single gesture, by the way he answers a simple question or touches his head with his finger, and by the way he moves his eyes" (*Letter* 52.12). Seneca's *Letters* are the product of a politically active aristocrat's cultivated retirement. We may imagine him coolly scanning the body language of humble petitioners or uneasy dinner guests. Control of one's own deportment must have been at a premium in such encounters. Physiognomy, the art of reading character from face and gesture, was, like astrology and dream interpretation, a recognized technical specialty in the ancient world. A Greek-speaking aristocrat from the eastern empire composed a physiognomical treatise that stressed the detection of a person's true location along a continuum of gender.

> You may obtain physiognomic indications of masculinity and femininity from your subject's glance, movement, and voice, and then, from among these signs, compare one with another until you determine to your satisfaction which of the two sexes prevails. For in the masculine there is something feminine to be found, and in the feminine something masculine, but the name "masculine" or "feminine" is assigned according to which of the two prevails. (Polemo *Physiognomy* 1 p. 192 Förster)

If there are masculine and feminine "types" that do not necessarily correspond to anatomical sex, then it should be possible to "slide" between genders. Hence the ancients had an intense cultural preoccupation with effeminacy: given that mixed gender signs are possible, how are we to know who is a real man? We may have to look very carefully: should someone's eyelids show the slightest sign of softness or slackening, or if his pupils move too rapidly, "then you may be sure that this is the profile of someone who is really feminine, even though you may find him among real men" (Polemo *Physiognomy* 1 p. 158 Förster). Strictly speaking, the physiognomist is telling us how to spot gender indeterminacy. The indeterminates are *androgynoi* ("men-women"). But such persons were also considered likely to practice sexual deviance. In this capacity they were known as *cinaedi* ("pathics"), males who prefer to play the "feminine," or receptive, role in intercourse with other men. Since, as we have seen, excessive indulgence in sexual intercourse of any kind was thought to cool the body down too far for the maintenance of proper masculine warmth, those who indulged too often with partners of either sex were in danger of becoming physically effeminate, no matter how manly they were to start with. Hence the ancients would judge that the innumerable conquests of a Hollywood stud endanger, rather than enhance, his virility. If one played an effeminate role in intercourse, this danger doubled.

Students always want to know whether homosexuality was permitted in Rome. The reality was too complex for this question. When modern people speak of homosexuality and heterosexuality, they are speaking from a belief system in which there are two kinds of people, homosexuals and heterosexuals, defined by their choice of sexual partners. Homosexuals choose partners of the same sex; heterosexuals choose partners of the opposite sex. In antiquity, however, what mattered, what defined one's place in the sexual scheme of things, was not the sex of one's partners but their social status. It was generally considered acceptable for a man of high status to have sex with persons of lower status, male or female, as long as he maintained the dominant, insertive role. Sex was about power. To have one's will with one's slaves was unremarkable. Let two men of equal status, however, be rumored to enjoy a sexual relationship, and the scandal was immediate: one of them must have surrendered his masculine prerogatives by renouncing dominance. He must be a *cinaedus*!

Complicating this basic scheme was, on the one hand, the preference of some upper-class Romans for all things Greek and fashionable and, on the other, the puritanical abhorrence felt by other upper-class

Romans for the same. "All things Greek and fashionable" included certain more fluid fashions in clothing (the toga being a rather stiff and heavy garment), as well as a wider range of sexual pleasures, especially homoerotic ones, toward which Greek culture had for centuries taken a more relaxed attitude.[2] In the bygone days of the Republic, a Roman aristocrat who considered himself a traditionalist would not allow his sons to learn dancing or play a musical instrument, "activities that our ancestors thought should be considered disgraceful for freeborn persons" (Macrobius *Saturnalia* 3.14.7). The reason these cultural refinements were felt to have a servile taint about them was that the Romans had originally acquired them from Greeks whom they had enslaved en masse during their conquest of the eastern Mediterranean (in the third and second centuries B.C.). Yet as the refinements of Greek decadence (to adopt the traditionalist's perspective) became more widely accepted in aristocratic circles, even a conservative Roman father might allow a little leeway in cultural matters so as not to handicap his sons socially. What leeway he might allow himself in sexual matters is hard to predict, since upper-class attitudes toward homoerotic behavior were all tangled up in a complex and ambivalent response to Rome's assimilation of Greek civilization.

People thought there were two kinds of effeminates, the flagrant ones, whose deportment plainly showed their deviance, and the hidden ones, who might be anywhere. Depilation was a possible sign of effeminacy. Body hair was thought, in science, folklore, and philosophy, to be the product of a man's natural heat. Those who tampered with it invited accusations of effeminacy. Yet there were also cultural pressures in favor of a little refinement in masculine grooming. Different accommodations were possible: Cynic philosophers rarely washed, let alone shaved, while Seneca attests a compromise: depilate the armpits, of course, but not the legs. Besides their suspiciously hairless limbs and genital area, *cinaedi* were thought to reveal themselves by a mincing gait, a tilted head, and an enervated voice. We are also told to suspect someone who shifts his eyes around and touches his nose when

2. Roman codes of sexual behavior differed most strikingly from Greek in their disapproval of pederastry—the sexual courtship of free-born youths by older men (see Williams 1995). On evidence for homoerotic relationships between social equals see Taylor 1997. Greek attitudes toward homoerotic behavior were themselves quite complex, and the curious reader should consult Dover 1978 and Winkler 1990, chaps. 1 and 2.

he speaks, laughs immoderately, "or has the annoying habit of grabbing other people by the hand" (Anonymous Latin *Physiognomy* 98 Förster). But these signs are evident among just the obvious *cinaedi.* A handbook on horoscopes lists multiple permutations of the stars under which one might be born a "hidden *cinaedus.*" These crypto-*cinaedi* are harder to spot: "they practice their vices in secret" (Firmicus Maternus, *Introduction to Astrology* 7.25.21). A physiognomist discusses their affected deportment: "Although they certainly are *cinaedi,* they actually try to remove suspicion from themselves by straining to assume a more virile appearance. They imitate a youthful stride, hold themselves with a peculiar firmness, intensify their gaze and voice, and with their whole body they adopt a rigid bearing (Anonymous Latin *Physiognomy* 74 Förster). Although the experts claimed to be able to uncover these impostors, what strikes us as somewhat unsettling is the universal atmosphere of suspicion that such a system implies. A man could be accused of effeminacy if his self-presentation was too "soft" (a dead giveaway) or too "hard" (overcompensating). What we are to imagine in practice is a limited number of frankly role-reversed men who may have enjoyed deliberately "camping it up" and a lot of anxious "normal" males, who cultivated various degrees of refinement while eyeing one another warily for signs of weakness. Certainly accusations of effeminacy were a standard ingredient in political invective. Cicero earned Antony's undying enmity by accusing him publicly of being a *cinaedus:* "At first you were just a public prostitute, with a fixed price: quite a high one too. But very soon Curio [an older politician] intervened and took you off the streets, promoting you, one might say, to wifely status, and making a sound, steady, married woman out of you."[3] In private life, poets who wrote satiric epigrams pulled no punches.

> Look at that guy, Decianus, with the matted hair,
> Whose stern-looking face intimidates even you,
> The one who's always going on about the Old Roman Heroes—
> Don't believe in looks: why only yesterday,
> he was a bride!
>
> (Martial 1.24)

3. Cic. *Philippics* 2.18.44 (translation by M. Grant from *Cicero: Selected Works* (Harmondsworth, 1971), 122. On this kind of invective see Edwards 1993.

The mannerisms that the physiognomists and the satirists considered effeminate are just the mannerisms that the orator Quintilian told his pupils to avoid.

> The eyes should never look rigid or bulging, languid, torpid, or lasciviously rolling. They should not swim about looking watery and voluptuous, with sidelong sexy glances. Nor should they ever look as if they were asking or promising anything (*Oratorical Precepts* 11.3.76).

A student should control his eyebrows so that they are neither too rigid nor too mobile. He should hold his head in such a way as to indicate neither rude stiffness nor limp passivity. He should never touch his nose or sway in such a way that he be mistaken for a dancer. The fundamental paradox seems to be that the orator had to persuade his audience without seeming to try to please them, for ingratiating mannerisms would look inappropriately subservient and feminine. Deportment was a balancing act for which the rhetorical education of aristocratic youths provided invaluable training.

Public speaking was an essential skill for propertied persons in Roman society. An aristocratic patron was expected to take care of his dependents' needs for representation in the public arena. Ideally, he ought to be able to defend their interests in court. If he lived in the provinces, he would need to be able to transact business effectively with the city council of his native town, of which he would automatically be a member. He ought to know how to welcome imperial officials—the provincial governor, for instance—with an impressive show of oratory. He might even be sent on an embassy to plead for earthquake relief from the emperor. In every public encounter—at the baths, at dinner, or at law—he had to be able to present himself unflinchingly to the scrutiny of his competitive male peers. To this end he was trained in oratory.

The process began when a young man began to wear the toga of manhood, at about age sixteen. In the old days of the Republic, young men were informally assigned a mentor whom they would follow about in his round of daily activities, picking up legal knowledge, rhetorical skills, and, it was hoped, the proper sort of moral values by precept and example. Greek civilization, however, had elaborated a much more systematic method of teaching rhetoric, which, despite resistance from traditionalists, eventually became the model for Latin rhetoric also. In Italy, North Africa, and the western half of the Empire generally, where Latin was the primary language of the educated, it was considered a mark of distinction to know some Greek as well. So young westerners, who might have learned their elementary Greek from imported nursemaids and other slaves, would, in their teens, attend the rhetoric lectures of both Greek and Latin teachers.[4]

A rhetoric student would learn to tell fables, to extemporize on familiar themes (e.g., whether one should marry), and to impersonate mythological characters (e.g., Juno upon learning that she cannot prevent Aeneas from sailing to Italy). The young Augustine made a terrific splash with his Juno. "The contest," he says, "was to be won by the boy who best expressed Juno's grief and rage in words appropriate to her majesty" (*Confessions* 1.17). The prize was glory and the applause of one's fellow students and their fathers gathered round; the forfeit for those who failed was public disgrace and perhaps a beating. Rhetorical education was a competitive sport, focused around contests and performance. Teachers competed publicly with one another, and many students continued declaiming into adulthood. Augustine's budding schoolboy talent blossomed into an imperial professorship in Milan, where he taught the sons of courtiers and delivered panegyrics in the presence of the emperor himself. It did not desert him after his conversion, whether he thundered against heretics from his North African pulpit or debated with a Manichaean missionary in the public baths.

After fables and other preliminary exercises, students would progress to more elaborate role-playing, where they gave advice to the heroes of the past (e.g., urging Cicero not to try to save his life by begging pardon of Antony). One might set out to prove that it was (a) expedient, (b) honorable, and (c) necessary for him to die. Such a speech ought to be sprinkled with well-turned epigrams that earned extra points if they involved well-known Ciceronian tags (e.g., *O tempora, O mores!*). Thus book learning, the dutiful perusal of Virgil's *Aeneid* and Cicero's classic speeches, was transmuted into live performance.

---

4. In Greece, Turkey, and the Near East, Greek-speaking aristocrats seldom deigned to learn Latin, so for many generations Greek was really the empire's dominant international language. After the reforms of Diocletian, however, at the end of the third century, the imperial civil service became an ever more tempting route to wealth and power, and the sons of Greek aristocrats set sail for Beirut to learn Latin, law, and shorthand.

The most popular exercises of all were mock trials in which the teacher set the facts of the case and the students came up with speeches for both sides. For example, the teacher might present a fictitious law, such as "A sexually dissolute man shall be barred from public speaking." The teacher might then offer a fictitious situation: "A good-looking youth made a bet that he would go out in public in women's clothes. He did and was gang-raped by ten young men. He accused them in court of assault and won. Then the magistrate prohibits him from speaking in public. He accuses the magistrate of injury" (Seneca the Elder *Rhetorical Disputations* 5.6). The teacher might then ask the student to take the side of the magistrate, and the student might say, "In our fathers' time, it was considered an abomination for aspiring lawyers to leave even an arm uncovered by the toga!" Next the teacher might ask the student to take the side of the youth, and the student might say, "He was so well known for sexual modesty that no one would have believed him unless he had made the bet." Students were judged on the convoluted cleverness of their legal reasoning, on the imaginative "spin" that they were able to put on an unpromising case, as well as on their epigrams and purple passages describing the excesses of rapists and tyrants and the sufferings of their victims. All in all, it was a highly colored spectator sport. What is particularly fascinating about these fictitious cases is the way they refract, through a fantastical lens, some of the abiding social tensions of upper-class life. Stories of sons falling out with their fathers and of fathers disinheriting sons and adopting alternates are commonplace in the repertoire, as are tales of wifely faith or infidelity and problems involving the acknowledgment of illegitimate children fathered on slaves and concubines. In the case just cited here, the transvestite youth embodies a culturally telling paradox: by winning his case against those who raped him, he has vindicated his interests verbally in public, a quintessentially "masculine" feat, but in so doing he has convicted himself of effeminacy and thus risks losing the gendered privilege of public speech.

Romans harbored a fascinated ambivalence about "effeminate" rhetorical style. When commenting on each other's performances, they frequently invoked gender stereotypes in their criticism, saying this speaker's rhythms are "soft," "broken," or "unmanly" or that one's voice displays an unwholesome flexibility, "dissolving into effeminate modulations." Even stylistic comment that has nothing specifically to do with performance gets drawn into the polarized language of gender.

When Quintilian wants to convey the incongruity of style mismatched with content, he chooses a metaphor of cross-dressing: "It's as if men deformed themselves by wearing necklaces, pearls, and long dresses, which are feminine adornments, or as if triumphal robes (the most distinguished things that can possibly be imagined) should sit becomingly on women!" (*Oratorical Precepts* 11.1.3). Too much pliability, in voice or posture, evokes both the subservience of women and the suspect versatility of the professional performer. Cicero insists that the orator carry himself with a "vigorous and manly posture of the upper body that derives not from actors and the stage but from the army or even the wrestling grounds" (*Oratory* 3.59.220). Actors were a socially despised group, although certain superstars had fans among the powerful. The problem with Cicero's recommendation was that while fewer and fewer upper-class young men were doing a stint in the army, more and more of them went to the theater, whence all sorts of exaggerated mannerisms were indeed infecting their oratory.

Public speaking had always been a spectator sport, and the censorious comments of the elite males who practiced it remind us that they were aware of a need to distinguish themselves from entertainers. Though some heedless youths might, like actors, seek too much to please by voice and gesture, the refinements of educated language itself were not easily imitated or painlessly acquired. The language of rhetoric set one apart from one's social inferiors. It amounted to a specialized dialect whose complexity and ties to the literature of the past gave it cultural authority. Grammatical gaffes, the casual use of a word lacking a classical pedigree—errors like these exposed one to the ridicule of one's peers, and fear of such ridicule kept boys in school.

In addition to their command of educated language, the aristocrats of antiquity also commanded vast wealth. They preferred to spend it in ways that highlighted their social position. Conspicuous consumption in food, clothing, slaves, and real estate, the forms of Roman excess that have most captured the modern imagination, were not the whole story. Most of the amenities of urban life were financed out of pocket by local aristocrats themselves. Imperial taxes, in money and kind, went to feed the imperial army and the city of Rome. In other cities, the leading citizens, whose wealth generally derived from landed property, were personally responsible for the collection of imperial taxes from the peasantry on their estates (they collected as much as they could, paid the emperor his due, and kept what was left over). They also allocated amongst themselves the financing of public baths and entertainments. This could involve large annual expenditures for wood to heat the baths and oil for the anointing rooms. (Oil was the ancient world's soap and was used in great quantities.) Games and shows were even more expensive: there were actors, musicians, and troops of gladiators to hire, and arrangements had to be made for the capture and transport of wild beasts. Another common form of beneficence was the release of stored grain as free donations or at subsidized prices during times of scarcity. Such distributions tended to favor the city populace, whose support was more important for a leading citizen's reputation, over the country people, whose labor had produced the grain in the first place.

Bread and circuses—these transitory delights produced instant popularity for the donor, but some rich men preferred to make capital improvements in their city's repertoire of public buildings; they donated temples, arcades, and bridges, as well as statuary, ornamental columns, and gilding for buildings already there. Emperor Antoninus Pius wrote to the Ephesians, who seem in this case to have been insufficiently appreciative of a particular donor's "love of honor": "I have agreed to all his requests for supplemental funding and welcomed the fact that he has not chosen the usual method of those engaged in political life who, for the sake of immediate prestige, lavish their funds on shows and grain distributions and prizes for the games, but has chosen a way by which he may make the city more imposing in the future" (*SIG*³ 850). Most of the architectural remains of the Roman world that still draw the gaze of tourists from Turkey to Gibraltar are the product of this "love of honor" on the part of leading citizens and the emperor himself.

What was in it for the donor? He invested in the goodwill of his fellow citizens, with results that were immediately gratifying and occasionally even protective. It was good to be acknowledged in holiday parades or in the theater as a public benefactor. At times of food shortage or civil unrest, the town houses and granaries of philanthropic citizens were less likely to be looted or burnt than those of rich men thought to be hoarding. Popular goodwill also made a donor less vulnerable to jealous or vengeful peers. Officials of the imperial government who judged major cases tried not to make too many unpopular moves. Beyond these temporal advantages there was the lure of immortality, as pagans conceived it: a man's name and fame in the eyes and on the tongues of his fellowmen. Generous donors were rewarded by their town with honorific thank-you notes inscribed on stone, many of which have survived to this day. Best of all was a public statue; most of these have been looted, but their inscribed bases remain.

Manius Megonius Leo, who served his native town in southern Italy in many capacities (as aedile, public treasurer, member of the Board of Four), was already the proud recipient of two public statues when he wrote his will. In this document, he promised that if his fellow citizens erected a third statue in his honor (he stipulated that it be placed in the upper forum but wrote that an equestrian statue was not necessary; a pedestrian one would do), he would bequeath to the township one hundred thousand sesterces. Out of the interest on this money, every year on his birthday, the town councilors were to hold a feast in his memory with a cash honorarium of three hundred denarii for the attendees (minus the cost of the food). To the rest of the town's ordinary citizens, male and female, he bequeathed one denarius annually, as well as a communal stipend to buy a sacrificial victim for the Feast of Departed Souls (his soul included).

> From you, best of townsfolk, I earnestly seek, in the name of the most sacred Emperor Antoninus Pius and his children, that you hold in perpetuity to my purpose and dispositions, and that you inscribe this whole chapter of my will on the pedestal of my pedestrian statue, which I besought you above to set up for me, that it may be the better known also to our descendants or, again, that it may act as a reminder to those who may be munificent towards their native city.[5]

Manius was not, outside his local region, a famous man. He wrote no books, and he had no notable connections with the imperial court or Rome's highest aristocracy. Rated as a public performance, however, his life was a success. We cannot know how he subjectively made sense of his role as a man, but now at least we know a little bit about the culturally accepted "languages" of flesh, voice, and gesture, through which he, his father, his grandfather, and his great-grandfather expressed their entitlement to social dominance.

5. *ILS* 6468 (second century A.D.); the translation is from Hands 1968, 189.

CHAPTER THREE

Roman Demography

Bruce W. Frier

Demography is a social science that specializes in the statistical measurement of human populations: their size, structure, and change over time.[1] Demographic statistics are, of course, a familiar part of the modern world; they are reported in newspapers and discussed on television talk shows. Governments also make heavy use of such statistics to assess the current well-being of their populations (e.g., what is the average life expectancy at birth?) and to plan for the future (e.g., how many high schools and teachers will be needed to educate teenagers ten years from now?). Demographers, for their part, lay heavy stress both on obtaining accurate measurements and on developing statistical tools that permit reliable projections. In lesser-developed countries, where the modern transition to low birth and death rates is still in progress, demography is central to virtually all policy making for economic growth.

The Roman world was fundamentally different, of course. The central government was tiny by modern standards, and it had little capacity to collect the sort of data that we today regard as essential. Further, the methods that modern demographers use to analyze statistics did not then exist; the systematic examination of risk and probability, on which all demography depends, was unknown to the Romans and did not, in fact, come into existence until late in the Renaissance, although the Greeks were already aware of the basic problem of risk (Bernstein 1996, 11–22). The Roman government did try to keep track of its population; most of us will immediately recall, for instance, the census of Palestine that the Gospel of Luke associates with the birth of Jesus. But Roman efforts were undoubtedly crude and incomplete.

1. For a good introduction to demography see Newell 1988. On Roman demography see Parkin 1992.

Modern demographic studies of the Roman Empire therefore examine its population through an intellectual prism that is alien to the Empire's culture and the form of its government. Nevertheless, the hope is that such studies will permit us not only to see the Roman Empire from an important new perspective but also to comprehend better the basic material problems that Romans were forced to confront, even if they themselves had no better than a limited understanding of these problems. In effect, we are seeking to use fragmentary surviving evidence and modern methods in order to reconstruct a demographic regime that at least approximates the actual experience of ordinary Romans during the early Empire.

As it turns out, this is no easy task. And once it is completed, a still more difficult task awaits us: to bring Roman culture into a clear relationship with this material reality. For instance, as we shall see later in this chapter, on her twentieth birthday a typical Roman woman would probably have been married for some years; she might well have borne one or two children already; and she had a life expectancy of only about thirty additional years (as compared with about sixty years for a twenty-year-old American woman today). Even if facts of this sort were not always sharply apprehended in the past, they had vital and immediate significance to the members of the Roman community. Accordingly, we would expect Roman cultural, social, and legal institutions to lay considerable stress on the interpretation of such facts, as part of an effort to explain and justify existing social reality.

But the task of linking culture to reality is always and everywhere difficult and extremely controversial. The goals of this chapter are far narrower. It aims simply to describe the main statistical characteristics of the population of the early Roman Empire and to offer some evaluation of their historical significance.

Mortality

The modern industrial world has been profoundly shaped by the demographic transition, a quiet revolution in which both birth and death rates have fallen dramatically from their former levels.[2] This revolution began in Europe and the European world during the later eighteenth century, and it still continues today in many lesser-developed

2. See Chesnais 1992.

countries. The Roman Empire lies, of course, on the "other side" of the demographic transition. What does this distinction mean in concrete terms? We may start by looking at patterns of mortality, the rates at which persons die.

In the United States today, newborns have an average life expectancy of just over seventy-six years.[3] This means that if current mortality rates at various ages continue unchanged into the future, all children born at this time will live an average of about seventy-six years. This figure is obviously not a prediction with regard to individual persons; many might die before age seventy-six, and others might live longer, but on average they would live about 76 years. But further, and much more important, it is also highly improbable that mortality rates will in fact continue at their present levels. Current mortality rates may conceivably rise in the future (for instance, if new diseases cause heightened death levels), but it is more likely that they will fall, especially as medical advances conquer or ameliorate the major causes of death. Average life expectancy is best thought of, therefore, as a theoretical measurement not of what will be but of what is—that is, of the existing health and social welfare of the American population.

Before the demographic transition, average life expectancy at birth was far lower than its modern level: it was most commonly within a range from about twenty to forty years, with most populations of the past probably falling into the lower half of this range. This difference is initially almost impossible for us to comprehend, and nowhere is this more true than with regard to infant mortality rates (the probability that newborns will die before their first birthday). In the United States today, despite the extreme vulnerability of newborns, very few of them—less than 1 percent—will die during their first year of life. Populations of the past experienced much higher rates; quite commonly over 20 percent of newborns died in their first year of life, and levels as high as 30 or 35 percent are not unknown.[4] Similar though less dramatic differences in mortality levels persisted throughout the entire human lifespan. The result, of course, was much lower average life expectancy not only at birth but also later in life.

Where does Rome fit into this picture? We cannot be completely sure, since the evidence is meager. Our best "official" source is a table

3. United Nations Development Programme 1996, 188, based on UN estimates. The United States is fairly typical of developed countries.

4. Livi-Bacci 1991, 72–78, summarizing modern studies.

given by Ulpian, a Roman jurist of the early third century A.D.[5] Ulpian's table gives multipliers that were used in estimating the tax value of annuities at various ages; but since the present value of annuities is closely related to the life expectancy of annuitants, it seems likely that the table is in fact estimating life expectancy. The values in Ulpian's crude "life table" are extremely low, consistent with an average life expectancy at birth of about twenty-one years, and a life expectancy at age ten of about thirty-five additional years. (By contrast, contemporary American life expectancy at age ten is about sixty-three years for males and seventy years for females.)

Can such low figures possibly be correct for the Roman Empire? Our best source seems to confirm that Ulpian's life table is at least not far removed from reality. From early imperial Egypt have survived more than three hundred census declarations of ordinary households (figs. 6, 7).[6] These census returns, which contain more than a thousand entries, appear to be quite accurate, at least by premodern standards, particularly in giving ages. The age distribution in these returns is heavily skewed toward younger ages, which is symptomatic of a population in which mortality levels are high. For instance, persons less than fifteen years old are about 35 percent of the total population, while persons aged sixty-five and older are only about 3 percent. If we assume, as seems likely for most pretransition populations, that population growth was very slow in Roman Egypt (about .2 percent per year would be usual), then the likely average life expectancy at birth in Roman Egypt can probably be set at about twenty-two and a half years for both sexes.

Other sources are considerably more questionable but tend to the same conclusion. A few well-analyzed village cemeteries from Hungary have a distribution of ages at death that is consistent with life expectancy at death in the low twenties; and the same is also true of the mature adult ages at death on the numerous gravestones from Roman North Africa (Frier 1983).

All this evidence should be treated with some caution. In particular, our data relate only to adolescent and adult mortality, from about age ten onward. We have no good evidence for Roman infant mortality levels, which tend to be extremely variable before the demographic transi-

5. Frier 1982. The source is Aemilius Macer *Digest* 35.2.68 pr., citing Ulpian.

6. Bagnall and Frier 1994, on which the following discussion draws heavily. Mortality is reconstructed at pp. 75–110. A sample return is discussed in the appendix to this chapter.

Fig. 6. The excavation of Karanis. Much of our most important evidence for Roman demography comes from Egypt, discovered in excavations such as this one from Karanis. We can see here the houses of the ancient town as they reemerge from the sand. (Courtesy of the Kelsey Museum.)

tion. Further, even for adult mortality, the Roman Empire embraced an extremely large and geographically diverse territory, and considerable regional variations and temporal fluctuations in mortality are certainly to be anticipated, even if evidence for differences is still lacking.

Nevertheless, today it seems safe to posit that Roman mortality levels were very high even by pretransition standards. If, as seems likely, Roman average life expectancy at birth lay in the lower twenties, then Roman mortality levels were much higher than those found usually in early modern Europe, and indeed they were only marginally lower than those usually associated with anthropological populations of the prehistoric period (Weiss 1973, 48–51). This is of major historical importance since average life expectancy is today usually regarded as one basic measure of quality of life: it indicates, although in highly compressed form, how well a society is doing in providing its general population with basic health services and other essentials to achieving long life. By using just this single measure, we can suggest that the Roman empire provided its subjects with no real improvement in their overall social well-being.

But how is it possible that the Roman empire, despite all its undeniably impressive cultural and political achievements, would not have offered appreciable material benefit to its inhabitants? Looking at the evidence from another perspective, historians have frequently hypothesized that the empire itself may well have contributed to high mortality levels. We know it to have been characterized, for instance, by an extreme maldistribution of income and wealth, which might easily have lead to poor nutrition in the general population; thus, there is good evidence that the Roman social and political elite had appreciably lower mortality than the lower classes.[7] Further, the empire's elaborate web of roads and its concentrated urbanism, for which the empire is so justly famous, could also have indirectly provided a network that facilitated disease in taking hold and then rapidly spreading from city to city.[8] Finally, the empire's central government was small by modern standards and hence bureaucratically inadequate when it came to implementing the draconian measures that are required to fight disease.

However, while the collective force of such factors was doubtless considerable, it is admittedly difficult to isolate and quantify the potential contribution of each one. And even in their sum, such causes may be insufficient as a complete explanation, particularly granted the presence of other factors (e.g., the long imperial peace) that ought to have worked in the opposite direction. It is in this context that we must turn to examine another type of cause that may also have had considerable impact on Roman mortality levels: the patterns of marriage and childbirth.

Marriage

In the Roman Empire, marriage was basically a private event only loosely regulated by the state. Two persons could meet and marry usually with the counsel of their families but without direct involvement

7. Hopkins 1983, 146–47: the method of recruitment to the Roman senate implies that senators had an average life expectancy at birth of about thirty years.

8. On sanitary conditions in Roman cities see Scobie 1986.

by the state, which did not even maintain marriage registers.[9] Roman law did set criteria for marriage, including minimum ages (twelve for women, puberty or age fourteen for men); and the government also actively encouraged the formation of marriage as a matter of public policy. But beyond that it did little to interfere with private arrangements. Even divorce was virtually unregulated and could occur, in principle, on the demand of either party.

In pretransition populations, much depends on entry into marriage, because for most women marriage marks the beginning of the sustained sexual contacts that lead to childbirth. Most pretransition societies exhibited an "early marriage" pattern in which women usually married by age twenty and thus were married during the period of their highest fecundity (from age twenty to age twenty-nine). In much of early modern Europe, by contrast, female entry into marriage was delayed into the middle or late twenties, with the consequence that women were commonly unmarried during a large portion of their period of highest fecundity; this has the obvious effect of reducing overall fertility rates. Further, in "early marriage" populations it was normal for almost all women to marry; but in "late marriage" populations a substantial proportion of women never married, and this too tended to hold down general fertility.

It is now clear that the Roman Empire was an "early marriage" population. In the western Empire, gravestones giving women's ages at death show a clear progressive shift during the late teens and early twenties, from parents to husbands as commemorators of the deceased woman; this shift clearly reflects the steady passage of women into marriage during their late teens (Shaw 1987). The Egyptian census returns display a strikingly similar pattern: free women began to marry at age twelve, but by their fifteenth birthday only about 12 percent of women were married. The bulk of female marriage took place between ages fifteen and twenty; by age twenty more than 60 percent of women were married, and by age twenty-five somewhat over 85 percent. Both in the western Empire and in Egypt, almost all women eventually married.

This pattern implies that Roman women most commonly married for the first time while one or both of their parents were still alive. For such women, marriages were often probably arranged; the women

9. On Roman marriage see especially Treggiari 1991.

themselves were too young to make an independent choice, though Roman law required at least their formal consent. In this respect, Rome differed little from most other premodern societies, in which "marriage for women . . . was almost universally a life-cycle stage in a physiological as well as a social sense[,] in that it occurred at or close to menarche. Few women failed to marry and those who married moved into their new state because of physical maturation" (Wrigley 1987, 7).

The demographic aspects of this "early marriage" pattern are important, but the pattern also has many other aspects that are of social and cultural significance. Behind the fact of early female marriage, there necessarily stood many social and legal institutions that aimed to explain and ease the transition out of the paternal household and into the marital. The leading historian of Roman marriage has sensitively characterized them.

> The wedding itself acted as a *rite de passage* for the bride, who set aside childish things when she dedicated her toys to the household gods and became a *matrona*. The ritual retained its sacramental character even when *confarreatio* [the ancient patrician wedding ceremony] was not involved. The veil and the torches had resonances for the Romans which they scarcely have for us. The bride, through outward and visible signs, perhaps through ritual words and through the giving of consent, implied dedication to the particular role of wifely virtue.[10]

The nature of this "passage" was reinforced by the pattern of male marriage. Though men began to marry in their mid- to late teens, their entry into first marriage was often slower than that of women, and it was usual for men not to marry until their middle twenties or even later.[11] There was thus often a considerable gap in age between husbands and wives, though with sizable variations. One has the distinct impression of marriage as a strongly patriarchal institution, especially because it was the almost invariable custom for brides to leave their parents' home and move into that of their husbands; and at least lower-class couples seem usually not to have founded a new house-

10. Treggiari 1991, 180; cf. 161–70.

11. See Saller 1987 for the western Empire. The same general pattern is found in Roman Egypt, but males begin marrying somewhat earlier. Saller (1994) has reconstructed a useful model of typical Roman families.

hold (in the manner of modern "nuclear" families) but instead to have dwelled in the home of the husband's father if he was still living. Thus, in Roman Egypt, a large percentage of households are typically complex multifamily units, with several coresident families. Even after the death of their father, surviving brothers might continue to live together, along with their wives and children. Only among the upper classes, where individualistic values had taken firmer hold, was this pattern less common.

But Roman marriage was much more fragile than this patriarchal image might imply. It may have been fairly rare for a woman, once married, to remain married for the remainder of her reproductive life. For one thing, high mortality rates meant that many marriages could end fairly quickly through the death of a spouse; and this problem was certainly aggravated by the advanced age of many Roman husbands. Widows and orphans were therefore a common feature of the Roman world, and many legal institutions were intended to provide for them, though with what effectiveness it is hard to judge.[12] Likewise, the ready availability of divorce resulted in the early dissolution of many marriages; this was particularly true among the Empire's upper classes, but the Egyptian census returns indicate that even lower-class couples frequently divorced.

After the loss of a spouse through death or divorce, many Romans sought to remarry, at times more than once. But at least the Egyptian census returns indicate that women rarely remarried after about age thirty-five. Because of the heavy burden of childbearing, this could often have been a matter of personal choice; but it is also evident that older men tended to prefer marriage (or remarriage) to much younger wives, sometimes as much as thirty years younger. The principal result of this remarriage pattern was that a large number of older, but presumably still fertile, women were unmarried; by age fifty, only around 40 percent of surviving Egyptian women were still married.

The Roman marriage pattern is thus a bit more open to personal choice than it may at first appear. But in general the marital regime is typical of Mediterranean countries before the fertility transition, and many elements of this pattern still survive today in the Islamic nations of northern Africa. For demographers, the most important aspect of this pattern is negative: the Romans do not attempt to control fertility

12. Krause 1994.

through resort to delayed female marriage. They were obliged to live with a marital regime in which women were regularly married during the peak period of their fertility; and so any controls on fertility had to occur within marriage itself.

One final point that needs to be made regarding Roman marriage is that some Romans could not marry. Large numbers of Romans were slaves who could not legally marry and who therefore could not bear legitimate offspring. But there is evidence from inscriptions that many slaves did enter into informal slave unions *(contubernia)* that received at least a degree of social recognition and respect. A similar informal institution, called concubinage, existed also among free Romans, for persons who either were forbidden to marry (e.g., soldiers on active duty) or were socially discouraged from doing so (e.g., patrons with their ex-slaves). Because of such informal arrangements, illegitimate children were not uncommon in the Roman world, but little social stigma seems to have attached to illegitimacy.

Fertility

Because mortality was very high in the Roman Empire, one might easily suppose that fertility also had to be very high. On this view, the Roman population was obliged to mobilize maximum fertility if it was to replace itself, and accordingly women, especially married women, had to bear children as frequently as possible. But however intuitively plausible such a proposition might seem, it is in fact untrue. Even at levels of mortality that we today would regard as exceedingly high, virtually all human populations retain quite considerable reserves of reproductive capacity. Throughout human history, control of population has always been an ordinary—almost integral—part of domestic life.

What changed during the modern fertility transition was not the fact of population control but rather the way in which it occurs.[13] Today we think of family planning and fertility control as largely a matter of individual choice. In the case of a family, a husband and wife usually have children within a few years of their marriage, and they determine, often in advance, the number of children that they will have. Couples regulate the timing of pregnancies through contraception and (to a lesser

13. For a good introduction to the fertility transition see Alter 1992.

degree) abortion; and they have fairly readily available to them the means for achieving fertility control, as well as expert and confidential medical advice on all aspects of conception and pregnancy. Although couples may have large families if they wish, the great majority opt for relatively few children; indeed, in many industrialized countries, average family size has fallen below—in some cases, far below—the level required for population replacement.

This regime of individually controlled fertility is today so universal in the industrialized world that we easily forget how recent it is. Basically, it is the product of the fertility transition, which began in some areas of France during the late eighteenth century and then spread throughout Europe and the European-influenced world during the nineteenth and twentieth centuries.[14] Before the modern fertility transition, marital fertility was also controlled, but in a much different way—through traditional social institutions and customs that placed little if any emphasis on individual choice within marriage. This traditional fertility regime is found everywhere within pretransition populations, and it still exists today in some lesser-developed nations.

For the Roman Empire, although we know much less than we would like to know about marital fertility among ordinary Romans, it now seems clear that a traditional fertility regime was also in force. The starting point for such a regime was widespread social acceptance of the view that the primary purpose of marriage is procreation; as the Romans put it, marriage exists "for procreating children" *(liberorum procreandorum causa),* a phrase often repeated in both official and lay sources. As one Roman doctor puts it with stunning candor, "women usually are married for the sake of children and succession, and not for mere enjoyment." Although many Roman sources also occasionally speak of marriage as a lifelong companionship between spouses, this more individualistic (and, to our way of thinking, more advanced) idea is apparently largely confined to the upper classes.[15]

Historically, the close and conscious linking of marriage to procreation produced a marital fertility regime in which it seems that individual control of fertility through direct means, such as contraception and abortion, was virtually unthinkable, a contradiction of the very idea of marriage. Once they had entered into marriage, women bore

14. See especially Coale and Watkins 1986.

15. Treggiari 1991, 205–28; Dixon 1992, 61–71. The doctor is Soranus (*Gynecology* 1.34).

children at a more or less regular rate until one of three things happened: they became infertile through menopause or otherwise; their marriage ended through divorce or the death of their husband; or they themselves died in childbirth or otherwise. In such traditional regimes, therefore, marital fertility rates (births per thousand married women of a given age) remained more or less constant for women in their twenties; but these rates declined gradually for married women in their thirties and then rapidly for those in their forties, as a direct and immediate function of the onset of infertility among adult women. The resulting curve of marital fertility is found universally in pretransition populations, and the Egyptian census returns reveal it in Roman Egypt as well (Frier 1994).

A "natural" marital fertility regime of this type confronts the intrinsic danger of overpopulation: too many children may be born, leading to rapid population increase. But in fact this has only rarely been the outcome, because these regimes usually have indirect controls on fertility, controls that act to "dampen" fertility across the entire span of female fecundity, but without altering the basic "natural" pattern of childbirth. Ancient sources indicate, for instance, that ordinary Roman women usually breastfed their children for two or three years after their birth; lactation tends to delay the resumption of ovulation after a birth. These sources also recommend against sexual relations between spouses during the period of breastfeeding, on the specious folk theory that semen would contaminate breast milk. Both breastfeeding and abstinence during breastfeeding are widely found in other pretransition societies as well.

The importance of such indirect controls on fertility is that they act to space births without regard to the number of children that a woman has previously borne; that is, they are just as effective whether a woman has previously borne, for example, one, four, or seven children. Hence such controls are not part of any conscious effort at family planning or limitation in the modern sense; they seem, in fact, to be regarded as entirely consistent with the assumed procreative purposes of marriage. All they do is delay a new pregnancy once childbirth has occurred.

Nonetheless, in pretransition populations indirect controls of this type frequently had considerable effect in reducing fertility rates from the maximum levels that are known to be socially sustainable. On present evidence their exact effectiveness cannot be determined for the

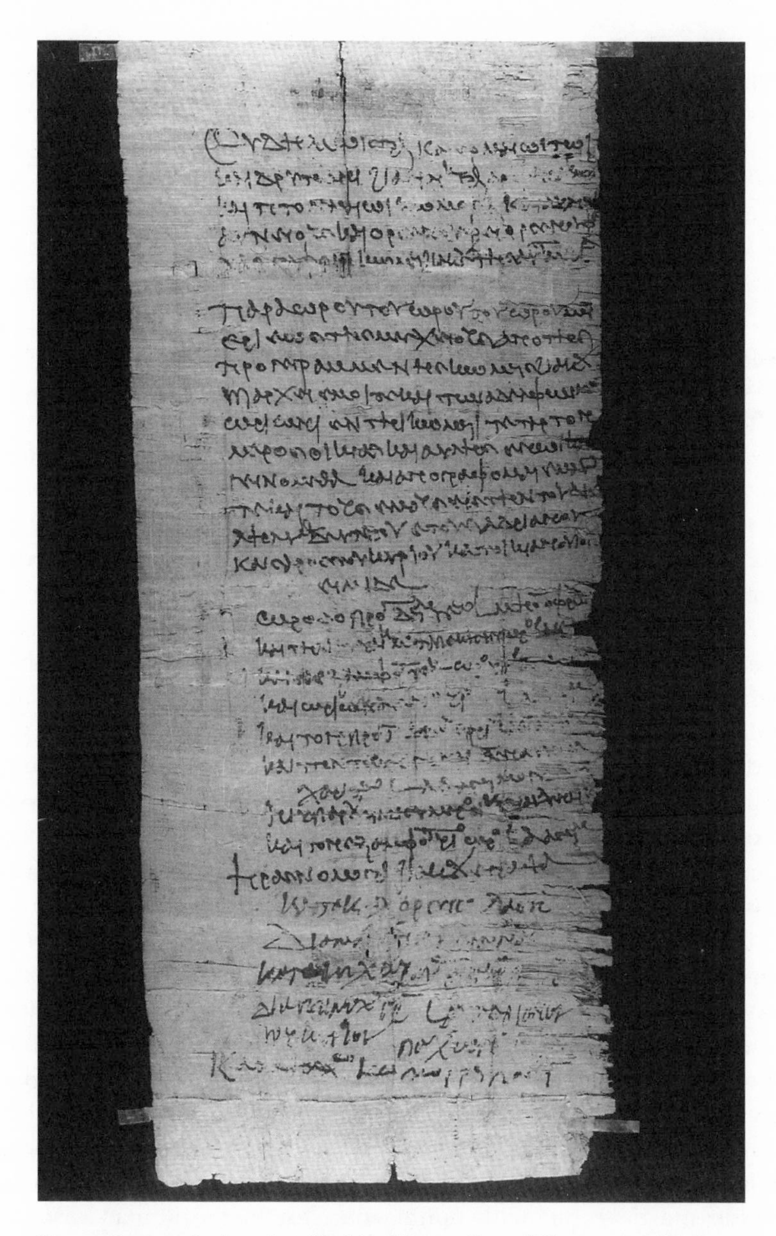

Fig. 7. Census declaration filed by Horos, Son of Horos, and Herieus, daughter of Menches, on May 5, A.D. 119. (P. Mich. Inv. 106, courtesy of the Rare Books Collection, Graduate Library of the University of Michigan.)

Roman Empire; but in a few instances the Egyptian census returns do suggest a normal birth spacing of two to three years, which is typical of pretransition populations. Other sources suggest that Romans were generally quite conscious of the importance of birth spacing; if births followed too closely on one another, the health of both mother and children could be endangered.

Where such indirect controls failed, the Romans also resorted to infanticide or exposure (Harris 1994). Exposure, apparently the more common of the two practices, differs from infanticide in that the exposed child is given at least a theoretical chance of being taken in by a stranger—often to be raised then as a slave. Infanticide and exposure were not commonly considered immoral in the Roman world, nor were they made illegal until the later Empire; even the upper classes often put newborn children to death if they were deformed or unlikely to survive, and the lower classes allegedly exposed newborns also for economic motives or on the basis of sexual preference. The frequency of exposure cannot be determined, but plainly it was not rare.

The Romans were not unaware of contraception and abortion as means of birth control. Indeed, to judge from ancient medical writings and other sources, the Romans, like the Greeks before them, were fascinated both by the reproductive process and by contraception and induced abortion as means to control it. One scholar has recently argued that many of the suggested potions might have been effective if they were taken in exactly correct dosages.[16] This argument is inconclusive, because we cannot be sure what the ancient dosages were, much less how consistently they were used. But even if it were the case that ancient couples had access to accurate information about contraceptives and abortifacients, would it necessarily follow that they would have made use of them to effect family limitation?

As the marital fertility pattern in the Egyptian census returns shows, the answer to this question is assuredly negative. Rome is not the only pretransition society in which direct mechanisms of birth control have been widely discussed. But in all these societies abortion and contraception have normally been associated not with pregnancy within marriage but with nonmarital sex. In the Roman case, this would have included adultery, prostitution, informal unions short of

16. Riddle 1992. The prescribed abortifacients are more likely to have been effective than are the contraceptives. Surgical abortion is attested but was probably too dangerous under ancient medical conditions.

marriage, and sexual relations with and between slaves—a fairly large territory in which the desire of women to curb pregnancy was often particularly acute. The domain of nonmarital fertility was more than sufficiently large to have developed a technology of its own. Abortion and contraception are in fact sometimes referred to as "the secrets of the prostitutes."

Some confirmation for this view comes from an unexpected source. Condoms were apparently unknown in antiquity, but some literary sources do refer to withdrawal (coitus interruptus) as a means to avoid pregnancy. Significantly, these sources describe withdrawal as a "woman's procedure," meaning that the active partner in withdrawal was not the man but the woman (Parkin 1992, 193 n. 159). To us this ascription of the action to women seems strange; but it makes perfect sense if withdrawal was most commonly used by, for instance, prostitutes.

But it is also possible that direct forms of birth control spread beyond the confines of extramarital sex into the upper classes of the Empire. Here, as we have seen, a more individualistic conception of marriage appears to have taken hold, and this conception might well have been consistent with the earliest appearance of family limitation; indeed, the few ancient sources that speak expressly of family limitation are clearly directing their remarks, which are usually disapproving, toward the upper classes. Further, we have good evidence that the upper classes were not reproducing themselves. For example, three-quarters of early imperial senatorial families disappear altogether after one generation (Garnsey and Saller 1987, 123, 141–45). Since the Roman elite probably had lower than normal mortality rates, it is hard to explain that group's population "crash" except on a hypothesis of unusually low marital fertility—a phenomenon that is also found among some elite groups in early modern Europe.

We are probably justified, therefore, in thinking of a two-tiered regime of marital fertility—the upper classes experimenting (perhaps disastrously) with conscious family limitation, while the vast majority of the Roman population remained captive to more traditional ways of thinking about marriage and childbirth. The Roman satirist Juvenal, writing in the early second century A.D., comments bitterly on exactly this point: noting that while poor women must inevitably give birth to their children, wealthy women enhance their promiscuous "lifestyle" by seeking out drugs that induce sterility or abortion. Augustan legislation that offered material inducements to marriage and childbirth was immediately aimed, it seems, at increasing procreation among the upper classes, though it was framed to influence free citizens generally.[17]

But this differentiated picture may still be too simple. There is much that is still unknown about ancient fertility, a subject that is usually veiled from our notice by considerations of class and propriety. For instance, it cannot be ruled out that ordinary Roman couples did in fact occasionally make some use of contraception and abortion, although not for family planning and limitation, but rather to ensure a safe interval between successive births when the more indirect methods of fertility control had for some reason failed. Whatever the truth in such matters, it remains certain that by and large the Roman Empire was a traditional fertility regime. Even in the absence of confirming evidence, this is exactly what we would have anticipated.

Beyond the immediate impact of indirect controls on fertility, it is also possible that the failure of older Roman women to remarry may also have had a dampening effect on fertility. But this effect would probably have been small, since older women are increasingly likely to be infertile in any case.

Finally, we must deal, at least briefly, with the difficult problem of reproduction among slaves (Bradley 1987). By law, the offspring of a slave woman were slaves themselves, the property of her owner; and birth is accordingly recognized as one means whereby people became slaves. Since slaves were a source and indicator of wealth, many Roman slave owners are known to have encouraged their slave women to bear children; but it remains deeply problematic whether, in general, the slave population reproduced itself naturally. Even if it did so, slave fertility rates would have been well below those of free married women.

An Assessment

Historians have made considerable progress in unraveling the deep mysteries of Roman demography, but there remain many topics on which we are inadequately informed. We know surprisingly little, for instance, about the dynamics of migration within the Roman Empire,

17. Treggiari 1991, 77–80. The Juvenal passage is *Satires* 6.592–598.

not only between provinces, but also, more particularly, between cities and their surrounding territories. Yet even here pioneering efforts are underway.[18]

More generally, it is still very difficult to determine, with any degree of precision, the population of the Empire and its regions. The prevailing view among historians is that the total population of the early Empire probably lay in a range from about forty-five to sixty million persons, consistent with the Mediterranean's likely "carrying capacity" (its ability to support population) under ancient social and economic conditions; and it also seems clear that population generally rose, although slowly, as a consequence of imperial peace and the external and internal security that it brought about. But for human populations "carrying capacity" is a notoriously elusive concept. Recently, at least one historian has vigorously argued for much higher population levels in Roman Italy and in the Empire generally (Lo Cascio 1994).

This controversy will not be resolved for many years, if not decades, to come. In the meantime, however, it is worth making a few more general observations about the demographic background of the controversy. These observations are intended to clarify why historians are today so interested in obscure topics like the sexual practices of Roman married couples. Their interest is not, as one might perhaps have supposed, some sort of arcane voyeurism. Great issues are at stake here, issues that stem from our attempts to evaluate the social performance of the Roman Empire, its institutions, and its culture.

First of all, as we have seen, Roman mortality rates were extraordinarily high, nearly "off the scale" when compared to the populations of early modern Europe. As was observed earlier in this chapter, historians who consider this problem usually try to explain low Roman life expectancy through reference to external circumstances (e.g., concentrated urbanism and the maldistribution of social resources) that may have contributed to causing high mortality; and such explanations have the merit of intuitive appeal.

Demographers, however, while not denying the possible contribution of disease and malnutrition to high mortality, are likely to see the matter within a wider perspective. Under the mortality regime described earlier, annual Roman death rates are likely to have been on the order of forty to forty-five per thousand persons, though undoubt-

18. See Morley 1996, especially 33–54.

edly with considerable fluctuations from year to year and region to region. In the long run, in order for the Roman population to remain stationary or to grow, birth rates had to equal or exceed these death rates. A slow annual growth rate would have required a steady excess of births over deaths; if, for instance, the long-term annual growth rate was .2 percent (which is typical for pretransition populations) and if the death rate was about forty-three per thousand, the birth rate had to be forty-five per thousand.

Such a birth rate is high by the standards of modern industrial nations; the current American birth rate is about sixteen per thousand. But human populations do not find it especially difficult to attain Roman levels of fertility. The forty-eight least developed countries of the world, for example, today have a cumulative birth rate of just under thirty-six per thousand (but forty-three per thousand if India is excluded), and twenty-two of these countries have birth rates higher than forty-five per thousand.

These countries, however, are now generally faced with potentially devastating population growth, mainly because, as a result of improved health delivery systems, their annual death rates are far lower than their birth rates—usually around ten to fifteen per thousand. Accordingly their populations are swiftly growing, by a cumulative average of about 2.3 percent per year (2.9 percent excluding India), a rate that doubles the population every generation. Such population growth often outstrips these countries' resources and the growth of their economies. As a consequence, many least developed countries face stagnant or even declining per capita income levels. One obvious solution for these countries is to bring down fertility rates. But their governments have found this difficult to achieve, in part because of the widespread persistence of attitudes toward marriage and childbirth that are deeply rooted in culture and religion.

These countries are confronting a quandary that demographers have worried about at least since the time of Thomas Malthus (1766–1834). As is well known, Malthus hypothesized that rising population levels would inevitably lead, in the long run, to an increase in food prices and a decline in real income. Malthus thought that this problem could only be resolved in one of two ways: either through preventive checks whereby a population finds ways to reduce its fertility levels or through the positive check of increased mortality. As we have long since learned, of course, the Malthusian dilemma is not inevitable;

through industrialization and the deployment of technological breakthroughs, societies can sustain and even dramatically improve the economic well-being of their growing populations. Still, in the end, all of us recognize that the stupendous population growth of the past century will not continue indefinitely.[19]

The Malthusian dilemma becomes more acute, however, when we turn to examine premodern societies like the Roman Empire, for which, as historians now agree, dynamic economic development was largely foreclosed as an option. The Roman Empire did not, of course, face the modern plight of extremely rapid population growth; its death rates were far closer to balance with its birth rates. Still, over a very long period the early Empire appears to have experienced gradual population growth, and its mortality levels were also very high. Historians are bound to inquire as to the possibility—the bare possibility, at least—that these two facts (if they are facts) are related to one another. In other words, is it possible that low Roman life expectancy was somehow the consequence of overpopulation?

It is in this context that my earlier discussion of Roman marriage and fertility becomes important, for this is the locus of the Malthusian preventive checks on population growth. Many populations in early modern Europe used such checks: they delayed female entry into marriage, especially when economic times were adverse; and eventually they resorted to direct means of fertility control through contraception and abortion. But as we have seen, the Roman population still largely remained within a traditional pattern of early marriage and "natural" fertility. Restraints of fertility were not unknown, but they were indirect, crude, and probably somewhat inflexible. On present evidence we cannot precisely determine how well the Roman combination of restraints operated in practice, nor can we estimate their resilience in the face of varying demographic challenges. But if Roman modes of fertility control are regarded as Malthusian preventive checks on population growth, they were probably much less responsive to short- and perhaps even long-term demographic challenges than were those methods widely used in early modern Europe.

And so we are left with the positive check of increased mortality. The Roman Empire was immensely large: on one estimate, it constituted as much as one-fifth of all persons then living, though its popula-

19. Cohen 1995.

tion was concentrated in less than 3 percent of the land area of the earth. To a considerable extent, the wealth of the Empire was, in the last analysis, simply the huge size of its population, which, even if it still widely lived in poverty, could fairly easily provide the resources that the state required for governance and protection. This consideration alone may perhaps be enough to explain the pronatalist policies of the emperor Augustus and his successors.

But such policies were arguably shortsighted. On the most plausible demographic reading of the situation, not underpopulation but overpopulation constituted the greatest threat to the Empire, particularly to the older, more densely settled areas at its core. The threat was that high fertility rates, induced by social conventions of early and universal female marriage, might gradually have led to high mortality rates, with exactly the effect we may in fact be observing if the standard interpretation of Roman mortality evidence is correct. On this hypothesis, Roman mortality gradually rose until it was high enough that a kind of equilibrium was established with fertility.

Only time will tell if this tentative hypothesis of Roman overpopulation is correct. The question is hard to settle decisively. For the Roman world, as for premodern societies generally, when population levels are reliably known, much of the other circumstantial evidence about population gradually (if often still controversially) falls into place within a broader causal framework. But in the absence of such accuracy, circumstantial evidence often remains incurably ambiguous and hence susceptible to diverse understandings. For example, a recent collection of the evidence for Roman Egypt has pointed to a considerable rise in both land and grain prices during the first two centuries of our era; this rise can be taken as ominous if, as seems not improbable, it implies a decline in real wages among the general Egyptian population (Duncan-Jones 1990, 143–55). But the collection is incomplete, and its implications are still subject to debate.

Help may eventually come from archaeology, particularly from paleopathological studies of Roman graveyards and from field surveys of inhabited Roman sites. Paleopathology, which resembles forensic medicine, may yield precious information about nutritional and health levels among ordinary Romans. Field surveys can be expected to provide us with evidence for the classic indirect signs of population growth—occupation of new territory, clearing and cultivation of marginal land, urbanization, and emigration—and more particularly for the geographical distribution of these signs within the Mediterranean basin. Considerable work has already been done along both these lines, but a comprehensive synthesis is still many years in the offing.

Finally, it deserves stress that even in premodern societies, rising population was not necessarily an evil. For example, some economists have forcefully argued that population pressure has often been historically responsible for changes in technology and patterns of land use that eventually raised the economic productivity of labor while bringing about more intensified forms of cultivation and land-augmenting investment, including the drainage of swampy lands and irrigation for multiple cropping.[20] Roman historians have recently applied such economic thought to the surviving evidence for agricultural practices in Roman Egypt and elsewhere.[21] This line of research has a great deal to recommend it, and the results thus far have been impressive. However, it would still take a brave soul to argue, on the basis of present evidence for the state of the early imperial economy, that such increased rationalization could possibly have sufficed to offset any major surge in population levels.

The Antonine Plague

Demographers fear excessive population growth not only because it can progressively sap the ongoing vitality of a people but also because it exposes that people to increased risk of sudden cataclysm. Therefore it is in order to end this admittedly rather grim chapter with a brief account of the Antonine plague, an event that can serve to symbolize the ambiguity that still surrounds Roman demography.

Ancient sources refer vaguely to widespread epidemics under Domitian and Hadrian, but the early Empire was apparently spared a true pandemic until A.D. 165, when a Roman army, returning from war on the Eastern frontier, brought with it a disease that was probably smallpox, now for the first time establishing a firm foothold in the Mediterranean basin.[22] This plague, the first of many that enervated the later Empire, raged for a quarter century; in 189, at the height of its sec-

20. E.g., Boserup 1981.

21. Kehoe 1988, 1992; Rathbone 1991.

22. Littman and Littman (1973) give the evidence for smallpox, but the identification depends on descriptions in ancient sources and is not entirely certain. For deaths in Rome see Dio 72.12.3–4.

ond outbreak in the city of Rome, an eyewitness says it caused two thousand deaths per day.

Although the consequences of the Antonine plague should not be exaggerated, they were clearly severe (Duncan-Jones 1996). Various sources attest the plague across the entire breadth of the Empire, in Egypt, Syria, Asia Minor, Greece, Dacia, Noricum, Italy, Gaul, and Germany; only Roman North Africa, less connected to the main avenues of trade, may have escaped its full force. Our sources also stress the plague's heavy toll on human life both in cities and in rural areas, its persistence and recurrence, and the widespread famines that broke out in its wake.

These sources cannot be understood except on the assumption the disease fell on a population that was vulnerable because it altogether lacked an inherited or acquired resistance. As a result, mortality was very heavy. If the Antonine plague resembled other similar pestilences in later history, it is not at all inconceivable that as much as 10 percent of the empire's total population perished from it; in concentrated settlements, such as cities and military camps, the death toll may well have been twice as high. The Roman Empire was not dealt a mortal blow, but the sudden drop in population ushered in or immensely aggravated a host of social and economic difficulties that would trouble the Romans for more than a century to come.

How should the plague be interpreted? One historian, noting that precisely in this period Roman merchants are recorded as having made their earliest contacts with the Han Empire in China, has suggested a spillover between hitherto isolated "disease pools" similar to the well-known spillovers in both directions as a consequence of the voyages of Columbus to the Americas (McNeill 1970, 109–15). This ingenious proposition cannot be verified, of course, but it is very tempting. There is also the possibility that the Antonine plague originated in the jungles of sub-Saharan Africa, as many diseases (including AIDS) were later to do, and that it entered the Empire through the Nile Valley.

Whatever the plague's source, for our purposes the more burning question is whether casualties were so high because this catastrophic plague preyed on a society already dangerously debilitated by the stresses of excessive population growth during two long centuries of imperial peace. We will never be able to answer the question. In this, as in so many other matters concerning Roman demography, we must content ourselves with speculation.

Appendix: A Sample Census Return

The following translation is of a fairly typical (but unusually completely preserved) census return written in Greek and filed on A.D. 15 May 119 by an Egyptian family from the village of Tanyaithis. The return is addressed to Apollonios, the governor *(strategos)* of the district in which Tanyaithis is located. The declarant is Harpokration, a seventy-year-old scribe. He declares his wife (aged thirty-nine); his son, who is a doctor (at age seventeen!); and his daughter (aged fifteen).

> To Apollonios, *strategos* of the Apollonopolite district:
> From Harpokration son of Dioskoros (son of Harmais) and of Senorsenouphis (daughter of Psenanouphis), from Tanyaithis:
> I register for the house-by-house census of Lord Hadrian Caesar's second year (A.D. 117/118), in compliance with the commands of Rammius Martialis the most noble prefect, in a house and vacant land belonging to Senonnophris (daughter of Harpokration) and her siblings, in the southern quarter of Tanyaithis:
>
> myself, scribe, aged 70, scar on the shank of the left leg;
> Dioskoros, a son, his mother being Senpachoumis daughter of Anompis, without scar, doctor, aged 17;
> Senpachoumis daughter of Anompis, wife of Harpokration, aged 39;
> Tazbes the Younger, a daughter, aged 15.
>
> And I swear by the fortune of the Emperor Caesar Trajan Hadrian Augustus that I have honestly and truthfully presented the above return, and that no one is left unregistered, or may I be liable on my oath.
> In the third year (A.D. 118/119) of Emperor Caesar Trajan Hadrian Augustus, 15 May. I, Harpokration son of Dioskoros, presented the return above.

The family reported in this return is a "nuclear" family and is somewhat small by Egyptian standards. The group is living in a rented house belonging to a woman named Senonnophris, who, despite the coincidence of her father's name, is probably no kin to the declarant, Harpokration. Both Harpokration and his son, Dioskoros, have Greek names, and both are "professionals"; theirs is probably a middle-class family. But Harpokration's wife, Senpachoumis, and his daughter, Tazbes, have Egyptian names. Intermarriage between Greeks and Egyptians was not uncommon, but by this date names alone are in any case rarely a reliable guide to ethnic background. Harpokration's parents also have mixed names. It should be noted how careful declarants were to declare exactly the lineage of themselves and their family members. This usually makes family reconstruction quite easy, but the authorities may have been more concerned about possible confusion caused by the small repertory of common personal names; most residents of Roman Egypt have no "family" names.

What stands out immediately is the large gap in age between Harpokration and his wife: thirty-one years. Judging from the age of their oldest child, she married him at least eighteen years before, when he was fifty-two and she was twenty-one; but it is possible that they married somewhat earlier and that any previous children had already left their home. We have no way of knowing whether this was Harpokration's first marriage, but many males did marry quite late.

In the census returns, occupations are given only for males, who were probably the main support of most families; and adult males alone were subject to the head tax levied by the government. The tax began at age fourteen and continued to age sixty or sixty-two. This indicates, as other evidence confirms, that boys began to work soon after they reached puberty, without passing through a period of "adolescence"; Harpokration's son is not unusual. Since there was no formal medical education, the boy probably had been apprenticed out to an older doctor before beginning his own practice. As for Harpokration, his occupation involves no physical labor (most of his neighbors were probably farmers), and he has perhaps continued working as a scribe past the normal "retirement" age.

Harpokration's daughter is not yet married at age fifteen, but she probably will marry and move out of the household within a few years. Harpokration's son may well not marry for another decade or so, but even after marriage, he, his wife, and his children will probably continue to live with his father, if Harpokration is still alive then—which is, however, unlikely (only one person in the census returns is attested as having reached age eighty).

Like all census declarants in Egypt, Harpokration swears to the truth of his declaration. There were severe penalties for filing false returns, but we have evidence that many Egyptian families attempted to conceal younger children, particularly to avoid the head tax. Harpokration appears to have written out the declaration himself, without aid; but many villagers state in their returns that they are illiterate in Greek and that their returns have been written for them by officials or by scribes like Harpokration.

The brief description of physical markings on males is interesting. This information was used by the Egyptian police to identify criminals.

Finally, it should be noted that Harpokration filed his return almost a year after the end of the official census year in 117/118. This was the usual practice, but we do not know the reason for it.

The papyrus is *P.Giss.* 43 = *P.Alex.Giss.* 14 = *SB* X 10630 (117-Ap-7).

PART TWO

Religion

CHAPTER FOUR

Roman Religion: Ideas and Actions

David S. Potter

Themes

Religion defined time, space, and relationships among the Romans. The festival cycle, through which the rites of the state religion were celebrated, determined the internal structure of months and years, while a variety of doctrines concerning the ultimate fate of the world offered a general framework for human existence. In the realm of physical space, distinctions between sacred and profane divided up territory, public and private, Roman and non-Roman. Human actions and the structures of human relationships were governed by observation of divine guidelines; manifest divine approval was needed for any action of significance, and divine advice was consistently sought on matters ranging from journeys abroad or the whereabouts of a slave to the future of a child or relationship. The wheels of the system were oiled by divination, which provided for constant divine manifestation in the lives of mortals.

Active and Passive Aspects of Roman Religion

Marcus Tullius Cicero (106–43 B.C.), wrote that "the whole religious practice of the Roman people is divided into rites *(sacra)* and prediction *(auspicia)*, to which a third is added, namely, whatever the haruspices

References to secondary literature have been severely restricted. I hope that I have not thereby done an injustice to any of the authors whose work has been utilized extensively in this article or to others from whose work I have benefited over the years. I thank Professors Maud Gleason and Brian Schmidt for reading and commenting on an earlier draft of this chapter, saving me from many mistakes. They are not to blame for those that remain.

and the interpreters of the Sibylline Books reveal for the sake of prediction from portents and monsters" (*The Nature of the Gods* 3.6). *Sacra* were the established cult observations of the Roman people; *auspicia* were predictions obtained by augurs by studying natural phenomena or the action of birds. The haruspices and the interpreters of the Sibylline Books—quite distinct groups—dealt with other forms of divine communication.

The separation between the rites connected with the celebration of the gods and efforts to communicate with the divine through divination is extremely important. It underlines the difference between the acceptance of old knowledge and the search for new, between the passive religious experience that is concerned with maintaining and celebrating the established relationship between human and divine, on the one hand, and the active religious experience, the search for new knowledge about this relationship, on the other (Potter 1994, 4–15). The integration of the two varieties of religious activity, the "active" and the "passive," is fundamental for the success of any religious system. A successful religious system must be able to provide its adherents with a coherent program of activities to celebrate the existing social, political, and natural order of their community, and it must offer an inherent, internally logical, readily controllable mechanism for change that enables the community to respond to new ideas and situations without having to consciously abandon existing tenets.

Gods

In the Roman world the mechanism for religious change was prophecy, and its use for state purposes was strictly controlled by the governing class, through the creation of offices that allowed its members to oversee the use of prophecy for public purposes. Under most circumstances, the state did not try to regulate the use of prophecy by private individuals, any more than it attempted to regulate the worship of gods outside of the civic pantheon.

In the Roman view, there was an enormous number of gods, and it was possible for a new god to be born at any time; the gods of classical antiquity had active sex lives, and most Romans felt that if one god could beget another god in the distant past, there was no reason why a god could not have a divine child in the present. In the second century A.D., there is good evidence for the birth of at least two new gods—one of them in the form of a human-headed snake that gave oracles—and there is considerable evidence for claims to divinity being made by or for a number of others at various other times (Robert 1980, 393–422). Thus several authors tell us of Apsethus the Libyan, who is said to have trained a number of parrots to fly around North Africa uttering the words "Apsethus is a god" with the result that the Libyans began to offer sacrifices to Apsethus. This went on until a "clever Greek" caught one of these parrots and trained it to say instead that "Apsethus, having caged us, compelled us to say Apsethus is a god," and Libyans then burned Apsethus at the stake.[1] The story may be apocryphal, but it represents the sort of thing that was thought possible, and in many instances the cases for and against a claim to divinity were less straightforward.

The addition of new gods could lead to changes in the way that the preexisting pantheon of gods could be understood. The situation was made all the more complex by the fact that there was no Roman version of the Hebrew or Christian bibles or of the Islamic Koran. There was no central body of texts that could link together all aspects of polytheism throughout the Roman world. Scholars who were interested could assemble lists of cults for individual cities and speculate upon the relationship between the gods on these lists to each other; philosophers could theorize on the nature of the divine. But there is no reason to think that the results of their endeavors had a great impact on the way that the average person thought about the divine world that he or she might contact on any given day.

Marcus Terentius Varro, the greatest scholar of the first century B.C. attempted to bring order to the chaos that he perceived in the structure of Roman cult when he wrote his *Divine Antiquities.* He said he was providing an immense service to the Romans by telling them who their gods were and what they did (Augustine *City of God* 4.22); and the work earned praise from Cicero who said that Varro had enabled Romans to realize who they were (*Posterior Academics* 9). But evidence that Varro's book had a significant impact on the practice of state or private cult is lacking. Most of what we know about Varro's book comes from quotations by later Christian writers who treated his work not as the schol-

1. Hippolytus *Against the Heresies* 6.3; cf. Maximus of Tyre *Essays* 35 (giving the Libyan the name *Psapho*). A similar story is told about Hanno the Carthaginian in Aelian *Historical Miscellany* 14.30; for a summary see also Koskenniemi 1994, 216.

Fig. 8. The Capitolium from Ostia. This temple, which, in its present form, dates to the second century A.D., would have housed the cult of Jupiter, Juno, and Minerva, modeled on the cult of the Capitoline triad at Rome. (From Potter 1983.)

arly enterprise that it was, but rather as a sort of pagan bible that could be used to make fun of polytheism. Varro had tried to reconcile local forms of worship with a scheme of "greater" and "lesser" gods, providing a list of twenty gods who were "select" because they had more important responsibilities in the universe than the others (Augustine *City of God* 7.2). He claimed that gods originally worshipped in alien cities had agreed to become Roman gods because they recognized the superiority of those at Rome and because they recognized the superior religiosity of the Roman people (fig. 8). The structure of the divine world, for Varro, thus prescribed the order of the physical world where conquered cities looked to Rome for leadership. He may even be the ultimate source for what we know about a ritual known as the *evocatio*, described for us by the fifth century A.D. antiquarian Macrobius. Through this ceremony, enacted at the beginning of a siege, the gods of the enemy city were "called out" and offered a place at Rome if they deserted their current worshippers (*Saturnalia*. 3.9.2), and of the belief that the chief god of Rome had a secret name so that Rome's enemies could not summon him forth in turn.

To the modern reader, Varro's attempt to explain the gods may appear to be a desperate effort at reconciling the "active" aspect of Roman religion with his desire to create a coherent framework for the structure of the cycle of cults celebrated at Rome. Another Roman, the poet Ovid, offered a somewhat different view on the structure of Roman religion by writing a poem (of which only the first half seems to have been finished) in which he described the religious structure of the Roman state in terms of the festival cycle. In this Ovid may have been influenced by other contemporary work on the calendar, and his approach had the strength that it enabled Romans to see how their history was deeply implicated in divine action. Ovid plainly had a poetic agenda that went well beyond this, and poetic models that were Greek as well as Roman. But, for present purposes, it is important simply to note that we know of several books from the second half of the first century B.C. that were taking different approaches to the problem of describing the gods of Rome. To later Christian writers, the failure of Romans to present a coherent picture of their gods, and a coherent doctrine for their worship was taken as a sign of the futility of the whole project (see, e.g., Tertullian, *Apology* 25.2–3). The gods worshipped by polytheists could not be real gods. A more generous reading would suggest that the complexity of civic cults illustrated the plurality of interests that the gods were thought to serve. There could be no straightforward system of understanding in a society as diverse as that of Rome, or in one that was constantly evolving. The gods of Rome were understood in diverse ways as they were relevant to their worshippers.

Ideally, no Roman would worship a god, either new or alien, unless that god had been officially recognized, and a Roman would worship the gods whose cults had been established by their ancestors (Cic. *Laws* 2.19). New cults could be admitted to the state pantheon at any time, and their addition to the multitude of acceptable divinities did not mean that other gods were necessarily thrown out: the number of gods was potentially infinite. The process of admission was itself quite straightforward. The first criterion for membership was a recommendation from an existing member of the pantheon, given through an officially recognized prophet or some other manifestation (e.g., victory in a battle). Once the recommendation had been received, the senate checked to make certain that it was authentic and then moved to ensure that the new cult would have a cult site where it could be celebrated. So, too, the Roman senate could determine (again either as a result of prophecy or in gratitude for some favor) that new *sacra* should be celebrated in honor of an existing god. The fact that humans decided if some divinity should receive cult in the city did not detract, as some modern scholars (following in the tradition of Christian apologists) assert, from the "religious" character of these transactions. The initiative was always with the gods, who told mortals that it was time to do something, and who could be counted on to act again if their first message was ignored. The role of the senate in certifying a new cult is simply an illustration of the fact that religion runs along a two-way street: recognition of a new cult was a promise to worship the god correctly. It is a feature of the "active" aspect of religion discussed earlier in this chapter.

Beyond the distinction between officially recognized civic and noncivic cult, no effort was made to control worship unless the ruling class decided that a cult was promoting immorality or rebellion, as happened with the cult of Bacchus in the early second century B.C., the cult of Isis in A.D. 19, and Christianity at a number of points. The Romans seem essentially to have been satisfied with the notion that "public *sacra* are celebrated at public expense for the people, and whatever is done for mountains, towns, cures, and shrines; but private *sacra* are those that are celebrated for individuals, households, and families" (Festus p. 284 L).[2] Similarly, the Roman state made no effort to control private divination unless officials felt that it threatened the social order. In principle, there was nothing wrong with individuals trying to get information for themselves. There was only a problem when they

2. See also the excellent discussion in Beard 1994, 732–33.

asked a divinity to do something to someone else or if they were seeking knowledge that could upset the public order. There are numerous efforts to ban "magic" on record, and there are several cases where the state actively intervened to stop the circulation of prophetic books on the grounds that they were fakes and were promoting public disorder (Potter 1994, 171–82).

Belief and Social Control

Belief in the gods functioned on a number of levels. At one level there was a predisposition to suppose that any inexplicable phenomenon was an act of some higher power. At another level there was a predisposition to suppose that because something was remarkable, it must therefore be divine (Price 1969, 445). In both cases the initial predisposition was based on the observation of a phenomenon that lead to the conclusion that a supernatural being was involved (Rives 1995, 15). Rituals provided a model for the order of society and for a human being's relationship with the vast, uncontrollable forces of nature. Human existence in a preindustrial society was extraordinarily tenuous. Life expectancy at birth was somewhere around twenty-five years (or less), meaning that the world was full of dying children and that those who survived had to confront the facts of mortality, hunger, and chronic injury or illness on a daily basis. The extraordinary number of medicinal remedies that have survived in sundry works are testimony to humanity's virtual impotence in the face of illness of any sort. The ritual of passive cult provided psychological reassurance that there was help and reason to hope in the face of all this. The urge to control the uncontrollable manifested itself in devotional exercises of all sorts. But the cults of the Roman world were often more than this. Classical polytheism existed on a plane beyond that of simple grunt and sacrifice in an effort to control the weather. Although the ancient world produced intellectuals of all sorts who laughed at the idea that the gods took an interest in human affairs and at the assumption that the gods could be influenced by the slaughter of animals by their altars, by far the greater number of intellectuals in this world believed profoundly in the gods. They evolved their own, complex explanations of the way that humans could deal with the gods and developed complex models of the way that the divine world was ordered, seeking to explain the multitudinous manifestations of divine action that they perceived.

While belief in the divine was an important feature of Roman religion, the Romans could and did think that their religious system had mundane applications. It was perfectly possible for a person to believe that the gods existed, to believe that the gods had established the basic tenets of their own worship, and to think that the existing religious system had some very practical social applications. It was the very fact of belief that made this possible, and it was possible for a person to sneer at one or another aspect of the system and still know that the gods could intervene in his or her daily affairs. The emperor Vespasian is said to have made fun of the imperial cult as he lay dying, remarking as his life slipped away that he thought that he was becoming a god. Ten years earlier he had exploited the sensibilities of his subjects by engaging in some fake healing miracles at the temple of Serapis in Alexandria. But he had also taken the Jewish rebel Josephus into his confidence when the latter predicted, right after his capture, that Vespasian would be emperor, and he had sought the council of an oracle when he was worried about the powers of a German prophetess named Veleda.[3]

Writing at the height of the Republic, some two centuries before Vespasian, the Greek historian Polybius compared the Roman state with others.

> The quality in which the Roman commonwealth is most distinctly superior is in my opinion the nature of their religious conviction. I believe that it is the very thing that among other peoples is an object of reproach—I mean *deisidaimonia* (superstition)—that maintains the cohesion of the Roman state. These matters are clothed with such pomp and introduced to such an extent into their public and private life that nothing could exceed it, a fact that will surprise many. My opinion is that they have adopted this course for the sake of the common people. It is a course that perhaps would not have been necessary had it been possible to form a state composed of wise men, but as every mob is fickle, full of lawless desires, unreasoned passion, and violent anger, the mob must be held in by invisible terrors and suchlike pageantry. (Polybius *History* 6.56.6–12)

3. For his dying remark see Suetonius *Life of Vespasian* 23.4: *vae, inquit, puto deus fio.* For the miracles at Alexandria see Tacitus *Histories* 4.81; Suetonius *Life of Vespasian* 7.2; Dio *History of Rome* 66.8.1. For Veleda see Merkelbach 1981.

This statement appears to be the straightforward expression of an explicitly rationalist approach to religion. In other parts of his history Polybius suggests that he believed that Tyche, the personification of Fortune, played an active role in human affairs and that men who desecrated the shrines of the gods were visited with divine retribution. Thus when the Macedonians rose in revolt against Rome in 146, Polybius says that "the thing was a heaven-sent infatuation and that all the Macedonians were visited by the wrath of god" (*History* 36.17.15), and in two other cases he suggests that rulers of the Hellenistic east were smitten by divine vengeance (*History* 31.9.3–4, 32.15.14). It seems that Polybius believed that the gods did act in this world but that the rites with which they were honored were human inventions. Furthermore, even though he thought these rites were human inventions, Polybius also plainly believed that the gods would avenge themselves on mortals who violated their sanctuaries or otherwise dishonored their worship (Walbank 1972, 65).

Polybius was not alone in his belief that the gods existed and that the religious institutions of the Roman state were connected with the social and political order. This view appears to have been commonplace among members of the ruling classes in the Republic, and it lies behind some significant imperial initiatives from the time of Augustus through the conversion of the empire to Christianity in the fourth century A.D. According to a view of Roman history that became standard by the first century B.C., Numa Pompilius, the second king of Rome, was the originator of most of the religious institutions of the state. The selection of Numa for this role is typical of the thought process of the Roman world that routinely endowed important institutions with founders in the distant past. This view is all the easier to understand if one sees the central areas of Rome, as of most ancient cities, as vast museums of civic history. The houses of great nobles displayed the trophies won by former owners, and the public areas of the city were filled with memorials that appeared to be and were extremely ancient even by the second century B.C. Ancient, too, were some of the rites, and some hymns were in such an archaic form of Latin that people did not know what they said. Such a festival as the Lupercalia, during which young members of the nobility ran through the streets dressed in skins and hitting women with leather thongs, suggested an origin in a society that was at a stage well before the evolution of civilized life. In addition to the hymns and conduct associated with various celebrations, the sacrifices to the gods were often very simple, suggesting that they too were devised at a time when Rome was still a very small place. Thus Dionysius of Halicarnassus (a Greek who wrote a book on Roman antiquities for the education of other Greeks in the time of Augustus) noted that he had seen "meals set before the gods in the sacred precincts on old wooden tables, in baskets and on small earthen plates, consisting of barley bread, cakes, and smelt, with the first offerings of some fruits, and other things of a like nature, simple, cheap, and devoid of vulgar display." He continued, "I have seen also the libation wines that have been mixed, not in silver and gold vessels, but in little earthen cups and jugs, and I greatly admire these men in that they retain their ancestral customs, not exchanging the ancient rites for boastful and expensive display (*Roman Antiquities* 2.23.5). Romans, in constant physical contact with the memorials of their past, considered their ancestors, who had built the city up from its small beginning and left them these memorials, people of great wisdom and models for their own conduct.

Antiquity conferred authority, and it stood to reason among educated Romans that their institutions must have been the work of a single great legislator in the earliest years of the city's history and that this legislator must have shared their understanding of the way that these institutions worked. The most serious question about Numa seems to have been whether he had made up these institutions himself or received them directly from the gods. Thus in the twenties B.C., the historian Livy wrote:

> closing that temple [the temple of Janus] after he had secured the disposition of all the neighboring peoples through treaties and alliances, he [Numa] decided that, lest the minds of the Romans, minds that fear of enemies and military discipline had once restrained, should decline under conditions of leisure once they had put aside concerns for external perils, the first thing to do was to instill fear of the gods, a thing most effective with a multitude that was ignorant and, in that age, crude. Since this fear could not descend into their hearts without some miraculous story, he pretended that he met at night with the goddess Egeria and that with her advice he instituted the *sacra* that were most acceptable to the gods and established special priests for the service of each god. (Livy, *History of Rome* 1.19.4–5)

Cicero had earlier implied the same view when he wrote that Numa had quenched the ardor of the Romans for war by the introduction of religious life (*Republic* 2.26), and he firmly expressed the view himself that a common religion was important to a well-ordered state. His clearest statement of this doctrine—a statement that may well sum up the attitudes of his contemporaries, ancestors, and heirs toward the social function of the religion of the state—comes in another of his dialogues, *The Laws.*

> From the start the citizens must be convinced that the gods are the lords and moderators of all things, that whatever is done is done with their authority and will, that they deserve the best from the race of mortals, that they perceive how each man is, what he does, and whatever he allows himself, with what mind and what *pietas* he observes the cults, and that they take note of the pious and the impious. Minds that are imbued with these principles will scarcely shrink from useful or correct opinions. (2.15–16)

In Cicero's view it is really not possible to separate the human from the divine: the legislator creates the rites that people will observe, but the gods are also involved, keeping watch over society. It is up to them to decide what to do if mortals do not observe the rites that were created to make them mindful of the divinities. Mortals can have a role in this, by recognizing evil behavior and punishing it—for if they do not the gods surely will—and the actions of the gods could have serious implications for the community as a whole. Under the empire, for example, people were often moved to take action against such groups as the Christians because they thought that their behavior was immoral and offended the gods. So, too, in all periods, difficulties that Rome encountered could be explained as the result of human transgression against the gods. According to a view that was well established in the first century B.C., the Roman people had declined from piety to crime, and this caused the political crisis that brought down the Republic.[4] Augustus saw to it that he appeared to people as the restorer of the traditional religion, perhaps in part to remind the Roman people that the

4. See Wiseman 1992 for an important discussion of concerns about religious propriety in the Late Republic.

civil wars stemmed from the general decline in public morality. Throughout the thirties B.C., as he was seeking to establish his position as sole leader of the state, he was constantly restoring temples, temples whose condition could be taken as visible proof of the decline in state morality. Nearly three hundred years later, the emperor Decius seems to have adopted the same line when he ordered all the inhabitants to sacrifice to the gods and to obtain certificates proving that they had done so.[5]

Did Augustus really believe his own rhetoric, did Decius really believe that his edict would make the gods happy, and did all those who executed Christians actually think that if they did not do so the gods would punish their community? It is impossible to know. Certainly Augustus had once made fun of the gods at a banquet when he was a young man, and we know of a number of governors who were not interested in Christians.[6] The emperor Decius has left us no way to judge his inner thoughts (if he had them). In the rough world of Roman republican politics, many were aware that the institutions of the state religion were abused in efforts to prevent things from happening, and sometimes they just did not care.[7] But the Age of Augustus followed on from that of Julius Caesar and Cicero, which suggests that the value of proper observation of the state religion was enhanced rather than destroyed by the events of the fifties B.C.: the civil wars could be taken as proof of how the gods felt about the way things were going. And it was the Roman populace, the humble inhabitants of the city rather than the exalted members of its ruling class, who first decided that the murdered Julius Caesar was actually a god. So, too, after a great fire destroyed Rome in A.D. 64, the Roman people turned to Sibylline verses to express their feelings about Nero, whom many blamed for the disaster, just as centuries before many had turned to the *carmina Marciana,* oracular verses bearing on the disasters that Rome was suffering at the hands of Hannibal. Despite its failings, the Roman religious system

5. For Augustus see Liebeschuetz 1979, 55–100; for Decius see Potter 1990, 41–42.

6. Suetonius *Life of Augustus* 70; for Christians see Potter 1993.

7. For the abuse of the religious system in Republican politics see Taylor 1971, 76–97. But see now Beard 1994, 739–42; and see Wiseman 1992 for the suggestion that there was rather more concern about abuse of the system than is allowed for in Taylor's classic discussion.

continued to work as a social institution because people believed that the gods took an interest in human affairs.

In practical terms there are two primary functions of a religious system. One is to define the relationship between humans and the divine through a series of sacred acts whose performance enables mortals to predict the reaction of the divinities implicitly believed to have ordained these rituals. The other is to provide divine guidelines that reinforce a society's conception of permissible social and political behavior.[8] It is not coincidental that the dominant role in organizing both these aspects of the religious system on the human plane ordinarily falls to the dominant social and political class within a given society (Rives 1995, 9). Likewise, though the actual working of the process may not always be a fully conscious act of manipulation, this group will take the ideology with which it endowed its religious system and either employ it to restrict the use of that system by outsiders working for change or use its tenets to help define acceptable avenues for reform. Similarly, it is not unusual for groups excluded from political power to try to exploit the dominant ideology to justify their demands for reform. It is time now to turn to some of the basic concepts through which the system worked.

Pietas and Impietas

In the Roman state, acceptable and unacceptable religious conduct are subsumed in the notions of *pietas* and *impietas*. *Pietas* may be defined as dutiful respect toward members of one's family, toward others with whom a person shares social relations, and toward the norms of society. *Impietas* is a failure to observe those norms.

Although the Romans regarded *pietas* as a crucial virtue and allowed that the obligations of *pietas* could justify behavior that might otherwise be regarded as obnoxious violations of the social order, they did not feel that exemplary *pietas* necessarily brought someone any special favor from the gods. Just as Roman public religion was a matter of state, so, too, *pietas* was not simply a "religious" concept. It was one of the basic virtues that a Roman might seek to possess and display like a

8. Wiseman 1992 is an important corrective to the notion that divine sanction did not extend to the level of individual conduct. The notion that criminals were punished in Hades was plainly prevalent. Contrast Beard 1994, 729.

physical object. Thus after Caesar's murder in 44 B.C., the future emperor Augustus would justify the raising of a private army and his involvement in civil war as an act of *pietas*—he was obligated to pursue the murderers of his adoptive father. This *pietas* seems to have a physical quality: it can compel action, or it can be worn like a piece of clothing (Tacitus *Annals* 1.10).

Pietas was defined through action, and so was *impietas*. It was not until the later years of the reign of Augustus or his successor, Tiberius (A.D. 14–37), that one could think or speak *impietas*, and this expansion of the definition of *impietas* stems directly from politics: *impietas in principem*, or *impietas* toward the emperor, became a definition for treason that involved thought as well as deed (Bauman 1974, 1–24). Before this, *impietas* had to be something that one did to violate the implicit agreement between the state and the divinities that humans would actively observe proper conduct. The worst possible form of *impietas* was the murder of a close relative, *parricidium*. The human vengeance for this crime was horrific, and it was generally thought that someone who committed it was also tormented by the anger of the gods. Tacitus tells us that after the emperor Nero murdered his mother, he was constantly tormented by guilt, and Cicero suggests that "the punishment of the gods is a double one because it comes from their tortured souls while alive and a reputation after death, such that their deaths are approved by the judgment and pleasure of the living" (Tacitus *Annals* 14.10; Cicero *The Laws* 2.43–44).

After *parricidium*, other forms of *impietas* involved the knowing violation of divine rites. By the first century B.C., young Romans were brought up on tales of massive disasters stemming from failure to take the gods seriously, such as that of Appius Claudius, the consul of 249 B.C. who gave battle to the Carthaginians despite the sacred chickens' refusal to eat. The observation of the feeding habits of these birds, an operation known as the *tripudium* (which technically involved observing the way that grain fell to the ground from the beaks of feeding birds), was a traditional form of consulting the gods. If Claudius had simply misinterpreted the way the chickens had acted, he would only have been the victim of his own error. But that he ordered them to be thrown into the sea with the words "If they will not eat, let them drink!" shows that he had recognized the implications of what the gods were saying and did not care. The disaster that followed also served to remind the Romans that the gods might avenge themselves not on the guilty individual but rather on the state as a whole.

The Roman response to another open act of *impietas* shows just how threatening such acts were thought to be even as Rome was emerging as the dominant state in the Mediterranean world. In 205 B.C., a Roman army recaptured the south Italian town of Locri from Hannibal's Carthaginians. After the city's surrender, they left a garrison behind under the command of Q. Pleminius, a bad choice. Pleminius proceeded to abuse the Locrians and then stole the treasury of the temple of Persephone. As Livy tells it:

> Avarice did not abstain from the theft of sacred treasures; among the temples that were violated was that of Persephone, whose treasury had been inviolate through the ages, save only that it is said to have been despoiled by Pyrrhus, who returned the treasures with a great sacrifice to expiate his sacrilege. Therefore, just as the royal ships, damaged by disasters at sea, brought nothing to land in one piece except for the sacred money of the goddess that they were carrying, so now that same money brought another sort of disaster, driving all those stained by contact with the violation of the temple to madness. (Livy *History of Rome* 29.8.11; see also 29.18.3–5, 16–17)

In 204 the Locrians sent an embassy to Rome to complain of their treatment, of the poor discipline of Pleminius and his men (they were fighting among themselves), and of the theft of the treasure. The final point made a deep impression on the senate, which appointed a commission to recover all of the stolen objects and restore them to the temple and then to deposit a matching amount of money. When this was done the commission performed expiatory sacrifices that had been decreed by the pontifices. The whole process reveals that the senate felt that the state as a whole was threatened by the actions of Pleminius (who was brought to Rome in chains to stand trial) and that the state had to act to make amends to the divinities to protect itself from the misdeeds of an individual.[9]

9. Livy *History of Rome* 29.21.4; see also 29.19.8–9, 20.9–10; This discussion depends in general on Scheid 1985.

The cases I have thus far noted were blatant, but *impietas* need not involve great moments in history or dreadful family crimes. *Impietas* involved any violation of divine law. *Impietas* could be committed, for instance, by failure to observe a holiday properly, and its definition could be the subject for learned discourse so that people would know what to watch out for. This is perhaps best illustrated by Macrobius' record of discussions of the subject by Q. Mucius Scaevola, *pontifex maximus* c. 130–115 B.C., who was renowned as an authority on sacred law.

> . . . it is affirmed that someone who does something unwittingly on such a day [a holiday] ought to offer a sacrifice with a pig. Scaevola the pontifex said that it was not possible for someone who knowingly did something on a holiday to expiate the crime, but Umbro denies that a person is polluted who does something pertaining to the gods or for the sake of the *sacra* or who does something looking to the urgent necessity of life. Scaevola, asked then what it was possible to do on a holiday, responded that it was possible to do what would cause harm if it was not done. Thus if a cow fell into a cave and the paterfamilias, summoning assistance, could free it, he would not seem to have polluted the holiday; nor would the person who saved a broken beam from imminent ruin by propping it up. (*Saturnalia* 1.16.10–11)

In Scaevola's view and that of other Romans, it was impossible for a person who had committed *impietas* to be free of the crime, and the state could only hope, as in the case of Pleminius, that the gods would be satisfied by its apology. But there were no guarantees.

Vitium and the State

In his discussion of holidays, Scaevola draws a distinction between witting and unwitting violation of divine law. In his view the former was *impietas* that could not be expiated; the latter was simple error, *vitium*, for which it was possible to make amends and to expect that the gods would accept the apology. It was not possible to undo what had been done, but it was possible to prevent something else from going wrong, and it was always necessary to apologize. The more important the person, the more serious the consequences of vitium could be, for, in

Varro's words, "a magistrate elected in spite of unfavorable omen is none the less a magistrate" (*The Latin Language* 6.30), and errors connected with magistrates, the very men charged with mediating the relationship between society and the gods could be catastrophic: all that could be hoped was that such a magistrate would not do anything that would lead to the ruin of the state, before he could be removed from office.[10]

But what constituted *vitium,* and how could one know that something was wrong before an army of the Roman people was annihilated by Gauls or a fleet sunk beneath the waves? It often took a great deal of thought, and there might be different ways of looking at things, as was the case with the consular elections in 163 B.C. When Tiberius Sempronius Gracchus (himself consul for that year) was overseeing the election of the consuls for the next year, an official charged with reporting the votes dropped dead. Such an event might well be taken as a sign, and Gracchus, who was an augur, and most proud of his learning, decided to consult haruspices to make sure that the election should continue. The consultation of the haruspices was presumably intended to reassure people that Gracchus' actions as an auger were correct. But it backfired when the haruspices told Gracchus to stop the voting. Gracchus took this as a direct insult, told the haruspices that they had no business telling him that he was in error, and continued about his business (Cic. *The Nature of the Gods* 2.11). Two consuls were duly elected and took office in January 162.

Several months later, after the new consuls had assumed office and left Rome to command their armies in the provinces, the senate suddenly received a letter from Gracchus, who was then governing Sardinia. Gracchus explained that when he had been reading the books of the augurs (discussion later in this chapter) he had suddenly realized that he had been wrong to continue holding the election, because he had in fact made an error in his taking of the auspices. This error, a clear *vitium* in his view, invalidated the election; the senate agreed and compelled the new consuls to resign.[11]

The issues of time and space here are remarkable. The original election seems to have been held in the mid-summer of 163, and Gracchus could not have written his letter to the senate before the end of January

10. I owe much of my understanding of this subject to Rosenstein 1990.
11. For the technical issues here, see Linderski 1986, 2204.

(at the earliest). By sending his letter to the senate, Gracchus was bringing the whole administrative apparatus of the state to a halt. It is this that makes the incident so valuable for understanding the views of his contemporaries. That he should have been taken seriously suggests that others agreed that the state was in danger from the gods.

Gracchus' error had consisted of his erection of his augural tent outside the *pomerium*, the sacred boundary of the city, in the gardens of Scipio, a very short distance indeed from the *pomerium*. It is fairly clear that this really was inadvertent: if Gracchus had been opposed to the election of the consuls who were elected, he could simply have canceled the election when the *rogator* died. But a *vitium* was a *vitium*, and the senate obviously took the situation very seriously indeed. It also appears that the issue here did not have anything to do with politics on the human plane but rather involved the perception that the state was in danger from the gods if something was not done to correct the situation.

Vitium was not always recognized in time, and its identification was a major feature of the ongoing discovery of divine intention that is the fundamental "active" aspect of Roman religion. Thus in 176 B.C. the consul Petilius set out to fight the Ligurians in northern Italy, not knowing that he had committed an error when he took the auspices before his departure. Just before giving battle, he committed *impietas*, because he attacked despite the fact that consultation of the sacred chickens failed to produce a favorable omen. The Romans were only saved from total catastrophe because of another error. In his prayer to Jupiter before the battle, Petilius said, "May I capture Letum [the place-name means "death"] today!" (Valerius Maximus *Memorable Deeds and Sayings* 1.5.9). If he had followed ordinary custom and included his soldiers in this phrase uttered before them—"May we capture Letum today!"—he would presumably have brought about the destruction of his whole army. As it was, Petilius died but the Romans won. The circumstances surrounding Petilius' actions only became clear when the senate ordered an investigation into the matter. The other consul had died a few months earlier, and the death of both chief magistrates during their year in office suggested that there had been a serious disruption in the state's relationship with the gods (Livy *History of Rome* 41.8). The senate's reaction was remarkable. No new consul was elected to take Petilius' place, and the senate challenged whether the consul who had been elected in place of Petilius' deceased colleague—in an election that Petilius had presided over—had the right to conduct elections for the next year. Presumably, anything that Petilius had done was felt to be extremely questionable after his *vitium* at the original auspices.

The search for errors was the responsibility of the augurs and, increasingly, the business of the haruspices (see discussion later in this chapter). They had to be on guard not only for mistakes being made in the present but also for any that might have been made but not detected in the past. The accidental repetition of an earlier, undetected mistake could be catastrophic. The process of discovering new faults was known as *coniectura,* while that of determining from past failures that there was about to be a problem was *observatio,* the careful collection of past signs.[12]

There were two basic difficulties with both processes. The first is that they were based on the human capacity to observe and process information, meaning that problems could remain undetected from disaster to disaster. The second is that it was still up to mortals to decide what to do once a sign had been noted. Thus, according to Roman tradition, not until the year after the battle at Allia in 390 B.C. in which Rome's army was destroyed by the Gauls did it became clear to the Romans that they should not give battle on the day after the ides (either the thirteenth or the fifteenth) of any month, and even then consultation with a haruspex was required before they could arrive at this conclusion. The story as it stands is probably an invention of the mid–second century B.C., as it seems to be connected with a vigorous debate that was going on at that time about the relative merits of haruspices and traditional augural discipline. But the way that the story is told reveals a great deal about how the Romans thought that they acquired new knowledge. The source for this tale is once again Macrobius, to whom the reasoning clearly still made sense in the fifth century A.D. His account is as follows.

> In the three hundred and sixty-third year after the founding of the city a debate was opened in the senate by the tribunes of the soldiers with consular power[13] Virginius, Manlius, Aemilius, Postu-

---

12. Linderski (1986, 2231–34) notes that *observatio* could also mean simply the collection of signs in the present, though in an augural context it also meant "the establishment and recording of the positive knowledge concerning certain kinds of signs" and "the codified body of augural knowledge," and that the second meaning is its most important in this context.

13. On numerous occasions in the fifth and fourth centuries military tribunes with consular power were elected instead of two consuls.

> mus, and their colleagues on the question of why the state had been afflicted with so many disasters in recent years, and, upon the suggestion of the senate, the haruspex L. Aquinius was ordered to appear before the senate to explain the divine reasons for this, and he said that Q. Sulpicius, the tribune of the soldiers with consular power, when he was about to fight against the Gauls had made a sacrifice with reference to battle on the day after the ides of April, the same thing had happened at Cremera[14] and many other places, and the battle had always come out badly after a sacrifice made on the days after [the ides]. The senate then ordered that the day after all the calends, nones, and ides should be considered *dies atri* [dark days], so that on these days there would be neither battle nor sacrifices nor elections. Moreover, Fabius Maximus Servilianus the pontifex [c. 140 B.C.] claimed in his twelfth book that it was not fitting to offer sacrifice to the spirits of the dead on *dies atri* either, because it was necessary to call upon Janus and Jove, whom it was not right to call upon on *dies atri.* (Macrob. *Saturnalia* 1.16.22–25)

At first glance the senate's action appears to be a case of ritual overreaction. Apparently all it had been told was that a sacrifice offered on the day after the ides was a bad idea, but the senate proceeded to decide that nothing should be done on the days after the calends, nones, and ides of every month. Each of these days was significant for religious reasons. On the calends, the first day of the month, rites to Juno were observed. The nones, the ninth day before the ides, were traditionally set aside for the announcement of sacred events, and the ides were sacred to Jupiter. The senate therefore concluded that if disaster struck when sacrifices for undertaking a major operation were held on the day after one sacred day, then disaster could perfectly easily result from taking actions on the day after any sacred day. It therefore instructed the pontifices who were in charge of the sacred records of the state to make note of this and ensure that this prohibition was remembered. Finally, in the second century, another pontifex arrived at the further view that even private rites for the ancestors should be forbidden on the day after any sacred day. His view does not seem to have

14. The main strength of the Fabian gens had been destroyed in battle at Cremera in 477.

become law, because the senate, as far as we know, never instructed the pontifices to observe this prohibition. Even though the reasoning seems to have been consistent with precedent, others did not seem to have thought that observation of the facts justified such a prohibition, no matter how logical the argument in its favor.

The role of the senate in determining religious regulations for the state is plain, but its significance remains a matter for dispute. According to one recent study of Roman priestly institutions, senatorial determination in these cases shows that the senate as a body, rather than any group of priests, mediated between the human and the divine and thus that the religious system consisted of "a series of interpretations and reinterpretations—satellites around an elusive and intangible core."[15] According to another view, the role of the senate suggests that the gods should merely be seen as "special citizens" of the state and that the power of the gods is subject to that of the magistrates (Scheid 1985, 51). In defense of these views, it is clear that the senate often decided if *impietas* had been committed or if a trial for sacrilege was necessary, the senate decided if it was necessary to investigate the possibility that a *vitium* had been committed, and the senate decided if a *vitium* had indeed been committed after it had listened to reports on the subject. The senate decided if something was a *prodigium* that the state had to take account of, and the senate decided on the admission of new gods to the pantheon. The senate decided on the regulations for the cults of the state and oversaw contact with oracles. These prerogatives remained with the senate even after the emergence of the monarchy—it is not until the reign of Trajan (A.D. 98–117) that we find a new divinity being admitted to the pantheon by imperial fiat and without prior senatorial approval (the divinity in question was Trajan's sister).[16] In acting as it did, the senate also acted to preserve the hierarchical fabric of the political order. Only the most respectable citizens could be members of the senate, and the common people depended on the good judgment of the senate to ensure that the state's relationship with the gods remained intact. Moreover, until the emperors assumed a dominant position in the religious hierarchy of the state, the location of control in the senate as a body, rather than with individuals, reflected the ideology of the senate, whereby no one individual senator could dominate

15. Beard 1990, 30–34.
16. For this see Price 1987, 92.

his peers. But to suggest that the senate is "mediating" here—that is, that the senate is negotiating the relationship between human and divine—and that there was no fixed center to this system is not correct. In all cases the senate (at least in theory) acted on the best information that was available to it about what the gods wanted. It was the senate's task to preserve a relationship whose parameters were entirely determined by the gods. Whatever the senate might decide, the initiative that sparked its action came from the gods. The best that humans could hope for was that they could keep the gods in a good mood.

The actions of the senate diffused responsibility if things went wrong and diffused credit if things went right. The fact that there were numerous gods complicated human response, but it did not alter the locus of power. The senate's role in administering the affairs of the cults on the earth did not make the gods into great citizens. Rather it showed that the maintenance of the *pax deorum* (the peace of the gods, or the goodwill of the gods toward the Roman people) was an issue of outstanding importance. The senate's role was not to mediate between god and man but to harmonize the "active" and "passive" aspects of the system. It was to isolate the diverse strands of divine communication and orchestrate them into a coherent symphony. The senate stood between the state's prophets, who listened to the music of the gods, and the state's priests, who recorded the score for the future so that the Roman people could always hear what the gods had desired in the past and could continue to listen to them in the future.

Practice

Priests

In describing his ideal constitution for the Roman state, Cicero wrote that "the several gods will have their several *sacerdotes*, there will be pontifices for all the gods, and flamines for the individual gods" (*The Laws* 2.20). This seemingly simple formulation masks some real complexities in the actual Roman state (Wissowa 1912, 413–14). The term *flamen* is very ancient, and it was not the designation of a priesthood but rather defined a function within the system of worship. In the high classical period (c. 100 B.C.–A.D. 300) people seem to have been satisfied with the notion that the flamines were so named because since "they always kept their heads covered and had their hair girt with a woolen *filium* [band], they were originally called *filimines*," and that they took their names from the rites that they celebrated (Varro *The Latin Language* 5.84). Their function was therefore to preside over sacrifices. In fact the word *flamen* descends from an Indo-European root meaning "priest" and is connected with, for instance, the Sanskrit word *brahman*. As we will see, some flamines had duties that were significantly different from those of other priests. In classical Latin, the generic word for any sort of priest had come to be not *flamen* but *sacerdos*, a word that the Romans of the classical period believed was derived from *sacer*, meaning "rites" (Varro *The Latin Language* 6.83). The flamines could thus be said to constitute a subcategory of priest specifically connected with sacrifices. Unfortunately, this was not always the case. The word *flamen* seems to have dropped out of general usage in Latin by the end of the sixth century B.C., only to be revived by students of the language in the first century B.C. Thus flamines are found in association with the very oldest cults of the Roman state and with the very newest, the cults of the emperors and cults in provincial communities. The word *sacerdos*, rather than *flamen*, is found in association with the worship, for instance, of the Great Mother, whose cult arrived in Rome in the late third century, and other gods who came to Rome had *antistes* (whose name is etymologically connected with the verb meaning "to stand before," since priests stood in front of temples while making sacrifices). There were also some cults that were celebrated by fraternities and, in one case, a sorority.

The pontifices were not associated with the worship of any single divinity. The word *pontifex* seems to be derived from *pons* meaning "bridge" and the verb *facere* meaning "to make," and it appears that the pontifices' original function was to look after Rome's first bridge over the Tiber, the *pons Sublicius* (bridge on piles), and hence to celebrate rites connected with it. From this it appears that the pontifices acquired oversight over other crossing points, including that between life and death. The pontifices were intimately (and extensively) concerned with burial habits and then, it appears, more generally with the rules governing communication between human and divine. Thus in some of the incidents described already, they are charged with recording decisions about rites to be offered to the gods.

It appears that within this collection of officials are four basic categories, probably representing one or two different stages in the early development of Roman religion.[17] One category is that of the "priest statue," or a priest who stood as the representative of the divinity in the city (Scheid 1985, 39–42). The second type is the apotropaic performer, a fraternity member who performed symbolic actions to avert evil and promote health. The third sort is the ritual overseer, a variety that includes the vast majority of other priests at Rome. The fourth includes priestly colleges whose primary function was to act as guardians and interpreters of specific traditions. Thus the pontifices acted as guardians and exegetes of the *ius pontificum,* the tradition of the pontiffs; the *fetiales* interpreted the *ius fetialis* that governed Rome's relations with the outside world; the augurs interpreted the *disciplina auguralis* (augural science); and the *quindecimviri* interpreted the Sibylline Books (Wissowa 1912, 475).

The *flamen dialis* was the archetypal "priest statue." In explaining why the flamen was forbidden to touch or name either the dog or the goat, Plutarch says that this is because the goat was lascivious, of an unattractive color, and susceptible to epilepsy (a theory based on the notion that the bleating of a goat sounded like the utterance of a human suffering an epileptic seizure) and because the dog is "a belligerent creature" and thus kept away from sanctuaries. The flamen himself had to stay away from these creatures because he was "the animate embodiment and sacred image of the god," he was in effect a walking sanctuary (*Roman Questions* 111), and his house was a place of refuge (*Roman Questions* 111; Aulus Gellius *Attic Nights* 10.15). The restrictions on the flamen's actions, including prohibitions against his seeing the Roman people drawn up in order of battle outside of the *pomerium* and against his riding a horse (Aulus Gellius *Attic Nights* 10.15), meant he tended to be put in office at a very young age and that, although he had to be a

17. The value and, indeed, the practicality of studying the chronological development of Roman cult is challenged by Beard (1990) on the grounds that her chart of Roman priests (pp. 20–21), a chart that purports to list the significant priesthoods at Rome, shows nothing later than the end of the regal period. This chart is extremely misleading because it omits all *antistes* and *sacerdotes.* The argument is further flawed by failure to take account of Rome's development from a small collection of villages into a major urban center in the regal period (c. 800–500 B.C.). It nonetheless is extremely risky to assert much of anything about the early development of cult, even to the extent that I have done here. For an intelligent discussion of the problems with the evidence see North 1989, 573–82.

patrician, he was not usually a person who could be expected to do much with his life. But personal character did not matter as long as the flamen observed the taboos connected with his status, and even though he was rarely a senator (the taboos made the pursuit of a normal senatorial career in the republic a virtual impossibility), he was entitled by tradition to a seat in the senate house as Jupiter's representative.

There were several early festivals that required ritual performances by groups of people to avert evil. In the late Republic, and under the monarchy, the most notable of these was the Lupercalia. This festival was celebrated each year on the fifteenth of February by two colleges of male priests, the luperci quinctiales and the luperci fabii, and by the vestal virgins (Wiseman 1995).

As befits any religious institution of enormous appeal, the Lupercalia was anything but a static celebration, for while it always retained three basic features—a sacrifice, a dinner for the colleges of priests associated with the festival, and a race through the streets—the meaning and practice changed. Of the three elements, two remained consistent: the sacrifice and the feast. At the sacrifice, goats and a dog were sacrificed and portions were burned along with sacred cakes prepared by the vestal virgins from the first ears of grain taken at the previous year's harvest (the cakes, called *mola salsa,* were used in several other festivals as well). The sacrifice and feast took place at the Lupercal, a spot located on the southwest foot of the Palatine and thought to be the place where a she-wolf had nursed the infant founder of the city, Romulus, and his brother, Remus. After the sacrifice, several of the luperci then took the bloodstained knives that had been used to sacrifice the animals and smeared it on the foreheads of two young men, and others wiped it off with wool that had been saturated with milk. When this happened the two young men who were the objects of these ministrations laughed, and all the luperci sat down to eat. After this they ran through the streets striking people with thongs cut from the skins of the sacrificial beasts.

In the earliest period it appears that there was only one college of luperci. In the early third century B.C., a period of intense social reorganization, whereby the plebs gained access to virtually all the institutions that had previously been restricted to patricians, a second college was added. Also, in the earliest period, the priests dressed like Lupercus, the eponymous god of the festival; that is, they undressed and ran around in the nude waving their thongs (Wiseman 1995, 10–16). About the time that the second college was added, some clothes were added as well—if loincloths cut from the skin of the sacrificial animals not needed for thongs can qualify as clothing. In the earliest festival, it had also been the case that the luperci struck anyone that they met. In 276 B.C. (probably) this was changed, almost certainly as the result of divine revelation, so that the luperci directed their attention to women of childbearing age, who would strip to the waist to receive a blow from a Lupercus in order to enhance their chances of having a child. The combination of nudity and overt sexuality (the blow was thought to represent sexual penetration by the god) appears to have catapulted the festival to the forefront of popular celebration—and it was this that drew the attention of the emperor Augustus, who reformed the festival once again to ensure that the luperci were better dressed (wearing a more concealing form of loincloth). He did nothing about the nudity of the women, who now appear to have been expected to strip to the waist and kneel in a submissive posture to await the attention of the priests, rather than to throw themselves at the priests. Female nudity and the connection with fertility ensured that even after most traditional festivals had ceased, the Lupercalia continued to be one of the events that bound the citizens of Rome together. Its celebration was not discontinued until the late fifth century A.D., when Pope Felix III finally had it stopped (he instituted a festival for the purification of the Virgin Mary in its place) (Wiseman 1995, 17).

When they celebrated the Lupercalia, the luperci stood as representatives of the Roman people before the gods. The safety of the city for the coming year depended on their proper performance of the ritual. This appears to have been true of other colleges as well. In all cases it is significant that they actually had to perform ritual actions in a public capacity, that they physically participated in the worship of the divinity on behalf of the state rather than just presiding over the performance of sacrifice, the role of priests in the third category. Unlike some of the flamines or the vestals, but like other priests, they were expected to do this in addition to their other duties. The fratres Arvales, the Arval brethren, are a case in point. The group was theoretically established by Romulus, even though they came to occupy a significant place in the Roman priestly scene when the emperor Augustus "restored" (or invented) a series of rites for them to perform. During a three-day festival, they would touch crops during a ritual banquet over which the goddess Dea Dia presided, and they would dance a three-step dance while reciting a hymn in Latin that was so archaic by the time of Augustus that it is difficult to believe that many of them actually understood what they were saying.[18] But this really did not matter, and it may even have made the ceremony more impressive, enhancing the notion of continuity with the distant past. More important was that the Roman people could see the leading men of the state (and several of their male children, who had a place in the rites on two of the three days of the festival) acting to guarantee the harvest and external safety of Rome—interestingly (and probably not coincidentally) the two areas that Augustus had made the particular spheres of his activity as *princeps.*

The role of the ordinary priest was much less active. The priest's job was to lead a sacrificial procession, initiate the sacrificial activity, and watch as others, generally people of low social status, did the work. In these circumstances the physical act of sacrifice represented the proper working of the social order, where responsibility for the worship of the gods lay with the members of the senate and where the actual work was done by the people (Gordon 1990, 203–6). Such priests stood as representatives of their class, and it was not even expected that they would necessarily have a precise knowledge of what it was that they were to do. The fact that a person was the *antistes* of Apollo would not mean that he was necessarily expected to know even the right form of prayer to offer. The responsibility for knowing such things rested instead with the state's overseers of matters divine, the pontifices. The *antistes* were not expected to be innovators in any way, nor were they expected to retain an accurate knowledge of the religious traditions of the state so that they could correctly instruct those who were celebrating the rites.

In the late Republic the idea developed that three of the groups who acted as overseers of tradition were more important than the others. These were the pontifices, the augurs, and the *quindecimviri sacris faciundis* (I will use the post-Sullan title for this collegium, *quindecimviri,* as a matter of convenience hereafter), respectively the subjects of books 2, 3, and 4 of Varro's *Divine Antiquites.* In the reign of Augustus another college joined this group: the *septimviri epulonum,* the board of seven charged with organizing banquets in honor of the gods.[19] Together the

18. See now Scheid 1990, especially the brilliant analysis of the significance of the first day's ceremonies on pp. 506–46.

19. Wissowa 1912, 414–16, 446; Szemler 1972, 28.

four colleges were simply known as "the four greatest colleges of *sacerdotes*" *(sacerdotum quattuor amplissima collegia)* (Wissowa 1912, 414). Any member of one of these colleges could also be the *antistes* or *sacerdos* of a specific god, and it was possible for a member of one of the four colleges to be a member of another in the Republic. Augustus, who was concerned to spread priestly dignities more widely in the aristocracy and who was a member of all four colleges himself (*ILS* 107), ensured that no senator could hold more than one.

Originally membership in the three "greatest colleges" was limited to patricians, but in 300 B.C. plebeians became eligible for membership. With the admission of plebeians the number of pontifices was increased from three to six, the number of augurs from three to nine, and the number of the future *quindecimviri* from two to ten. Sulla raised the number in all three groups to fifteen. Once plebeians had been admitted to these groups, the only official requirements for membership were Roman citizenship, free birth, and the absence of bodily defects. The unofficial requirements were much more strict. Whether the colleges were filled by election or by admission on the decision of the existing members (the method of selection changed from time to time, until selection by the existing membership through a process known as co-optation became standard under Augustus), only the most distinguished members of the senatorial aristocracy or members of the greatest aristocratic families at Rome ever found a place in one of the colleges during the Republic, and selection was a mark of imperial favor after Augustus.[20]

The members of the great priestly colleges, although many of them took their duties extremely seriously, were no more "professionals" than any other priests, aside from the three major flamines and the vestals. But the fact that members called on to give advice did so as a college had some important implications for the way that they functioned in the state as a whole. It meant that there was no single religious figure or group controlling the system, and it tended to reinforce the importance of precedent. This was also useful since the principle of consultation could absolve any one individual from sole responsibility if things did not work out. The ability to share the blame for divine anger was just as important to a monarch as it was to the government of the Republic (Rosenstein 1990, 85–87). The way that this worked in

20. Szemler 1972, 30–31; Syme 1986, 4–5.

practice may be seen, for example, in the events surrounding Rome's declaration of war against Philip V of Macedon in 200 B.C.

Right after the declaration of war, the senate decreed that there should be a three-day period of *supplicatio* (prayer) to the gods during which the two consuls should go to all the *pulvinaria,* couches or platforms on which the images of the gods stood, and ask the gods to grant victory in the war with Philip (Livy *History of Rome* 31.8.2). This rite appears to have been developed under the influence of Greek practice at the end of the fifth century B.C. and was ordered by the senate either because, as on this occasion, senators felt that it was necessary to ensure the goodwill of the gods, or because, as on other occasions, the *pontifices* or prophets whom the state decided to take note of advised it. Which people participated in supplications varied depending on the reason that the *supplicatio* had been ordered. In this case it appears that only the consuls (with their assistants) were involved. At other times we hear that participants included anyone in the city older than twelve (and that they were wearing crowns and carrying laurel branches) or the *matronae* (married women) (Wissowa 1912, 358). When the *supplicatio* was finished the consul charged with the war against Philip asked the *fetiales,* the college of priests charged with the ritual oversight of Rome's relations with the outside world, if it was necessary to announce the declaration of war to the king in person, or if the announcement could be delivered to the first garrison that he encountered in Macedonian territory (Livy *History of Rome* 31.8.3). The *fetiales* replied that he could do either, and the senate decreed that he could send whoever he wanted as an ambassador to make the declaration, so long as that person was not a member of the senatorial order. The fetial decision represented an interesting development in the tradition of fetial law.

The consultation was necessary because it was impossible to carry out the ancient procedure for declaring war. The procedure had developed in early Latium when Rome was but one of a number of states occupying the Latin plain that were bound by the *ius fetiale,* an agreement not to go to war without having first sought redress of grievances (Watson 1993, 7). It was the duty of the fetial priests to ensure that Rome went to war for just cause and that it behaved properly in the period leading up to the actual outbreak of war. Like the pontifices and other priests, they could not themselves declare war (that was the business of the senate and people); their job was to make certain that procedures designed to ensure divine agreement with the human decision were carried out correctly. In the end, it was Jupiter who decided the justice of Rome's case by either granting victory or permitting disaster to strike.[21]

In the earliest period of the city's history, when an offense had been committed by one state (or citizens of one state) against another, three ambassadors would be sent to demand redress (and act called the *rerum repetitio*). There would then be a thirty-day waiting period, at the end of which, if satisfaction was not obtained, the *fetiales* prayed to the gods for success in war (a prayer known as a *testatio*). On the thirty-third day after the *rerum repetitio,* ambassadors were sent to deliver the declaration of war by throwing a spear into enemy territory (an act called the *indictio belli*). By the time that Rome had conquered Italy, this last action was no longer practical, and an area was consecrated as enemy territory in front of the temple of Bellona (a goddess of war) so that the spear throwing could take place there. By the time that Rome went to war with Carthage in 218, the ambassador who was sent to deliver the initial demand for redress after the Carthaginian general Hannibal had sacked a city that was allied to Rome was empowered to deliver the declaration of war when satisfaction was not received. In 200 it appears that the consul had decided that Rome had already made its demands to Philip perfectly clear, that he had no interest in listening to them, and that all that remained to be done was to deliver the actual *indictio* (Livy *History of Rome* 36.3.10).[22] This was one change in procedure; the other arose from the difficulty of actually finding Philip (who was in the eastern Mediterranean) so that he could receive the declaration in person. It was obviously impractical for the Romans to sail around with a large army waiting to find Philip before they could do anything, but there was still the nasty question of what the gods would think if they did not. The consultation of the *fetiales* could absolve the consul of personal responsibility for *vitium* if he was defeated (and they could argue that their decision was based on changes in the *ius fetiale* that had not proved fatal in the past). The debate about the way to declare war was repeated on the orders of the senate in 193 B.C., when the consul was told to ask the *fetiales* three questions about the declaration of war with king Antiochus III and the Aetolians in Greece. With

21. See Watson 1993, 19 on the role of the god as a judge in the dispute.
22. For the history of the rites in general see Wisowa 1912, 475–79.

the passing of time we hear of further debates about the proper procedure, and we can see here how the *fetiales* continued to emend the formula to suit changed circumstances, but it remained a feature of Roman war into the later second century B.C., when Polybius comments on its observance (Pol. *History* 13.3.7).[23] A form of the rite was used when Augustus declared war on Cleopatra in 32 B.C., and it was employed even when the emperor Marcus Aurelius set out on his final campaign in the Balkans during A.D. 178 (Dio *History of Rome* 50.4.5, 71.33.3).

A similar question of ritual propriety was raised shortly after the consul's consultation of the *fetiales,* when the same consul vowed games and an unspecified monetary gift to Jupiter once victory was won. At this point the *pontifex maximus* intervened, saying that a vow could not be offered from an unspecified amount of money because it was impossible to use the money that was vowed in the war: it had to be put aside immediately and could not be mixed in with other money (Livy *History of Rome* 31.9.7). Since the *pontifex maximus* was merely delivering an opinion (albeit one that was supported by precedent) rather than handing down a binding decision concerning the vow (which he did not have the power to do), the consul asked the collegium as a whole to rule on this matter. The pontifices returned a *decretum* (opinion) to the effect that the consul's vow was permissible. The collegium did not initiate action; it acted in response to an inquiry put to it by a responsible official or body. Its responses were binding on points of religion if the facts were as presented to it, the standard phrasing of a pontifical decree being "if facts of the case as presented to us are true then . . ." As this phrasing suggests that pontifices were supposed to reach their decision by majority vote through rational consideration of precedent, dissenting opinions did not matter. Thus in a case mentioned earlier, the opinion of a *pontifex maximus* about the celebration of family rites on days after the calends, nones, and ides, although logical, never seems to have become an accepted feature of state ritual, because his colleagues are not on record as having agreed with him.

After the pontifices had decided that the consul could vow the games, it was up to the *pontifex maximus* to instruct the consul on the wording of the vow. Since the pontifices were not themselves directly

---

23. See also the accounts of debates in the senate in 187 (Livy *History of Rome* 38.46.12) and 171 (Livy *History of Rome* 42.47.5).

involved in the campaign, they could not undertake the vow themselves. This had to be done by the person who was. The job of the pontifex was to ensure that he got the wording of the prayer correct so that the gods would be favorably inclined to the undertaking. In all cases it is significant that the collegial decisions ratified changes in ancient procedure.

Prophecy

Priests were responsible for the passive operation of cult; prophets were the agents of "active cult." While the various groups charged with oversight of the religious traditions of the state could initiate changes, they could only do so on the basis of the interpretation of precedent; they could not and did not seek knowledge directly from the gods. The integration of fresh divine revelation into the existing system was in the hands of others. It was the responsibility of Rome's prophetic overseers to interpret the messages that the gods were sending, and like the pontifices, they were supposed to do this on the basis of experience.

The aristocracy that dominated Roman politics was loath to admit that any of its members could be in personal communication with a god. The Roman people, on the other hand, seem to have been deeply fascinated by this possibility. Thus there was a constant tension between the claims of individuals and the claims of the state. In the eyes of the senate, and later in the eyes of the emperors, only those prophets and prophecies that had been duly investigated and determined to be reliable by experts could be admitted into public life. No emperor was any more interested in finding that one of his subjects was in direct communication with a higher plane than the Republican senate had been in finding that one of its members was closer to the gods than others. The system of dealing with divine revelation was therefore set up to control access to the divine. It was not and could not be completely successful: the subject was just too interesting.

In the early Republic two collegia oversaw divine communication, the augurs and the *quindecimviri sacris faciundis.* The augers were concerned with revelations that could be obtained through the observation of natural phenomena. The *quindecimviri* were concerned with *prodigia* and divine advice as to how to respond to them. Since they sought this information through consultation of the *libri sibyllini,* which were written in Greek, they were, by extension, concerned with "foreign rites." In the middle Republic a third form of divination began to become popular at Rome, *haruspicium,* an Etruscan form of divination based on the detailed examination of the internal organs of sacrificial animals and other natural phenomena.

The *quindecimviri* acted when the senate received a report of a prodigy that it thought was genuine, and they were charged with the authentication of new oracles (the Romans were aware that there might be more Sibylline oracles than were in their collection). In the first century B.C., when the *quindecimviri* were charged with assembling a new collection to replace the one that had been lost in a fire, an important test of legitimacy was the presence of acrostics in the texts, but there may have been others: it is hard to believe that the board would admit a prophecy that Rome would be destroyed just because it contained an acrostic. In general terms the Roman collection seems to have been primarily concerned with oracles that concerned prodigies (although there are some exceptions), and it may well be that this was what the *quindecimviri* were also looking for. It is notable that the final decision did not rest with them, for when the board had assembled its collection it reported its findings to the senate (Dionysius of Halicarnassus *Roman Antiquities* 4.62; Tacitus *Annals* 6.12.3; Cicero *On Divination* 2.111–12).

About fifty years after the *quindecimviri* had assembled their collection, another investigation of oracular texts was carried out by Augustus. Great as the authority of Augustus may have been in this matter, his purification of Roman prophetic books did not put an end to the process of selection. Tacitus reports that the tribune Quintilianus complained in the senate when the *quindecimvir* Caninius Gallus had wrongfully caused a book to be included among the Sibylline oracles in A.D. 32 and that the senate wrote to the emperor Tiberius asking his advice as to the way it should handle the situation. Tiberius responded, "moderately criticizing the tribune on the grounds that he was ignorant of ancient custom because of his youth," and he "rebuked Gallus because he, a man experienced in religious lore and ceremonies, had brought the matter before a badly attended meeting of the senate, on dubious authority, without the approval of the collegium and not, as was customary, after the oracle had been read and evaluated by the magistrates" (Tacitus *Annals* 6.12.1–2).

It is likely that a fair amount of time was spent discussing precisely these issues, for it was as essential to the emperor as it had been for the Republican senate to control the record of "authentic" divinely inspired prophecy. This is why Augustus had burned in the Forum two thousand prophetic books that were deemed "false," and it is why he had moved the books from the Capitoline to the temple of Apollo on the Palatine (Suetonius *Life of Augustus* 31). The temple was located next to his house, and Apollo was credited with special interest in the welfare of Augustus himself (Liebeschuetz 1979, 83).

There was reason for the state to try to control the material that offered its subjects alternative paradigms to its own view of history and inspired public distress. The state could do no more than take occasional exemplary action in this regard and could exert no real control over the books that were in circulation; it could merely seek to question their authority. Given that there was a clear distinction in Roman thought between the official cults of the state, on the one hand, and private religion, on the other, it is perhaps not curious that the state only took action against these books—as it only took action against forms of private worship—when they seemed to threaten the political order. Individuals were left to make their own arrangements so long as they did not clash with those of the community as a whole. In the realm of prophetic books, there was ordinarily no reason for the senate to bother to act.

The augurs, the second group connected with oversight of the state's relations with the gods, were not directly concerned with the future. Rather, they were concerned with establishing the view of the gods about the propriety of actions as they were being taken. Although the augural art itself was plainly not a purely Latin phenomenon, it came to be regarded as the characteristically Roman form of interpreting communications from the gods, more specifically communications from the god Jupiter.[24] The art consisted primarily of interpreting the actions of birds who were thought to be Jupiter's messengers and the ability to determine when a natural phenomenon such as a clap of thunder affected the outcome of a ceremony. Errors in the interpretation of divine signs, *vitia,* were offensive to the gods and could lead to disaster if they were not corrected. The distinction between the work of the augurs and other specialists in prognostication is between what may be termed inductive and subjective prediction. The primary characteristic of inductive divination was that it did not depend on direct divine inspiration but was founded upon facts known from observation

24. Linderski 1986 is fundamental for what follows here.

(Cicero *On Divination.* 1.34, 127). Subjective divination depended upon divine impulse, actual contact between a god or his or her messenger and mortals (Cicero *On Divination.* 1.18.34).

The art of taking the auspices, *auspicium,* was not solely the province of the augurs. All Roman magistrates were expected to take the auspices whenever they undertook any public business. Since they would not necessarily be augurs, it was expected that they would be able to interpret basic signs. These signs were of two sorts, "requested" *(imperativa)* and "offered" *(oblativa).* Requested signs were granted as a result of actions made by the person taking the auspices; "offered" signs were portentous events that took place while the magistrate was taking the auspices or engaged in public business. The observation of the eating habits of the sacred chickens was an effort to obtain a "requested" sign; a sudden clap of thunder, hailstorm, or other natural phenomenon could be an "offered" sign. It was up to the magistrate to decide if something that could be interpreted as an "offered" sign was in fact significant. The only time that a magistrate had no choice in the matter was when an augur was present to instruct him. A sign of either sort was good only for one day.

Aside from their participation at sacrifices, augurs oversaw the conferral on magistrates of the ability to take the auspices, the designation of sacred areas, and the interpretation of signs that were brought to their attention. In cases of the inauguration of a magistrate or a sacred area, a single augur could be empowered to administer the ceremony. In cases where questions about the auspices were raised, the collegium as a whole had to speak. It was then up to the senate to decide what to do.

The augurs had books containing records of past results, appropriate prayers, and the tricks of their trade, to help them decide the answers to questions. These books were regarded not as books of prophecy but rather as instructional manuals. Similarly books by individual augurs on their trade were no more than technical treatises: they might interest other augurs and even other members of the Roman aristocracy, but they could not be used as guides to the future. As a result, while augural divination could serve to defuse potentially explosive political events either by bringing them to an end (if an augur perceived a problem at any point in an election, for example, he could stop it) or by diffusing the blame for a disaster by revealing problems in the state's relations with the gods, it was not an effective device for mediating change. By the beginning of the second century B.C., the augurs had serious competition in interpreting divine will.

Haruspicium offered the prediction of the future and description of the present state of human and divine relations. We do not know when the haruspices began to be recognized as accurate diviners who were worthy of Rome's attention, but it is clear that even the senate thought that their advice should be sought by the time of the Hannibalic War (Livy *History of Rome* 23.36.10, 25.16.3). The loss of ten books of Livy's history covering the later fourth and the bulk of the third century makes it impossible to know when consultation of the haruspices actually became common at Rome, but it is possible that the practice only became important at Rome after the final conquest of Etruria in the early third century B.C.

The haruspices could be consulted about the innards of sacrificial animals *(exta),* lightning *(fulgura),* and prodigies (fig. 9). Their prognostic ability depended on books that seem to have recorded what had happened in cases involving similar signs. Before consulting the books, it was necessary to make as careful an observation as possible of the phenomena that were to provide the clues to the future. In the case of a prediction on the basis of *exta,* a haruspex had to be present at the slaughter of the animal.[25] When the animal was killed, he took the liver in his left hand, stood with his right foot on the ground and his left foot on a stone, and "read" the liver clockwise. In dealing with lightning, the haruspex would try to determine which part of the heavens the lightning had come from. For predictive purposes the haruspices had divided the sky into sixteen regions, and the significance of a lightning bolt depended on which sixteenth of the heavens it appeared in and on what, if anything, it hit. The interpretation of portents appears to have been based primarily on the ability to assess an event in light of precedent. Thus in our last sighting of the haruspices on campaign (with Julian in A.D. 363) they appear with their books of "portents in time of war" after the emperor has been brought a dead lion and tell him that the sign prohibits an invasion (Ammianus Marcellinus *History of Rome* 23.5.10). Julian, advised by philosophers who seem to have convinced him that they could alter the prescriptions of fate, ignored the warning. He died in battle while trying to withdraw from Persia a few weeks later.

Haruspical responses could be quite long and complex, as is evident

25. Van der Meer 1987, 157–64.

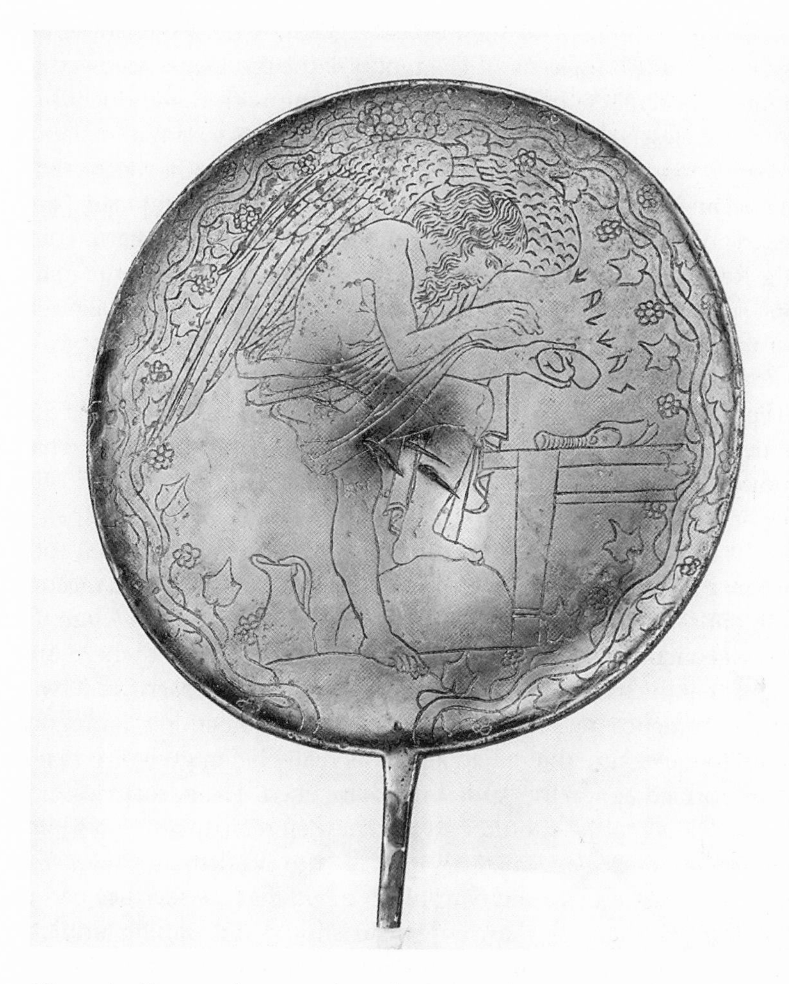

Fig. 9. An Etruscan bronze mirror depicting a haruspex reading a liver. The haruspex is holding the liver in his left hand, and his left foot is on a stone. (MEG 12240; courtesy of the Monumenti musei e gallerie pontificie.)

from those that can be reconstructed on the basis of a speech in which Cicero suggests that they referred to the actions of his political enemies (rather than to himself as they had proposed). The speech opens with a description of the prodigy and continues with a number of general suggestions about what this prodigy signifies about the state of Roman affairs. The opening words are "Whereas in the Ager Latiniensis a loud noise and a clashing has been heard, expiations are due to Jupiter, Sat-urn, Neptune, Tellus, and the heavenly gods" (Cicero *Concerning the Responses of the Haruspices* 20). The report of the prodigy is followed by a number of remarks on just what was wrong with Rome (including "games carelessly celebrated and profaned," "envoys slain in violation of earthly and heavenly law," "good faith and oaths neglected," "ancient and secret sacrifices carelessly performed and profaned," and "dissensions among the *optimates*") and by warnings "lest harm come to the Republic by occult designs" and "lest further honor accrue to the worst sort and the rejected." At the very end is a warning to take care "lest the constitution of the Republic be changed" (Cicero *Concerning the Responses of the Haruspices* 34, 36, 37, 53, 55, 56, 60).

The construction of new responses for each new event sets the discipline of the haruspices apart from that of the *quindecimviri,* who had to be content with the oracles that they found. The difference in the information that could be obtained from an augur and a haruspex is brought out very well by Livy's account of a consultation that took place in 213 B.C. involving the consul Tiberius Sempronius Gracchus (the grandfather of the consul in 163 B.C.). Livy reports that when the sacrificial victim was killed, two snakes came out of nowhere and began to eat the liver. The haruspices advised another sacrifice (it was standard practice to repeat a sacrifice once something had gone wrong, to make sure that a bad sign was really being given). When it was performed again, the same thing happened. The haruspices then told Gracchus that he should beware "hidden men and veiled plots" (Livy *History of Rome* 25.16.2–4). He failed to heed their advice and was killed. An augur would simply have said that the sacrifice had to be performed again or that the consul should do nothing until he could get a sacrifice to come out correctly, since it was clear that the gods were displeased about something. This is the same sort of difference that we have already seen in the two responses to the death of the *rogator* at the consular election of 163 B.C. As an augur, Gracchus insisted that only augural precedent was relevant and that, as he thought that he had properly observed the signs, the death of the *rogator* could have no meaning. To the haruspices, the death was obviously a *prodigium* that indicated that something was wrong. This could be taken, as Cicero takes it in his account of the incident, as a sign that both forms of divination were correct. But elsewhere Cicero, who had much to say in favor of augury after he became an augur, is scathing about *haruspicium*. Like a number of Romans of his class, he sneered at haruspices as foreigners, and there may be more to his objections than their provenance.

The haruspices had no official standing in the Roman state until the emperor Claudius created a specific *ordo* of sixty-one haruspices in A.D. 47. They spoke either when the senate decided that it needed to consult them (which would mean that neither the *quindecimviri* nor the augers could provide the needed information on some point) or when an individual asked them. Indeed, the rise of haruspices as personal advisers to Roman aristocrats appears to parallel the decline of aristocratic government at Rome in the late Republic. Great individuals like Sulla and Caesar had personal haruspices.[26] Julius Caesar also seems to have taken a particularly dim view of Etruscan senators who claimed expertise in *haruspicium* and who served the cause of his political enemies.[27] Cicero, when expressing his true thoughts on the subject, seems to have disliked the haruspices for very similar reasons: their wisdom was all too often at the ready disposal of his adversaries (Linderski 1982). All of this mattered because people felt that the gods could intervene in human affairs whenever they felt like it and because these communications were more detailed and less susceptible to collegiate interpretation by members of the Roman aristocracy. It is also interesting that haruspices were only integrated into the state system of divine interpretation under Claudius, a man personally fascinated with Etruscan antiquity. His excuse for doing so was to preserve a discipline that was being lost. This may not be surprising: with the emergence of the monarchy, prognostication that bore on political events was dangerous if it was not banal, and the members of the class from which the important haruspices of the Republic emerged, the upper class of the cities of Etruria, could find other, safer things to do until their learning could be used by the emperor.

---

26. See Torelli 1975, 122–24 for a useful list of haruspices. The opposition between *haruspicium* and augury does not seem to have been felt as strongly in Etruria; note fragment 2 of the *fasti LX Haruspicum* (Torelli 1975, 108): *[fu]lmine pr[ocuravit ostenta suo] | [c]armine et augurales d[iviniationes] | complures fecit.*

27. Rawson 1978, 132–52; see also Wiseman 1992, suggesting a rather more extensive record of personal prophecy in the fourth and third centuries (as well as the regal period) that was consciously suppressed by procedures adopted by the senate in the second century.

Time and Space

One crucial feature of the divine connection with the Roman people was the definition of time and space. It is symptomatic of the diffusion of responsibility throughout the administration of the religious system of the Roman state that no one group had authority in these matters. The augurs, as we have seen, were responsible for the definition of space that was under the protection of the gods: their observations enabled the establishment of a *pomerium* (the sacred boundary within which the Roman people were under the protection of their gods) and of the areas where the gods were worshiped. The pontifices were responsible for determining where bodies could be buried (in ground that was by definition outside of the *pomerium*), how people should act on certain days, and calendar issues. As we have seen, there could be considerable disagreement among members of the collegium on matters of conduct, and its management of the calendar was extraordinarily inept.

The traditional Roman year, which may have been instituted c. 450 B.C., had twelve months and was, in theory, lunar. It had four months of thirty-one days (March, May, July, and October), seven months of twenty-nine days (January, April, June, August, September, November, and December), and one month of twenty-eight days (February). In order to bring the calendar into line with the phases of the moon, an extra, or "intercalary," month of twenty-two or twenty-three days and the remaining five days of February were theoretically inserted every third year, after the feast of the Terminalia on 23 February. Intercalations were not always made as they were supposed to be, and the system was in perpetual chaos until Caesar threw the whole calendar out with his institution of the solar year of 365¼ days in 45 B.C.

The Romans absorbed from the Etruscans the notion that time was divided into *saecula,* which should be marked with significant festivals. According to a tradition reported by Varro, *ludi saeculares* (commemorating the beginning of a *saeculum*) were instituted after *prodigia* were reported and the wall between the Colline and Esquiline gates was struck by lightning. When the *quindecimviri* were consulted they found a Sibylline oracle that prescribed sacrifices to Pluto and Proserpina every one hundred years. According to another tradition, the *ludi* were first celebrated in 509, after the expulsion of the kings, and again in 449, 249, and 149 (though contemporaries reported that they were really celebrated in 146). A tradition that almost certainly does not predate Augustus' celebration of the games in 17 B.C. by very long was said to have been contained in the books of the *quindecimviri* and to have placed games in 457, 347, 237, 127, and 17. An Etruscan tradition asserted that the first four *saecula* were 105 years long, the fifth 123 years, and the sixth and seventh 119 years and that the Etruscan name would perish after ten *saecula* had been completed. I will return to another aspect of the role of religion in defining temporal relationships when I discuss the internal organization of the year through the festival cycle.

Sacrifice

Roman sacrificial ritual developed with the passing of time. The point and type of a sacrifice could vary according to the god to whom it was offered and the reason for the offering, though, for the most part, there appear to be four main reasons for offering one: to implore a god's assistance, to thank a god for assistance, to propitiate an angry god, and to commemorate some earlier divine action. Sacrifices of the first three varieties could or might have to be offered at any time; sacrifices of the fourth variety took place at established annual festivals.

When they offered sacrifice, humans asked the divinity to join them at a meal. The divinity would take part of the sacrificial object, and the humans would get the rest. The sort of thing that was offered varied with the importance of the person making the offering and the occasion of the sacrifice. In addition to making the offering, a person might also want to dedicate something to the god in thanks for the god's help. Thus someone who had survived a disease might offer a sacrifice to the divinity that he or she thought was responsible and then dedicate a model of the affected body part in the temple. After victory in war, the Roman state would offer sacrifices to thank the gods for assuring the victory and would dedicate some of the spoils taken from the enemy in the temple of the god or god's concerned (the result was that the temples of the gods often had substantial sums of money to lend to the state in times of emergency).

The actual form of sacrificial ritual is a very useful guide to the way that the Romans thought about their relationship with divinities. There are some variations here, depending on the age of the ritual, and thus the change in sacrificial ritual is also something of a guide to the evolution of Roman cult. I will begin, therefore, with a discussion of sacrificial ritual that was typical in the high Republic and empire and then move on to look briefly at some other sorts of sacrifice. This will lead into the next section of this chapter, that on Roman festivals, where I will be arguing that the festival calendar provides a model through which Romans could understand the evolution of their society and of their society's relations with the gods.

Dionysius provides an account of some of the standard features of a Roman sacrifice as part of his argument that the early Romans were really Greek (an argument designed to make Greeks feel better about being ruled by Rome).

> . . . the manner of performing the sacrifice was the same as with us. For after washing their hands, they purified the victim with clear water and the fruits of Demeter *[mola salsa]* on their heads, after which they prayed and gave orders to their assistants to sacrifice them. Some of the assistants, while the victim was still standing, struck it on the temple with a mallet, and others received it with knives as it fell. After this they flayed it and cut it up, taking off a piece from each of the inwards and also from every limb as a first offering, which they sprinkled with grits of spelt and carried in offering baskets to the officiating priests. These placed them on altars and, making a fire under them, poured wine over them while they were burning. (*Roman Antiquities* 7.72.15)

The illustration of a sacrifice scene from the Arch of Trajan at Beneventum illustrates the social ideology connected with the act of sacrifice (fig. 10).[28] On the relief from the arch, the emperor is standing on the right and pouring an offering of wine from a small dish onto a fire that is burning on what was, when the relief was complete, a small altar. Two young boys, *camilli,* stand to his left, one of them carrying a small box, an *acerra,* from which the emperor will take some incense to burn once he is through pouring the wine. The togaed people who stand behind the emperor, directing their gaze (and thus the viewer's

28. For the procedure here see Wissowa 1912, 351–53; this analysis of the iconographical message of the Beneventum relief depends on Gordon 1990, 203–6.

Fig. 10. Sacrifice scene from the Arch of Trajan at Beneventum. The division of action, with the members of the procession concentrating on the emperor who is in charge of the sacrifice rather than on the actual slaughter of the animal, is illustrative of the ideology connected with animal sacrifice. (Alinari/Art resource AL 116715.)

gaze) toward him, are other priests. Their posture reminds viewers that the most important character here is the person in charge of the sacrifice and that his actions will determine whether or not the gods will be satisfied. The process at this point is described by the elder Pliny.

> It does not accomplish anything to sacrifice victims without a prayer, and it is not the right way to consult the gods. Furthermore, there is one form of words for asking an omen, another for averting one, and another for commendation. We see that our highest magistrates address the gods with fixed prayers; that to prevent a word being left out or spoken in the wrong place, one

> person reads it out first from a script; that another is posted as a guard to keep watch; that a third is given the responsibility to see that silence is maintained; and that a piper plays so that nothing but the prayer is heard. (*Natural History* 28.3.10)

The focus of the action remains the magistrate, who, for all the help he receives, is responsible for mediating the contact with the god, and without him the whole event would be pointless. The ritual formality of the prayer is connected with the concept of *vitium,* for it was often through error in the recitation of a prayer that disaster struck; and it is notable that the process appears to assume a wide variety of possible reasons for a mistake being made, not all of them caused by the person offering the prayer. Talking to the gods was clearly a very difficult business.

Returning to the sacrifice, the emperor on the Beneventum relief is looking off to the left where some public slaves (generically known as the *victimarii,* "victim handlers") are preparing for the next stage of the ceremony, the killing of the sacrificial animal. One of these slaves holds the head of the animal down, while another, the *popa,* prepares to stun the beast with the blow of a mallet. When this is done the animal's throat will be slit by a third attendant, the *cultrarius.* Here, as in Dionysius' account, it is plain that the person in charge of the sacrifice, like a proper Roman aristocrat, should not be seen as participating in the dirty work of killing and butchering the animal. This sort of manual labor had to be performed by social inferiors, inferiors whose comparative nudity separates them from their superiors. After the animal had died, it was cut open and its innards (the *exta*) were inspected to make sure that everything was in the right place. If there was a problem, the animal was thought to have been rejected by the gods and another would be killed. If there was another problem, the sacrifice would be postponed. If everything appeared to be in good order, the liver would be handed to the haruspex. He would not actually stick his hands in the animal but would wait until a servant handed him the object of his science. If the haruspex found no unfavorable sign, the *exta* would be placed on the altar to be burned as a meal for the god. If the haruspex found something wrong, the sacrifice would be repeated, and if a second problem was discovered, the sacrifice was postponed. As the passage from Pliny just quoted suggests, a new prayer might also be necessary to avert the evil omen.

This prognostic element of a sacrifice was a relatively late development at Rome, for, as we have seen, the haruspices do not seem to have been significant actors on the Roman religious scene until the third century B.C. Initially, observation that everything was in the right place seems to have been sufficient for the sacrifice to proceed.[29] After the *exta* were inspected, they were placed on the altar and the sacrificant said a prayer to the god. Here again, if there was any problem, a second sacrifice would have to be performed: the elder Gracchus' failure to heed the signs at his second sacrifice in the incident described earlier ensured that he would die—but his failure may have been because he felt that since the *exta* had been found in the correct place, the additional warning of the haruspices was irrelevant (an attitude that his grandson shared). Once the successful sacrifice had been made, the sacrificant would sit down to a meal with his associates at which the remains of the successfully sacrificed animal formed the main course.

The selection of appropriate sacrificial animals was important, and some ceremonies called specifically for cattle, others for sheep, and others for pigs. It was also necessary that the animals chosen be of only one color, white for sacrifice to the gods of the upper world and black for sacrifice to those of the underworld. There was also some ranking of animals according to the divinity to whom the offering was to be made—an offering of cattle to Jupiter should, for instance, consist of oxen, while bulls should be offered to Mars and a calf to Vulcan (Wissowa 1912, 347–9)—and it was a general rule that female animals should be offered to female divinities, male animals to male divinities.

So far I have only discussed public sacrifice. A private individual who wanted to make an offering to the gods would simply show up at the temple, find the priest, pay a fee, receive instruction as to the proper form of sacrifice to offer and the proper form of prayer to offer, and then allow the *victimarii* who were assigned to the temple slaughter the animal. If he wanted a haruspex to inspect the liver, however, it seems that he himself would have to hire one for the occasion. The necessity of paying a fee to the priest and supplying an animal to be slaughtered may have prevented the mass of poor Romans from making an offering at a temple. There was also cult offered to household gods (the Lares and Penates), the household genius, a household Vesta, and the spirits of the dead (Manes), which would be overseen by the head of each fam-

29. Schilling 1962, 1371–78.

ily (paterfamilias) (Wissowa 1912, 141–59). Household sacrifice required a small shrine in the household and a much less elaborate offering. The simplest summary of their worship is in fact provided by an edict of the Christian emperor Theodosius banning these practices in 392 A.D. with the words "A person shall not by more secret wickedness venerate his Lar with fire, his genius with wine, his Penates with fragrant odors; he shall not burn lights to them, place incense before them, or suspend wreaths for them" (*Theodosian Code* 16.10.12). The average Roman would be much more likely to engage in regular cult in the home (the "secret wickedness" that Theodosius refers to here) to preserve the well-being of the household than to take part in public acts of worship at the temples. Furthermore, in an aristocratic household it would be commonplace for slaves, freed people, and clients to offer cult to the genius and Lares of the paterfamilias.[30] In doing so they defined their position as subordinates within the establishment.

The ideology of a public sacrifice is made clear by the relief from Beneventum described earlier. The ruling class at Rome was acting on behalf of the Roman people to ensure the goodwill of the gods toward the state as a whole. The priests and pontifices, themselves members of the upper classes, had the specific knowledge that was needed to make this work, both for the state and for private individuals. In this respect the essential, "passive" act of worship served to illustrate and maintain the social order.

This account of sacrifice describes the great majority of public sacrifices in the Roman empire, but not all of them. The rites of the luperci described earlier worked quite differently, and we know that a large number of other sacrificial rites connected with extremely ancient festivals depended on the physical intervention of the priests. In these cases we also find a very wide range of offerings that appear to be connected with the specific purpose of the festival. Thus we learn that on the Fordicidia (15 April) pregnant cows were originally sacrificed to the male divinity Tellus (at some point the dissonance with normal practice was found to be too disturbing and the offering was made to Terra Mater, or Mother Earth, instead) and the unborn calves were torn from their mothers wombs by the vestal virgins. The vestals oversaw the incineration of the calves and collected the ashes for use at the Parilia on 21 April, where they were mixed with bean stalks and the blood of a horse

30. Orr 1986.

that was sacrificed in October. At the Parilia this mixture was thrown onto a fire and a worshiper leapt through the fire. While we cannot be certain as to who did the leaping on behalf of the state (it may well have been the *flamen Palatualis,* since the festival was primarily connected with this divinity), the act was plainly important (Wissowa 1912, 165–6). While the purification of the community as a whole took place in the city and was thought to mark the anniversary of the city's foundation, the day was also used for the ritual purification of sheepfolds by private individuals who prayed to Pales that he/she (there was some question here and Pales was sometimes referred to as if two gods) protect and increase the flock in the year to come, a process that also culminated with people leaping over a fire (Scullard 1981, 104–5). Rites of this sort reinforced the sense of participation in a community that had endured through the favor of the gods for an extremely long time.

Festivals

As I have already indicated, the festival cycle at Rome was extremely complicated, describing the shape of the year in a way that also offered a description of the history of Rome through the wide variety of festivals that were celebrated within it. As a matter of convenience, these festivals may be divided into three types, representing three different stages of the development of the Roman state. The earliest variety appear to have been family festivals that were initially connected with the well-being of the household but became state festivals connected with the general well-being of the community as a whole and involving broad participation throughout the community, as individual families performed rites to secure their future even as the representatives of the state engaged in rites that propitiated the gods for the state. I have already discussed several of these events, the Lupercalia (15 February), the Fordicidia (15 April), and the Parilia (21 April). Festivals of the second variety were instituted by the state for the general safety of Rome. Their foundation dates fall after the end of the regal period (509 B.C.), and they appear to have become more lavish as Rome became a major power in Italy. They also tended to honor "foreign" cults or to adopt features of "Greek ritual," chiefly a banquet at which the statues of the relevant gods appeared on couches to dine with the celebrants and a series of public entertainments. The third variety were festivals instituted to commemorate the acts of the emperors.

The earliest festival of the second type was held in honor of Jupiter Optimus Maximus (Best and Greatest) on 13 September. It appears to have begun as a votive festival in the late sixth century and to have become an annual celebration no later than 366 B.C., by which time it had come to include the Roman games *(ludi Romani)* that gradually expanded to fill the period from 5 to 19 September (Scullard 1981, 183–6). It is in connection with this festival that we get one of our best descriptions of a sacrificial procession that joins elements of ancient Roman cult with aspects of Greek worship. The source is once again Dionysius of Halicarnassus, and he describes these proceedings to show his Greek audience that the Romans are indeed a civilized people, because they knew how to celebrate the gods like the Greeks. The difference between this sort of cult activity and that connected with a festival like the Lupercalia or the Parilia, with their apotropaic performances, is immediately apparent (I omit Dionysius' comparisons with Greek practice throughout).

> Before beginning the games the principal magistrates conducted a procession in honor of the gods from the Capitol through the Forum to the Circus Maximus. Those who lead the procession were, first, boys who were nearing manhood and of an age to participate in the ceremony, the sons of *equites* riding horses, on foot if they would fight in the infantry, the former in cavalry formations, the later in infantry formations as if they were going to school, so that the number and beauty of those who were approaching manhood would be plain to foreigners. These were followed by charioteers—some of whom rode four-horse chariots, some two-horse chariots—and others riding unyoked horses After them came contestants in both light and heavy games, their whole bodies naked except their loins . . . the contestants were followed by numerous bands of dancers arranged in three divisions, the first consisting of men, the second of youths, and the third of boys. These were accompanied by flute players . . . and lyre players. . . . The dancers were dressed in scarlet tunics girded with bronze cinctures, wore swords suspended at their sides, and carried spears of shorter than average length; the men also had bronze helmets adorned with conspicuous crests and plumes. Each group was lead by one man who gave the figures of the dance to the rest, taking the lead in representing their rapid and

> warlike movements . . . after the armed dancers others marched in the procession impersonating satyrs and portraying the Greek dance called *sicinnis* . . . after these bands of dancers came a throng of lyre players and flautists, and after them people who carried censers in which perfumes were burned along the whole route of the procession, and also the men who bore the display vessels made of silver and gold, both those that were sacred to the gods and those that belonged to the state. Last of all in the procession came the images of the gods, borne on men's shoulders. (*Roman Antiquities* 7.72.1–13)

The performers here represent those who appeared in the *ludi Romani*. The significance of the games is that they provided a way for the Roman people to join in the celebration of the gods, whose approval for this form of celebration is signified by the participation of their statues in the procession. The fact that participation was entertaining is an important characteristic of Roman cult. The games were paid for by members of the senate, and they once again reminded the average Roman that their happiness and the well-being of Rome were ensured by the actions of their political and social superiors. It is symbolic of the union between the political and religious order that the expenses of the games were met by magistrates (the aediles) while the organization of the banquet of Jupiter was the province of priests.

Another such festival was the Megalasia (4 April), instituted to honor the Magna Mater (Great Mother), whose cult was introduced at Rome during 204 B.C. as the result of a consultation of the Sibylline oracles in the previous year. Livy says that in this year a sudden outbreak of religious emotion swept Rome when the occurrence of frequent hailstorms caused the Sibylline Books to be inspected. A prophecy was discovered to the effect that whenever a foreign enemy invaded Italy, it would be possible to defeat him and drive him off if the "Idaean mother" was brought from Pessinus in Asia Minor to Italy. Livy goes on to suggest that this was taken particularly seriously because envoys who had been sent to Delphi after the battle of the Metaurus had returned with an oracle of Apollo that promised an even greater victory than they had already won over the Carthaginians. An embassy was duly sent off to Rome's ally, Attalus of Pergamon, who controlled Pessinus, to ask for the image of the divinity. On the way they stopped off at Delphi and received a response in which the god told them that they would obtain their desire and that when they brought the divinity (in the form of her cult image) to Rome, they should make sure she stayed as a guest of the best man in the city (while a suitable temple was built to house her). Despite the obvious political overtones of these negotiations, it is significant that, from the Roman point of view, the initiative for the establishment of the festival came directly from the gods speaking through oracles (an "active" religious experience insofar as it is the gods who are giving new information about the way that they should be worshiped). The day selected for the celebration of the cult, 4 April, thus commemorates the arrival of the new divinity and the whole course of events leading up to her arrival.

The actual worship of Cybele, as far as the Roman state was concerned, was to be thoroughly Roman. It consisted of (1) the praetors' offering of a vegetable relish (known as a *moretum*) on the grounds that in earliest times mortals had lived on milk and vegetables and (2) the institution of a custom by which members of various sodalities invited each other to dinner at each other's houses (the changing locations commemorating the goddess' move from Asia Minor to Rome) (Wissowa 1912, 264). This was not, however, the way that the cult was celebrated in Asia Minor, for there the goddess had professional priests (often individuals who had engaged in autocastration) who led extraordinarily lively processions. At some point in the Republic the senate forbade Roman citizens to participate in such activities, but the cult became too popular, and in the empire we find many eminent Romans holding priesthoods of the goddess (castration having gradually been forgotten as a requirement). These priests do not ever seem to have had official standing in that they were not the ones responsible for the state worship, but rather they were involved in private celebration of the rites, rites that continued to develop throughout the imperial period (Wissowa 1912, 266–67). Indeed, in the fourth century, with Christianity becoming the dominant religion at Rome, some of our best evidence for the non-Christian religious sympathies of Roman aristocrats, who seem to have worshiped the goddess as a symbol of their devotion to the ancient traditions of the state, comes precisely from the shrine of the Magna Mater on the Vatican (Matthews 1973). The distinction between the state cult and other worship of the Magna Mater is characteristic of Roman religion, for state cult was concerned with the relationship between the community and the divinities; an individual's relationship was up to that individual (so long as this did not involve practices that the state deemed dangerous or disgusting). An aristocratic devotee of the Magna Mater who might be tempted to dash through the streets of Rome beating a tambourine in a procession for other worshipers of Cybele would, if elected praetor and charged with the celebration of the rites on 4 April, show up in a toga and deposit the *moretum* (he would have to leave his tambourine at home).

The third sort of festival, the commemorative festival, married events ordinarily connected with celebrations of an individual's life or deeds (e.g., a triumph or a funeral) with those connected to the *sacra*. It is a process that first becomes significant with Julius Caesar, in honor of whose victories the senate voted that annual games should be held—on the Parilia to commemorate the victory at Munda in 45 B.C. and for the ten days between 20 and 30 July to commemorate the victory at Pharsalus in 48 B.C. Neither of these events replaced earlier festivals that fell during their course (there were several in the last ten days of July), and it seems that neither one lasted for very long. Indeed, it was typical for festivals that commemorated the deeds of one monarch or dynasty to be forgotten under a successor or succeeding dynasty. By the fourth century A.D., while the calendar of Rome was filled with festivals commemorating the victories of the emperors of the late third and early fourth centuries, those connected with earlier monarchs appear to have been forgotten.[31]

Commemorative festivals were the essential feature of the imperial cult. Award of the trappings of divine cult and commemorative festivals to living human beings had a long history in the Greek east, where it derived from the inflation of honors offered to individuals for service to the community.[32] In those cases, as in the case of the imperial cult, whether or not the recipient was actually a god was occasionally questioned after the recipient had passed from the mortal plane: as we have seen, people were aware of the possibility that new gods could appear at any time and that one did not need to be an emperor to be one. But these cults are not, strictly speaking, a feature of Roman religion, for

31. Salzman 1990.

32. Habicht 1970. See also Gauthier 1985. The connection with civic honors has received strong support in a Clarian inscription published in Robert and Robert 1989, in which see Menippos col. 1, ll. 22–23, with pp. 77–85. For the spread of the imperial cult in the west see Fishwick 1987; for the cult in the east see Price 1984. Rives 1995 offers much of general importance in the context of a discussion of North African manifestations.

they defined the relationship between the people of the empire and their ruler rather than that between humans and divinities. Thus it was possible for a loyal subject of the empire to observe, "In my time, when evil has grown to such a height and has come over every land and every city, no god arises from man, except in the speech and flattery addressed to the powerful" (Pausanias *Description of Greece* 8.2.5). In the view of the author of these lines, gods were preternaturally great and beneficent beings (Habicht 1985, 152–53). On a slightly less refined view, as we have seen, gods were all-powerful and difficult to deal with.

Mortals also knew what an emperor could do. Quite simply, he was not like a real god. Therefore, while his cult had the same social functions as other cults and while expressions of respect to him were modeled on the institutions of cult, his cult lacked the awesome element of the divine. When the Christian Pionius refused to sacrifice to the gods, the priest of the provincial cult at Smyrna suggested that he could "at least offer a sacrifice to the emperor" (*Acts of Pionius* 8), who, as this phrase suggests, was not on the same plane even in the eyes of his own official. This view is also reflected by the fact that as a general rule (though there are exceptions that may be no more than carelessness) sacrifices were offered not to an emperor but on his behalf.

Every city was free to choose the way that it honored the emperor: the terms were not dictated from Rome, though the emperor could indicate preferences, choosing to recognize a manifestation of the cult or not. The provincial assembly could offer a model but could not prescribe a form; this was up to people in each city. The diversity of the cult is perhaps the most important indication of its nature, for no cult could function without the approval of the god to whom it was offered. The imperial cult, representing a community's participation in Romanness, was a thing apart, filling a central role in the Roman state by providing a vehicle for communicating with the central power and for distributing news about the emperor's deeds. As a political and cultural institution, the imperial cult had no equal, involving the provincial elite with the imperial administration in a way that was simply inconceivable in the context of local cult. It ensured the spread of a common ideological system while maintaining a degree of autonomy for local dignitaries (Rives 1995, 95–96). The use of the trappings of cult placed the emperor, quite literally, in the heart of every significant urban area in the empire (Price 1984, 133–69).

Divine Friends

The emperor may not have been a god, but it was readily believed that he had very powerful gods for friends. The precise nature of this relationship was expressed in various ways at different periods of classical history.[33] In the Homeric epics the gods are shown as actual companions of chosen humans, lending physical aid to them in their struggles. In the fifth century B.C. the notion that a human being was protected or assisted by a personal daimon became more prevalent, and later writers tended to interpret the Homeric picture of divine aid in allegorical terms or to suggest that what Homer meant to say was that his heroes were protected by lesser beings that were representing the gods. In Latin this relationship was expressed either in terms of a personal daimon, as in Greek, or through reference to a personal genius. Particularly important people might also expect to have a personal relationship to a greater god (even though this might be mediated by the divinity's lesser agents).

The emperor Augustus was the personal favorite of the god Apollo; the emperor Domitian was the favorite of Minerva. Just before he died, it is said that Domitian dreamed that Minerva left her shrine and told him that she could no longer protect him since she had been disarmed by Jupiter (Suetonius *Life of Domitian* 15.3). The emperor Julian is said to have had a similar experience with the genius of the city of Rome shortly before his own death in 363. The genius had earlier appeared to him and urged him to take the throne (Ammianus Marcellinus, *History of Rome* 20.5.10, 25.2.3). Various emperors in the third century A.D. explicitly use the word *comes* (companion) to describe divinities with whom they wanted to suggest that they had especial connections. This tendency took on a new aspect after A.D. 285 when the emperors Diocletian and Maximian took the names *Jovius* and *Herculius*, the adjectival forms of the names of Jupiter and Hercules, to emphasize the point that these particular divinities were assisting them in putting the empire back on its feet.

Emperors were not the only people to have personal relationships with divinities. Aelius Aristides, a successful orator in the second century A.D., wrote an entire book about the dreams that he had received

33. Nock 1947 remains fundamental on this point, and the following discussion depends on it.

from various gods (chiefly Asclepius) at various points in his career, and the greatest doctor of the imperial period, Galen, wrote that he performed an operation on advice that he had received from Asclepius in a dream.[34] People actively sought divine protectors and even wore protective amulets of all sorts that were thought to be able to channel the force of a divinity toward a human being in need. Such amulets may have been the most common form of personal adornment in the Mediterranean world.

The ubiquity of the belief that mortals could and did arrange personal protection for themselves by gods or their agents is one of the crucial aspects of "active" religious practice in the Roman world. The fact that this belief was still commonplace and very important in the early fourth century is one reason why it is wrong to think that classical polytheism was in decline around the year A.D. 312, when an incident connected with this belief forever changed the religious balance in the empire. In that year an ambitious young man who had claimed a portion of the empire for his own in A.D. 306 had an experience that led him to cross a crucial religious frontier,[35] the boundary that separated the inclusive faith of classical polytheism from the exclusive faith of Christianity.

Constantine, for this is the young man in question, appears to have felt that he had been under the personal protection of the Sun for some time before he launched the invasion of Italy that was destined first to make him ruler of the western portion of the Roman world and then to provide the base from which he would claim the whole of the empire twelve years later. At about that time something happened to convince Constantine that he was wrong about his protector—we will never be sure what happened (he himself told different stories about it). He became convinced that his protector was in fact the Christian God rather than the Sun. This quintessentially active variety of contemporary Mediterranean religiosity spelled the end of classical polytheism, for Constantine established the Christian faith as the central faith of the empire, the Christian god (who permitted no rivals) as the protector of emperors.

The religion of the Roman people did not go away overnight, and it plainly exercised a profound influence on the Jewish sect that was

34. For Aelius Aristides and Galen see the evidence collected in Bowersock 1969, 61, 74.

35. For this view see Liebeschuetz 1979, 277–91.

Christianity, in its formative years, to make it a faith that could be more readily understood and used by the diverse inhabitants of the empire. Not everyone felt that the traditional forms of worship and those of the Christians needed to be opposed to each other. But the opinion that these forms of worship could coexist came to be a minority view, and what may be the most poignant expression of traditional belief was uttered in a losing cause, when in a letter composed in A.D. 384, the senator Symmachus asked that the altar of Victory that Augustus had placed in the senate house after Actium not be removed.

> Each person has his own custom, his own practice; the Divine Mind has distributed various guardians to the various cities; as particular souls are given to mortals at birth, so, too, are heavenly geniuses divided among peoples. Utility, which is the clearest proof of the existence of the gods to mortals, adds to this argument. For as all human reason moves about in the dark, whence can knowledge of the gods come better than from the memory and documents of favors done in the past? If the long passage of time lends authority to religion, faith must be kept with so many centuries, and our parents must be followed by us, as they so fortunately followed theirs. . . . What does it matter by what rational system the truth is sought? It is not possible to come by one path to so great a truth. (*On the Altar of Victory* 3.8–9)

PART THREE

Bread and Circuses

CHAPTER FIVE

Feeding the City: The Organization, Operation, and Scale of the Supply System for Rome

Greg S. Aldrete and David J. Mattingly

One of the most impressive achievements of the Roman Empire was simply the fact that for several centuries it managed to sustain and supply its capital city, which had a population of around one million people.[1] This was a notable accomplishment in a largely unmechanized preindustrial society where long-range transportation of goods was hazardous and costly.[2] The requirements of the city of Rome far outstripped the available local resources, however, and necessitated imports on an enormous scale. The most essential of these imported items was food. But while the supply of grain and, in particular, the operation of the grain dole have received considerable attention, grain was only one of many foods imported on a large scale.[3] From the reign of Augustus onward, Rome imported very great quantities of marble and other decorative stones, which adorned its public buildings and the houses and villas of the rich.[4] Timber was another bulky item that was imported in vast amounts in all periods of Roman history, for use

1. On the population of Rome in the early empire see Hopkins 1978, 96–98.

2. On the debate about transportation in the Roman world and on the relative costs of water versus land transport see n. 11. On sea travel in general see Casson 1971 and Rouge 1981. On the speed of communication by water see Duncan-Jones 1990, 7–29. On roads see Chevallier 1976.

3. On the grain supply in general see Rickman 1980; Garnsey 1983, 1988. On the administration of the grain dole see d'Escurac 1976; Casson 1980; Sirks 1991. For the separate issue of military supply in the early empire see Remesal Rodriguez 1986. On grain as food see Foxhall and Forbes 1982. On wine and oil see our n. 7. On fish products see M. Ponsich 1988; Curtis 1991; Corcoran 1963.

4. See Dodge 1988; Ward-Perkins 1971.

in cooking, heating, construction, and cremation and for a variety of other purposes (Meiggs 1982).

While we shall focus primarily on food-related supply problems, it must be stressed that the supply of food was but one part of a larger logistical structure for the city. The minimalist nature of the central Roman administration has often been emphasized,[5] and some scholars have questioned whether the bureaucracy of Rome's supply system was ever very sophisticated. We shall argue, on the contrary, that the sheer scale of the system, together with what we can infer about the complexity of its organization, strongly suggests that the state took an active role in encouraging and overseeing the supply of both foodstuffs and other materials to the city of Rome.

The Problem

By the end of the Republic, Rome's greatly increased population had far outstripped local resources and was ever more dependent on imported goods to sustain itself. The dietary needs of the approximately one million people in the Roman population at the time are normally assessed in terms of grain consumption, though modern estimates of this consumption vary since it is impossible to be certain of the precise proportion of daily calorie intake fulfilled by cereals. The normal assumption is that cereals provided at least two-thirds of calorie intake. Figures have been advanced in recent years of between 200 and 270 kg of grain per person per year.[6] Other principal forms of nutrition included olives (and especially olive oil) and wine.[7] The advantage of all three of these crops was that their products were relatively easy to store, an important consideration in an age when methods of food preservation were fairly rudimentary. For this reason in particular, grains, oil, and wine were the key components in the Roman diet, sup-

5. For example, Hopkins (1983a, 186) estimates that in the Roman empire there was only one elite official for every three hundred thousand provincials. Nevertheless, when the lesser officials and servile civil servants are taken account of, the bureaucracy appears less skeletal.

6. Garnsey 1983, 118 (200 kg); Foxhall and Forbes 1982, 69–72 (212–37 kg); Panella 1985, 180 (260 kg); Rickman 1980, 3–8 (270 kg).

7. On wine see Tchernia 1986; Rossiter 1981. On olive oil see Amouretti 1986; Mattingly 1988a, 1988b, 1996.

plemented by other foods as and when in season or available on the open market. Meat was not a significant component of the everyday subsistence of the poorer sectors of society, and in a huge city such as Rome, their degree of reliance on the three staples (oil, wine, grains) was probably very high, especially during the winter months. The total annual requirement of these foodstuffs was thus colossal, in excess of 400,000 metric tons.[8] Even if the government had wished to avoid direct involvement in the mechanics of the food supply, the scale of the problem and the potential of food shortages to spark serious unrest impelled the state to play an increasingly active role in the logistical arrangements for feeding the city. The supply system that was developed is commonly referred to as the *annona.*

A further problem related to the demography of the city was that the poor had limited means with which to buy food, particularly at the inflated prices that often operated in the capital. There is a common misconception that the urban plebs led an entirely indolent existence, surviving on a diet of free shows and handouts of cash and grain. In reality, it is clear that work was a necessity for most people, though many jobs were seasonal in nature and continuous employment for unskilled workers was hard to come by. The state, particularly from Augustus onward, was able to generate jobs in various sectors (notably the construction industry), but there was also a necessity for more interventionist policies. In the late second century B.C., the Roman state adopted the principle of distributing some food free or at reduced prices to qualifying male citizens in times of shortage. Although not at first a commitment to regular distributions, the tendency over time was for the citizen plebs to expect increased state involvement in the food supply of the city. The precedent of distributing some free food was in a sense a point of no return for the Republican government. The state thus assumed responsibility not only for ensuring that adequate food was on sale at reasonable prices in the markets but also for the collection, transport, and distribution of a proportion of the total foodstuffs required.

---

8. Our figures for order of magnitude (explained in more detail later in this chapter) are minimum estimates, based on bare subsistence needs. Changing the proportion of the main elements of the diet or substituting other commodities would not greatly affect the overall tonnage of food required.

Even meeting the minimum needs for these commodities imposed severe burdens on a preindustrial state. Food shortage and famine were recurrent threats to an urban population as dependent on imports as that of ancient Rome. Incidents of food shortage frequently led to riots and other social disturbances. In the period from the end of the Second Punic War to the start of the Principate (201–31 B.C.) there are at least thirty-seven attested incidents of food shortage in Rome.[9] The causes of these shortages were varied, from crop failure in the main producing areas, to the effects of war (both external and civil), to disruption of the shipping lanes by pirates, to official negligence or corruption, to natural disasters such as fire or floods destroying supplies. A common response to the early signs of impending shortage was for merchants to hoard supplies, causing food prices to soar. Such shortages often resulted in serious social unrest and rioting, since basic foods quickly became unaffordable or unobtainable for the poorer people in society while large stocks were known to remain in the warehouses.

Food crises continued to afflict the city of Rome even after the creation of the Principate, with ten incidents attested in the reign of Augustus alone and a total of twenty-three in the period down to Septimius Severus (31 B.C.–A.D. 193).[10] For much of Roman history, then, the availability of food and its cost on the market at Rome was a necessary preoccupation both of the populace at large and of those responsible for maintaining public order. The Roman state, notoriously noninterventionist and unbureaucratic in many areas of life, was forced to address the problems associated with feeding the city.

Overland transport of bulk foodstuffs was clearly expensive in antiquity, and the major part of Rome's needs beyond what was sup-

9. See Garnsey 1987, 193–217 for incidents of food shortage or crisis in the years 189 (?), 182, 165, 142, 138, 129, 123 (?), 104, 100, 99, 91, 90, 89, 87, 86 (?), 82, 75, 74, 73, 67, 58, 57, 56, 54, 49, 48, 47, 46, 44, 43, 42, 41, 40, 39, 38, 37, 36 B.C. Since we lack detailed historical sources for much of this period, it is likely that we have considerably underestimated the scale of the problems. We should note that because the state did take measures to alleviate these crises, true famine was rare. On famine at Rome see also Virlouvet 1985.

10. See Garnsey 1988, 218–27 for crises under Augustus in the years 28 (?), 23, 22, and 18 B.C. and A.D. 5, 6, 7, 8, and 9; for crises under later emperors in A.D. 32, 41, 51, 62, 64, 69, 70; and for undated incidents in the reigns of Domitian, Hadrian, Antoninus Pius, and Marcus Aurelius in 161 (?), 189, and 193.

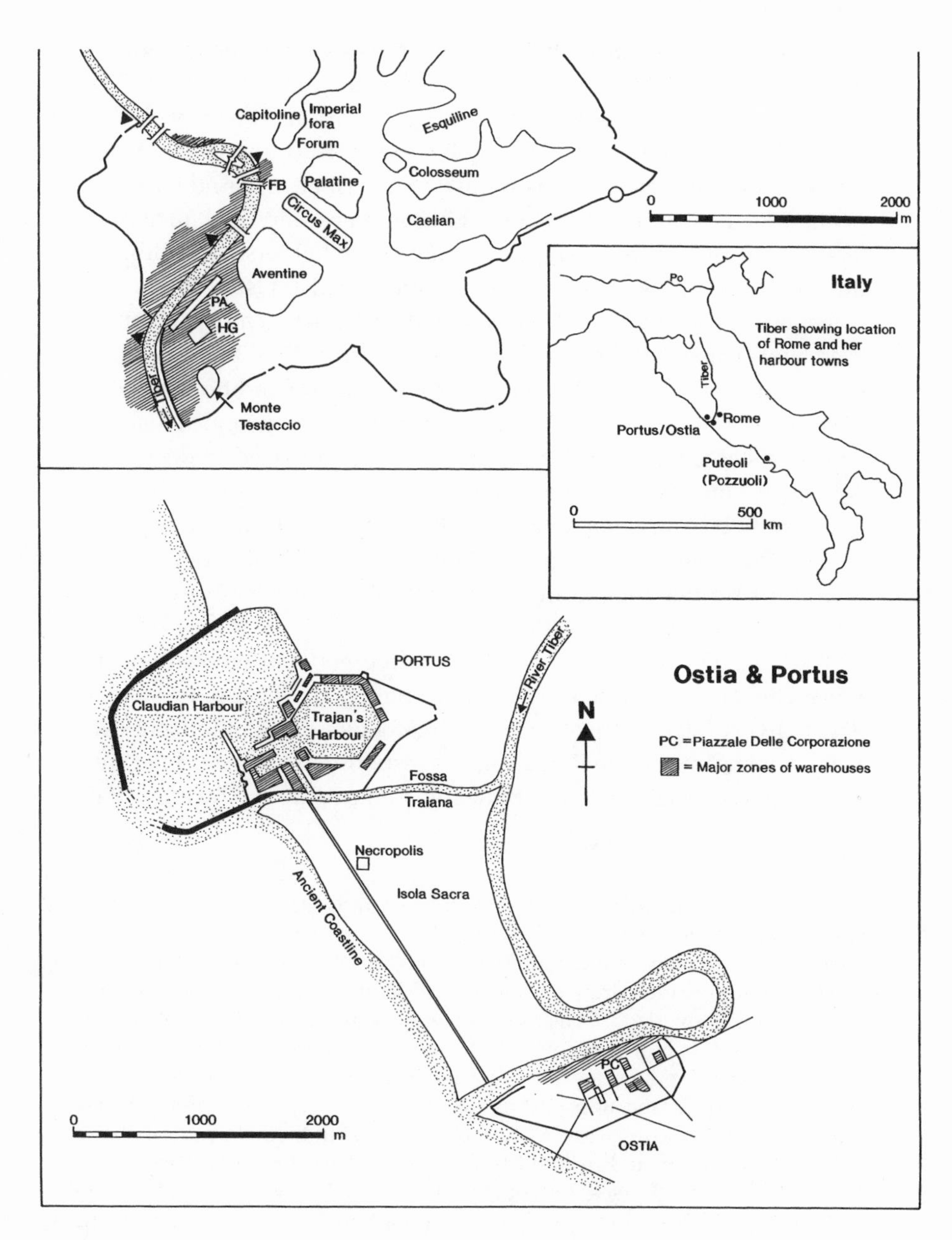

Fig. 11. Commercial quarters at Rome and Ostia, showing areas of wharves and warehouses, with (inset) locator map showing Rome's ports.

plied by her immediate hinterland came by water.[11] Rome was located about 15 miles inland as the crow flies, on the left bank of the Tiber River (fig. 11). The river was navigable for ships and boats of shallow draft, though not for the larger seagoing ships. Unfortunately there was no good natural harbor at the mouth of the Tiber, where the town of Ostia served as Rome's port. In Republican times ships tied up at riverside wharfs or had their cargos off-loaded onto lighters while riding at anchor offshore.[12] Some of the goods were stored at Ostia; others were transported upstream to Rome in small riverboats. Only the smaller merchant ships could proceed directly upriver to Rome without unloading in the hazardous and poorly sheltered conditions at Ostia. Because of the inadequate facilities, crowded berths, and dangerous conditions at Ostia, many of the largest ships preferred to dock some way from Rome, at Puteoli on the Bay of Naples. From there, their cargoes had to be transshipped into smaller boats for onward transport to Rome. The absence of more substantial harbor installations close at hand thus further complicated the considerable problems involved in supplying the city.

The uncertainties of crop production, the perils of navigation, and the organizational difficulties of coordinating the transport, storage, and delivery of the huge quantities of foodstuffs required imposed major constraints on the Roman state's response to the recurrent threat of shortage. These problems are neatly summed up by Tacitus: "Italy

11. The classic calculation of costs by Jones (1964, 841–45) suggested that a wagonload of wheat would double in price after 300 miles of overland haulage charges. He also notes that the comparatively low charges for sea freight made it "cheaper to ship grain from one end of the Mediterranean to the other than to cart it 75 miles overland." His figures were calculated in relation to cereals, however, and less bulky commodities would have been more competitive for overland transport. Duncan-Jones (1982, 366–69) has calculated relative cost ratios for sea:river:land transport as 1:4.9:34–42; that is, it was probably five times as costly to move goods by road as it was to shift them the same distance by inland waterway and from thirty-four to forty-two times more expensive than moving them by sea. Of course, the risk of loss was far higher with seaborne traffic. See also Greene 1986, 39–40; Spurr 1986, 144–46; Hopkins 1983b.

12. Dionysius of Halicarnassus (3.44) and Strabo (231–32) describe ships unloading offshore of Ostia while stressing the dangers of this procedure.

relies on external resources, and the life of the Roman people is tossed daily on the uncertainties of sea and storm."[13]

The Solution

The Dole

The problem of the food supply for the city of Rome was closely related to the availability of the main staples. Through the acquisition and governance of empire, Rome was in an unrivaled position to regulate and direct trade in foodstuffs. Rome also received a considerable volume of surplus cereal production as tax or rent from the provinces, notably Egypt, Africa, and Sicily. Surplus production of other needed commodities expanded in the provinces; for example, Spain and Africa emerged as major exporters of olive oil under the Principate (Mattingly 1988a, 33–55).

The state did not seek initially to develop its own merchant fleet, relying instead on private shipping agencies to transport the goods to Rome. It is clear, however, that a number of inducements were offered to encourage this trade: direct payments and subsidies, tax breaks, and social distinctions (such as the grant of citizenship). The stages by which these measures were introduced and the details of their application are hazily understood, but it is evident that in the late Republic and early Principate the state did adopt measures that amounted to the underwriting or subsidization of transport costs on a significant amount of goods being brought to Rome. Much "trade" activity at the ports of Rome was thus founded on redistributive principles, or could be described as "tied" in nature. In this manner the state sought to guarantee that adequate supplies of a range of foodstuffs were available in the city.

The distribution of food (whether free or at a reduced price) is a separate but related issue. The first grain law in Rome was passed at the urging of Gaius Gracchus in 123 B.C. and introduced the principle of monthly sales of grain at a reduced price. The main threats to the grain supply in the first century B.C. came from the series of civil wars that led

13. Tacitus *Annals* 3.54. The sentiment is repeated in *Annals* 12.43: "The life of the Roman people has been entrusted to ships and disasters."

to the demise of the Republic, and at various points the Gracchan system of subsidized cereals fell into abeyance, only to be revived in modified form through popular pressure when conditions allowed.[14] It is important to stress that the initial schemes were all limited to "adult" male citizens (with some citizen groups, such as freedmen, perhaps excluded) and provided grain at a reduced price, not free. Due to poverty, a large percentage of the free poor, even if eligible, may not have been able to take full advantage of these schemes.

A major change occurred in 58 B.C. with the passage of the grain law of Clodius. This seems to have introduced a number of novel concepts: the free distribution of grain, the inclusion of freedmen of citizen status, the lowering of the minimum qualifying age to ten. All these measures greatly expanded the list of those eligible to this form of state assistance, while for the first time making the system more favorable for poorer citizens. The cost of such an expanded system was seen by many conservatives as exorbitant, and the new measure met some determined opposition in the senate. By 46 B.C. there were 360,000 people eligible for the individual allotment of 5 *modii* per month (an annual total of c. 400 kg per person—enough to keep two people at subsistence level). Consequently, Caesar reduced this number by half, and Augustus likewise seems to have limited his distributions to a male citizen pool that numbered around 150,000–200,000, excluding some groups, such as recently manumitted slaves, from those eligible. Although there were some additions and some growth in the size of this privileged group under the Principate, it probably never exceeded 250,000 again. To put it another way, only one-quarter of the estimated populace of the city was eligible for free grain (though perhaps twice that number could be sustained on the grain distributed). At the beginning of the third century A.D., Septimius Severus added a ration of free olive oil to the grain dole, and later in the same century, Aurelian added pork and wine to the list of foods given to dole recipients.[15]

---

14. Grain laws were passed in the 90s *(lex Octavia)*, in 73 *(lex Terrentia Cassia)*, and in 62 *(lex Porcia)*. The law of 62 either raised expenditure on grain distribution to 7,500,000 denarii or increased total outlay by this amount. In either case, it is evident that the state was by this date investing heavily. Perhaps as much as 50,000 tons of wheat could have been purchased outright for this sum. On the grain supply in the Republic see Garnsey, and Rathbone 1985, 20–25; Garnsey, Gallant, and Rathbone 1986, 30–44.

15. HA *Septimius Severus* 18.3; HA *Aurelian* 35.2, 48.1.

The needs of those ineligible for the grain dole, notably the noncitizen free poor, could not be ignored entirely by the state. As we shall see, the supply system that was developed to bring the dole grain to Rome had a wider remit. To an increasing extent, the state undertook to ensure that adequate supplies of a range of foods were available in the markets of Rome at reasonable prices. It is important not to focus on the detail of the dole to the exclusion of this significant additional role of the annona system.

Harbors and Warehouses

The unsatisfactory harbor arrangements for Rome continued until A.D. 42, when the pressing need for a good harbor at the mouth of the Tiber compelled the emperor Claudius to undertake the construction of an enormous artificial harbor (fig. 11). About 4 kilometers north of Ostia, Claudius excavated out of the coastline a gigantic basin over 1,000 meters wide. He also cut canals connecting the new harbor with the Tiber and had two moles built up to shelter the harbor from the sea (Tacitus *Annals* 15.18.3). Even in this new harbor, known as Portus, ships were still not immune from storms, since Tacitus records that two hundred ships within the moles were sunk in a storm in A.D. 62 (*Annals* 15.18.3). Evidently, some part of the important Alexandrian grain fleets continued to unload at Puteoli.[16] The problem of storms was finally solved by Trajan, who excavated a hexagonal inner harbor basin 700 meters in diameter, within which ships were evidently safe.[17]

At Rome itself, both banks of the Tiber to the south of Tiber Island served as an extensive unloading zone for ships. Excavations have revealed quays of finely dressed stone along the riverbanks, with giant stone rings to which the ships tied up, as well as ramps to facilitate unloading. Such facilities were especially concentrated in the area to the south of the Aventine Hill, known as the Emporium district.[18]

---

16. Seneca *Letters* 77. The excellent harbor and associated facilities at Puteoli ensured that this port continued to be used even after the construction of Rome's new harbors.

17. For a full discussion of Ostia's role prior to Portus see Meiggs 1973, 16–54. Meiggs 1973, 149–71 has a useful description of the construction and layout of Portus.

18. Castagnoli (1980), Le Gall (1953, 194–204), and Rodriguez-Almeida (1984, 23–106) discuss Rome's port installations.

Ostia, Portus, and Rome all contained numerous warehouses *(horrea),* and the sophistication, number, and size of these storage structures are eloquent testimony to the scale and importance of Rome's imports.[19] Although there is some variation, the structure of most *horrea* consisted of an open courtyard with small rooms opening onto it from four sides. Warehouses were frequently multistoried structures, with the upper levels accessible by staircases and ramps. Some of the Roman warehouses were truly enormous structures. The *Horrea Galbana* contained 140 rooms on the ground floor alone, which covered 225,000 square feet.

These *horrea,* particularly those used to store grain, seem to have been constructed with considerable care. Since grain must be kept dry and cool to preserve it from spoilage and vermin, many warehouses had raised floors, which helped to keep the grain free of moisture and at an optimal temperature. In addition, warehouses were very solidly built, with thick walls (at least 60 centimeters, and frequently 1 meter, thick), and usually a space was left between adjoining warehouses as a deterrent to fire. Finally, in keeping with the value and importance of the items stored within them, the Roman *horrea* demonstrate a great concern with security. Within the structure, large square windows connected one room to another for ventilation, but the windows that pierced the outer walls were always placed high on the wall and were very narrow, to prevent theft. There were also only the minimum number of exterior windows necessary for ventilation. The door frames of the *horrea* at Ostia preserve traces of elaborate systems of locks and bolts on both the doors to the individual rooms and those to the warehouse complex as a whole. Also, probably for security purposes, entrances connecting the *horrea* to the outside were remarkably few, and these doors had locks that were fastened from both the outside and the inside. Often, there were only two or three external doors, even for very large complexes. In addition, the doorways themselves were quite narrow, often less than 1.5 meters in width. As Rickman stresses, the narrow entrances and multiple levels of Roman warehouses demonstrate that goods were transported by human power alone, without the use of carts or draft animals. Such a system would have required an enormous number of laborers employed solely as porters.

---

19. All information for this section on *horrea* is derived from Rickman 1971, particularly 1–15 and 76–86.

Commercial Organization of the Supply System: The Guilds

The complexity of Rome's logistical system can be illustrated by tracing the path of commodities once the ships carrying them arrived at the mouth of the Tiber.[20] As Casson points out, when a ship arrived at the mouth of the harbor, "it had to present its ship's papers, be acknowledged by the harbourmaster, be assessed the appropriate port fees, and, most immediately, be assigned and conducted to a berth" (Casson 1965, 35). He suggests that the boat that met the incoming ship was also the one that would tow it to its assigned berth. Once the ship was tied up, the cargo had to be unloaded by gangs of men and then transported to and stored in a warehouse. Eventually, the cargo was taken from the warehouse and loaded into specialized riverboats, which were then towed up the Tiber to Rome; this stage could, and probably often did, take place a considerable time after the ship had first been unloaded. Once at Rome, the process of unloading and storing at warehouses had to be repeated. Finally, of course, the cargo was distributed to its actual place of consumption. At every stage of this process, there were officials and overseers monitoring the exchanges, comparing the commodity to official weights and measures, perhaps collecting taxes, and insuring that none of the cargo mysteriously disappeared. This process involved many thousands of people, including imperial officials, commercial associations, individual merchants, various guilds of boatmen, and a great many porters and dockworkers.

There appear to have been three main types of boats used in the harbors and on the Tiber: the *scaphae* and *lintres,* the *lenunculi,* and the *codicariae.* The *scaphae, lintres,* and *lenunculi* seem to have all been rowboats; *scaphae* and *lintres* simply designate any one of a variety of light rowboats used for a myriad of purposes around harbors, whereas the *lenunculi* were larger boats with multiple oarsmen (Meiggs 1973, 297). There were five guilds of *lenuncularii* at Ostia (*CIL,* xiv, 352). The largest and most important of these was the *lenuncularii tabularii auxiliarii.* In A.D. 192 this guild had 258 members and listed Roman senators among its patrons.[21] The *lenuncularii tabularii auxiliarii* were probably the boat-

20. Subsequently in this chapter, we shall limit our discussion to the period after Portus superseded Puteoli, although Puteoli continued to be a port of importance and to serve as an auxiliary port for Rome for a long time. For the role of Puteoli as a harbor for Rome see D'Arms 1970, 73–165; D'Arms 1981, 121–74; Frederiksen 1984, 319–58.

21. *CIL,* xiv, 251, 341.

men who met incoming merchant ships at the mouth of the harbor and towed them to their assigned berths (Casson 1965, 35). A second guild was the *lenuncularii pleromarii auxiliarii,* which in A.D. 200 had only sixteen members (*CIL,* xiv, 252). Meiggs identifies this guild's boats as those that lightened larger merchantmen at sea before entering the Tiber (Meiggs 1973, 298). This was undoubtedly a much larger guild prior to the construction of Claudius' harbor. A third guild was the *lenuncularii traiectus luculli,* who were ferrymen (*CIL,* xiv, 409). The function of the remaining two guilds of *lenuncularii* is uncertain, although there are three additional ferry services mentioned in inscriptions: the *traiectus marmorariorum,* the *traiectus togatensium,* and the *traiectus rusticelius.*[22]

The final important group of boats was the *naves codicariae.* These were highly specialized vessels used to transport goods from Ostia and Portus up the Tiber to Rome. They were hauled upriver by men trudging along towpaths running alongside the Tiber. The 22-mile trip up the Tiber took three days, and the average size of these boats may have been about 70 tons (Rickman 1980, 19). *Codicariae* are easily identifiable in sculptural reliefs and mosaics by their lone, lowerable mast stepped extremely far forward, which was used for towing. Another distinctive feature of *codicariae* was a series of cleats on the mast, which enabled the crew to climb the mast. These cleats were necessary since, because the mast could be lowered, the ship lacked standing rigging, which was normally used for this purpose.[23] The guild of the *codicarii* lasted at least through the fourth century A.D., indicating the vital role they played in supplying the city's food (Meiggs 1973, 293–94). The *codicariae* were apparently hauled by human power rather than by animals (LeGall 1953, 257). Martial alludes to the rhythmic chant of the boat haulers, known as *helciarii,* as they trudged along the towpaths by the Tiber (4.64.22). In addition to the Ostian *codicarii,* there was an entirely separate group of *codicarii* that transported goods between Rome and points further upriver.[24]

---

22. *CIL,* xiv, 425, 403; xiv, supp. 1, 4053–56.

23. Casson 1965 discusses these and other characteristics of *codicariae* in greater detail as well as analyzing all the known iconographic representations of this specialized type of boat.

24. This distinction is suggested by two inscriptions, one of which refers to *codicari naviculari infernates* (*CIL,* xiv, 131), and the second of which specifies *codicari nav(iculari) infra pontem S(ublicium)* (*CIL,* xiv, 185).

The size, variety, and specialization of the boats used at the harbors and on the Tiber were impressive. However, the boatmen represented only one group of guilds out of many. Their subdivisions and duties have been described at some length to serve as a representative example illustrating the complexity of the Ostian guilds involved in the transportation of goods to Rome. In the other guilds as well, a similar degree of specialization and complexity probably existed. There were many guilds associated with the construction and maintenance of ships. The *fabri navales,* the shipbuilders' guild, listed 320 ordinary members in the late second century A.D. (*CIL,* xiv, 256). Other related guilds include the *stuppatores,* the caulkers, and the *restiones,* the rope makers.[25] Not surprisingly, porters' guilds were particularly numerous; among these were the *saccarii,* the carriers of sacks of grain; the *phalangarii,* the carriers of amphoras; the *saburrarii,* who carried sand (used for ballast) on and off the ships; and the *geruli,* the stevedores. Other important guilds connected to the harbor activity included the *mensores frumentarii,* who measured grain as it was unloaded from the ships and also when it was loaded onto the *codicariae;* the *horrearii,* the warehouse workers; the *custodiarii,* the warehouse guards; the *lignarii,* the timber dealers; the *collegium fabrum tignuariorum,* the general construction workers, whose guild listed 350 members in A.D. 198; and finally, the *urinatores,* divers whose job was to recover goods that fell overboard while being unloaded.

These were some of the guilds associated with the actual physical handling of merchandise or with the construction of equipment and buildings around the docks. There were, of course, also guilds for the owners of the goods, most notably the grain, wine, and oil merchants. In Ostia, many of these guilds appear to have had offices located in the so-called Piazzale delle Corporazioni, a large rectangular colonnade with sixty-one small rooms opening off of it (Meiggs 1973, 282–89). In front of each room was a mosaic apparently illustrating or advertising the type of guild or the commercial services of the owner. Also, many of these offices seem to have been occupied by merchants or shippers from various cities in Gaul and North Africa associated with the supply

25. For a complete listing of the many inscriptions mentioning these guilds as well as the epigraphic citations for those guilds referred to in the remainder of this paragraph see Frank 1940, 248–52. On Ostian guilds see Meiggs 1973, 311–36.

of commodities to Rome.[26] Grain merchants are heavily represented, but so are shippers in other goods, including exotic animals.[27]

Merchants and Shippers

The role and particularly the identity and status of the "middlemen" who brought the grain and other foodstuffs to Rome are matters of debate. Moreover, the distinctions between shipowners, captains, and merchants are not always clear.[28] The state possessed a navy, but not a merchant marine. Therefore even state-owned grain from imperial estates intended for the dole had to be shipped by private merchants and shippers working under contract to the state. The very fact that there were enough shippers to keep Rome supplied with sufficient food indicates that there were profits to be made in shipping foodstuffs to Rome. The potential for making a considerable profit in overseas trade is attested in numerous literary sources.[29] One way to attempt to determine who these traders were is to consider who possessed the capital necessary to invest in such ventures.

Overseas trade entailed a substantial risk in terms of capital, due to

---

26. See, for example, *CIL*, xiv, supp. 1, 4549[32] (Gaul); 4549[10, 12, 17, 18, 34] (North Africa).

27. One mosaic from Sabratha depicts an elephant (*CIL*, xiv, supp. 1, 4549[14]), and another from an unidentified city shows a boar, a stag, and an elephant (Meiggs 1973, 287 and plate xxiiib).

28. See Rickman 1980, 124–27, 141–43 for a discussion of such distinctions and their complexity. He also gives examples of men who combined categories, such as Sextus Fadius Musa, who was both a *navicularius* as well as a *negotiator* (*CIL*, xii, 4393; cf. Rickman 1980, 125). It is interesting to note that even the *codicarii* were sometimes also merchants; M. Caerellius Iazymis of Ostia identifies himself as a *codicarius* and a grain merchant: *codicarius item mercator frumentarius* (*CIL*, xiv, 4234).

29. For example, Pliny the Elder comments that innumerable people were engaged in trade, hoping to make a profit (*Natural History* 2.118). Juvenal mocks those who, lured by dreams of enormous profits, sail the seas as merchants, and he says that wherever hope for profit calls, fleets will follow (*Satires* 14.267–78). In a list of ways to gain wealth quickly, Seneca the Younger puts overseas trade first (*Epistle* 119). Petronius' vulgar fictional freedman, Trimalchio, increased his inherited fortune by shipping wine to Rome (Petronius *Satyricon* 76).

the expense of both cargo and ships.[30] However, the group that probably possessed the most wealth, the senatorial aristocracy, was at least technically forbidden from engaging in overseas trade by the *plebiscitum Claudianum* of 219–218 B.C., which decreed that no senator or senator's son could own an oceangoing ship with a capacity of more than three hundred amphorae, since trade was thought to be beneath the senators' dignity.[31] Perhaps a stronger impediment to senatorial involvement in trade, however, was the prevailing social ethos that considered trade a sordid occupation in which gentlemen should not participate. According to this ethos, the only proper source of wealth for aristocrats was landownership and agriculture. According to Cicero, "of all things from which one may acquire wealth, none is better than agriculture, none more fruitful, none sweeter, none more fitting for a free man" (*De Officiis* 1.151). The most eloquent description of this attitude, and the most forceful expression of its primacy, is in M.I. Finley's influential book *The Ancient Economy*.[32] In Finley's view, the possibility of loss of status effectively precluded direct senatorial involvement in trade for profit.

Most of the *negotiatores, mercatores,* and *navicularii* engaged in trade

---

30. Hopkins 1983b, 100–102. There were, however, several methods widely used by the Romans to reduce these financial risks. Often merchant ships were owned by a number of individuals who bought shares in the ship, thus spreading the potential losses among multiple investors (see, e.g., Plutarch *Cato the Elder* 21). Also, to reduce the loss incurred by any single shipwreck, a merchant could transport his goods in several ships rather than putting all of them into one vessel. One result of these strategies was that ships typically carried mixed cargoes consisting of a variety of different goods belonging to multiple owners. On mixed cargoes in general see Parker 1984, 1992. For a case study of a wrecked ship with an extremely varied cargo see Colls et al. 1977. Sometimes a number of merchants would even pour their grain together into one ship's hold (*Digest* 19.2.31). On maritime commerce in general see Casson 1971; Sirks 1991.

31. Livy 21.63. Livy records that this measure met with considerable hostility from the senators, indicating that at least at this time senators were involved in overseas trade. On this law see D'Arms 1981, 31–39; Yavetz 1962. By the late Republic, although this law was still on the books, it seems to have lost its force, since Cicero refers to it as "outdated and dead": *Antiquae sunt istae leges et mortuae* (*Second Verrine* 5.45).

32. Finley 1985; see particularly pp. 35–62. Finley's analysis of Roman social attitudes is based on close reading of upper-class literary sources, especially Cicero.

appear to be freedmen, foreigners, and other low-status individuals.[33] One solution to the dilemma of funding is the suggestion that senators served as invisible partners in commerce, providing the financial backing for the freedmen and slaves whose names appear on inscriptions as merchants and shippers. Thus the freedmen and others act as "agents" for the senators.[34] While the solid evidence for such transactions is meager, it certainly seems possible that silent partnerships between senators and their agents existed. It is unlikely, however, that the majority of merchants and shippers were simply agents for senators, if for no other reason than the scale of trade.[35] It seems entirely possible that many of these merchants and shippers were independent operators, as suggested by the numerous dedications and funerary monuments that they left behind.[36]

Although the state did not have a merchant marine service of its own, the emperors were clearly concerned with ensuring that there were adequate numbers of shippers bringing essential supplies to the city of Rome. Claudius passed legislation aimed at encouraging shippers to import grain to Rome. His legislation decreed that anyone who owned a ship with a capacity of at least 10,000 *modii* (about 70 tons) and who employed that ship in bringing grain to the city for at least six years would, if he were a Roman citizen, gain exemption from the *lex Papia Poppaea,* which penalized the childless; if the owner were a woman, she would gain the privileges granted to mothers of four children; and finally, noncitizens would be rewarded with Roman citizenship itself.[37] Similar incentives offering exemptions from various taxes

---

33. See Finley 1985, 58–60.

34. On such senatorial agents see D'Arms 1981, 154–59; d'Escurac 1977. For a skeptical view of the use of agents, see Garnsey 1983, 129–30.

35. Although senators were concentrated at Rome, and while they certainly possessed a disproportionate amount of wealth, this class was numerically quite small. MacMullen (1974, 88) has estimated that only about .002 percent of the population of the Roman empire was of senatorial rank. There were many equestrians, successful freedmen, and provincial aristocrats who amassed considerable fortunes, as attested by their numerous, often lavish public dedications. See, for example, the lists compiled by Duncan-Jones (1982).

36. Meiggs 1973, 275–98 cites many of these inscriptions from merchants found at Ostia. On merchants as independent operators see also Garnsey 1983, 121–30.

37. Suetonius *Claudius* 18–19; Gaius *Institutes* 1.32c; Ulpian 3.6.

and liturgies were added by Nero and by several second-century emperors.[38]

It has also been suggested that a considerable percentage of Rome's population was supported by an "internal supply" operating outside of regular market mechanisms. This "internal supply" consisted of the senatorial and equestrian upper classes acting out the aristocratic ethos of self-sufficiency by importing foodstuffs from their own estates for the consumption of themselves and their extended households, including such dependants as slaves and other retainers (Whittaker 1985). Again, while this mechanism may have accounted for some of the supply for the city, the size of the overall demand was much greater.[39] Additionally, even if a sizable percentage of Rome's supply were privately imported from the estates of the wealthy for consumption by their households, the foodstuffs still had to be transported to Rome by shippers, most of whom were probably private contractors.

One likely source of merchants and shippers is the local provincial elites around the empire, particularly those from important port cities in regions that exported goods to Rome. The wealthy *Augustales* found in coastal cities in Spain, Gaul, Italy, and Africa, whose benefactions adorned their local towns, may well have made their fortunes in overseas trade.[40] For these men the wealth gained in trade and then invested in land led to local magistracies, particularly for their sons, and sometimes ultimately to high status in Rome itself. The prosperity of gateway cities such as Lepcis Magna in Tripolitania, with their luxurious public buildings and private villas adorned with expensive marbles, indicates the wealth that could be gained by local elites controlling large-scale agricultural surpluses and engaging in maritime trade.[41] Therefore, while trade was viewed as an improper occupation for an aristocrat, wealthy men, including senators, were probably often at

38. Tacitus *Annals* 13.51; *Digest* 50.5.3, 50.6.6.5–6 and 8–9.

39. On the scale of foodstuffs necessary to sustain the city see our calculations later in this chapter, in the section titled "Scale."

40. On such local elites who were clearly connected with overseas trade and whose wealth led to local aristocratic status see Garnsey 1983, 124–26; D'Arms 1981, especially 121–48, 175–81. For a detailed view of two such men see Tchernia 1980. See also Rodriguez-Almeida 1980 (for study of the *tituli picti* on amphorae from Monte Testaccio), 1984.

41. Mattingly 1988c, 1988a.

least indirectly involved in overseas trade, and such commerce offered an opportunity for others to join the ranks of the wealthy, which could lead ultimately even to elite status itself.

The Administration of the Supply System

Another way to gauge the complexity and sophistication of Rome's supply system is to attempt to determine the size and the degree of active involvement by the imperial administration.[42] In the Republic, there was a *quaestor Ostiensis,* whose job was to oversee the transport and storage of grain at Ostia (Rickman 1980, 47–48). Around A.D. 7 or 8, Augustus first created the office of *praefectus annonae,* the official primarily responsible for overseeing and ensuring an adequate grain supply.[43] It is interesting to note that the first *praefectus annonae,* C. Turranius Gracilius, held the post of prefect of Egypt immediately before being assigned the prefecture of the annona. Because of the importance of Egypt to the grain supply, his experience and connections in Egypt certainly made him a logical choice for the job of overseeing the food supply of Rome.[44] Various subordinate officials quickly multiplied. In the first century A.D., the chief assistant to the *praefectus annonae* was termed an *adiutor.* By the end of the second century, this official had become the *subpraefectus annonae,* was directly appointed by the emperor, and received a salary of 100,000 sesterces (Rickman 1980, 221). From the time of Claudius, there were various special financial officers based at the main harbors, including the procurator of the port *(procurator portus)* and the procurator of the grain supply at Ostia *(procurator annonae Ostis).*[45] It is somewhat surprising that in addition to the numerous honorific inscriptions dedicated to the *procurator annonae Ostis* by the corn merchants,[46] there are many dedications from the *fabri tignuarii,* the construction workers' guild.[47] These honorific inscriptions certainly suggest that the official duties of these procura-

42. On all aspects of the imperial administration's role in the supply system of Rome see first d'Escurac 1976.

43. Suetonius *Claudius* 24.2. On the dating of the creation of the prefecture of the annona see d'Escurac 1976, 29–32.

44. For the career of C. Turranius Gracilius see d'Escurac 1976, 317–19.

45. On imperial procurators see Pflaum 1960–61 and supplement (1982).

46. For example, *CIL,* xiv, 154.

47. *CIL,* xiv, 160. See Meiggs 1973, 300 for further examples.

tors extended beyond simply overseeing the grain annona. Beneath each procurator were a variety of lesser officials, such as *cornicularii, dispensatores, beneficiarii,* and a whole range of *tabularii,* official measurers.[48] One of these *tabularii* of Ostia advanced through a series of financial posts, eventually rising to the procuratorship of Belgica.[49]

Many of these officials seem to have made careers specializing in supply posts. Sextus Julius Possessor was, at various points during his career, assistant to the prefect of the annona in charge of warehouses at Portus and Ostia *(adiutor praefecti annonae ad horrea Ostiensia et Portuensia),* procurator in charge of the banks of the river Baetis in southern Spain *(procurator ad ripam Baetis),* procurator of the annona at Ostia *(procurator Augusti ad annonam Ostis),* and procurator *ad Mercurium,* a district of Alexandria associated with grain storage.[50] Plainly, he fashioned an entire career in the administrative posts involved with the supply of the city. He began at Rome itself as an *adiutor* to the prefect of the annona. After this post he was dispatched to Spain. Baetica, in southern Spain, was one of the most important suppliers to Rome of several essential commodities, including olive oil, wine, metals, and *garum,* a popular salty, fermented fish sauce. The river Baetis (modern Guadalquivir) was the main transport link between the agricultural heartlands of Baetica and the sea.[51] As procurator of the riverbanks, Possessor's primary duty would probably have been to facilitate the steady movement of these supplies, whose ultimate destination was Rome. His next post was back in Italy as a procurator at the port of Ostia. Finally, since the single most important part of Rome's supply

48. These include the offices of *tabularii, tabularii adiutor, tabularii portus,* and *tabularii Ostis ad annonem.* For a complete analysis of the imperial offices involved in the supply of the city see particularly d'Escurac 1976, 89–152. For a more succinct description, see Meiggs 1973, 298–310; Rickman 1980, 218–25.

49. *CIL,* vi, 8450, cited by Meiggs (1973, 301).

50. *CIL,* ii, 1180; *PIR*² I 480. See also Pflaum 1982, no. 185, pp. 50–51; Rickman 1980, 224.

51. The scale and complexity of the trade mechanisms at work on the river Baetis are suggested by epigraphic evidence indicating the existence of guilds of boatmen and of others involved with river transport similar to those that operated on the Tiber. The link between these guilds and the imperial administration is made explicit by dedications by the guilds to imperial officials involved with the annona and food supply (*CIL,* ii, 1168–69, 1180, 1183). On the importance of Baetica as an agricultural region in general see Blasquez-Martinez and Remesal Rodriguez 1980 and 1983. On the Tiber guilds see Le Gall 1953, 216–83.

system was probably the annual grain fleets from Alexandria in Egypt, it is no surprise to find that this specialist in the supply of Rome is next known to have been in charge of the Alexandrian grain warehouses. Although his career comprised a variety of posts both in Rome and in several provinces, Possessor clearly specialized throughout his life in the supply of the city of Rome.

There were probably many other imperial officials with specialized duties. One example of this is recorded on the tombstone of T. Flavius Stephanus, who is described, between inscribed pictures of two camels and an elephant, as having been the *praepositus camelorum*.[52] Meiggs suggests that this was a post in charge of overseeing the supply of exotic animals to the city (Meiggs 1973, 302). There was certainly an active trade in animals for beast hunts and arena displays, so the existence of such a post is not surprising.[53] It does, however, indicate the extensive and active role of the state in supervising the supply of all commodities, no matter how unusual or specialized. The presence and involvement of such administrators was not limited to Ostia alone. There were officials in charge of the banks and riverbed of the Tiber itself, the *curatores alvei Tiberis et riparum* and their *adiutores*.[54] They had a variety of duties, including the drawing of boundaries along the riverbank (Braund 1985, 810a and b), the monitoring of the *lenuncularii* (*CIL*, xiv, supp. 1, 5320), and also probably overseeing the dredging of the river and towpath maintenance. The annona officials had offices at both Ostia and Rome, and many of the other imperial officials undoubt-

52. Bloch 1953, n. 37.

53. The capture and difficult transport of exotic wild beasts for the games at Rome must have been a considerable industry in its own right. Numerous animals, including elephants, tigers, lions, panthers, rhinos, hippopotamuses, crocodiles, giraffes, bears, and even ostriches, were slaughtered in the arena, often in staggering numbers. Even the transport of a single elephant or hippo cannot have been an easy matter, and Augustus alone claimed that he gave twenty-six beast shows in which thirty-five hundred animals were killed (*Res Gestae* 22). Trajan is said to have given games that lasted 123 days and included the slaughter of eleven thousand animals (Dio 68.15). On the subject of the capture and transport of wild beasts for the games in Rome see most recently Bertrandy 1987. An older work on the same topic is Jennisson 1937. The mosaics at a villa in Sicily dating from the early fourth century A.D. vividly depict the capture, caging, and shipping of wild beasts for the arena and provide useful iconographic information on these subjects; see Carandini, Ricci, and de Vos 1982.

54. Le Gall (1953, 135–86) describes these officials and their duties.

edly did as well. The imperial organization formed a coherent unit encompassing Portus, Ostia, the Tiber, and Rome itself.

Dedications by construction workers to the *procurator annonae Ostis* suggest that the duties of officials connected with the annona extended far beyond simply overseeing the supply of grain for the dole. The construction and maintenance of port and warehouse facilities is but one such area of their work. The comprehensiveness of their duties is best illustrated by examining the interest shown by annona officials in ensuring and promoting the supply of olive oil to the city long before this commodity was first officially distributed by the state by order of Septimius Severus.[55] An inscription dating to the reign of Hadrian, three-quarters of a century before the olive oil dole was instituted, records an honorific dedication to the *praefectus annonae* C. Junius Flavianus by the grain and olive merchants of Africa, the *mercatores frumentarii et olearii Afrari* (*CIL*, vi, 1620). That the grain and olive merchants would set up a joint monument to the *praefectus annonae* indicates that these two groups had parallel relationships to the prefect (d'Escurac 1976, 189). It is easy to think of reasons why the grain merchants would be grateful to the *praefectus annonae*, but the fact that the olive merchants were similarly grateful strongly suggests that he also played an active role in the importation of olive oil and that the olive merchants had frequent interactions with him even before olive oil became a part of the dole. This type of connection is made even more explicit by an honorific inscription to M. Petronius Honoratus, the prefect of the annona from 144–146/7, in which he is hailed as a patron (*patronus*) by the olive merchants from Baetica (*negotiatores olearii ex Baetica.*) (*CIL*, vi, 1625b). He subsequently went on to become the prefect of Egypt, in which post the experience and connections he had developed as prefect of the annona were no doubt very useful.

Not only were annona officials interested in and involved with the oil supply, but there were also state officials specifically charged with guaranteeing an adequate supply of olive oil. During the reign of Antoninus Pius, one C. Pomponius Turpilianus is identified as the *procurator ad oleum in Galba Ostiae portus utriusque* (*CIL*, xiv, 20). His job was evidently to supervise the passage of oil through the enormous *Horrea Galbana*.[56] Because oil was constantly moving through these

55. HA *Septimius Severus* 18.3. Aurelian subsequently added rations of pork and wine to the dole (HA *Aurelian* 35.2, 48.1).

56. D'Escurac 1976, 191. Rodriguez-Almeida 1984, 53–65.

warehouses, and since ensuring a sufficient supply of oil was clearly a concern of the state, his appointment to this post represents not merely a short-term or exceptional case but probably a permanent position. Antoninus Pius once gave free distributions of grain, wine, and olive oil to the populace, and no doubt such imperial distributions were greatly facilitated by the existence of imperial officials such as C. Pomponius Turpilianus who were already deeply involved in the supply of these basic foodstuffs (HA *Antoninus Pius* 8.11).

Finally, there is even evidence that the state dispatched officials to the provinces to promote the export of olive oil in the period before it had become a part of the annona. An inscription from Hispalis dating to about A.D. 166 records that Sextus Julius Possessor was assistant to the prefect of the annona, Ulpius Saturninus, and that Possessor was in charge of counting and perhaps meeting quotas in Spanish and African oil, for overseeing its transportation, and for paying the shippers.[57] That a high official of the annona, an *adiutor praefecti annonae,* was sent on a mission to Spain and Africa to promote the supply of olive oil is a clear indication that the officials of the annona were intimately involved in ensuring an adequate supply of a range of foodstuffs to Rome—not just grain.[58] Additionally, it is important to note that this inscription contains an explicit reference to shippers being contracted and paid by the state to transport oil to Rome long before oil had become a part of annona distributions.

Scale

In addition to its complexity, a second significant aspect of the supply of Rome was its scale. Although attempts at quantifying ancient trade

57. *Adiutor Ulpii Saturnini praefecti annonae ad oleum Afrum et Hispanum recensendum item solamina transferenda item vecturas naviculariis exsolvenda* (*CIL,* ii, 1180).

58. Rickman (1980, 224) disagrees with this interpretation. He believes that Possessor never left Rome but was simply in charge of keeping the accounts of Spanish and African oil that reached Rome. Rickman is unable, however, to offer any support for his view, and it seems rather difficult to understand why the inscription honoring Posssessor would be erected in Hispalis if he never left Rome. There is evidence that annona officials were indeed sent to the provinces from Rome; a second-century inscription from Arles refers to a *procurator Augusti ad annonam provinciae Narbonensis et Liguriae* (*CIL,* xii, 672). The availability of surplus oil in Spain and Africa is attested by archaeological evidence for large-scale production; see Mattingly 1988a, 1988c.

are highly dangerous and the results are often questionable, determining general orders of magnitude can be illuminating as long as one keeps in mind that these are only rough approximations. Undoubtedly, the three main foods imported to Rome were the staples of the Mediterranean diet: grain, olive oil, and wine.[59] In this section, we shall attempt to determine a rough order of magnitude for the scale of imports of these three essential items to the city of Rome and then point out some of the implications that can be drawn from these calculations.

Assume that the average inhabitant of Rome consumed 237 kg of wheat per year. With one million people in Rome, 237,000 metric tons of wheat were required for the city per year.[60] If this number is divided by the estimated average ship capacity of 250 tons, the wheat supply of Rome would necessitate a minimum of 948 shiploads of wheat each year.[61] The risk of a high rate of loss or spoilage at sea would have required the state to arrange for transport of substantially more than this minimum figure. The total number of ships carrying grain to Rome would have been higher still since large amounts of barley were also being imported, particularly for use as animal fodder.

59. On the ancient diet see above all Foxhall and Forbes 1982. On grain, oil, and wine see our n. 3. On Roman agriculture in general see Spurr 1986; Moritz 1958; White 1970. Interesting comparative data is offered by studies of modern diets in underdeveloped Mediterranean areas: see Allbaugh 1953; MacDonald and Rapp 1972.

60. For grain consumption, we have used the average figure suggested by Foxhall and Forbes (1982, 72). Other modern estimates range from 150,000 to 400,000 tons of grain consumed per year. For a summary of these alternative views see Garnsey 1983, 118–19.

61. The average size of Roman merchant ships is a matter of considerable debate. Hopkins (1983b, 97–102) suggests an average cargo capacity of 250–400 tons. Casson thinks that the majority of ships had a capacity of 100–150 tons. He believes, however, that some ships, in particular the largest of the grain freighters from Alexandria, could have had a capacity of over 1,000 tons (Casson 1971, 170–73, 183–200). In our calculations, we have used a figure of 250 tons capacity, since although the average merchant ship was likely to have been much smaller, the largest ships were probably the very ones that we are concerned with in this study—those engaged in the transport of staples to the city of Rome. While larger capacity ships may have been most efficient, efficiency alone may not have been the most significant factor in determining ship size. A ship and its cargo were very valuable, and therefore the larger the ship, the greater the financial risk. Due to the hazards of ancient maritime travel and the apparent frequency of shipwrecks, in many cases modestly sized ships may have been preferable to larger ones (Hopkins 1983b, 100–102).

Fig. 12. Large storage vessels *(dolia)* for storage of olive oil or wine, set into the floor of a warehouse in Ostia. Such warehouses attest the scale of oil and wine consumption in ancient Rome.

For olive oil, we have used an average consumption rate of 20 liters per person per year.[62] As a figure for personal consumption, this could easily be a low estimate. In a study of modern Methana, average olive oil consumption was 50 kg per person per year (Foxhall and Forbes 1982, 68). In addition to its value as food, olive oil had many other significant functions in antiquity, such as its usage in baths, for lighting, and for perfumes. In Rome, with its gigantic imperial baths and its concentration of elite households, many thousands of liters would surely have been consumed for these purposes.[63] But the minimal figure of 20 liters per person per year multiplied by a million people yields 18,000 metric tons of oil (fig. 12). To this weight must be added an additional 8,000 metric tons to account for the weight of the 285,714 amphorae in which the oil was

62. Amouretti 1986, 177–96; Mattingly 1988b; 1996.

63. One hint at the amount of oil used in baths and gymnasiums is that the gymnasium at Tauromenium from 195–167 B.C. consumed about 3,700 liters of oil each year (*IG*, xiv, 422). In the fourth century A.D., Rome contained over eight hundred baths of varying sizes.

Fig. 13. Monte Testacchio in Rome's commercial district—a mountain of discarded olive oil amphorae.

transported (fig. 13),[64] for a total annual cargo of 26,000 tons. Divided by 250 tons per ship, this yields an absolute minimum of 104 shiploads of oil per year. Once again, the transport of larger quantities will have been necessary to guarantee this minimum level of provision.

For wine, we have somewhat arbitrarily chosen an average rate of consumption of 100 liters per person per year. While adult males probably drank more, this figure allows for children, women, and slaves, all

64. We have based these calculations on Dressel type 20 amphorae with an average capacity of 70 liters of olive oil and an empty weight of 28 kg. See Peacock and Williams 1986, table 1, p. 52. See also Rodriguez-Almeida 1984, 186–87.

of whom most likely consumed far less than adult males.[65] Again, multiplied by one million inhabitants, this results in 100,000,000 liters per year of wine, or about 100,000 metric tons. Adding another 60,000 tons for the weight of the four million amphorae results in a total weight of 160,000 metric tons per year.[66] Again, dividing by an average ship weight of 250 tons yields a total of 640 shiploads of wine per year.

Therefore, an absolute minimum figure for the number of shiploads necessary to carry a year's supply of wheat, oil, and wine for the city of Rome is 1,702. The prime sailing season, when most of Rome's imports arrived, probably lasted only about one hundred days; thus, during this period an average of around seventeen ships per day would need to have arrived at Rome's ports.[67]

As a check on our computations, we calculated the calories provided by our hypothetical diet of grain, oil, and wine. If we use the caloric values of 9,000 cal/kg of oil, 3,000 cal/kg of wheat, and 500 cal/kg of wine, our hypothetical diet results in a daily intake of 2,326 calories per person.[68] This figure is lower than those suggested by modern subsistence data: 3,822 cal/day for an extremely active male, 3,337 cal/day for a very active male, and 2,852 cal/day for a moderately active male (Foxhall and Forbes 1982, 48–49). However, once adjusted for the presence of other foods in the diet, such as fruits and vegetables, as well as for the lower requirements of women and children, our average caloric figure of 2,326 cal/day seems reasonable, or at least of the right order of magnitude for a minimum value.

Such quantifications are also useful for attempting to estimate the scale of labor necessary to move all of these goods from the ships to

65. Foxhall and Forbes (1982, 68) note that in modern Methana, the adult males drank well over a liter per day of homemade wine.

66. Based on Dressel type 2–4 amphorae with an average volume of 25 liters and an empty weight of 15 kg (Peacock and Williams 1986, table 1, p. 52).

67. Our calculations, although arrived at independently, tally very closely with similar calculations made by Panella (1985, 181), who estimated that eight ships per day would arrive carrying wine, one and a half with oil, and ten with grain, compared to our figures of six ships per day of wine, one of oil, and nine and a half of grain. In reality, many (perhaps most) ancient ships carried mixed cargos, not a single commodity. One wrecked ship, for example, was found to have been carrying a cargo of metal, pottery, oil, wine, and fish sauce (D. Colls et al. 1977).

68. The extremely high nutritional value of olive oil for a given unit of weight makes it one of the most efficiently packaged foods available to the Romans. This was certainly a significant factor in its ready marketability in long-distance trade.

Rome. Since this transportation involved numerous loadings and unloadings between the merchant vessels and the warehouses in Rome, amphorae and grain sacks were made to be about the maximum weight that an individual porter or pair of porters could carry. A year's supply of 20,000,000 liters of oil translates into about 285,714 amphorae, and 100,000,000 liters of wine would require 4,000,000 amphorae.[69] For wheat, 237,000 tons equals 4,740,000 sacks.[70] Totaling the number of annual individual man-size loads of these commodities results in over 9,300,000 "porter-loads" per year.[71] Although the eventual transport of these commodities up the Tiber could be stretched out over the entire year, the ships had to be unloaded as soon as possible and the goods stored in a nearby warehouse. If the ships were unloaded in the hundred-day peak sailing period, this process would necessitate ninety-three thousand porter-loads per day. To push this calculation a bit further, if each trip by each porter took fifteen minutes and if each porter worked nine hours a day with one hour off for lunch and other breaks, simply unloading the ships in the most basic way would have demanded a force of around three thousand laborers.[72] This process of

69. These numbers of amphorae are certainly not improbable. South of the Aventine, in the Emporium district of Rome, is Monte Testaccio, a triangular artificial hill 180 meters wide, 250 meters long, and almost 50 meters high, entirely composed of broken olive oil amphorae discarded over a period of approximately 150 years. Rodriguez-Almeida (1984, 109–19) has estimated that Monte Testaccio contains the remains of over fifty million olive oil amphorae. For a similar quantitative study of amphorae fragments from Ostia see Panella 1983.

70. At 50 kg/sack after Casson 1965, 32.

71. Since a Dressel 20 amphora loaded with olive oil would weigh about 91 kg, we have assumed that it would require two porters to transport each oil amphora. Examples in Roman art illustrate how two porters could transport a large amphora by passing a stick through one of its handles and then carrying it suspended between them on the stick. We have assumed that the 50 kg grain sacks and 40 kg loaded wine amphorae were carried by individual porters.

72. Fifteen minutes is perhaps an optimistic estimate for a single trip, which would have consisted of the porter picking up his burden of a sack or an amphora; checking it off with an official on the boat; carrying it down the narrow gangplank; bearing it to a nearby warehouse, where he would again need to have it checked off and perhaps inspected by an official; depositing it in the warehouse, which often entailed bearing it up narrow stairways to upper levels; and finally returning to the ship for another load. He may well have had to wait in line at the many narrow passages involved in this route, such as the gangplank and the warehouse entrance, as well as at the official measuring and accounting posts. Naturally this procedure would be considerably complicated and lengthened if the warehouse were not immediately adjoining the dock.

loading and unloading had to be repeated many times before the commodities eventually were distributed at Rome. While this type of calculation is extremely speculative, it does suggest the enormous amounts of labor demanded by the system.

The trip up the Tiber in the *codicariae* offers another opportunity for quantification. Assuming an average tonnage of 70 tons per ship (Rickman 1980, 19), 6,043 Tiber trips would be required to transport the 423,000 metric tons of grain, oil, and wine to Rome. At a minimum round-trip time of one week, allowing time for loading and unloading, and assuming that this transport was spread out evenly over the entire year, a minimum of 116 *codicariae* would have been needed. Since the Tiber's ease of navigability varied throughout the course of the year, river transport was probably concentrated in the more favorable months. If the river shipping season were ten, eight, or six months long, the number of *codicariae* needed would have been 151, 189, or 252, respectively. How much of an underestimate these calculations are is indicated by Tacitus' comment that in A.D. 62 a tempest sank two hundred vessels at Portus and a fire destroyed an additional one hundred at Rome itself (*Annals* 15.18). All of the boats destroyed at Rome, and probably many of those lost at Portus, were *codicariae.*[73] Yet, despite the loss of three hundred boats, enough remained to ensure that there was no resultant food shortage (Tacitus *Annals* 15.18).

Another commodity imported to Rome in huge quantities during the Empire was marble and other decorative stones. While it is impossible to guess the total amount of marble imported for use in public and private building, a few case studies are suggestive. Trajan's forum made extensive use of foreign marbles. Its design included eighteen 50-ton cubes of Parian marble for Trajan's column; fifty cipollino marble columns; another fifty granite columns, weighing 40 tons each, for the basilica; sixteen columns of giallo antico marble from Chemtou; and many thousands of tons of other exotic marbles. Altogether it has been estimated that 50,000 tons of marble were imported.[74] At the standard

73. Casson firmly believes that all three hundred of these boats were *codicariae.* While the ones burned at Rome probably were, it seems likely that a good number of the ships sunk by the storm at Portus were other types of vessels.

74. All figures for Trajan's forum are taken from Frank 1940, 222.

250 tons per ship, Trajan's forum required over two hundred shiploads and over seven hundred riverboat-loads of marble.[75]

On a similar note, the Colosseum used about 200,000 tons of travertine over a four-year period (Cozzo 1970, 98). This stone probably traveled down the Tiber to Rome on the boats of the *codicarii* of the upper Tiber. At 70 tons per boat, transporting the travertine for the Colosseum would have taken 2,857 trips.[76] By the end of the first century A.D., Rome and Ostia had apparently developed marble yards where blocks of standard sizes and varieties were stockpiled. Eventually the marble yards in Rome, which were located in the Emporium district, became known as the Marmorata quarter. From quarry marks on the stones, it is evident that blocks could lie in these yards for many years prior to the time they were actually used in building. Two blocks of Numidian marble found at Ostia evidently lay in the yards for three hundred years before they were used (Ward-Perkins 1980, 327). These marble yards and the standardization of the blocks demonstrate considerable mass production of even exotic imported marbles and are suggestive of a very high volume of imports of decorative stones.

All of these calculations are probably underestimates. As previously mentioned, we have not taken into account oil used for noningestive purposes or other grains, such as barley. Certainly considerable spoilage and loss occurred during shipping and at all stages of transport, necessitating arrangements for overprovision of these commodities above and beyond the minimum requirements. There were innumerable minor goods also passing through the system, ranging from exotic foods to manufactured goods to luxury wares. The daily requirements of the city were frequently augmented by lavish imperial handouts at public feasts or religious festivals. In 46 B.C., in celebration of one

75. One cargo of Docimean marble shipwrecked at Punta Scifo has been estimated at 150 tons (Pensabene 1978, 107), while another shipwreck of Cipollino marble in the bay of Giardini only weighed 95 tons (Basile 1988, 138). Although it is impossible to generalize on the basis of only two ships, our standard ship size of 250 tons may well be too large. The limiting factors governing transport of marble by ship were probably not only weight but also the bulkiness of large slabs as well as the considerable danger to the ship caused by the shifting of the slabs in the hold.

76. Since the Tiber above Rome got shallower and narrower, these boats may well have been even smaller, entailing a proportionate increase in the number of trips.

of his triumphs, Julius Caesar is said to have given away 10 *modii* of grain (about 67 kg) and 10 Roman pounds of olive oil (about 3.3 kg) to every member of the Roman plebs then receiving the grain dole, a group of people who at this time may have numbered over three hundred thousand.[77] Only a few distributions of this scale would quickly boost the import calculations, and the emperors often exhibited such largesse.[78]

The confusion and bustle at Portus and Ostia would have been even more intense than we have described, because the ships tended to arrive in bunches or even great fleets rather than being spread evenly through the sailing season. If we accept that at the peak of the season, ships were arriving at Ostia and Portus far in excess of our notional average of seventeen ships per day, then it follows that in order to cope with the volume of traffic during that peak, labor provision, storage capacity, and river haulage must have been organized on a far grander scale than we have described. Seneca offers an eyewitness account of the arrival of a fleet of supply ships at Puteoli.

> Unexpectedly, today, Alexandrian ships appeared within sight, those which are usually sent ahead and announce the arrival of a fleet behind them; they call them mail-boats, a welcome sight in Campania. A vast mob stood on the docks at Puteoli and spotted the Alexandrians from the configuration of their sails, despite the great mob of ships. . . . In the midst of this turmoil, as everyone rushed to the water's edge, I took great pleasure in my leisure. (Seneca *Ep.* 77)

This passage reveals a number of important points. First, the arrival of the grain ships was unexpected; this stresses the uncertain nature of ancient sailing. Second, the fleet sent messenger boats ahead, clearly to give the port time to prepare for its arrival (and perhaps to allow time for people to gather from the countryside in expectation of employment unloading the ships). Finally, the arrival of the main supply fleets was exciting and important.

---

77. Suetonius *Julius Caesar* 38, 41. Conversion from Roman measures is based on tables in Foxhall and Forbes 1982.

78. On imperial distributions see Van Berchem 1939. Augustus, for example, twice gave grain distributions equivalent to a year's worth of the grain dole (in 23 B.C. and A.D. 6): see *Res Gestae* 15.1; Dio 55.26.

Food Supply and Labor Provision

As has been demonstrated in this chapter, the Roman supply system would have demanded thousands of unskilled laborers in Ostia, Portus, and Rome, especially at the peak periods of activity during the summer. The sporadic nature of this demand required a large number of unemployed, or at least underemployed, people to be available whenever demand surged. The only group of potential laborers that appears to have met these two requirements of size and constant availability is the urban plebs.[79] As P.A. Brunt has shown, the urban plebs cannot have subsisted solely on the grain dole. They would have both needed and wanted at least occasional employment as wage laborers.[80] While it would be theoretically possible for a segment of the urban populace to subsist on the grain dole, the urban plebs would have needed cash to pay for other basic essentials, such as lodging and clothes. They would also certainly have wanted to earn money to supplement their free diet of bread and water with other foods, such as wine, oil, fish, and the occasional vegetable or piece of meat.

The sheer number of workers required, together with the erratic nature of the demand, rules out the exclusive use of slave or criminal labor. Although some of the more permanent or skilled jobs were probably held by slaves, most of the labor cannot have been servile, because the great seasonal fluctuations in labor would have left the slave owners with masses of idle or severely underemployed slaves to be fed, clothed, and housed during the periods of low labor demand. Therefore much of this labor must have been provided by the urban plebs themselves. That they also worked in addition to receiving the dole is supported by Suetonius, who records that Augustus was concerned about the loss of work that occurred on the days when the plebs went to receive their ration. He attempted to alleviate this loss by distributing the grain three times a year rather than every month, but protests were so great that he abandoned the scheme (Suet. *Augustus* 40). There may be another reference to this loss of work in a letter of Cicero to Atticus, in which Cicero complains that the builders working on his house

79. On the urban plebs in general during the early empire see Yavetz 1988; Veyne 1990. On urban living conditions see Scobie 1986.

80. Brunt 1980. Although Brunt's article focuses on casual employment on imperial building projects, his arguments apply equally well to employment opportunities in the supply system of the city.

have temporarily left to go collect their grain dole.[81] Clearly substantial numbers of the urban plebs found employment on public works. That they did so is evidenced by Vespasian's famous rejection of a suggestion for a laborsaving device to move columns: he said that he had an obligation to feed the plebs.[82]

In general the supply system of Rome must have provided employment for thousands both at Rome and all over the Mediterranean, particularly in the regions that were major exporters of foodstuffs, such as southern Spain, North Africa, and Egypt. In each of these regions thousands of people were employed not only in farming but also in a variety of related occupations, such as making amphorae, operating presses, transporting the agricultural products by land and river, overseeing production and transport, and shipping the goods to Rome. Most of these people would have been aware that their livelihood was the result of the needs of the capital city and of the special interest and involvement of the emperors and of the state in ensuring an adequate supply of food. This awareness and the resulting gratitude is exemplified by an incident in which Augustus, who had been a prominent figure in the institutionalization of Rome's supply system, was sailing in the gulf of Puteoli near the very end of his life. As his ship passed by a newly arrived Alexandrian ship (quite possibly a grain freighter), the crew of the Alexandrian ship, crowned with garlands and burning incense, hailed Augustus with lavish praise and good wishes and declared that it was because of him that they lived, sailed the seas, enjoyed liberty, and made their fortunes (Suet. *Augustus* 98.2).

Conclusion

The size and complexity of both the guilds and imperial bureaucracy concerned with the supply of Rome, coupled with even minimalistic calculations of the scale of the goods that moved through this system, strongly suggest that the entire system was more complex and more

81. The meaning of this passage is uncertain; all the Latin says is that they went off *ad frumentum* (Cicero *Letters to Atticus* 14.3 = SB 357). Casson (1978, 47) suggests that the meaning could not be that they went off harvesting, since the letter was written at least a month before harvesting could have begun. His interpretation is that they went to buy corn. This passage is admittedly ambiguous, but it may well refer to the same problem that concerned Augustus.

82. Suetonius *Vespasian* 18. See Brunt 1980 for a more detailed discussion of this passage.

deliberately organized than has often been admitted. The supply of the capital city was clearly an issue of concern to the emperors, who expended huge resources to ensure that its inhabitants were fed.[83] The interest of the state was not limited to grain alone: the duties of the *praefectus annonae* and his subordinates clearly extended to other foodstuffs. In addition, the variety of officials concerned with often rather specialized commodities, such as wild beasts, is another indication of both the size of the system and the involvement of the state. Another notable aspect of the imperial administration was the considerable professionalism achieved by some of its officials, particularly middle- and lower-level ones, who seem to have made entire careers specializing in the supply of the city. The contacts and informal networks with guilds and merchants that these officials built up in one post undoubtedly carried over into subsequent ones and played a role in the smooth operation of the system. Although much attention, both ancient and modern, has focused on food riots and shortages,[84] a far more significant point is how well the system worked. Despite the shortages, there were no real instances of widespread starvation for hundreds of years. Overall, the logistical institutions of Rome were remarkably successful in achieving the difficult feat of feeding a million people year after year in a preindustrial society. The very success of the system and the enormous scale on which it operated imply a high degree of sophistication and organization. The size of this system demanded vast amounts of labor at all stages. Much of this labor was drawn from the freeborn population rather than from the slave sector, and this factor provides at least a partial counter to the popular image of a huge mass of idle urban plebs concerned only with "bread and circuses."[85] Many of them must have found at least occasional work in the organization that existed to pro-

83. Even Tiberius, who of the Julio-Claudians was the least interested in the people of Rome and who spent the most time away from the city, is reputed to have called the supply of Rome a particular concern of the *princeps* (Tacitus *Annals* 3.54). On Tiberius and Rome see Yavetz 1988, 103–13.

84. See, for example, Garnsey 1988, 198–211; Evans 1981.

85. Juvenal *Satires* 10.81. This image has haunted the urban plebs from antiquity to the present. Typical of modern historians who accept this view is Carcopino (1941, 210), who states, "In the city of Rome there were 150,000 complete idlers supported by the generosity of the public assistance." Both halves of this image are incorrect, since the plebs were not unemployed, nor did they spend all their time at public amusements. In the early empire, a mere 3 percent of the total populace could have attended the theaters at the same time (if all the theaters were in use simultaneously), 5 percent could fit into the Colosseum (in

vide subsidized or free handouts of food for them. Much of the information gathered in this chapter is fairly well known, but it is often presented separately; when put together, a coherent picture emerges of a system that was complex and sophisticated and in which the state must have played an active role. The perception that the network that supplied commodities to Rome was a random or improvised patchwork is at odds with the realities of the organization and scale of the system itself.

---

which most of the seats were reserved for the upper classes, with room for only about five thousand of the poor out of the Colosseum's total capacity of around fifty thousand), and although around two hundred thousand could be present at the Circus Maximus, there were only about twenty days per year on which races were held. However the plebs may have used their time, only a very small portion of it could have been spent at the games (Balsdon 1969).

CHAPTER SIX

Amusing the Masses: Buildings for Entertainment and Leisure in the Roman World

Hazel Dodge

Panem et circenses, "bread and circuses," were the two things that the Roman satirist Juvenal, writing in the late first and early second century A.D., said the Roman mob yearned for.[1] The significance of *panem* is dealt with by Greg Aldrete and David Mattingly elsewhere in this volume; the importance of entertainment and leisure in the Roman world can be judged by the plethora of theaters, amphitheaters, bath buildings, and the like that survive across the Empire. Huge amounts of money were poured into providing the cities of the Empire with fitting venues. The finance for these projects came from a variety of sources, but by the second century A.D. the elite had identified such facilities as appropriate vehicles for self-advancement. The financial input could vary from providing free oil or free entrance at the baths for a day to paying for the construction or decoration of a theater or providing all the performers and entertainers at the games.[2]

In this chapter, I shall describe the structures that were used to stage

1. Juvenal *Sat.* 10.80–91. This is obviously an oversimplification of the situation. See chap. 7 in this volume for the performers and performances associated with the physical structures that are the subject of this chapter. I thank David Potter and David Mattingly for the opportunity to contribute to this volume and for reading and commenting on a draft of the text. I am very grateful to Professor Kathleen Coleman, who has also read and commented on the text, saving me from many errors. Alison Wilkins drew most of the figures. I thank Jon Coulston for all his help, support, and advice, as always. Any remaining errors are my own.

2. This practice of civic munificence became more and more common in the imperial period, particularly in Asia Minor and North Africa.

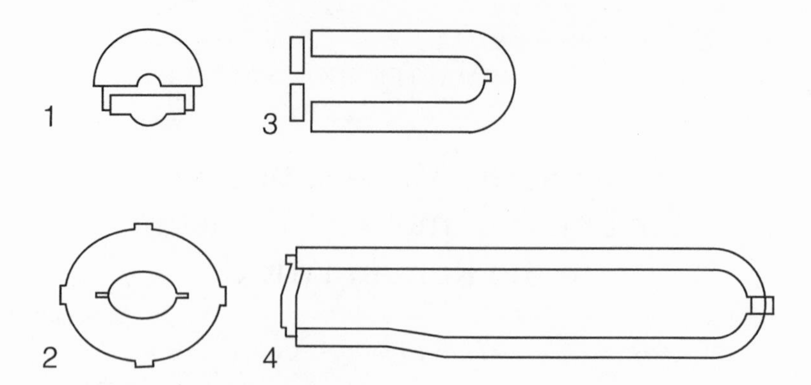

Fig. 14. The relative sizes of Roman entertainment buildings in Rome: (1) the theater of Marcellus; (2) the Colosseum; (3) the stadium of Domitian; (4) the Circus Maximus. (After Humphrey 1986, fig. 1.)

Roman entertainments, making some reference to the form of spectacles involved (fig. 14). The latter theme and the social history of Roman entertainers are more fully reviewed by David Potter in chapter 7.

The buildings associated with public entertainment and leisure were distinguished by their function and the activities that they housed, as much as by the building technology employed to construct them. Some structures had a very long history and were adapted over time as cultural and social changes occurred. There was also wide variation in the provision and form of these facilities across the Empire.

The Origins of the Games

Although religious in origin, the Roman games quickly acquired secular and political importance. Such mass public entertainment took a number of different forms: *ludi circenses* (chariot racing in the circus), *venationes* (games with animals, also in the circus, but later they took place in the amphitheater as well), and theatrical performances, *ludi scaenici.* The gladiatorial games were not part of the public games and had no religious association. These were *munera,* public spectacles. The early gladiatorial games were associated with aristocratic funerals, and by the Empire they took place in the amphitheater or the circus, though occasionally also in theaters or other public spaces (Humphrey 1988, 1153–54).

The contrast between Greek and Roman games is marked. The games in Greece essentially involved freeborn male citizens of individual city-states competing in athletic contests for symbolic and monetary prizes. Events in the Olympic Games and the other major contests at Nemea, Isthmia, and Delphi included running races over both long and short distances, with and without armor; boxing; and the pentathlon (discus, javelin, long jump, sprint, and wrestling).[3] Equestrian events, including two- and four-horse chariot races, were also contested. Such games were held at regular intervals at religious sanctuaries and remained essentially religious celebrations.

These contests continued to be important in the Greek-speaking part of the Roman world. Nero competed in the Olympic Games, having postponed them from A.D. 65 to A.D. 67 so that he could participate during a visit to Greece.[4] In A.D. 131/2 Hadrian instituted a new set of games, the Panhellenic Games in Athens, as part of the cultural organization of Greek cities, the Panhellenion.[5]

However, at Rome athletic games in the Greek style were slow to arrive and never achieved the popularity of the other *ludi* and *munera*. Competitors and performers in Roman games were for the most part slaves or criminals, competing out of necessity; free Roman citizens were stigmatized if they appeared on the stage or in the arena.[6] Many theatrical performers in the Empire formed trade guilds to protect their interests as they traveled around; these organizations are some of the best-attested guilds from antiquity.[7] The participants in the arena or circus usually performed for the organization to which they belonged, for example, a gladiator school or circus faction.[8] The performers, if they survived long enough, could gain in time their liberty as well as considerable sums of money and retire as wealthy people.[9]

---

3. See, for example, Swaddling 1980; Olivova 1984.

4. Suetonius *Life of Nero* 24. He took part in a chariot race, driving a ten-horse chariot. He fell from the chariot and did not actually complete the course. However, he was declared the winner because he would have won if he had not had the misfortune to fall!

5. Spawforth and Walker 1985, 1986.

6. Csapo and Slater 1995, 275–85.

7. Roueché 1993, 50–57

8. Cameron 1976; Humphrey 1986; Golvin 1988, 149–52; Roueché 1993, 49–80.

9. Wiedemann 1992, 120–24. A particularly successful charioteer in the second century was Gaius Appuleius Diocles (*CIL* 6.10048).

In the early Republic, games often formed the final part of the celebrations of a triumph of a victorious general, but from 366 B.C. these games became a separate institution and were particularly associated with Roman festivals.[10] First of all these were the *ludi Romani* associated with Juno, Jupiter, and Minerva, centering on 13 September, and commemorating the anniversary of the dedication of the Capitoline Temple. These games were unique for nearly 150 years, but after the end of the third century B.C., five more games were added: *ludi Plebei* (honoring Jupiter); *ludi Apollinares* (honoring Apollo); *ludi Megalenses* (honoring Cybele, the Great Mother goddess of Asia Minor, whose cult statue was removed from Pessinus according to the prophecy of the Sibylline Books); *ludi Ceriales* (honoring Ceres); and *ludi Florales* (honoring Flora).[11] At first the games lasted one day only, but by the late Republic seventy-four days in the year were devoted to public games. In the imperial period it became common practice for the emperor to put on special games to commemorate victories and anniversaries. It was an accepted obligation of members of the local elites throughout the empire to put on games for public entertainment at their own expense. Indeed, it was often a requirement while holding public office.

The Theater

Greek Origins

The earliest venues for the drama associated with Greek religious festivals were merely flat areas in the open, often near the sanctuary or temple of the deity concerned, with a convenient hillside close by for the audience, which was sometimes accommodated on temporary wooden stands. Gradually these areas became monumentalized and made permanent. The oldest known auditorium resembling the developed type of theater was the Pnyx in Athens, where the whole body of citizens met in assembly.[12] Another area associated with drama in Athens, one that would house the Theater of Dionysus, lies on the southern slopes of the Acropolis. The earliest phase of this area's use dates to the end of the sixth century B.C.; a disaster involving a temporary structure in the early fifth century B.C. is said to have induced the Athenians to give the auditorium a more permanent form. However, the oldest part of the

10. Humphrey 1988, 1153–54; Stambaugh 1988, 225–140.
11. Scullard 1981.
12. Travlos 1971, 466–67.

actual structure dates to the second half of the fourth century B.C. (Lawrence 1983, 362–64).

Greek drama and the associated buildings spread in the Mediterranean as the sphere of Greek influence broadened, and it was presumably through contact with the Greeks of southern Italy and Sicily that the idea of the theater and drama was first introduced to the Romans. At this stage it would be worthwhile to summarize the different characteristics of the Greek and Roman theaters (Bieber 1961, 189) (fig. 15).[13]

Characteristics of the Greek Theater

Theaters of either the Greek period or Greek inspiration can be recognized by a number of characteristics (fig. 15a).

1. They were built against a hillside without the use of vaulted substructures.
2. The auditorium, or *cavea,* extended past the shape of a semicircle.
3. The auditorium partially enclosed a flat circular area, the orchestra, where the action of the play took place.
4. Access to the orchestra from outside was via two open passages, *parodoi,* on either side of the *cavea.*
5. In the early theaters there was no stage building.

It should be emphasized that these are common elements and that there was a great deal of variation in the plan, size, and features of a Greek theater.

Various technical terms are used to describe the different parts of the *cavea* of both the Greek and Roman theater. The *cavea* was divided by horizontal walkways (Greek *diazoma,* Latin *praecinctio*) into the *media* and *ima cavea.* Sometimes a third, upper section of seating was present, the *summa cavea.* The seating itself was divided into wedge-shaped areas (Greek *kerekides,* Latin *cunei*) by stairways.[14]

The architectural history of the Greek theater was dictated by changes in dramatic technique principally in Athens (Pickard-Cambridge 1988). At first, all the action took place in the orchestra, and the

13. Bieber 1961 is the only standard work on the subject of Greek and Roman theater. It is still useful but now rather out-of-date.

14. Bieber 1961, xii–xiii.

backdrop was provided by the surrounding natural scenery. (This accounts for the spectacular setting of some Greek theaters.) The development of some form of stage building for scenery can be traced back to the later fifth century B.C. The chorus and actors performed on the circular piece of ground that comprised the orchestra, the name of which means literally "dancing place"; this had been the original function of the orchestra when dancing and singing made up the entire performance. No raised stage was required, but a background of scenery was provided; for example, in the Theater of Dionysus at Athens, the back wall of the stoa associated with the Temple of Dionysus and the theater was used to hang scenery on.[15]

Gradually the stage building took on a more formalized design. From the Hellenistic period, it became the practice to provide an artificial backdrop, a *scene.* As well as allowing the use of different scenery, the *scene* also facilitated such devices as *deus ex machina,* where a particular character (usually a deity) could appear from above to the rest of the company. From the *scene* the more developed idea of a raised stage apparently developed. Epidaurus, in the Argolid, has one of the best surviving theaters in Greek world. Built by Polyclitus the Younger in the later fourth century B.C., it provides a good example of developments in theater design at this time. The auditorium has two distinct slopes, the upper part being steeper. The *scene* is ruined, but many scholars date it to the original construction. If this dating is correct (and it is disputed), the theater at Epidaurus provides the earliest example of an important development, that of a raised stage, the *proscaenium* (Lawrence 1983, 364–68).

The *proscaenium* was usually stone, often incorporating rows of short columns, and stood on a low stylobate several meters in front of the *scene* wall, the whole structure being normally around three to four meters in height. Vitruvius states that the roof of the proscenium was the stage on which the actors moved. Archaeology strongly suggests that from the second century B.C. this was true.[16]

---

15. Lawrence 1983, 363–64. This is an area of hot debate among scholars as it relies on the marriage of the archaeological evidence (which given the subsequent history of many of these structures is very difficult to interpret) and what the plays themselves are apparently implying.

16. Vitruvius *Concerning Architecture* 6.2; Bieber 1961, 54–79 (classical theater), 108–28 (Hellenistic theater); Lawrence 1983, 364–68. For the height of the proscenium see Pickard-Cambridge 1946, 192.

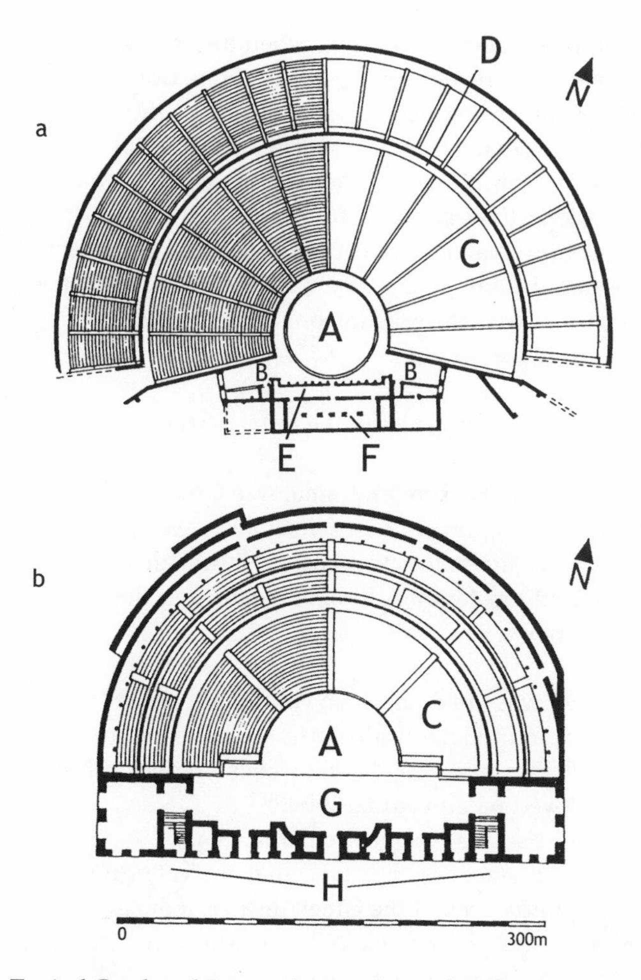

Fig. 15. Typical Greek and Roman theater plans (after Ward-Perkins 1981, fig. 163): *a,* Epidaurus, mid-fourth century B.C.; *b,* Orange, first century A.D. A = orchestra, B = *parados,* C = *cuneus,* D = *diazoma* or *praecinctio,* E = *proscaenium,* F = *scene,* G = *pulpitum* or stage, H = *scaenae frons.*

The Hellenistic-period theater at Priene in Asia Minor clearly demonstrates the way in which the use of the building influenced changes in design in both the auditorium and the *scene.* The structure originally dates from the fourth century B.C., and special seats with backrests *(prohedria)* were placed around the orchestra for city magistrates and other dignitaries. All the action took place in the orchestra, and there was probably a *scene* that functioned as a backdrop. At the beginning of the second century B.C., when the still extant *proscaenium* and *scene* were constructed, some parts of the performance must have taken place on the *proscaenium*. The front wall of the upper *scene* was pierced by three openings, and access from the ground was via a staircase. The large openings made possible a variety of scenic effects, and doors at the side allowed actors to approach the stage from several directions. From the later second century B.C., all performances were held on the stage building, and a new *prohedria* was built five rows up from the orchestra so that the action on the stage was at the eye level of the most privileged spectators.[17]

Characteristics of the Roman Theater

The Roman theater, like Roman drama, was Greek in origin, but in its earliest known examples and in Vitruvius' description (*Concerning Architecture* 5.6), it differs in several aspects from all known Greek and Hellenistic-period theaters.[18] A Roman theater had the following characteristics (fig. 15b).

1. The theater was often raised on vaulted substructures so that it no longer required a hillside for its construction (though, obviously, hillsides could cut down on construction costs and were still employed wherever possible).[19]
2. The *cavea* was usually semicircular in shape.
3. There was a stage, or *pulpitum*, that projected much further than the *proscaenium* of the Greek theater, reducing the orchestra to a semicircle. The *pulpitum* was low (c. 1.5 meters high), usually with a solid front wall.
4. The action no longer took place in the orchestra.
5. The orchestra was part of the auditorium (Vitruvius *Concerning Architecture* 6.2), the paving often incorporating broader steps

17. Akurgal 1993, 196–201. While there is no doubt about the sequence of the changes to the theater at Priene, there is much debate about the dating of those changes. Lawrence (1983, 368) postulates a date for the stage as late as the early second century B.C. De Bernardi-Ferrero (1966–74, 4:241) gives a date of 250–225 B.C. for the construction of the *cavea* and for the first stage of the theater. Architectural moldings have been dated to the early third century B.C.; see Shoe 1936.

18. See in general Mitens 1988; Sear 1990.

19. The first known theater raised up on substructures is that at Teano built at the end of the second century B.C.; it formed part of a sanctuary, and a temple was placed at the back of the *cavea*. See De Caro and Cireco 1981, 236–37.

for the accommodation of movable seating for distinguished members of the audience.[20]

6. There was always a stage building, often with an elaborately decorated back wall, the *scaenae frons*. The stage building rose to the height of, and was attached to, both sides of the *cavea* to create an enclosed building. Vaulted passages were necessary to make the orchestra accessible at the point of junction covering the *parodoi* of the Greek theater. The elevated flat areas above these passages, *versurae*, provided special seating areas for local dignitaries, somewhat akin to private boxes at the sides of the stage in modern theaters.[21]

The origin of these Roman features is conjectural, but it is clear that they were not all the result of a steady evolution in the design of the Greek and Hellenistic theater. As late as the second century B.C., long after adaptations of Greek plays were first performed in Rome, the Large Theater at Pompeii was built on a purely Greek plan.[22] The solution must be partly sought in the long period when Roman theaters were constructed of wood, and it has been suggested that the farces popular in southern Italy and much-performed in Rome, the Greek *phlyakes* and the Oscan *Atellanae*, may have influenced stage construction. Vase paintings depict scenes from the *phlyakes* showing actors on a wooden stage, which varies in height.[23]

20. For example, as preserved at Sabratha and Lepcis Magna in Tripolitania, Vienne in Gaul, and Merida in Spain.

21. Bieber (1961, 189) makes the point that the Roman theater is much more of a class theater with more seats for local dignitaries and that where the audience sat depended on their status. The *lex Iulia theatralis* of Augustus (Suetonius *Augustus* 44.1) certainly meant that in Rome you were seated in the theater according to your status within society; this also applied to the amphitheater but apparently not so much to seating arrangements in the circus. How far-reaching this legislation was in both time and geography is not really known. See Rawson 1987; Scnurr 1992.

22. Mitens 1993. Theaters of more Greek design were still built in the eastern provinces in the Roman period; an example was at Caunos in southwest Turkey.

23. Bieber 1961, 129–46 (for the *phlyakes* and Atellan farces), 167–89 (for theater development in the Republic); Mitens 1993; Lawrence 1983, 368. A terracotta relief (c. 300 B.C.) from a southern Italian town and now in the Santangelo Collection in the National Museum of Naples apparently depicts a permanent stage building of Roman type; see Boethius 1978, fig. 180.

One of the basic distinctions between a Greek and a Roman theater advanced by the modern textbooks is that the auditorium of a Greek theater is extended beyond the shape of a semicircle around a circular orchestra, while a Roman theater had a D-shaped, or semicircular, *cavea* and a semicircular orchestra. This appears to be a fair distinction on comparison of the theater at Epidaurus with those at Aspendus or Orange. However, there are a number of D-shaped theaters from the Hellenistic world, particularly in Sicily and the Greek west; an example is Hieron's theater at Syracuse, constructed in the second half of the third century B.C. (and incidentally one of the largest in the Greek world).[24] The theater at Metapontum in southern Italy, dated to the end of fourth century B.C., may represent the earliest example of a Greek theater with a semicircular orchestra.[25] In Asia Minor, the Hellenistic theater at Miletus seems to have had a semicircular orchestra.[26] It is interesting to note in this context that the first permanent theater in Rome, built by Pompey, was supposed to have been copied from the Greek theater at Mytilene on the island of Lesbos.[27] The development of the stage building and the movement of the action from the orchestra onto the raised *proscaenium* or *pulpitum* may have influenced the design of the *cavea*. When all or most of the action took place in the orchestra, the performance was visible from all seats. However, once the use of an elevated stage became common, many of the audience members seated at the ends of the *cavea* in a Greek-style theater would have had a much restricted view of the performance, looking on sideways or even from behind; the D-shaped, or semicircular, design certainly rectifies this problem.

Vitruvius mentions a colonnade or portico behind the stage building, a *porticus post scaenam*.[28] One example of this arrangement was at Lepcis Magna, where the portico surrounds a temple dedicated to the Dii Augusti, the deified members of the imperial family. A similar

24. Wilson 1990, 60–63.

25. Wilson (1990, 68) suggests that it may represent an early prototype of the strictly semicircular theater.

26. Akurgal 1993, 207–9; Krauss 1973. The theater originally dates to the fourth century B.C.

27. Plutarch *Life of Pompey* 42.2. Though, as Mitens (1993, 100) points out, there is no similarity at all to be detected from the archaeological remains.

28. Vitruvius *Concerning Architecture* 5.9. He says people could retire to this area if the weather interrupted the performance, but it could also be used for stage props.

arrangement can be seen associated with the Large Theater at Pompeii.[29]

Rome and Italy

The earliest theaters in Italy were, of course, those built by the Greek colonies in the south and in Sicily, for example, the theaters at Syracuse, Catana, and Metapontum. The majority of these date to the fourth to third centuries B.C., and many were remodeled in the Roman period.[30] Nearly all theater building of the imperial period in Italy dates to Augustus and the first century A.D.; very few date to the second century. The latest theater built in Italy is that at Ventimiglia (late second/early third century A.D.).[31]

In 154 B.C. the construction of a permanent theater in Rome by the censors was blocked by the senate under the consul P. Cornelius Scipio Nasica, and from then on spectators were apparently barred from remaining seated during performances.[32] From this time, by law (presumably before this by custom), all theaters built at Rome were temporary wooden structures, demolished after the conclusion of the festival for which they were erected. There is much literary evidence for these temporary structures, which became increasingly sumptuous in the late Republic (Boethius 1978, 201–3). Pliny the Elder describes the structure erected by Marcus Aemilius Scaurus during his aedileship of 58 B.C. Despite its temporary nature, it was clearly a magnificent structure, with marble columns and gilded decoration.[33]

Tacitus remarks that in the end it proved more economical to build a permanent theater than to go to the expense of these temporary struc-

---

29. For the Lepcis Magna theater see Caputo 1987; for the theater at Pompeii see Coarelli 1976, 152–55. At the time of the volcanic eruption in A.D. 79, the portico was used for gladiatorial training.

30. Mitens 1993 lists some of the modern archaeological publications on the subject.

31. Cavalieri Manasse, Massari, and Rossinari 1982, 217.

32. Valerius Maximus *Memorable Deeds and Sayings* 2.4.2. According to Valleius Paterculus (*History of Rome* 2.15.3) this theater was to be located on the southwest slopes of the Palatine.

33. Pliny the Elder *Natural History* 36.113–15. Other temporary structures mentioned and described in the literary sources are the theater constructed by Lucius Mummius in 145–144 B.C. after his victory in Greece and that constructed by Claudius Pulcher in 99 B.C. (Pliny *Natural History* 35.102).

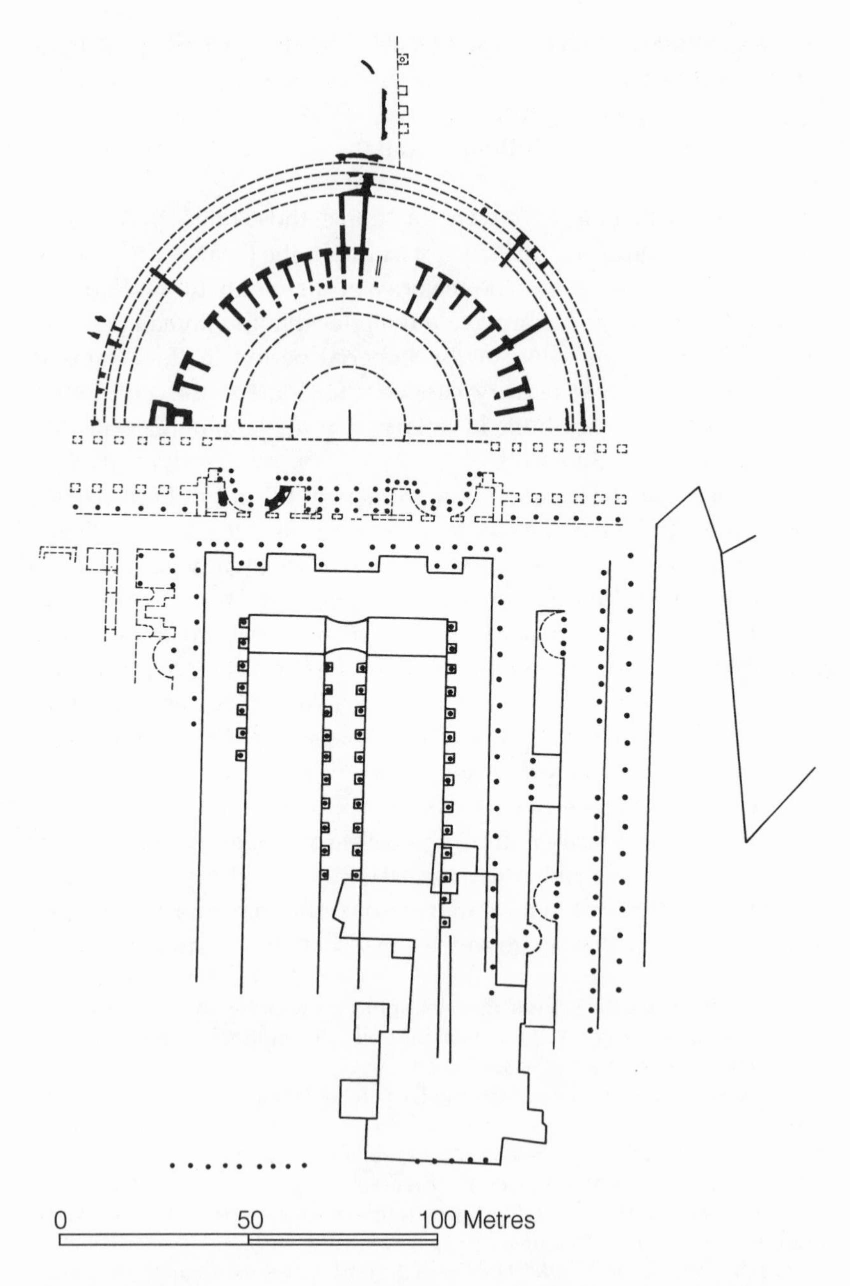

Fig. 16. The theater of Pompey (first century B.C.). Plan reconstructed from actual state, old drawings, and fragments of the Severan map of Rome [*Forma Urbis Romae*].

tures that were demolished each year.[34] The first permanent theater was dedicated by Pompey in the Campus Martius in 55 B.C., though he claimed that the theater structure was a monumental stairway to the Temple of Venus Victrix. Tertullian actually says that Pompey built the Temple of Venus in order to elude the senate's ban.[35]

The plan of Pompey's theater is known from the Severan marble plan (or *Forma Urbis Romae,* dated to the early third century A.D.), and some of the substructures are preserved in the cellars of later buildings in the Campus Martius; the plan is certainly preserved in the later street plan (fig. 16). The theater was built of Roman concrete faced with *opus reticulatum.* It had a semicircular orchestra and *cavea.* From the *Forma Urbis* it appears to have a low, wide stage. The shrine of Venus was axially placed at the back of the *cavea* along with a number of other shrines to Virtus, Honor, and Felicitas. Beyond the stage building was a large colonnaded portico with gardens, where works of art were displayed.[36]

Pompey's theater was followed by the Theater of Balbus in 19 B.C. and the Theater of Marcellus, dedicated in 13 or 11 B.C.[37] The latter building was constructed over the eastern end of the area of the Circus Flaminius, and the semicircular *cavea* was supported on vaulted substructures of concrete faced with *opus reticulatum.* The stage building still lies buried, but to judge from the Severan marble map of Rome, it was, and remained through successive restorations, a very simple building. The facade of the *cavea* was built of travertine and comprised a system of superimposed arches framed within the compartments of orders that were purely decorative. The lower story is Doric and the upper is Ionic, which foreshadows the decorative scheme of the Colos-

---

34. Tacitus *Annals* 14.20–21; he says it was feared that if people were provided with seats in the theater they might be tempted to spend all day in indolence. There was always concern that the construction of permanent theaters would lead to riots and sedition; see Nippel 1995.

35. Hanson 1959, 43–55; Tertullian *On the Public Shows* 10. It was built partly to commemorate his eastern campaigns, although he was not actually hailed a *triumphator* that year (Pliny *Natural History* 34.36; 36.113–15).

36. The ancient sources are Plutarch *Life of Pompey* 42; Pliny *Natural History* 7.34; 34.41. For the architecture and plan see Boethius 1978, 205–6. The stage building was elaborate by the early third century A.D.; Boethius suggests that it was constructed of wood initially. For the *scaenae frons* see Sear 1993.

37. The Theater of Balbus was built in the southern Campus Martius, and its remains lie beneath the Palazzo Caetani. For a reconstruction of the theatre of Marcellus see Connolly and Dodge 1998, 186–88.

seum ninety years later; on comparison with the later building it has been suggested that the theater had a third story that now no longer survives. This may have been of stone or timber (Ward-Perkins 1981, 26–28).

In the late Republic in central Italy, Campania, and Samnium, a particular type of theater complex developed which had no Greek antecedents, though it perpetuated, at least in its physical form, a major Greek association: that of drama and religion. These are the theater-temple complexes such as those at Gabii, Pietrabbondante, and Tivoli.[38]

At Gabii is a second-century B.C. complex with a temple possibly dedicated to Juno. The temple stood approximately in the center of a long rectangular *temenos* (sacred enclosure or precinct) The entire front of the *temenos* was taken up by a monumental semicircular staircase measuring about sixty meters in diameter. About twelve rows of steps or seats led up to the level of the temple podium. A wall cut off the orchestra, and it is thought that this wall belonged to some kind of stage building.[39]

The Temple of Hercules Victor at Tivoli was very similar to the sanctuary at Gabii but was much more elaborate in design. The entire complex was built on an imposing series of vaulted concrete substructures.[40] At the back of the sacred area was the temple, surrounded on three sides by two-storied colonnades. The fourth side was cut into by a large semicircular staircase of twelve steps on the axis of the temple, and there is evidence for a stage building.

High on a mountain hillside in Samnium, twenty kilometers northeast of Isernia, Pietrabbondante was originally a Samnite sanctuary, but under Hellenistic influence two temples with a theater placed in front were built. Another example of this type of complex can be seen in the Sanctuary of Fortuna Primigenia at Palestrina.[41]

The inclusion of a shrine or temple in theaters in the Roman world is not an uncommon arrangement. The theater at Lepcis Magna in Tripolitania was built in the Augustan period, dedicated in A.D. 1–2 by a member of the local wealthy elite, Annobal Tapapius Rufus. At the top of the *cavea*, on the central axis, was a small shallow temple, at the

38. Hanson 1959; Coarelli 1987; Mitens 1993, 95–97.

39. Hanson 1959, 29–31; Boethius 1978, 165–66.

40. Hanson 1959, 31–32; Boethius 1978, 167–69.

41. Boethius 1978, 169–74; Mitens 1993, 95–97.

same level as the portico surrounding the top of the *cavea*. The shrine was dedicated by Annobal Ruso in A.D. 35–36 to Ceres, the goddess of cereals, who was a popular deity in North Africa and was assimilated with the Phoenician goddess Tanit.[42] Similar shrines occur in the theaters at Dougga, Timgad, and Cherchel. Instances of a *cavea* shrine are rarer in other provinces, but at Vienne on the Rhône a shallow temple with a tetrastyle porch was built at the top of the *cavea* c. 15 B.C., and this exceeds in size the North African examples.[43]

Theaters and the Empire

Theater buildings are found all over the Empire, but their form can vary quite considerably. In Greece and Asia Minor most Greek theaters were adapted, many retaining their over-semicircular plan but being provided with a Roman style of stage building. Of course, there were many new structures built also. Further east, in Syria and Arabia, some of the earliest theaters are connected with Herod the Great—for example, the theater at Caesarea Maritima and the mud-brick theater near his winter palace in the Wadi Qelt near Jericho.[44] A particularly fine theater, built up completely on substructures, was constructed in the second century A.D. at Bostra, the provincial capital of Roman Arabia.

In Spain many of the theaters were built in the first century A.D. One of the earliest was that at Merida, donated by Agrippa in 16/15 B.C.[45] In Africa the earliest theater (apart from the Greek and Hellenistic theaters of Cyrenaica and Egypt) was constructed at Cherchel by Juba II at the end of the first century B.C.[46] Apart from such examples as the theater at Lepcis Magna (dated by inscription [*IRT* 321–23] to A.D. 1–2), most theaters in Roman Africa are dated to the second century. In Gaul and Britain Roman-style theaters were constructed (e.g., at Arles, Orange, and Lyon in France and at Canterbury and Colchester in Britain), but a more common practice, particularly in northern Gaul, was the con-

42. For Annobal Tapapius Rufus see *IRT* 321–23; for the construction of the shrine by Annobal Ruso, *IRT* 269; for the theater in general, Caputo 1987, particularly 24–28 for the shrine.

43. Hanson 1959, 67–70.

44. Ward-Perkins 1981, 310–12. For Herod in general see Holum et al. 1988.

45. Keay 1998, 56.

46. Picard 1976, 386–97. He was also responsible for the curious elliptical amphitheater (Golvin 1988, 112–13).

struction of a hybrid form of theater (often referred to as a Gallo-Roman form) to stage both theatrical and amphitheatrical performances—for example, Les Arènes in Paris and the theater at Verulamium (St. Albans) in southern Britain.[47]

Two particularly well preserved examples of Roman theaters are at Orange in the south of France (first century A.D.) and at Aspendus in southern Turkey (mid–second century A.D.). Both have semicircular auditoria and surviving stage buildings and are partially built against a hillside.[48]

The *cavea* of the theater at Aspendus was divided horizontally into two major parts by a *diazoma*—the lower *cavea* having twenty rows of seats, the upper twenty-one. The seats were of very good quality limestone, probably brought from the Taurus Mountains to the north. This stone was also used for many of the decorative details, especially on the exterior wall of the *scaenae frons*. The *cavea* was also divided by stairways into ten *cunei* in the lower part and twenty-one in the upper. A vaulted gallery ran around the *cavea* at the level of the *diazoma*, the primary function of which was not to facilitate circulation, though it must have helped to alleviate crowd congestion, but to provide structural support for the lower seats of the upper *cavea*. Around the top of the *cavea* was a gallery of fifty-nine vaults, providing an area in which to take a gentle promenade during a break in the performance and to find shelter in case of rain.[49]

The stage building of the theater still stands to its full height, the same height as the *cavea*. Five doors opened from the outside onto the stage itself. The stage would have been of wood and does not survive. Five smaller doors in the lowest part of the structure opened into the area beneath the actual stage (possibly to allow the building to be used for displays of animals). The inner back wall of the stage building, which formed the backdrop for the action on the stage, was originally entirely covered in marble and very richly decorated with two ranges of forty freestanding columns and numerous pedimented niches. The

47. For a general discussion of these structures see Grenier 1958, 754–65; Golvin 1988, 225–36.

48. Ward-Perkins 1981, 231–32, 302; Akurgal 1993, 333–35.

49. Vitruvius (*Concerning Architecture* 5.9) emphasizes the importance of colonnades attached to theaters to provide the audience shelter away from the performance area. See also my n. 29.

lower order was Ionic, and the upper, Corinthian. Much of the decoration no longer survives, but it followed a scheme of projecting orders with columns. The back wall of the stage building behind this applied decoration was flat, with no deep receding niches. Around the top of the *cavea* on the outside are sets of corbels, which would have carried the ropes for awnings (*velaria*).

The Stage Building of a Roman Theater

The application of architectural decoration as a permanent background to a raised stage first becomes habitual in the Roman type of theater—for example, in the theaters at Segesta and Tyndaris in Sicily, both dated early in the first century B.C. (Lawrence 1983, 372). Such elaborate decoration was also part of the temporary structures, if Pliny's description of Scaurus' theater (*NH* 36.113–15) is to be believed. The riot of sculptural details must have caused a distraction to the audience, but it did largely dispense with the need for scenery. Scholars have divided Roman stage buildings into two categories depending on whether the wall behind the decoration is flat or has curves and niches (Ward-Perkins 1981, 259–60). The so-called eastern type is distinguished by its continued emphasis on the rectilinear facade articulated about its three main and two minor monumental entrances, with applied columnar *aediculae* (small, ornamental, columnar niches) and continuous orders as at Aspendus. In the "western" type of stage building the wall is developed in depth with an elaborate alternation of projecting and reentrant features that throws emphasis on the decorative screen itself, as, for example, at Orange and Sabratha. All the stage buildings in Turkey are, logically enough, of the eastern type. However, this correlation between building type and geography does not work everywhere in the Empire; the vast majority of the Roman stage buildings in Syria (e.g., that at Bostra) are of the western type. As two different types of design, these categories can stand, but as geographical types they demonstrably do not.[50]

---

50. As Ward-Perkins (1981, 261) points out, the presence of so-called western stage buildings may reflect areas that did not have a long and essentially Greek theatrical tradition and that had to draw directly on the traditions of Rome and Italy.

Acoustics

A very important aspect of the design of ancient theaters was the provision of good acoustics.[51] The acoustics of the Greek theater at Epidaurus are still excellent today and rely entirely on the design and shape of the *cavea.* The acoustics of the Roman theater at Aspendus were boosted by the provision over the stage building of a wooden roof that was built out from the inner wall with a backward slope; this no longer survives. The prime purpose of this roof was not to provide protection for the actors but to act as a sounding board. With such perfect acoustics—normal speech in the orchestra can easily be heard at the gallery level—it is not surprising that a myth is associated with the construction of the theater at Aspendus and its acoustic qualities.[52] Another theater where it is today possible to test the acoustics is at Ephesus, where speech on the stage can be heard by an audience sitting in the top seats of the *cavea.* Unfortunately, as soon as a building falls into any degree of ruin, the acoustic qualities suffer considerably. Vitruvius discusses the use of sounding vessels in theaters to improve their acoustic capabilities. These, he says, can be made of bronze or earthenware and should be placed among the seats in the *cavea* (*Concerning Architecture* 5.5). No such vessels have been found from any ancient theater. However, compartments whose purpose is rather enigmatic if not used to house such sounding vessels are present at the *diazoma* level of the second-century A.D. theater at Aezani. A similar arrangement has been suggested for the theaters at Scythopolis (Bethshan) and Caesarea in Palestine.[53]

Velaria

From the mid–first century B.C., awnings, or *velaria,* were customarily used to cover the seating of temporary theater structures in Rome.[54] This practice became common in the permanent theater. Their use in

51. Vitruvius *Concerning Architecture* 5.3.5, 8; Bieber 1961, 127, 187–88; Plommer 1983.

52. Akurgal 1993, 334–35. The story goes that the king, wishing to find a suitable husband for his daughter, held a competition in which the victor would be the man who produced the most useful service for the city. The builder of the theater won the admiration of the king because of the theater's superb acoustics, thereby winning the competition.

53. Plommer 1983.

54. Lucretius *The Nature of Things* 4.75–83 comments on the patterns made by the sun shining through yellow, red, and purple canvas.

amphitheaters will be discussed later in this chapter. Physical evidence for their use in theaters can be seen at Aspendus, where corbels for masts project around the outside of the *cavea.* Interestingly, at Orange similar corbels are placed on the exterior of the stage building and were presumably part of the setup covering the stage.

Adaptation of Theaters

Nearly all the Greek theaters in the Mediterranean underwent some kind of remodeling in the Roman period, to give extra capacity and particularly to add a Roman style of stage building. Examples are the theaters at Ephesus in Turkey, the Theater of Dionysus in Athens, and the theater at Taormina in Sicily. Obviously the precise details of remodeling varied from one structure to another. Sometimes the *parodoi* were retained in a vestigial form, but an elaborate stage building was nearly always added.

Many theaters were further adapted to provide facilities for performances other than plays and comedies. These are dealt with in the next section.

The Odeum

The odeum (Greek *odeion*) was essentially a small-scale theater building that was entirely roofed. The incidence of odea is far less than that of theaters, and they tend to be more common in the east. A good example of an odeum in the west can be found at Lyon in France. More serious cultural performances, such as concerts, lectures, and poetry readings, were the domain of the odea, though these buildings could also serve public or civic functions.

In the Hellenistic east the *bouleuterion,* or council house, of a city often took the form of a small covered theater-like building, as do, for example, those at Miletus and Priene.[55] The mid-second century A.D. structure in the State Agora at Ephesus, erected by Publius Vedius Antoninus c. A.D. 150 and with an estimated capacity of fourteen hundred people, probably served as a venue for such refined entertainment as well as for council meetings.[56]

---

55. Lawrence 1983, 352–57; Akurgal 1933, 213–16 (Miletus), 194–95 (Priene).

56. *IE* 460. Its location next door to the Prytaneion, or town hall, strengthens this argument. There was an earlier *bouleuterion* in the city from the first century B.C., but its location is unknown.

In Athens two similar buildings were erected in the Roman period. Agrippa built an odeum adjacent to the Gymnasium of Ptolemy in the Agora (c. 15 B.C.).[57] It was essentially a large gabled hall surrounded by a roofed ambulatory. Except for a shallow entrance hall, the entire structure was taken up by the seating and stage of the concert hall. It was exactly square (twenty-five meters by twenty-five meters) with a height from orchestra to ceiling of twenty-three meters, and it would have seated about one thousand people. The unsupported span of the timber roof was remarkable, the only comparable building of this time being the Small Covered Theater at Pompeii with a span of 27.60 meters.[58] However, both these buildings were surpassed by the Odeum of Herodes Atticus built about A.D. 140 on the south side of the Acropolis in Athens. Herodes Atticus was a wealthy patron of the arts who was responsible for the construction and refurbishment of many structures in Greece (e.g., the fountain at Olympia and the Peirene Fountain and odeum at Corinth) and for the restoration of the stadium in Athens. His odeum was far larger than previous ones, seating about five thousand people, with a roof span of thirty-eight meters. The internal arrangement is that of a theater (Ward-Perkins 1981, 271).

The Amphitheater and Gladiatorial Displays

Origins of the Gladiatorial Games

Gladiatorial games *(munera)* had a completely different origin from the *ludi.* They seem to have developed in connection with aristocratic funeral games. Tertullian wrote at the end of the second century A.D. that "men believed that the souls of the dead were propitiated by human blood, and so at funerals they sacrificed prisoners of war or slaves of poor quality bought for the purpose."[59] The first recorded gladiatorial show in the city of Rome is attributed to the ex-consul D. Iunius Brutus Pera and his brother in 264 B.C. They held games in the Forum Boarium in honor of their father; three pairs of gladiators took part (Valerius Maximus *Memorable Deeds and Sayings* 2.4.7). Over the

57. Ward-Perkins 1981, 265–67; Camp 1986, 184.

58. Agrippa's odeum was radically remodeled in the second century A.D. after the roof collapsed.

59. Tertullian *On the Public Shows* 12; Humphrey 1988, 1159–63; Wiedemann 1992, 1–54. See chap. 7 in this volume for further references and a more detailed treatment of the games.

next two centuries the scale and frequency of gladiatorial shows steadily increased. Livy records of 174 B.C.:

> several gladiatorial shows were given. . . . Some were small. But one was notable above all the rest, namely, that given by Titus Flaminius to mark the death of his father. There was a public distribution of meat, a feast, and theatrical performances. The whole ceremony lasted four days. The climax of the show, which was large for the period, was fighting between seventy-four gladiators spread over three days. (Livy, *History of Rome* 41.28)

In 65 B.C. Julius Caesar gave elaborate funeral games for his long-dead father, which involved 320 pairs of gladiators; condemned criminals were also forced to fight wild beasts.[60]

In the city of Rome in the late Republic and early Principate the religious and commemorative elements of gladiatorial shows competed with the increasing importance of the political and spectacular. Gladiatorial shows were public performances, and before specific monuments were constructed to house them, they were held in the social and ritual center of the city, the forum, specifically, at least in the late Republic, in the Forum Romanum (Vitruvius *Concerning Architecture* 5.1). Under the Forum Romanum in Rome, archaeologists have found a series of well-planned corridors with the remains of mechanical hoists that would have been used to introduce animals and gladiators from beneath the Forum pavement.[61] The Forum probably continued to be used as an arena into the early imperial period, after which time other venues were more appropriate.[62]

Over time gladiatorial shows ceased to be held exclusively in a funerary context, but they were very rarely incorporated into the *ludi* in honor of various deities. The provision of a show became an obligation (or expectation) of certain public officeholders.

60. Pliny *Natural History* 33.53; Plutarch *Life of Caesar* 5. For *munera* and society in Rome see Edmondson 1996.

61. Carettoni 1956–58; Golvin 1988, 56–58; Welch 1991, 274–75 ; Welch 1994, 69–78.

62. The latest explicit reference to games in the Forum Romanum is when Tiberius hold games in honor of his father in the mid-twenties (Suetonius *Life of Tiberius* 7.2). By this time the Forum had become an architectural showpiece, unsuitable for these kinds of display and this size of audience.

Origins of the Amphitheater

The earliest known amphitheaters occur in Campania (central southern Italy), and it is normally assumed that the amphitheater is a purely Italo-Campanian monument without Greek architectural antecedents (Welch 1994). However, this does not explain how such a fully developed architectural form could have "suddenly" appeared. Recently it has been suggested that the early amphitheaters were modeled on the wooden structure erected in the Forum Romanum, which scholars have suggested was more or less oval in plan from the second century B.C.[63] In this context it should be remembered that temporary wooden structures for viewing contact sports, such as wrestling and boxing, existed in Greek and Hellenistic contexts. A recent find in the Roman forum at Corinth seems to have been such a structure, which took the basic form of an oval terrace cut into the bedrock. Associated postholes suggest that temporary wooden seating was erected when necessary (Williams and Russell 1981, 15–21).

It is not by accident that most of the earliest amphitheaters appeared in towns in Italy that had particularly close ties with Rome—notably, *coloniae* founded for army veterans, such as Capua (colonized in B.C. 83) and Paestum (colonized in 273 B.C.). The same may be true in the provinces (Welch 1991, 277).

In Rome the first permanent amphitheater was that of T. Statilius Taurus, dedicated in 30 or 29 B.C. in the southern Campus Martius. It was built of stone and wood and it was destroyed by fire in A.D. 64.[64] However, Pliny the Elder describes an extraordinary building put up by C. Scribonius Curio in 52 B.C. for the funeral games in honor of his father.

> [He] built close to each other two very large wooden theaters, each poised and balanced on a revolving pivot. During the forenoon, a performance of a play was given in both of them and they faced in opposite directions so that the two casts should not drown out each other's words. Then, at a certain point the theaters were revolved (and it is agreed that after the first few days

63. Golvin 1988, 56–58; Welch 1991, 274–76.

64. Dio *History of Rome* 51.23.1; Suetonius *Life of Augustus* 30.8; Golvin 1988, 52–53.

this was done with some of the spectators actually remaining in their seats), their corners met, and thus Curio provided an amphitheater in which he produced fights between gladiators.[65]

The permanent amphitheater was usually elliptical rather than circular in plan (the word *amphitheater* means seeing on all sides), with an oval arena (from the Latin *harena,* meaning "sand") completely surrounded by seating. It is a structure almost exclusively associated with the Romans.[66] Gladiatorial games, animal fights, and even sometimes aquatic displays involving the introduction of water into the arena were held in the amphitheater. The public execution of condemned offenders, including Christians, is associated above all with the amphitheater, although there were executions at various other venues. Gladiatorial games, hunting displays, and executions also took place in the Circus Maximus, even after the construction of the Colosseum (Humphrey 1986, 121).

Just as in other buildings, construction materials and techniques in amphitheaters varied according to local resources and traditions. By its very nature the construction of an amphitheater was far more complicated than that of a theater. The all-around seating required support, and access to seating needed to be provided for the audience. There had to be areas where animals and gladiators could be kept and assembled before performances, and these needed to be segregated from the auditorium. All of these needs were catered to in different ways. Advances in building technique in the last two centuries B.C. meant that it was possible to provide vaulted supports for seating, as seen, for example, in the Colosseum (travertine and concrete), in the amphitheaters at Nîmes and Arles in the south of France (stone), and at El Djem in Tunisia (stone and mortared rubble).[67] However, any available slope or hillside might also be used to cut down on the amount of building material required; for example, at Saintes (near Bordeaux) in France, the structure was built into a valley. Support for the seating might also be provided by digging down for the arena, the upcast forming earth banks on which the seating could be set (examples are at Pompeii, Trier

65. Pliny *Natural History* 36.116–20; Golvin 1988, 30–32.

66. Golvin 1988, 275–57 lists 186 such purpose-built structures in the Roman Empire with another 86 structures about which little is known.

67. Golvin 1988, 184–90 (Nimes and Arles), 209–12 (El Djem). For a reconstruction of the Colosseum see Connolly and Dodge 1998, 190–208.

in Germany, and, in Tunisia, Leptiminus). There are also a number of examples of wholly or partly rock-cut structures, for example, at Sutri in Etruria and Cagliari in Sardinia; the amphitheaters at Ptolemais in Cyrenaica and at Sabratha and Lepcis Magna in Tripolitania reused old quarries.[68]

The location of amphitheaters in towns depended very much on local topography and on when they were built. Structures such as these took up a lot of space, and it is common to find them on the fringes or outside the main urban area. However, some—for example, that in the Augustan colony at Aosta in northern Italy—were included within the city walls, presumably for security reasons (Frézouls 1990).

Amphitheaters in Italy

The earliest datable permanent amphitheater to be built in Italy was constructed at Pompeii soon after 78 B.C.[69] This structure, built on the eastern side of the city, within the Sullan wall circuit, measures approximately 460 feet by 345 feet. It does not have the complicated system of vaulted substructures characteristic of many later amphitheaters. The arena was sunk below the level of the surrounding ground, and the seats were supported on a solid mass of earth. At the upper level ran a retaining wall strengthened by external buttresses and incorporating external staircases. At the north and south ends were broad corridors leading into the arena, only the northern one giving access to the outside.

The most famous and most inspirational of all amphitheaters in the Roman world is the Flavian amphitheater, better known today as the Colosseum in Rome (fig. 17).[70] Its construction was begun by Vespasian between 69 and 79 on the site of the lake of Nero's Domus Aurea. It was dedicated in A.D. 80 by Titus, after his father's death.[71] Fittingly, it is the

---

68. Golvin 1988, 33–37 (Pompeii), 40–41 (Sutri), 83–84 (Lepcis Maga), 89 (Trier), 97 (Ptolemais), 124–26 (Saintes), 132 (Leptiminus), 208 (Cagliari); see also for El Djem Lachaux 1979, 137–41.

69. Golvin 1988, 33–37. It was funded by the *duovirs* Gaius Quintus Valgus and Marcus Porcius.

70. Ward-Perkins 1981, 67–70; Golvin 1988, 173–80; Conforto et al. 1988; Connolly and Dodge 1998, 190–217.

71. Dio *History of Rome* 66.25; Suetonius *Life of Titus* 7.3; Martial *Concerning Spectacles*.

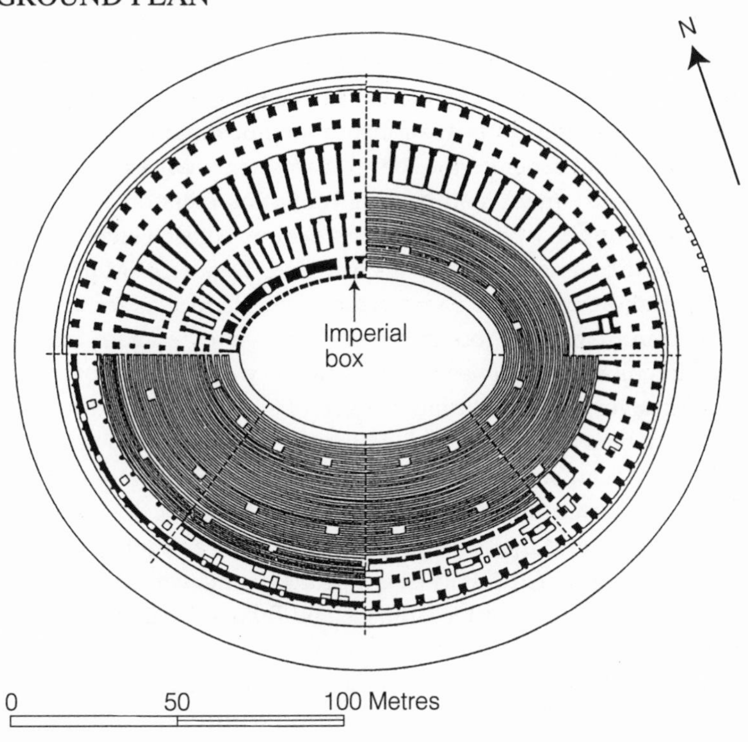

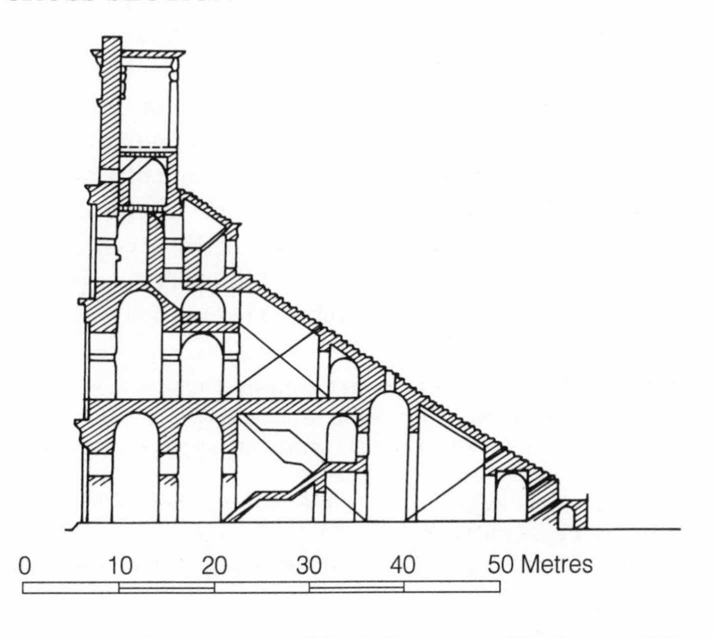

Fig. 17. Plan and cross section of the Colosseum, or Flavian amphitheater, at Rome (first century A.D.)

largest of all Roman amphitheaters, with outer dimensions of 188 meters by 156 meters; the arena measures 80 meters by 54 meters. It had an estimated seating capacity of forty-five thousand to fifty-five thousand people. The concrete foundations were 12 meters deep and supported the eighty main load-bearing travertine piers on which rested the facade, rising to a height of over 45 meters. At each level the arches were framed by engaged columns as in the Theater of Marcellus, the bottom story being of the Doric order, the second was Ionic, and the third, Corinthian. The fourth story consisted of a plain wall with Corinthian pilasters.[72] Beneath the arena, the wooden floor of which no longer survives, is an elaborate system of subterranean passages and chambers where animals and gladiators were kept in readiness.[73] Such substructures can be better appreciated in the amphitheaters at Capua and Pozzuoli in Campania, where the arena floors of Roman concrete are still in place and the trapdoors for hauling up animal cages can still be clearly seen. Outside Italy such arrangements can also be seen at Trier in Germany, El Djem in Tunisia, and Pula in Istria.

Amphitheaters in the West Provinces

Gladiatorial displays were extremely popular in Italy, North Africa, the Danube area, and the western Empire to judge from the number of amphitheaters and related structures surviving in those areas. These structures took a number of different forms. One of the earliest amphitheaters outside Italy was constructed at Lyon in Gaul and is a particularly interesting example. It was probably started in 19 B.C. and finished by the end of the reign of Tiberius. It was built by Gaius Julius Rufus, Grand Priest of the Three Gauls, and the amphitheater was designed to form part of the large sanctuary of the Three Gauls, adding a very Roman element to a pre-Roman focal point. At the beginning of the second century A.D. it was considerably extended, with the seating

72. There is a great deal of debate about the finished state of the Colosseum at the time of Titus' inauguration in A.D. 80. Almost certainly it was not completely finished. For a discussion of the evidence and supporting bibliography see Golvin 1988, 175–76.

73. Cozzo 1971; Connolly and Dodge 1998, 199–208. Some scholars have suggested that the arena substructures were far less substantial at the time of the inauguration and that they were completely enlarged and remodeled under Domitian (Rea 1988; Coleman 1993, 56–60).

capacity increased from three thousand to twenty-seven thousand people.[74]

A development particularly characteristic of Gaul, Germany, and Britain, areas far less Romanized, is a hybrid form of amphitheater and theater combined; some scholars call it a semi-amphitheater. One of the best known of such structures is in Paris, Les Arènes, consisting of an elliptical arena surrounded for the most part by standard amphitheater seating but on its west side flanked by a monumental stage *(scaena)*.[75] There has been much debate about such structures—about whether they were more amphitheater than theater and about what kind of performances took place in them. Similar types of theater/amphitheater are also located at rural shrines in Gaul (e.g., at Sanxay), and these should presumably be interpreted as a continuation of the classical connection between theater and religious ceremony as seen in the Greek sanctuaries at Delphi and Epidaurus, while also perpetuating the idea of a rural Celtic shrine.[76] The only example of this type of hybrid theater-amphitheater outside the northwestern provinces is at Lixus in Morocco (Golvin 1988, 230–36). The Hadrianic double theater at Stobi was built to serve a double purpose, with an arena that could be converted when necessary by the addition of a temporary wooden stage (Golvin 1988, 237–38).

Amphitheaters in the Eastern Provinces

By comparison, in the eastern empire there were fewer amphitheaters, though good examples do survive—for example, the rock-cut amphitheater at Corinth in Greece, the amphitheaters at Cyzicus and Pergamum in Asia Minor, and those at Caesarea and Beth She'an in Palestine (Golvin 1988, 237–50). As a result scholars have been quick to suggest that the bloodthirsty performances of the amphitheater were one aspect of Roman culture that did not find favor with the more refined Greeks of the eastern empire. However, it is quite clear from other archaeological evidence that gladiatorial and animal displays were just as popular in the Greek east as elsewhere in the Empire,

74. Golvin 1988, 117–18 and supporting bibliography.

75. Grenier 1958, 880–975; Golvin 1988, 225–36.

76. Drinkwater (1983, 179–81) suggests that these sanctuaries, which also have baths and other Roman urban-style facilities, provide a place for the rural population to enjoy such amenities.

though they may have taken longer to gain wide acceptance and may have been presented in buildings other than amphitheaters (see "Adaptation of Theatres as Amphitheatres").[77]

Many of the amphitheaters in the eastern empire do not survive very well, mainly because they were more often than not built with the arena dug down into the ground. However, at Pergamum the structure, which is unexcavated, was built so that it straddled a stream and so that the flanking slopes gave support to the lower seating. The rest of the auditorium was supported on vaults of mortared rubble with a good stone facing. The stream flowed through a vaulted tunnel beneath the arena.

Arena Substructures

Not all amphitheaters had corridors beneath the arena, but where present, these corridors did provide space to keep animals, scenery, and other equipment; Seneca mentions movable stage scenery (*Letters* 88.22). Trapdoors in the arena floor allowed both animals and gladiators to be hoisted up to various parts of the arena whenever required. The dramatic possibilities of such unexpected appearances were considerable.[78]

Flooding the Arena

It has often been argued that the Colosseum was flooded for the performance of aquatic displays during the hundred-day inauguration of the building in A.D. 80. The evidence comes from two sources, Martial (*Concerning Spectacles* 24) and Dio (*History of Rome* 66.25.4), but Suetonius makes no mention of this.[79] He does say that Titus gave a mock sea battle "in the old naumachia" (see "Naumachial and Aquatic Displays" below), and recent research suggests that the aquatic displays of A.D. 80 were entirely separate from the shows in the amphitheater. Moreover, it is quite clear that the structural evidence for the hydraulic system of

77. There are many mosaics, reliefs, and inscriptions testifying to the use of other buildings for arena displays; see Hornum 1993, 52–54.

78. Golvin 1988, 330–33; Cozzo 1971, 60–71; Connolly and Dodge 1998, 199–208.

79. Suetonius *Life of Domitian* 41 says that Domitian held naumachiae in the Colosseum. See my n. 73.

the Colosseum and other amphitheaters is open to interpretation.[80] Such systems have been postulated for a number of amphitheaters (e.g., those at Pozzuoli, Arles, and Nimes). However, the evidence for each seems to represent the normal system of drains that would be required for the drainage of rainwater from the seating. The only two amphitheaters where there does seem to have been provision for introducing water into the arena are at Merida in Spain and Verona in northern Italy, where large basins are sunk into the arena floor. At Merida the basin was definitely lined with waterproof mortar. These basins were effectively tiny naumachiae and could be covered up with wooden planking when the arena was being used for gladiatorial displays.[81]

Adaptation of Theaters as Amphitheaters

As early as the early first century A.D. there are literary references that attest to the staging of gladiatorial contests in theaters. In a number of cities, particularly in the eastern provinces where amphitheaters were not as common, other buildings, especially theaters (both pre-Roman and Roman), were either adapted to accommodate gladiatorial and hunting displays or built with a joint function in mind. Many Hellenistic theaters, already adapted to Roman design, were further modified by the addition of a high wall around the orchestra to protect the audience in the lower seating from wild animals.[82] At Ephesus in Asia Minor, the original iron railing was replaced by a wall two meters high; a similar structure was placed around the orchestra at Side. In the theater at Perge, a very attractive marble parapet in a latticework design was placed around the edge of the orchestra in the third century. Exactly when such adaptation takes place is often difficult to date, but it is usually not before the latter part of the second century A.D. At both Xanthus in Lycia and Corinth in Greece, the lower rows of seats were removed to create a high wall.[83] At Cyrene in Cyrenaica the magnificent Greek theater at the west end of the Sanctuary of Apollo was con-

80. Coleman 1993.

81. Golvin and Reddé 1990; Golvin 1988, 333–36, 109–10 (Merida), 169–71 (Verona); Golvin and Landes 1990, 94–97.

82. Golvin 1988, 237–49; Moretti 1992, 179–81.

83. Golvin 1988, 237–47. Golvin lists twenty-nine theaters in the east that are adapted in this way.

verted sometime in the second century A.D. by the elimination of the stage and the deepening of the small orchestra to form the arena of a small amphitheater. The seating on the north, seaward side, was carried on arches. The basis of the arena was of solid rock, so a tunnel had to be cut to allow the movement of animal cages around the arena (Golvin 1988, 96–97).

Some theaters (e.g., that at Corinth) were adapted even further so that they could be flooded and provide a venue for aquatic displays. The theater at Argos was in origin Hellenistic in date and rock cut. In the early Roman period the *cavea* was extended on both flanks and the circular orchestra was bisected by the addition of a Roman-style masonry stage building. At a later date a high wall was placed around the orchestra and an aqueduct was provided to flood the arena.[84]

Although very common in the east, this practice can also be found elsewhere in the Empire. At Ostia the theater associated with the Piazzale delle Corporazione was converted in the fourth century A.D. to accommodate aquatic displays, with water tanks placed beneath the seating. At about the same time the theater at Aïn Tounga (Thignica) in Tunisia was going through a similar remodeling.[85]

In addition to theaters, other buildings could also be adapted for arena games, as is very clear at Perge, where the curved end of the second-century A.D. stadium was surrounded by a wall that also crossed the lower seats, forming an arena. This was connected by five low doors to the vaulted substructures of the structure, for the passage of both gladiators and wild animals.[86] This practice of adaptation obviously has major implications for the change in use of these entertainment buildings and for changes in public taste.

---

84. For this practice see Traversari 1960. At Ptolemais in Cyrenaica an odeum-like structure that originally served as a *bouleuterion* was converted for theatrical use by the addition of a wooden stage, and sometime before A.D. 400 the entire orchestra was waterproofed to provide a tank for aquatic displays; see Kraeling 1962, 91–92.

85. Meiggs 1973, 424–25; Lachaux 1979, 123–26.

86. For a similar adaptation of the stadium at Aphrodisias see Erim 1986, 67–70, though the recent identification of cuttings all round the stadium for the supports for nets, has indicated that the building was used for animal displays from the beginning (pers. comm. K. Welch). Alterations were made in the stadium at Ephesus also; see Keil 1964, 61–63.

Velaria

Many theaters and amphitheaters from the Roman world have surviving evidence to indicate that they were provided with awnings (velaria) over all or part of the audience.[87] On the exterior of many structures (the Colosseum; the amphitheaters at Pula, Nimes, and Arles; and the theaters at Orange and Aspendus) are projecting corbels that supported the masts to which were attached giant awnings. In Rome these were the responsibility of a detachment of sailors from the fleet at Misenum, and it has been estimated that at least one thousand men were required to operate the capstan and ropes that enabled the awnings to be unfurled. The awnings themselves of course do not survive, but we do have a wall painting from Pompeii that provides the only depiction of such an awning in place. It depicts the amphitheater at Pompeii during a riot that broke out in A.D. 59 between rival supporters and that is referred to by Tacitus; the awning has been pulled out over the seating for the performance.[88]

Naumachiae and Aquatic Displays

Julius Caesar gave the first known mock sea battles (naumachiae) in a basin in the Campus Martius in 46 B.C., but such displays *(navales pugnae)* were held under Scipio Africanus in the context of military display and training. Dio reported that in 40 B.C. Sextus Pompey entertained his troops by giving a mock sea battle involving a fight to the death between prisoners of war.[89] Augustus built a much larger artificial lake (or *stagnum*) measuring some 1,800 by 1,200 Roman feet on the right bank of the Tiber, which was fed by a new aqueduct (the *aqua Alsietina*) for the performance of naumachiae.[90] Naumachiae at Rome are well

87. There is much epigraphic evidence in the form of grafitti from Pompeii that bears witness to the importance of these awnings. Advertisements for gladiatorial games proudly proclaim, *vela erunt* [there will be awnings].

88. See Golvin 1988, 17 for this whole subject; for the awnings of the Colosseum see Connolly and Dodge 1998, 198–99. For the riot at Pompeii see Tacitus *Annals* 14.17.

89. Suetonius *Life of Caesar* 39; Livy *History of Rome* 29.22; Dio *History of Rome* 48.19.1.

90. Augustus *Deeds of the Divine Augustus* 22–23; Coleman 1993 provides an excellent discussion of the subject; see specifically pp. 50–55 for Augustus' *stagnum*.

attested in the first century A.D., and the literary evidence suggests that the amphitheater was not the preferred location. It also suggests that naumachiae were more a phenomenon of the capital than elsewhere in the empire and were not common after the first century A.D.[91]

Not all aquatic displays involved the re-enactment of sea battles. The basins of the Verona and Merida amphitheaters would have permitted the use of small craft but could equally well have accommodated aquatic spectacles of a non-violent nature, such as those described by Martial. Such "water ballets" often involved nudity and themes of love and sex.[92]

At Jerash (ancient Gerasa) in Jordan a large double pool outside the city was used for aquatic displays of a particular nature; a small theater formed part of the complex. The pool in fact supplied water to the main *nymphaeum* (monumental fountain) in the city and was the location of the celebration of the notorious festivals of Maiuma (Browning 1982, 211–15). The Maiuma was probably of Phoenician origin, and by the late Empire it seems to have gained a reputation for promiscuous goings-on. Malalas described it as a "theatrical festival by night," and he thought its name meant that the festival was celebrated in May. The derivation is more likely to be from the Semitic word *mai,* meaning "water." Recent evidence from Aphrodisias, where a large pool was discovered in the Portico of Tiberius, may suggest that aquatic spectacles were part of the celebrations.[93]

The Circus and Chariot Racing

The Roman circus was the large entertainment building used first and foremost for chariot races, most commonly with four-horse *(quadrigae)* or two-horse *(bigae)* chariots. By the time of the Empire the circus had taken the form of a hairpin shape, but early on it had a far less formalized layout.[94]

91. Traversari 1960; Golvin and Reddé 1990; Welch 1991, 277–79.

92. Martial *Concerning Spectacles* 25, 26. For the amphitheaters at Verona and Merida see Golvin 1988, 109–10 (Merida), 169–71 (Verona); and see pp. 333–36 for *naumachiae* in general. For themes, subjects, and range of the aquatic displays see Coleman 1993, passim.

93. Malalas *Chronicle* 284–85; Roueché 1993, 188–89.

94. The most thorough treatment of the subject is Humphrey 1986. For the performers and performances see Cameron 1976.

Circuses in their canonical and monumental form were a later architectural development than theaters and amphitheaters. In archaic and classical Greece, chariot and horse racing were popular, but only the hippodrome at Olympia took a form that went beyond the minimal provisions that seem to be in evidence at other sites. There seems to have been two turning posts, an elaborate set of starting gates, and banks for seating the spectators, enclosing at least part of the track (Humphrey 1986, 5–11).

The most famous of all circuses is the Circus Maximus in Rome (fig. 18). Chariot racing was held as early as the Etruscan period in the area of what became the Circus Maximus, in the valley between the Palatine and the Aventine Hills. During the later Republic and the early Empire the Circus Maximus, to a greater extent than any other circus, also served as the venue for other events.[95]

The first structure on the site is said to date back to the sixth century B.C. (traditionally to the Tarquins), and for a long time all the seating and the starting gates were timber (Livy *History of Rome* 1.35.8). Claudius rebuilt them in marble, but under Trajan the biggest transformation took place. Including the racetrack and seating, the structure was six hundred meters long, with an average width of over one hundred meters. Estimates of seating capacity vary from 150,000 to 350,000; probably by the time of Trajan a figure of 350,000 was perfectly possible.[96] A maximum of twelve charioteers could compete in any one race, and they entered the arena simultaneously from the twelve *carceres,* or starting boxes, at the north end. The racers traveled counter-clockwise, normally circling seven times around the *spina,* the 344-meter-long barrier along the central axis of the circus. Thus, a normal race in the Circus Maximus was of just over three miles. Crashes were common, especially at the start of a race and on the turns, when the charioteers jostled for position. Statues and trophies adorned the length of the *spina,* and at each end was a *meta,* or turning point, in the form of large gilded bronze cones. On the *spina,* Augustus placed an obelisk of Rameses II brought from Egypt to Rome (now in the Piazza del Popolo), and in A.D. 357 Constantine II erected a second obelisk of Tuthmosis II (now in

95. There were other circus buildings in Rome, but none of them was as large or as important as the Circus Maximus. For a reconstruction of the Circus Maximus and the workings of the starting gates see Connolly and Dodge 1998, 176–81.

96. Pliny *Natural History* 36.103 says that it held 250,000 spectators.

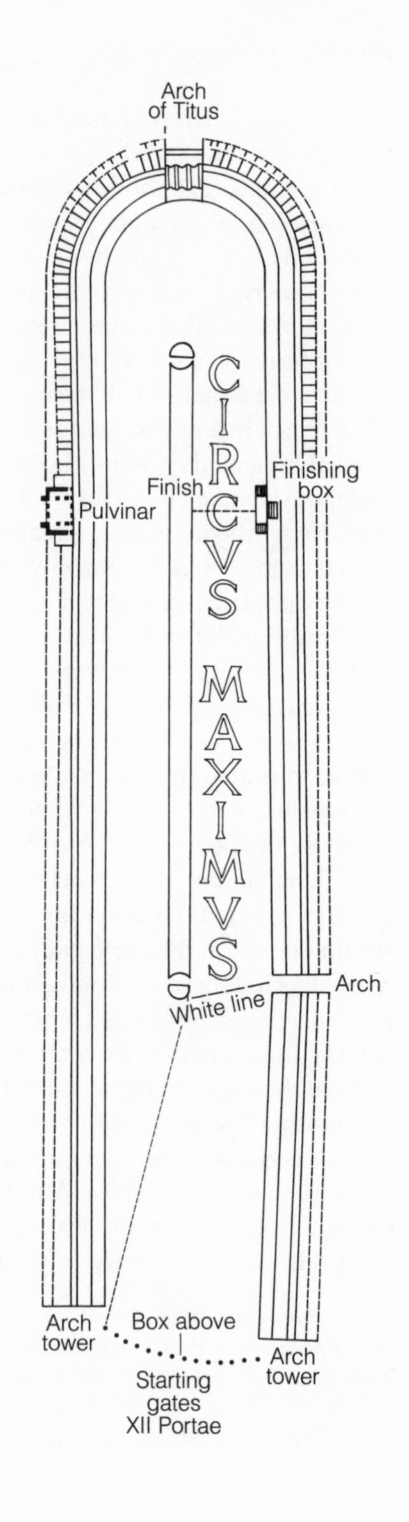

Fig. 18. Restored plan of the Circus Maximus at Rome, based on the Severan map of Rome (*Forma Urbis Romae*)

Fig. 19. Relief from Ostia showing details of the starting gates, including the fully equipped Herms (far right), the turning posts, and the dolphins that served as lap-counting devices (though it shows only four rather than the actual seven). The charioteer is accompanied by the *sparsor,* who is throwing water in the face of the horse, and by the *hortator,* who assisted the charioteer during the course of the race. Note that the victorious charioteer carries away the palm of victory in the background. (Ex-Lateran relief, Vatican Museums; DAI Rome neg. 39–557.)

Piazza San Giovanni in Laterano) (Humphrey 1986, 56–113). This relationship of obelisk and circus occurs at Caesarea Maritima in Israel, where fragments of a red granite obelisk can still be seen. In the later Roman period it was repeated at Constantinople, when Constantine shipped a great red granite obelisk of Tuthmosis III (1549–1503 B.C.) from Thebes to Constantinople (Humphrey 1986, 477–91).

As a result of their vast size, none of the many circuses in the Roman world has been completely excavated. One of the best-preserved and most thoroughly investigated is at Lepcis Magna in modern Libya.[97] The structure lay outside the city limits next to the shoreline. To the south was an amphitheater built in A.D. 56, and when the circus was

97. Humphrey, Sear, and Vickers 1972–73; Humphrey 1986, 25–55.

completed in the mid–second century, the two were interconnected by open passages and tunnels carved through the hillside. The unification of these two entertainment buildings in a single architectural complex is unknown elsewhere in the Roman world.[98] The arena of the Lepcis circus was almost exactly 450 meters in length. The starting gates were placed along a shallow arc so that all contestants had the same distance to travel to the beginning of the *spina,* at which point the track narrowed considerably. Gaining a good position in this initial gallop was often crucial to the outcome of the race. The preservation of the starting gates at Lepcis is good enough to allow the reconstruction of the mechanism by which they were opened at the start of the race. An attendant pulled a lever that activated a catapult system, which in turn jerked out the latches of the gates of each stall, allowing the gates to fly open simultaneously. At the end of the seventh lap, instead of returning down the track to the starting gates, the teams would round the turning point and head up to the finish line, which was roughly two-thirds up one side of the track.[99]

Other circuses in North Africa include those at Dougga, Cherchel, and Carthage. Elsewhere in the west circuses are located at Merida in Spain and Arles in the south of France. Although no preserved circus structures have been definitely identified in Britain, there is much evidence to suggest that chariot races took place there, perhaps on tracks lacking permanent grandstands.[100]

In the east, where horse racing was already well established, monumental circuses do not appear with the frequency that they do in the west. Eastern cities are known to have had chariot racing at one period or another, and some cities known to have possessed a monumental circus are Antioch on the Orontes, Bostra in Syria, Gerasa (Jerash in modern Jordan), and Cyrene. Interestingly, there are no attested monumental circuses in Greece, apart from at Thessalonike, where a hippo-

98. Humphrey (1986, 27) suggests that this location would have enabled a single magistrate or benefactor to give games in both venues on the same day. The potential of this double dose of popularity most assuredly would not have been missed by the elite of Lepcis Magna.

99. For the mechanism of the gates see Humphrey 1986, 157–68; Connolly and Dodge 1998, 178–79.

100. Humphrey 1986, 431–37. Fulford 1989, 189, suggests that the amphitheater at Silchester in southern Britain may have been used for horse displays of the kind that were more usual in the circus.

drome was built as part of the tetrarchic palace. This building location emphasizes the important relationship in later antiquity between imperial palace (in this case that of the tetrarch Galerius) and the circus, a relationship that had been established already in Rome with the Palatine and the Circus Maximus (Humphrey 1986, 579–638) and that was to become a basic feature of life in the new capital that Constantine built at Byzantium and named Constantinople.

The Stadium

The stadium was a well-established Greek type designed for footraces and other athletic displays. In plan it often resembled the circus, though on a much smaller scale. In general the stadium was close to one *stade* long (about 180–200 meters) and did not have a central raised *spina,* but the arena would be marked out with lanes, with a turning post at the end of each lane. In the Roman period only the very largest cities would have possessed both a circus and a stadium. In general, with some major exceptions, those in the west would possess only a circus, whereas those in Greece and Asia would possess only a stadium. Of course, it was always possible for a circus to double as a stadium if necessary.

Many of the Greek religious sanctuaries, such as Olympia, Delphi, and Epidaurus, continued to host major festivals in the Roman period, and they incorporated stadia as part of their original design, emphasizing the religious nature of the origins of the athletic games. The stadium at Priene represents a fine example of the Greek style of layout. It was actually attached to the Lower Gymnasium that was built c. 130 B.C., an open area 190 meters long and 6 meters wide, with a stoa of Doric design along the length of one long side. This stoa provided shelter for athletic training, lessons, and general social communication; the races were held on the track below. At the western end were the starting gates, so well preserved that it is possible to work out in general terms how a race was started. There are two rows of stones with holes through the center. The front row consists of eight stones, which were the starting posts for the races in Hellenistic times. The row behind has ten similar stones, but with smaller holes cut into them, which served the same purpose in Roman times. Corinthian columns stood on these Roman markers, and these columns carried an architrave. Examination of both the bases and the architrave reveals traces of grooves cut into them, which suggests that they held some kind of barrier in place in front of the runners until the umpire started them off. The finish line unfortunately has not been discovered.

Rome

In the early second century B.C., Greek athletics, wrestling, boxing, and footraces were included in the circus games. The first performance by Greek athletes in the Circus Maximus was in 186 B.C.[101] However, so-called Greek games and the idea of Greek athletics remained uncommon in Rome until imperial times, when such activities received something of a revival. The Greek sports *(certamina Graeca)* were usually included in the public games.

As an architectural type, the stadium arrived late in Rome. Temporary stadia had been built in the Campus Martius by Caesar and Augustus, but the first permanent stadium was the Stadium of Domitian dedicated by A.D. 86, the ground plan of which is preserved in the layout of the Piazza Navona. This stadium was built to house the Greek-style games developed by Domitian.[102]

Not only footraces but also the more heavyweight athletics disciplines of wrestling, the pankration, and boxing were held. The latter gained greater bloodshed and excitement (for the Romans at least) by the use of the *caestus,* a fist bandage with metal spikes.

The Stadium in the Empire

The second-century A.D. stadium at Perge in southern Turkey is one of the best preserved stadia of antiquity. The U-shaped construction extending from north to south is 234 meters long and 34 meters wide. The well-preserved rows of seats, twelve rows in all, were supported on inclined, stone barrel vaults and provided accommodation for about twelve thousand spectators. The entrance to the arena lay at the southern end, but of the monumental gateway marking this entrance, only a few fragments survive. Spectators entered through every third vault,

101. Crowther 1983. These were the games of M. Fulvius Nobilior and involved athletes from Greece who competed in the nude in the pentathlon events.

102. The first recorded stadium at Rome was a temporary structure built in the Campus Martius in 46 B.C. to celebrate Julius Caesar's triumph.

while doors between the vaults allowed access from one vault to another. These vaults, supporting the seating, were used as storerooms and workrooms and shops, especially during the festivals held in honor of Artemis. Inscriptions have been found giving the names and professions of the occupants of some of these shops.

At Aphrodisias a splendid example of a stadium survives. It was built entirely of stone and is 262 meters long and 59 meters wide at its broadest point, and calculations suggest that its thirty or so tiers of seats could accommodate about thirty thousand people. Unlike most other stadia it terminated at both ends in a curve, thus enclosing the whole building with seating. (Other examples of this arrangement are at Laodiceia ad Lycum and at Nysa in Turkey, and Nicopolis in Greece). The long sides were not parallel but bulged out slightly at their center to allow for better spectator viewing. At some later date the east end was converted into an amphitheater. Protective walls were added to the lowest row of seats (Erim 1986, 67–70).

One other stadium worthy of detailed comment is that of Aezani. Though nowhere near as well preserved, its association with the theater is noteworthy in itself. The stadium, built probably in the second century, is placed with its open end, where the starting line would be situated, up against the exterior of the stage building. The seating, of which a certain amount survives, is supported on earth banks.[103]

Baths and Bathing

The baths were an integral part of Roman urban life, in contrast to theaters, amphitheaters, and circuses, which were places of occasional entertainment. By the late Republic bathing became a daily occurrence for many inhabitants of Roman Italy, and from the early first century A.D. it became increasingly the custom for those of the Empire. Bathing became a symbol of being Roman, and thus the structures themselves became a symbol of Rome.[104]

It should be remembered that baths and bathing were not invented by the Romans. Bathing was very much part of the ritual of the Greek gymnasia. These complexes provided a social context for exercise and

---

103. There are other instances in Asia Minor of such theater-stadium complexes, for example, at Sardis. See Vann 1989, 59–65 for a general discussion of this arrangement.

104. For a scathing reference to this see Tacitus *Agricola* 21.

communal bathing and exerted a major influence on the subsequent history of bath development.[105]

The Greek Gymnasium and Baths

The gymnasium was the Greek public establishment for the athletic and educational training of young men and as such was a major focus of their lives. The only element connected with washing and bathing is the *loutron.* In early instances this was an open-air space set aside for cold ablutions; elevated basins and simple shower systems provided water. Scenes of these activities are depicted in vase paintings from the later sixth century (Yegül 1992, 17–19). The addition of hot-water facilities does not seem to have taken place until the Hellenistic period. Simple charcoal braziers would have provided the heat source.[106] During the Hellenistic period, many gymnasia were remodeled to incorporate facilities for hot bathing, and the idea of the gymnasium quite clearly changed in perception. The baths were beginning to take precedence.

Public baths (the *balaneion*) did exist in the Greek period, but they were small unpretentious structures provided with individual tubs or hip-baths. An example at Corinth (the Bath of the Centaur) dates to the fifth century B.C., and dating from the third century B.C. are examples in Magna Graecia, at Morgantina, Syracuse, and Gela. Excavation in the north wing of the Stabian Baths at Pompeii has revealed a public bath dating from the fifth century B.C., with hip-baths in separate cells.[107]

The heating systems in Greek baths were simple until the first century B.C. Charcoal braziers would have been sufficient to heat the small windowless structures, though there are some examples of more elaborate heating systems. At Olympia a furnace-boiler combination was used in the mid–fourth century baths. The boiler was located above a furnace in a service area between the two bathing halls, and supplied hot water to the new bathing unit comprising twenty-one hip-baths.[108]

---

105. See Delaine 1988 for a very useful discussion of bath studies.
106. Ginouvès 1962; Nielsen 1990, 6–14; Yegül 1992, 6–29.
107. Delaine 1989; Nielsen 1990, 6–7.
108. Delaine 1988, 14–17; Yegül 1992, 26.

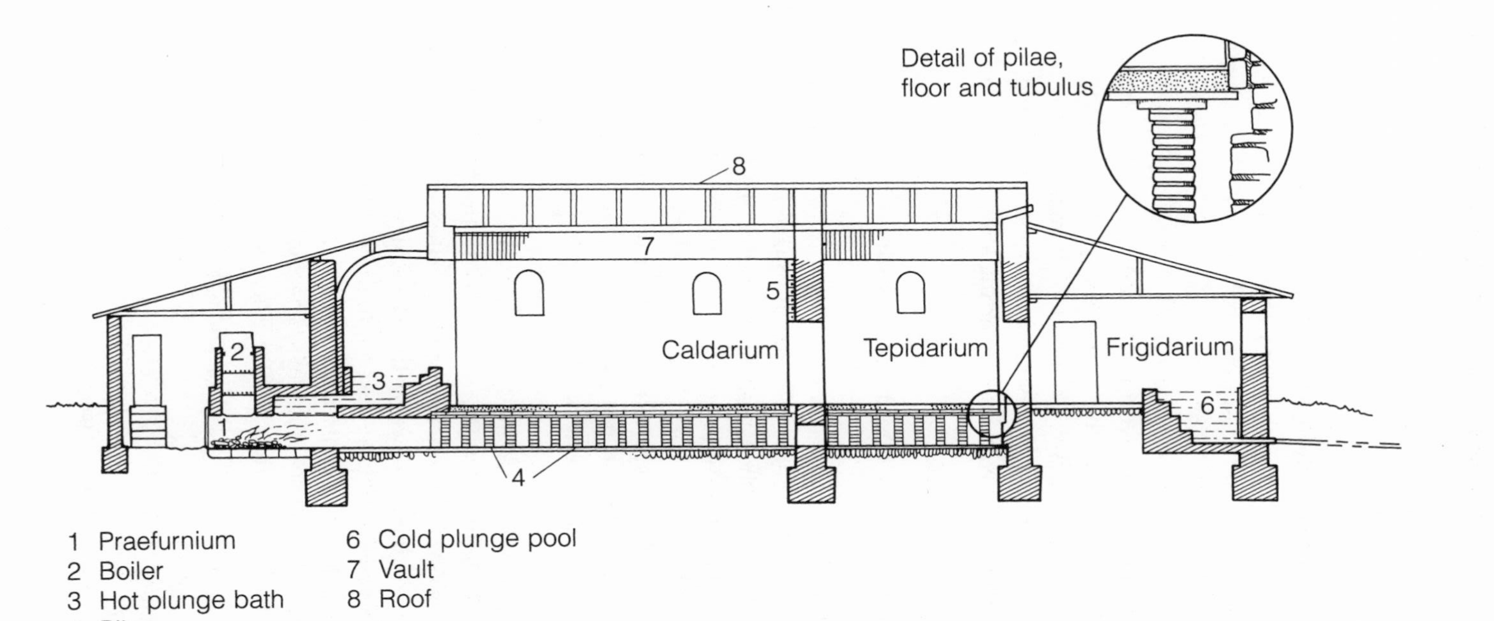

Fig. 20. Cross section through a bath. (After Nielsen 1990, fig. 14.)

Baths in the Roman Period

In the census of 33 B.C. carried out by Agrippa there were 170 small baths in Rome; by the early fifth century there were 856, as well as eleven large *thermae* (large public baths which in Rome at least were built by the emperors). For the Romans, bathing was both a luxury and a necessity.[109]

The early development of baths in Italy was strongly influenced by the Greek and Hellenistic world (Delaine 1989). Traditionally the Romans are credited with the invention of sweat baths and the hypocaust, underfloor heating. The popular claim is that Sergius Orata, a Roman entrepreneur of the early first century B.C., invented the heating system in connection with heating artificial oyster beds on the Bay of Naples.[110]

The Heating of the Baths

The earliest and clearest archaeological evidence for the true hypocaust comes from the Stabian Baths at Pompeii (phase IV, dated to the late second century B.C.) and the Greek Baths at Olympia (period IV, dated to c. 100 B.C.). The hypocaust could take a variety of forms, but in essence it was a system by which hot air could be introduced under the floor from a furnace area where the hot water was also heated (fig. 20). The floor was supported on *pilae,* small supporting pillars usually of bricks (though one-piece stone or terracotta *pilae* are found). The floor itself had to be thick so that it would not be too hot to walk on.[111]

Not only the floor but also the walls and vaults were usually heated. In the mid–first century A.D., Seneca refers to the "hollow walls" of vaulted baths as a recent development (*Letters* 90.25). The earliest archaeological evidence dates to the early first century B.C., when heated hollow walls were introduced into the Stabian Baths at Pompeii (fig. 21) and used in the construction of the Forum Baths. A hollow wall can be achieved in several ways. The commonest is with the use of continuous hollow box-tiles *(tubuli).* These were fastened to the wall using metal clamps and then plastered over. The bottom row of *tubuli*

---

109. Pliny *Natural History* 36.121; Nielsen 1990, 38.

110. Pliny *Natural History* 9.168; Delaine 1988, 15–17; Nielsen 1990, 14–17.

111. Delaine 1988, 15; Yegül 1992, 356–62.

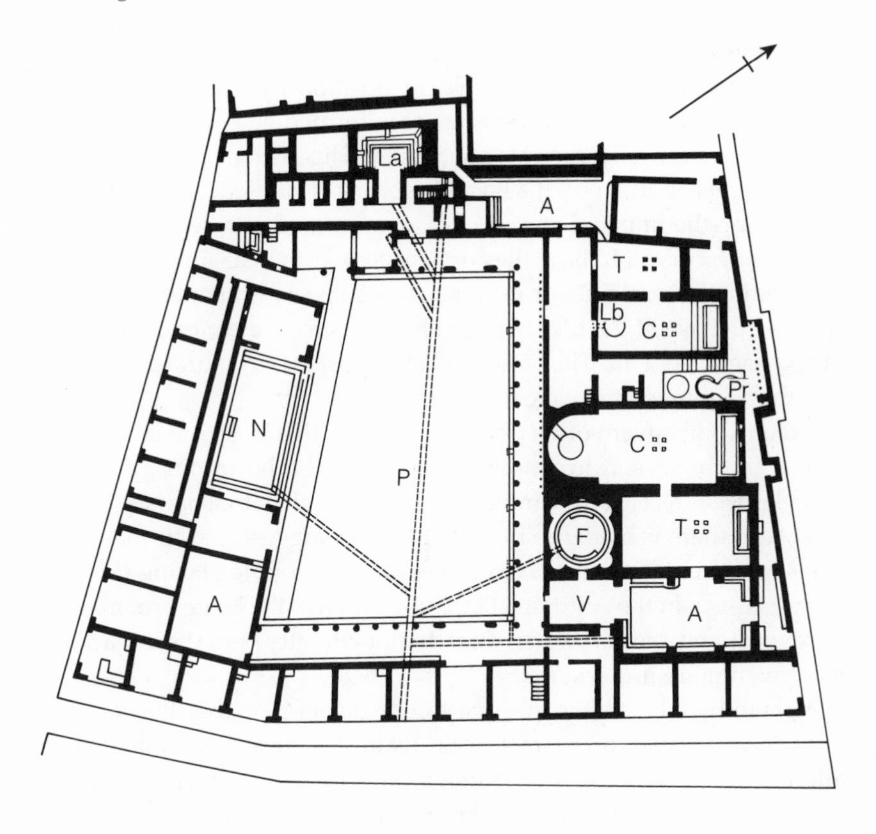

La - Latrine
N - Natatio
A - Apodyterium
V - Vestibule
F - Frigidarium
T - Tepidarium
C - Caldarium
Lb - Labrum
Pr - Praefurnium
P - Palaestra

Fig. 21. Plan of the Stabian Baths, Pompeii. Scale 1:500.

was set so that hot air in the underfloor area could naturally rise up the wall.[112] This method was used in the Forum Baths at Ostia and can still be seen in place there today. Another method was to use specially made tiles *(tegulae mammatae)* that created in the wall a cavity up which the hot air could rise. In Asia Minor and North Africa in particular (although examples are known from the Hadrian's Wall area in north-

112. Brodribb 1987, 63–83; Nielsen 1990, 14–16; Yegül 1992, 363–65.

ern Britain) spacers or bobbin-spacers were used. The spacers were made of fired clay and were held in position by a T-shaped metal cramp that ran through the spacer. This formed a space between the wall and a vertically mounted wall tile. The rising hot air escaped through flues in the roof. If a heated room was vaulted, as was usually the case by the imperial period, the hot air was channeled around the vault using curved hollow tiles or a system known as armchair voussoirs, either in terracotta or in stone. These specially shaped voussoirs allowed the use of flat tiles between them to create a series of voids for the passage of hot air. They also had an important structural purpose in that they lightened the weight of the whole roof.[113]

Roman baths were often oriented to take full advantage of the heat of the afternoon sun to amplify the heat in the hot rooms, a sort of greenhouse effect. For example, the Forum Baths at Ostia face southwest, and there is evidence in these baths to suggest that further measures to retain heat were taken in the form of double glazing (Meiggs 1973, 411–15). In the Antonine Baths at Carthage, the heated rooms face northwest and the sea; in the already hot climate, perhaps a sea view was given more importance.[114]

Roman bath buildings may vary in details of plan, but they accommodate a number of characteristic features. They were planned to allow logical progression from one room to another.[115] On arriving at the baths a bather would go to the *apodyterium* (dressing room), where he or she would leave his or her clothes. In the Forum Baths at Pompeii, open-fronted cupboard-like facilities clearly acted as the equivalent of modern lockers, albeit with a servant or slave paid to watch over the garments, instead of a lock and key (the system was anything but secure). From the *apodyterium* the bather might follow a number of different courses. One might oil oneself (usually with perfumed oil) and exercise in the palaestra. From there the bather would progress to the *tepidarium* (warm room), perhaps via the *frigidarium* (cold room), and then to the *caldarium* (hot room, closest to the furnace area). After the

113. For the different methods of heating walls see Brodribb 1987, 67–70; Yegül 1992, 363–65. For heating vaults see Yegül 1992, 365–68.

114. Yegül 1992, 192–96. For a general discussion of the Carthage baths see Lézine 1969.

115. For the different rooms of a Roman bath building and their technical terms and facilities see Nielsen 1990, 153–66. For the ritual of bathing see Yegül 1992, 30–47.

bather had spent some time sitting in the steam and in the hot-water plunge pools or splashing in the hot water from the *labrum*,[116] the next step would be to scrape off the oil using a strigil, taking with it the dirt and dead skin cells. This might be done by a servant. The bather would then return to the *frigidarium* and the *natatio*, where a cold plunge was an option. In the larger baths the *natatio* was a separate area.

The heat provided in the Roman baths was for the most part steam heat. Some baths had an additional heated room (the *laconicum*) that provided dry heat. Temperatures in this room could rise much higher than those in the more traditionally heated hot rooms, so time spent here would have been far less. Where these dry-heat rooms have been identified, they are reasonably small compared to other rooms (Nielsen 1990, 18, 158–59).

Imperial *Thermae* in Rome

In Rome the very large imperially built baths (imperial *thermae*) provided space for huge numbers of bathers at any one time (Yegül 1992, 128–83). There were often a series of subsidiary hot rooms. The plan of the imperial *thermae* was symmetrical about the main, short axis formed by the positioning of the *frigidarium*, *tepidarium*, and *caldarium*, allowing for the circulation of bathers through the building. These buildings provided not only bathing facilities but also libraries, meeting rooms, and gardens for promenading. Snacks, drinks, and a range of other services (such as prostitutes) were also commonly available.

The imperial *thermae* in Rome are some the most sophisticated and ambitious large-scale buildings from the ancient world. Traditionally the Baths of Agrippa built in the Campus Martius in 25 B.C. provide us with the earliest example of such baths. However, these were rebuilt in the third century, and it is not clear exactly what form the original plan took. The same is true of the nearby Baths of Nero. The Baths of Titus are known from a plan of Palladio, and although new excavations have taken place on the site over the last few years, a number of details are still uncertain.

116. In earlier baths plunge pools in the heated rooms were not a usual feature. A large shallow basin, or *labrum*, was filled with hot water instead. This is the setup in the Forum Baths at Pompeii (c. 80 B.C.). In the Suburban Baths at Herculaneum (c. 30 B.C.) both a plunge pool and a *labrum* are provided.

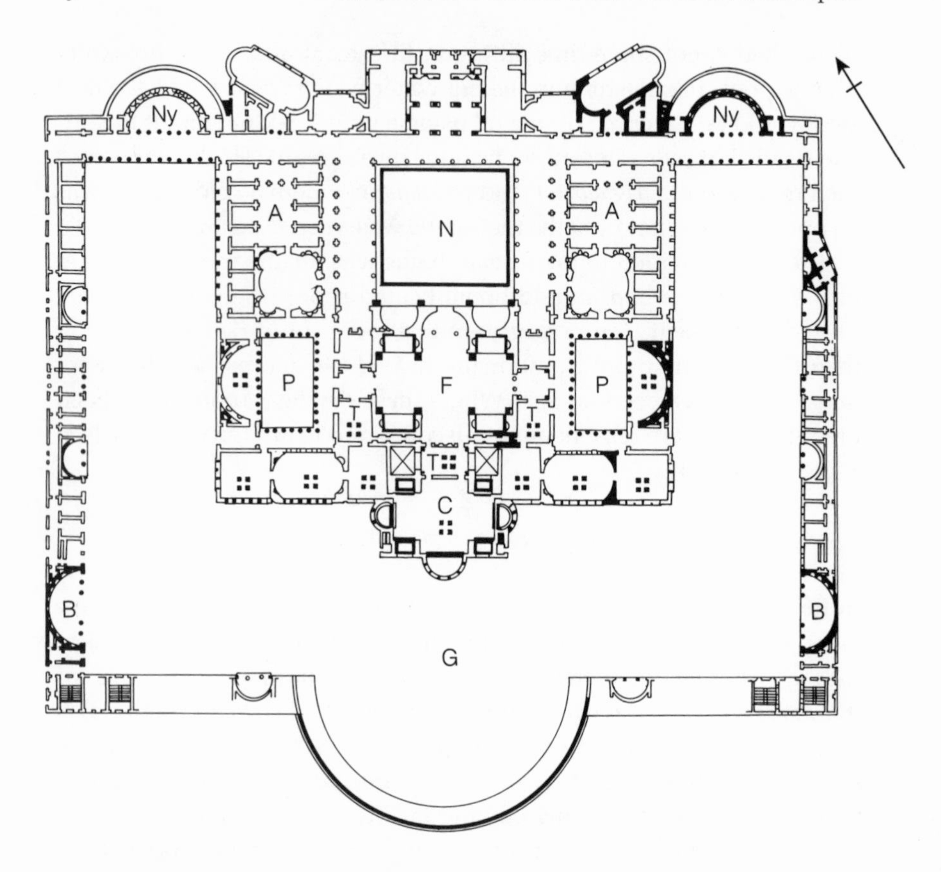

N Nymphaeum
B Library
A Apodyterium
N Natatio
F Frigidarium
T Tepidarium
C Caldarium
G Gardens

:: Denotes heated room

Fig. 22. Plan of the Baths of Trajan, Rome. Scale 1:2000.

The Baths of Trajan (A.D. 104–9) represent the earliest of the imperial baths whose plan we can be certain of (Connolly and Dodge 1998, 238–47). Clearly they are part of a long development and include a number of features that are in all the later baths of this type both in Rome (Baths of Caracalla, Baths of Diocletian, Baths of Constantine) and elsewhere in the Empire (e.g., at Trier, the Hadrianic Barbarathermen and the fourth-century Kaisarthermen).[117] The central bathing block is surrounded by an outer enclosure 330 meters by 315 meters in size. In the Baths of Trajan (fig. 22) the bathing block is attached to the outer enclosure on the northeast side; in the Baths of Caracalla the block stands totally within the enclosure. The *frigidarium* is positioned more centrally within the block and is covered by three cross vaults, and a large open-air swimming or plunge pool *(natatio)* was provided on the same scale as the main bathing rooms.

The Baths of Caracalla (completed A.D. 216–17) and the Baths of Diocletian (completed A.D. 305) were the largest of the imperial *thermae* in Rome.[118] Both covered a total area of about 120,000 square meters, though the actual bathing block of the Baths of Diocletian was larger. According to the fifth-century chronicler Olympiodorus, the Caracalla baths could accommodate sixteen hundred bathers; those of Diocletian, three thousand. (These figures should not be given too much relative significance, although they do still demonstrate the enormous scale of the activity [Yegül 1992, 146].) Both sets of baths were lavishly decorated with marble and granite columns, veneers, and mosaic. The *frigidarium* of the Baths of Diocletian has been preserved as Michaelangelo's Church of Santa Maria degli Angeli (1561); the great cross-vaulted hall was preserved intact, with its eight red granite columns that stand in front of the load-bearing piers. The overall huge scale of the construction of these imperial bath buildings can thus be fully appreciated.

Baths in the Provinces

In the provinces, the larger public baths were often designed more or less symmetrically, following the imperial *thermae.* This was obviously a practical expedient but may also represent influence from Rome. Examples can be found all over the empire and include the Large Baths at Djemila, dated to c. A.D. 183, and the large-scale baths at Cherchel (the West Thermae) and Carthage (the Antonine Baths).[119]

---

117. Wightman 1969, 82–85, 98–102; Yegül 1992, 172–73.
118. Delaine 1997; Yegül 1992, 146–69.
119. Nielsen 1990, 84–95; Yegül 1992, 193–96, 201–02; 205–6.

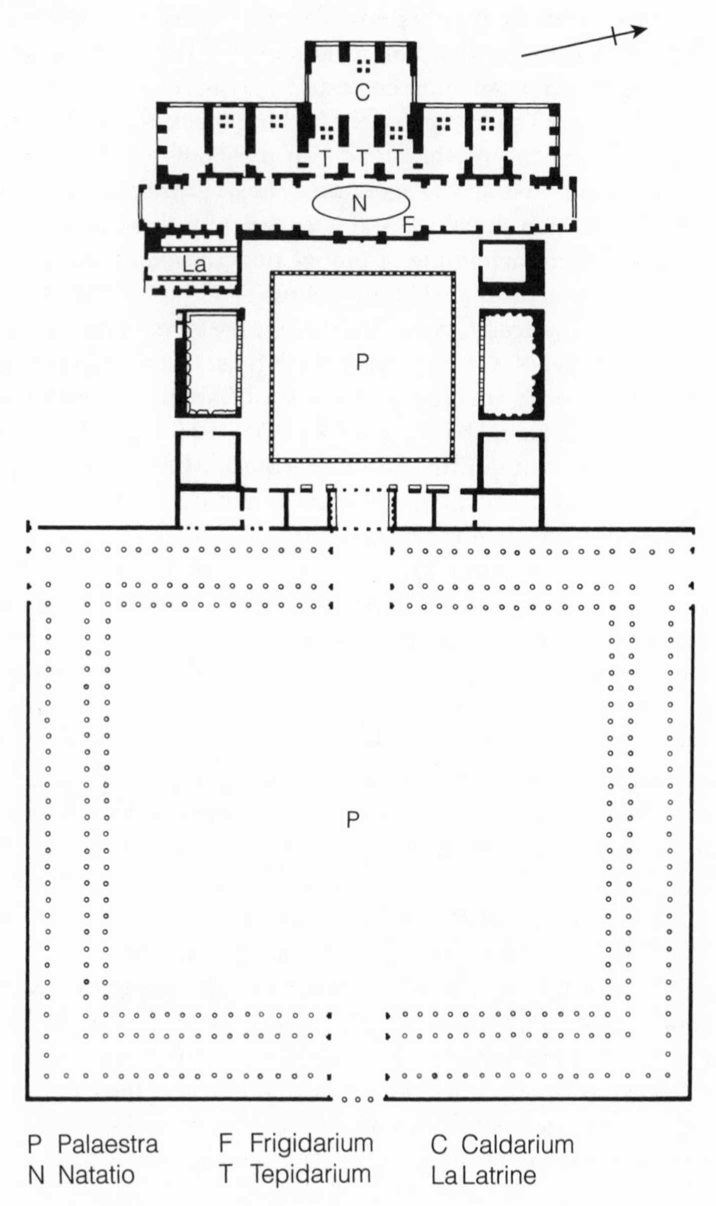

Fig. 23. Plan of the Harbor Baths-Gymnasium, Ephesus. Scale 1:2000.

In the eastern provinces and particularly in Asia Minor, large-scale baths were often provided along with Hellenistic-style gymnasia so that a more hybrid facility in terms of function and design was achieved.[120] A particularly good example of this can be seen at Ephesus in the Harbor Baths (Yegül 1992, 272–73). This complex was probably a Domitianic project in origin and included a large set of baths and a palaestra (fig. 23). On the east side was a huge peristyle (about 200 meters by 240 meters) that functioned as a gymnasium area and was known as the Porticoes of Verulanus. Other examples can be seen elsewhere in Ephesus (although not on the same scale), at Sardis (a second- to third-century A.D. construction), and in the Baths of Caracalla at Ankara.[121] However, there are also many examples of large bath buildings not designed on a symmetrical basis, although they provided very similar facilities: for example, the Baths of Faustina at Miletus (mid–second century A.D.), the third-century Large Baths at Aspendus, and the South Baths at Perge.[122]

There were obviously many smaller public baths *(balnea)* and private establishments as well as these large and lavish baths in both Rome and the provinces.[123] The plan and design of these, however, varied considerably, as they often had to take account of the building plot available. Such baths were common throughout the empire. Usually they did not have exercise facilities. From these smaller establishments the Turkish baths of today developed (Nielsen 1990, 114–18).

A particularly good and well-preserved example, although located outside the city, is the Hunting Baths at Lepcis Magna (fig. 24). This complex, whose first phase probably dates to the later second century A.D., comprises two identical bathing suites leading from one *frigidarium.* From the two hexagonal *tepidaria,* access was gained into two small rectangular *caldaria,* which were connected by a doorway. The rooms were covered by concrete vaults, an unusual feature in North African vault construction.[124]

120. Nielsen 1990, 95–118; Yegül 1992, 250–313.

121. Yegül 1986.

122. Yegül 1992, 291–301. There are also many examples in North Africa.

123. Yegül 1979; Nielsen 1990, 114–22.

124. Ward-Perkins and Toynbee 1949; Yegül 1992, 242–43. The name of these baths is derived from their very fine wall paintings depicting scenes of animal hunting.

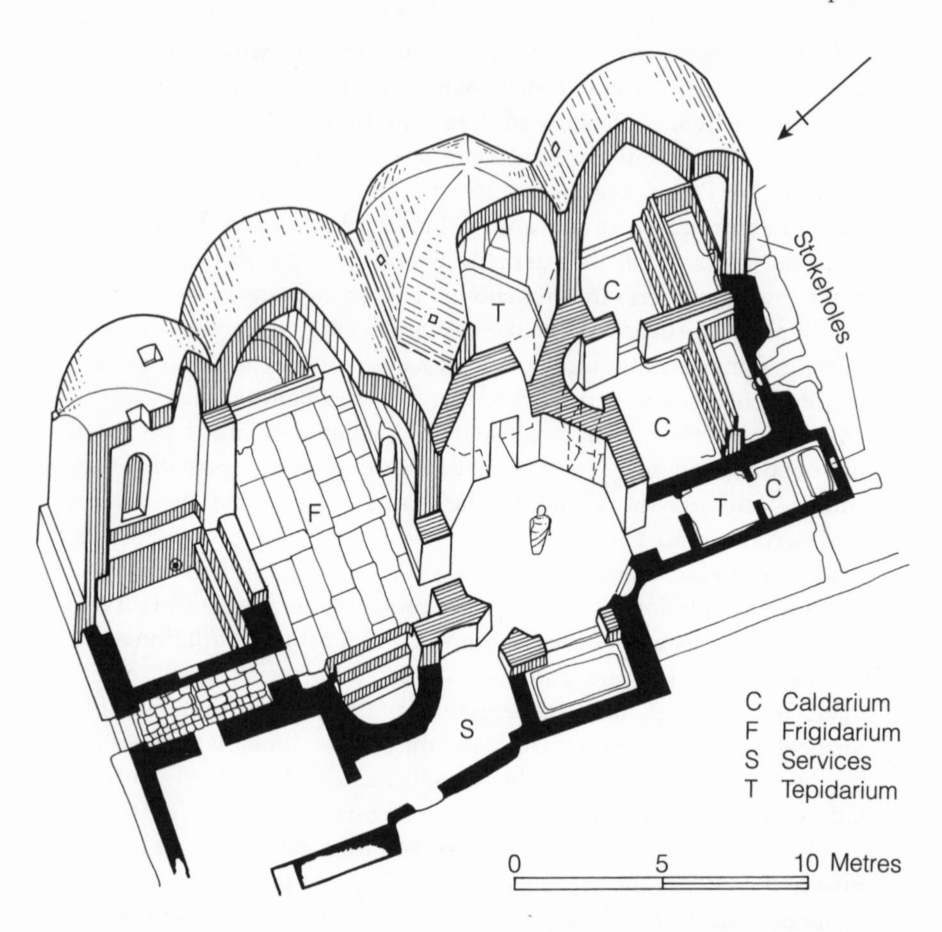

Fig. 24. Axonometric view of the Hunting Baths, Lepcis Magna. (After Ward-Perkins 1981, fig. 251.)

Roman bath buildings present some of the best opportunities to study building materials and techniques in the Roman world, but they also provide us with tremendous insight into a social practice that became a way of life for virtually every inhabitant of the empire. The myriad possible activities and facilities offered by these establishments—both the large and the small ones—is summed up in Seneca's famous letter written at a time when he had lodgings over a bath building; he is fervently wishing for peace and quiet!

> So picture to yourself the assortment of sounds, which are strong enough to make me hate the very powers of hearing! When your strenuous gentleman, for example, is exercising himself by flourishing leaden weights; when he is working hard, or else pretends to be working hard, I can hear him grunt; and whenever he releases his imprisoned breath, I can hear him panting in wheezy and high-pitched tones. Or perhaps I notice some lazy fellow, content with a cheap rub-down, and hear the crack of the pummeling hand on his shoulder, varying in sound according as the hand is laid on flat or hollow. Then perhaps, a professional comes along, shouting out the score; that is the finishing touch. Add to this the arresting of an occasional roysterer or pickpocket, the racket of the man who always likes to hear his own voice in the bathroom, or the enthusiast who plunges into the swimming-tank with unconscionable noise and splashing. Besides all those whose voices, if nothing else, are good, imagine the hair-plucker with his penetrating, shrill voice—for the purposes of advertisement—continually giving it vent and never holding his tongue except when he is plucking the armpits and making his victim yell instead. Then the cake-seller with his varied cries, the sausage-man, the confectioner, and all the vendors of food hawking their wares, each with his own distinctive intonation.[125]

Conclusion

While the activities of the theater, amphitheater, and circus were not everyday activities, those of the baths were. All, however, were integral to Roman life and can be found in varying shapes and sizes from one end of the Empire to the other. The design of the buildings were a product of Roman technological developments and local building resources and as such provide a wealth of information on building practices, inspiring much admiration, and often amazement, at the achievements of the mainly anonymous architects. But evidence of how the buildings were used, how they were adapted, and how their functions evolved provides us with the greatest insights; these buildings were the tools of Romanization.

---

125. Seneca *Letters* 56, 1–2, translated by R.M. Gunmore (Loeb Classical Library).

CHAPTER SEVEN

Entertainers in the Roman Empire

David S. Potter

Buildings for public entertainment remain some of the most spectacular monuments to survive from the Roman empire. Representing, as they do, an enormous expenditure of society's resources on pleasure they are a vivid reminder of the centrality of public entertainment for the exposition and formation of social values. It is thus not surprising that public entertainment and public policy should often become one and the same: the theater, amphitheater, and circus were the loci of imperial communication with the people, both in Rome and the provinces—the markers of assimilation to the dominant culture.

Neither the buildings, as Hazel Dodge shows in her chapter, nor the system of entertainment emerged overnight. Both are the product of long periods of evolution, representing the fusion of Italic and Greek cultural traditions. This fusion was not always precise; inconcinnities between the legal and social status of different entertainers remain constant throughout the eight centuries surveyed in this chapter, and developments in different forms of entertainment mirror those of Greco-Roman civilization as a whole.

There were, broadly speaking, four categories of public entertainer: the gymnastic, scenic, circus, and amphitheatral. Gymnastic entertainers were those whose activities were a feature of the gymnasium, the central institution of a Greek city, where all forms of exercise were indulged in the nude. Scenic entertainers were all entertainers whose activities fell within the theater or were translated from the theater to other venues. Also included with this group may be the rather large

I thank Kathleen Coleman, Christopher Jones, and David Mattingly for their comments on drafts of this paper. They are not to blame for problems that remain, especially those resulting from the author's stubbornness.

class of what can be termed "subtheatrical" entertainers: bear trainers, clowns, jugglers, tightrope walkers, singing ropedancers, and the like. Circus entertainers were, principally, charioteers and their assistants, though, after the beginning of the fourth century A.D., most other entertainments tended to be subsumed as sideshows to chariot races. Amphitheatral entertainers were those who engaged in combat with humans and beasts, initially in the architectural ancestors of the Italian amphitheater, and later in all manner of building, throughout the Roman world. We can gain some impression, albeit an imprecise one, of the relative standing of these different groups by looking at the way that they were organized. Amphitheatral performers were directly administered by people whose social status was closely akin to procurers, in groups whose title evoked that of a gang of slaves, the *familia*. Most of the charioteers were divided among four factions that were administered, in each city, by people of relatively high status and that appear to have maintained some corporate freedom. The most successful athletes in the empire obtained memberships in guilds, administered by other athletes and organized with charters that resembled Greek civic constitutions. The most successful members of these associations, or synods, as they were known, were people of quite high status indeed, ranking with town councilors in major cities. Actors occupied a sort of middle ground between athletes and charioteers (or even gladiators). On the one hand, some had their own synods (and had them for considerably longer than athletes); on the other hand, not all scenic performers were regarded as equally worthy. Thus, at one point some actors may be placed, at Rome, on a legal par with gladiators; at another we find them occupying the same space as champion athletes. There is no logical reason why, in a society where military virtue played as important a role in national self-definition as it did at Rome, participants in a form of entertainment that involved combat between armed humans or humans and beasts should be regarded as being of lower status than naked men who wrestled with each other. The explanation for this must be sought in the (often difficult to trace) historical development of the various forms of entertainment in the Roman world.

There are few, if any, constants on the sliding scale of status, and no one period in the history of public entertainment in the Greco-Roman world can be regarded as normative, though a number of trends appear in the course of the period under consideration here.

1. The primary forms of public entertainment were urban phenomena. Participation in them was a mark of participation in the Greco-Roman urban culture that evolved after the third century B.C. The decline of the ancient city was accompanied by a decline in the variety of public entertainments.
2. Developments in public entertainment were influenced by changes in political structures.
3. The evolution of entertainments in Italy and Greece were very different, a point most clearly reflected in the social status of entertainers. The tension between the Greek and Italic tradition was never fully reconciled.
4. The provision of public entertainments involved a substantial investment of the financial resources of the Greco-Roman world. The size of the investment of social resources in public entertainment is, in and of itself, a significant illustration of the predominance of the urban aristocratic value system of the Greco-Italian elite in shaping tastes throughout the Mediterranean world.
5. In the fourth century A.D., all forms of entertainment begin to be subordinated to the structures of circus chariot racing, which is little attested in the eastern part of the empire before the third century A.D. and in most of the west before the second century A.D.
6. The Christian church was hostile to most traditional forms of entertainment, and this had a significant impact on public entertainment from the second quarter of the fourth century A.D. onward (and cannot be studied in any detail here).

Actors and Athletes

The Civic Background

A wide variety of scenic entertainers are attested from a very early date in the history of the Italian states and Greece. In both areas it appears that the earliest contexts for their activities were at aristocratic festivals and in cult celebrations. The Italic tradition appears to have been dominated by dancers, while the Greek tradition, from a very early date, included performers in a variety of highly sophisticated genres of poetry. Down to the end of the second century B.C. these two traditions developed along quite different lines, and as many of the developments that proved to be most influential in the long term are of Greek origin, this survey will start there.

The most famous genre associated with public performance in Greece was epic poetry. Public performance by bards who either composed as they sang or, after the invention of writing, performed epics formed by others may have contributed to the development of other forms of poetic performance, such as symposiastic verse and elaborate hymns to the gods. In the sixth century a new form of entertainment evolved out of a form of ritual dance at festivals of Dionysus at Athens: the play.[1] The earliest form of drama appears to have involved a soloist acting out a story in conjunction with a chorus. By the early fifth century the genre developed so that two and then three actors split a variety of roles; it also led to the development of a new sort of building, as the actor(s) came to perform on a raised platform.[2] The theater, the building type that evolved from the needs of this sort of presentation, rapidly became the basic building type for all public artistic performances, and it remained so in the Greek World until at least the sixth century A.D. It does not appear to have been used outside of the Greek-speaking world until the third century B.C., when plays started to be written in languages other than Greek.[3] The extraordinarily rapid spread of drama and the theater among the Greeks may be connected with the political predominance of the Athenian state in the fifth century B.C.

Although the evidence for the early history of Greek drama is exceptionally poor, it seems that the earliest plays were on themes borrowed from the epic tradition: they concerned the actions of gods and heroes and were known as tragedies.[4] At some point in the early fifth century the tragedies were supplemented by plays that took a satirical look at contemporary history (sometimes with extraordinary fantasies) and at the epic tradition itself. These plays were known as comedies and satyr

1. For the view adopted here see Csapo and Slater 1995, 89–95 and the bibliographical note on 412–13.

2. For the evolution of acting see Pickard-Cambridge 1988, 135–56.

3. Bernard 1976, 318–22.

4. The issue of the origin of tragedy is separate from that of the origin of drama (the fact of drama does not dictate that tragedies will be performed), and the issue of why tragedy began to be performed as opposed to anything else remains open. For a survey of scholarship see Csapo and Slater 1995, 89–95.

plays. The soloists in all forms of drama were always men of citizen birth, as were the members of the chorus. The costs of their performances were born by wealthy citizens who sponsored plays in competitions at the great civic festivals. Other performers also competed in these civic festivals and in the major international festivals that had developed between the eighth and sixth centuries at Olympia, Nemea, Isthmia, and Delphi.[5] The competitive, or agonistic, tradition established at the early period remained a crucial feature of all Greek scenic events until the end of the third century A.D. It also gave rise to an emphasis on star soloists in all forms of entertainment.[6] Successful poets, choral flautists, singers with the lyre, performers of epic poems, actors, and the like traveled from city to city, festival to festival, contending with each other for prizes. Actors in particular achieved positions of considerable political importance, especially in the sphere of international relations. Their trade made them familiar figures in many cities, and their professional skills may have made them effective advocates.[7]

The development of athletic events parallels that of scenic entertainments in a number of important ways. Traditions of athletic contests associated with the funerals of great men are attested in both Greece and Italy at a very early period, but while the contestants in the Greek world were initially drawn from the highest social classes, those in Italy always seem to have been from the lower.[8] In both Greece and Italy, there also appears to have been a very early conceptual division between athletics as a form of moral and military training for young men and athletics for their own sake. In the Greek world it was asserted that humans were imitating the actions of the gods and earlier heroes; in the Italian world there appears to have been no such ideology, and it is likely that the two traditions began independently of each other. Competitive sports are widely attested in the cultures of the Mediterranean and Near Eastern worlds—as, indeed, they are in many other cultures—and it is perhaps best to see them as natural features of male

5. For the origins of the agonistic cycle (a problematic issue) see Hammond 1982, 350 with bibliography.

6. Csapo and Slater 1995, 222–24, 229–38.

7. Csapo and Slater 1995, 231–38 (and their discussion on 223–24); Pickard-Cambridge 1988, 279–81.

8. For the Greek world see Poliakoff 1987, 129–33; for the Italic world see Thuillier 1985.

society.[9] The inclusion of women in competitive athletics is less common: it seems to have been conceivable in some Greek states, but not in Italy or in other Mediterranean cultures.[10]

In the Greek world athletics involved a variety of track-and-field events and three "combat sports." These "combat sports" were wrestling, boxing, and pankration. Ancient techniques of boxing and wrestling were very similar to those now in use, while pankration might best be compared to North American professional wrestling, if the modern sport was truly competitive rather than staged. It combined boxing and wrestling, with none of the rules that governed those sports.[11] Boxing and wrestling were also common in Italy, though pankration only seems to have arrived with Greek influence.[12] The only other difference that is now apparent between Greek and Italian athletics at this period is that well before the end of the sixth century, Greeks competed in the nude, while Italians continued to wear a loincloth in competition.[13]

To understand the development of athletics it is useful to draw a distinction between a training and agonistic context. This is the same distinction that is observed today between, for example, members of the professional tennis tour and people who play regularly for fun, occasionally, perhaps, participating in a tournament at a local social/athletic association for a small prize. There does not seem to have been any ancient equivalent to "big-time" college athletics that exist in an intermediate position between professional and amateur sport. In ancient terms, the people who participated at events such as the Olympics tended to be professionals; the amateurs stayed home at the local gymnasium. An amateur could aspire to professional status by seeking to

---

9. Poliakoff 1987, 107–12.

10. For female athletes see Pausanias *Description of Greece* 5.16.1; Athenaeus *Wise Men at Dinner* 13.566; Scholia to Juvenul Satire 4.53 (a manifestly archaizing Greek event); Suetonius *Life of Domitian* 4, 13; Dio *History of Rome* 61.19; Moretti 1953, n. 63. For other possible evidence see Ginestet 1991, n. 27 (*CIL* 14.4014b?). Ginestet rather overestimates the attestation of collegia of young women—one of his examples is a reference to female gladiators (with the inaccurate claim that they were banned by Severus); another is a reference to *mulieres,* married women.

11. Poliakoff 1987, 54–63.

12. For the particularly Etruscan combination of boxing with dancing see Thuillier 1993, 38–39.

13. McDonnell 1993, 1991.

contend in festivals at cities other than his own, and there seem to have been athletes of regional importance, good enough to win in games at home or in neighboring cities, but not attaining to the status of those superstars whose careers took them to major international festivals on a regular basis.

For the purpose of the present survey, the context of "training" athletics can be dealt with very briefly, as it remained remarkably constant from the emergence of complex societies in Italy and Greece during the eighth century B.C. to the end of ancient civic structures as the Roman empire fell apart in the fifth, sixth, and seventh centuries A.D. Young men of social status high enough that they would be expected to take a leading part in civic defense were expected to keep in shape. Hoplite warfare, which became commonplace in both Greece and Italy during the seventh century, demanded a very high degree of physical conditioning if a person was to survive it. Since the basic tactical formation consisted of a line of armored infantrymen, usually eight deep, it was critical that everyone who participated be in roughly the same shape. People who lacked the stamina to keep in formation could wreck the battle line, at which point the battle would be lost.

In the late-fifth and fourth centuries B.C. the nature of warfare began to change. Armies became larger and more professional. In Italy this was marked by the emergence of the large armies of peasant proprietors that subdued most of Italy in the fourth and third centuries; in Greece, by the increasing dependence on mercenaries in the fourth century and then the creation of the great professional armies of the Macedonian kings. The result was that in the gymnasium the social aspect of the organization of young men of the property-holding classes in the Greek world became more important than the military. Here men under the age of thirty were usually organized into three age-groups: "boys" (adolescents between ages twelve and eighteen), ephebes (young men at ages nineteen and twenty) and *neoi* (young men between ages twenty-one and thirty).[14] The lower age-group was kept strictly separated from the two older ones, something that was reflected in the organization of athletic contests, which were ordinarily divided between those for the *paides* and those for "men," though there was occasionally a third category of "young men" corresponding roughly to the ephebes. It appears that all members of each category

14. Gauthier and Hatzopoulos 1993, 76–78, 85–87.

were expected to participate in the full range of track and "combat" events, though individuals might elect to specialize in one variety or the other for contests within the gymnasium.

The gymnasium building was the locus of athletic training for young men, and membership was controlled in accordance with social status. As a civic institution, it was funded by the community and the official, or *gymnasiarch,* who was selected each year to be in charge of its activities. Men older than thirty could exercise in private gymnasia if they chose to.[15] When Greek cities came to be founded in large numbers throughout the Near East and Egypt from the late fourth century B.C. onward, membership in the gymnasium came to be recognized as a fundamental marker of citizen status and social acceptability.[16] The groups of young men admitted to the gymnasium could also, it appears, be called on to act as the agents of social control and, occasionally, to play a significant role in local politics. In the Latin west, parallel organizations of young men, the *iuvenes,* are attested in similar roles as entertainers and political action groups.[17] That these groups existed in polite society shows that it is impossible to draw a strict dichotomy between Greek and Roman styles of athletic entertainment. Indeed, the corporate associations of *iuvenes* (young men) appear to have remained significant in the cities of, for example, Roman North Africa, well into the third century (fig. 25). The decline of the western *iuvenes,* like that of the Greek *neoi* may be associated with the general decline of civic support for all sorts of athletics at the end of that century. This was probably a function of both the economic difficulties of the period and the increasingly preeminent role that circus factions were playing in all entertainment. The rise of the circus factions also marked the beginning of the end of independent associations of professional athletes.

The Hellenistic World and Republican Rome (300–31 B.C.)

The late fourth century B.C. saw major changes in the political structure of the eastern Mediterranean world. Alexander the Great's conquest of the Persian empire and the two decades of war for control of that empire after his death led to the emergence of three major "supra-

15. Magie 1950, 855–60.
16. *P.Oxy.* 2186, 3276–84 with Lewis 1983, 42.
17. For local athletic events in North Africa see Wensch-Klein 1990, 27–29; for collegia of the *iuvenes* see Ginestet 1991.

regional" states: the Ptolemaic empire based in Egypt; the Seleucid kingdom that controlled Asia Minor, Syria, Iraq, and Iran; and a variety of political entities (ultimately the Macedonian kingdom) that controlled northern Greece, Thrace, and those portions of the Aegean that were not under Ptolemaic rule. The rise of these kingdoms had a major impact on the organization of both scenic and athletic entertainment. Kings controlled far greater resources than any previous Greek political entity. It was rare for an individual city, such as Rhodes, to be able to assert a significant independent place for itself in the world. Competition for civic status was thus channeled in new directions, away from the physical domination of neighbors to assertion of cultural and historical superiority. The civic festival became a central feature in such competitions for status, and the pressure to get the best entertainers took on a new intensity. In addition, both Philip II of Macedon and his son, Alexander the Great, were great fans of the theater and extended a long tradition of royal patronage for the arts and athletics.[18]

It is roughly at this time that we first have evidence for the formation of professional associations of scenic artists. The earliest evidence for interstate organization of performers comes from the island of Euboea in the early third century, where cities allied to provide entertainers at each other's festivals.[19] It may have been in response to such efforts at organization that the performers began to organize themselves. A guild of actors from Isthmia and Corinth is attested at roughly the same period as the Euboean pact, and so too is a guild of Athenian actors. A third guild is attested in Egypt by the end of the third century, and a fourth in western Asia Minor in the second.[20] These guilds, which had governing councils that were elected by the membership on the model of Greek cult organizations, presented themselves to the world as "artisans of Dionysus," the patron god of the scenic arts. The guilds negotiated the terms under which their members would appear at civic festivals and imposed fines on members who did not live up to the obligations of guild membership. The relations between a guild and a city that was holding a festival may be seen in the following decree of the Ionian guild.

---

18. Pickard-Cambridge 1988, 278–81.

19. For acting associations (not necessarily interstate) see Aristotle *Rhetoric* 1405a23; [Aristotle] *Problems* 956b11. For the association on Euboea see *IG* 12.9.207 with Pickard-Cambridge 1988, 281–82, 306–8.

20. Pickard-Cambridge 1988, 282, 287–88.

> Good Fortune. It seems to the assembly of the artisans of Dionysus; so that [. . .] salvation [. . . to owe] to Dionysus and to the people of Iasos in the festival that they celebrate to Dionysus, because of the existing friendship from ancient times of the registered artisans and of those who work with our synod, (we send) two flute players, two tragic actors, two comic actors, a citharode and a cytharist so that they will perform the choruses to the god in accordance with their ancestral provisions, providing (in addition) the equipment they require [. . .]. They will offer all the regular contests of the artisans of Dionysus for the specified time, providing everything in accord with the customs of the people of Iasos. If one of those who is sent by the artisans does not go to Iasos or does not perform in the contests, he will pay one thousand Antiochene drachmas as a sacred fine for the god to the assembly of the artisans of Dionysus, unless he was unable to perform because of illness or the weather. There will be an appeal of the fine for a person showing proofs for introducing and destroying the decree in accordance with the law. (*I. Iasos* 152)

The third century B.C. also saw important developments in the scenic arts at Rome. Until the middle of the third century, scenic entertainment at Rome was very similar to that in other non-Greek Italian cities. The emphasis was on dancers and some sorts of poetic performances that were considerably less elaborate than those of the Greek world.[21] The performers were not ordinarily people of social significance and did not compete with each other. They performed as part of celebrations offered by aristocrats as "gifts" to the people of their city *(munera)* or in connection with regular religious festivals financed by the community *(ludi)*.

The Romans appear to have developed a taste for plays even before they conquered the Greek states of Italy in the early third century and then achieved a dominant position in Sicily, with its largely Greek urban population, as a result of the First Punic War (264–241 B.C.). While we have virtually no direct evidence for the dramatic performances at Roman festivals in the fourth century B.C., a compelling case can be made suggesting that they included historical dramas and comedy. The comic performances were likely improvisations around stock

21. Massa-Pairault 1993.

characters, while the historical performances seem to have taken great events from the regal period and years immediately after that as their subject. A great change occurred when the native tradition was brought into direct contact with one from the contemporary Greek world: the use of a set script.[22] The two earliest Latin playwrights of significance, Livius Andronicus and Naevius, came from southern Italy, where literary drama already had a history. Their dramatic works, which included both tragedies and comedies, were adaptations of Greek works and quite probably also new versions of the sort of historical dramas that had been performed in earlier centuries.

The non-Roman origins of the early leaders of the classical acting profession at Rome are connected to another important issue, albeit one that is hard to detect in more than shadowy outline. As Hazel Dodge shows in her chapter, there were theaters in the Greek cities of Italy before the time of Plautus, and theatrical performances continued to be offered throughout the peninsula. A particularly nasty incident in the months immediately preceding the outbreak of war between Rome and its Italian allies in 91 B.C. involved a theatrical performance at Asculum, where Romans in the audience complained about a performance by a local comic actor (whom they lynched), provoking a violent response by the native population, which then attacked a Latin comedian, who tried to save himself by claiming that he had never performed in Rome (Diodorus of Sicily *Universal History* 37.12). Both actors appear to have functioned in an environment that was separate from that dominated by the aristocratic culture of the capitol. Tastes in Rome could and did influence tastes in the rest of Italy, but they could not and did not eclipse long-standing local traditions. Moreover, these traditions continued to exert an influence at Rome, in terms of both the identity of the performers and the shows that they offered. The prominence of individuals from the Oscan regions of south-central Italy is particularly striking: there is some reason to think that shows continued to be offered in Oscan as well as Greek and Latin in Rome during the time of Augustus (Rawson 1985, 476).

It may be that the prominence obtained by Italian performers influenced the Roman view that scenic performances were, as a class, in some way, non-Roman and potentially disruptive to the social order.

22. The early history of Latin drama is a controversial topic. The view adopted here may be found most fully in Wiseman 1995, 129–44.

Thus, while in the Greek world performers achieved greater independence and power, in the Roman world these entertainers remained clients of members of the aristocracy.[23] The resulting tension between the low social status of performers and their actual political importance was never fully resolved. Famous actors accumulated incredible fortunes, are often found in close proximity to very important members of the aristocracy, and were treated as objects of emulation by their aristocratic masters. The improvement in the status of Italian actors after the emergence of the monarchy, increasingly assimilating to the status of Greek entertainers, may be a consequence of this.

The development of scenic organizations is complicated by changes in taste and reciprocal influences between the Greek and Roman traditions. The two basic trends in this period are (1) the development of a "star" system with an emphasis on great solo performers and (2) the growth in popularity of amateur performance. These general trends had some impact on the development of the theatrical repertoire, leading to the eclipse of some styles of performance and the emergence of new kinds.

By the end of the third century B.C. the rise of tragedy and comedy on the Roman scene led to the formation of a *collegium scribarum et histrionum,* or guild of playwrights and actors.[24] The people who wrote plays were of very much the same status as those who performed them: Livius and Naevius were foreigners; in the next generation, the greatest of the Latin comic poets, Plautus, may have been a freedman; Ennius, who wrote plays as well as epics, came from Campania; and the two great playwrights of the succeeding generation, Luscius Lanuvinus and Terence, were likewise of non-Roman origin. By the time of Luscius and Terence there appears to have been a sort of competition between the authors of plays for top ranking in the city. But this competition appears to have been directed primarily at gaining the attention of prominent Romans who would purchase plays from them; and it does not appear to have lasted much beyond the lifetime of Accius in the early first century.[25] From the end of the second century onward there seems to have been a preference on the part of Romans who were offering *munera* for old plays. These men were not interested in competitions between playwrights or between actors: they simply wanted to

23. Leppin 1992, 71–83.
24. Jory 1970; Leppin 1992, 91–93.
25. See now Lebek 1996, 30–35.

win credit with the Roman people for putting on the best possible show. The result was that the works of authors like Plautus, Terence, and Ennius obtained the status of school texts, while the production of new theatrical literature passed from the hands of the disenfranchised to those of aristocrats, whose works may not ever have been intended for full stage performance.

At the same time that tragedy and comedy begin to appear on the Latin stage, there begins to be evidence for other sorts of performance, as well as for continuity with older forms. Thus pyrrhic dancing, a form of exercise that was allegedly created by the son of Achilles at Troy, continued to be performed both by groups of young men exercising in the gymnasia of the Greek portions of Italy and by professional performers elsewhere.[26] Pyrrhic and other sorts of dancing by troops of young men seems initially to have been adopted for military reasons among the Greeks and to have had religious overtones in the Italic tradition. Associations of Roman priests, such as the Salii and the Arval Brethren, danced at festivals that were relevant to them; though in the case of the *tripudium,* or three-step dance of the Arvals, the performance took place inside a temple and was for the pleasure of a divinity rather than the common public.[27] Dancers of various sorts appeared at other festivals, where their performances may have had an apotropaic purpose, symbolically expelling warfare from the community (Dupont 1993, 206–8). One exception to the overtly ritual context of Roman dances appears to have been a performance known as the *ludus talarius.* We know little about it save that it appears to have involved a troop of dancers who were accompanied by singing, cymbals, or a castanet.[28] Atellan farces, for which we have rather better evidence, were comic acts of Oscan origin that continued to be offered into the first century A.D., if not longer (Quintillian *Oratorical Precepts* 6.3.47). In the imperial period, the uneasy fusing of the Greek and Italic traditions of dancing

26. Plato *Laws* 814d–16e; Apuleius *Metamorphoses* 10.29; Plutarch *Moral Essays* 554b; Lucian *On Dancing* 9; Robert and Robert 1989, 58–59; Jory 1996, 24–26.

27. See chap. 4 in this book.

28. Cicero *On Duties* 1.150; Quintillian *Oratorical Precepts* 11.3.58; Fronto *To Marcus Antoninus Concerning Oratory* 14. For technical issues see Leppin 1992, 186–88 and the powerful case made by Jory (1995, 146–52) showing that the censors were banning forms of theater that derived from Greek theatrical traditions and retaining those of native Italic origin.

by troops led to a situation in which some sorts of dancing were permissible for young men of good standing, being sanctioned by ancient tradition, and others were for lower-status performers only.

The same uneasy fusion of traditions appears in connection with actors, or *histriones* (in Latin), the performers of comedy, tragedy, and particularly Italian forms of comic entertainment. Careful study of known *histriones* has shown that in the Republic, Italian troops of *histriones* who acted tragedies and comedies consisted of three to five players, led by an *actor,* who was also a participant in the performances; and that all members of such troops were either freed or slave (Leppin 1992, 50–51). At the same time, performers of mime, a form of comic performance that became extremely important in the course of the first century B.C., were organized in groups of seven, led by a star, usually male, though there were some women who gained great renown in this way. A person wishing to present a play to the public would negotiate with the lead actor of a troop, paying him the fee for the whole troop, and might negotiate further to get a particularly famous actor to appear as a soloist with them. The sums involved could be very high: L. Roscius Gallus is said to have been paid as much as 4,000 HS a day to perform in this way. His total annual income is put by one source at 300,000 HS per annum. The actor Aesop, the great star of the next generation is said to have left a fortune that would have placed him among the very richest people at Rome (200,000,000 HS), and a female dancer named Dionysia is said to have made 200,000 HS in one year.[29] In addition to their theatrical incomes, successful actors could also make money by assisting important Romans in other ways. Roscius and Aesop helped Cicero improve his oratorical skills, and much of what we know about Roscius is connected with the money that he received for training other actors. A slave who was purchased for 4,000 HS was turned over to Roscius under an agreement through which Roscius and the original purchaser of the slave formed a corporation whose assets consisted of the slave, whose value was held jointly by the two members of the corporation; Roscius' training increased the value of the slave to 100,000 HS (Cicero *On behalf of Roscius the Comedian* 27–28). A performer's chances of success on the stage could depend on public knowledge of his training. An actor named Eros, who was driven from the stage by a

29. Cic. *On Behalf of Roscius the Comedian* 23; Macrob. *Saturnalia* 3.14.13; Leppin 1992, 85–86; Lebek 1996, 36–43 and, for women, 43–44.

dissatisfied crowd, fled to Roscius' house, and when he reemerged before the public with a reputation as Roscius' pupil, his reputation was much enhanced.[30]

Roscius and Aesop were wealthy enough to finish their careers in the very upper echelons of Roman society. They do not seem to have been alone, and the aspiring politician was well advised to maintain good relations with leading members of the acting profession. Gnaeus Pompey, for all the power that he accumulated, does not seem to have been able to do this. His agents prosecuted the famous poet Archias, whose performances in Greek drew crowds that appear to have been every bit as enthusiastic as those at a modern rock concert, and lost the case (Cicero *On behalf of Archias* 5). An actor named Diphilus recited a line from a tragedy in 59 B.C. in such a way that everyone in the audience immediately took it as a negative reference to Pompey and demanded a dozen encores (Cicero *Letters to Atticus* 2.19.3). Mark Antony was better connected and got a famous mime, on very short notice, to play Caesar at Caesar's funeral and contribute to the riot that followed. At the same time, and on the same notice (less than a week), he had trained choruses reciting hymns in both Greek and Latin in Caesar's memory. Marcus Brutus, leader of Caesar's assassins, did not get the play that he wanted from a troop of actors a few months later.[31] Caesar appears to have been good to actors, and Antony appears to have enjoyed their company: this proved politically significant.

Antony was not alone in his patronage of performing artists. Most could be found as clients of great nobles, who would arrange for public performances as well as for private shows. Dinner parties at Rome were often turned into a sort of "dinner theater" through performances by a wide range of scenic artists. The host of the dinner party was essentially a benefactor and was a member of the class from which beneficence in both public and private was expected. The troops of entertainers that

30. Cic. *On Behalf of Roscius the Comedian* 30; Lebek 1996, 37.

31. For the performance at Caesar's funeral see Appian *Civil Wars* 2.146; Antony's own conduct was highly theatrical. For Brutus' problem (Accius' *Tereus* instead of the *Brutus*) see Cicero *Letters to Atticus* 16.5.1, 16.2.3 (he was happy enough with the *Tereus,* which would also have dealt with the theme of tyranny, but he was clearly at Accius' disposal). For Caesar's relations with actors see Lebek 1996, 46–48, also suggesting that Caesar broke significant barriers by engaging a mimographer of equestrian rank to perform on the stage at his triumph.

were supported in the home could also be exhibited in public—and the home of a wealthy person might, in the long run, be a preferable domicile for artists who, though talented, were not of the highest rank. But this could lead to difficulties, the line between public and private was often very hard to discern, and by the fourth century we find the Roman state intervening to prevent wealthy individuals from privatizing desirable entertainment commodities.[32]

International professional athletic associations (synods) emerge much later than similar associations of scenic artists. There is no obvious reason why this should be so, but a number of factors may be relevant. One of these is that victors in athletic events appear to have been better treated by their native cities. As early as the fifth century (if not earlier) we find some cities offering perpetual maintenance at public expense for victors at the international games.[33] We also have evidence that groups of victors within a city could form local associations to look after their own interests and that cities provided the expenses of other athletes in training (a practice that is attested as early as the fourth century B.C.) (Pleket 1973, 196–97). Furthermore, the continued connection between civic responsibility and athletic achievement may have restrained nascent desires for extracivic institutions. It may not, therefore, be accidental that we only begin to get evidence for international associations of athletic victors in the early first century B.C., when the traditional structures of the post-Alexandrine world were disintegrating before the new political reality of Roman domination, and when the economic relationships of the eastern Mediterranean were thrown into chaos by the wars waged by Rome against its enemies and by Romans against each other (Pleket 1973, 200–202). The first datable attestation of an international association of victors comes in a letter to the city of Ephesus from the triumvir Mark Antony in which he confirms an earlier grant of exemptions from public service for the association.[34] Who granted the original exemption? We cannot know at the present time,

32. Jones 1991, 185–98 is fundamental; for late imperial restrictions see *Theodosian Code* 15.7.5, 6, 10.

33. *IG* 1[3] 131; Robert 1936; Robert 1967, 16–17 = *OMS* 5:356–57 (discussing *I.Eph.* 1415).

34. The actual date, 43 or 33 B.C., is in dispute (see Pleket 1973, 201–2). I favor the higher date because of the possible connection with Caesar. See the next note.

but other evidence for the granting of exemptions to cultural figures (among whom athletes would rank) suggests that it may have been Julius Caesar.[35] Further evidence for the recent institution of a synod of international victors comes from an inscription in honor of a long-distance runner from Miletus who says that he was the first winner of the stadion race established by the "international association of crowned winners at the sacred games." Other evidence from this text (a reference to the games established by Augustus to celebrate his victory at Actium in terms that suggest their recent institution) places his career in the twenties B.C.[36] Shortly after this, we begin to get evidence for two quite distinct synods: that of the "international athletes" and that of the "international crowned victors." Both appear to have been based in Asia Minor, and both existed alongside of local associations of athletic victors in various cities. The chief distinction between the local associations and the "international" associations is that the former were primarily retrospective, providing benefits for people who had brought honor to a city through their victories, while the latter had a prospective element, in that they were concerned with both the privileges of members and the organization of contests.[37]

Developments from Augustus to Alexander Severus (31 B.C.–A.D. 235)

There were a variety of entertainments that had existed alongside theatrical events in traditional Greek festivals. On lists of festivals where the traditional "main events" were presented as "contests" *(agones)*, these are described as "exhibitions" *(epideixeis)*.[38] The performers included actors, dancers, puppeteers, and mimes. The latter acted in highly stylized comic acts in which actors played generically determined roles. The themes of their performances appear to have been

35. See Suet. *Caesar* 42; the provisions of this edict (which, on present evidence only affected educators in Rome) were extended by a grant of immunity to doctors and educators by a decree that may date to the period just after Philippi (see *I.Eph.* 223).

36. Moretti 1953, n. 59; Pleket 1973, 202.

37. See Pleket 1973, 203–6 on the distinction between local and international groups. He should not be blamed for the discussion of the functional distinctions offered here.

38. Robert 1936, 244 = *OMS* 1:680.

drawn from daily life, though there is evidence for mimes who specialized in "old stories" as well, and they were extremely popular. In, at the latest, the second century B.C., they had their own professional association at Rome, the Parasites of Apollo, and we know that there were aristocratic writers of new texts for them in the first century.

Shortly after the Mithridatic War, a dignitary at the city of Priene put on a theatrical display that included the pantomime Ploutagenes (*I. Priene* 113). This is the earliest extant specific record of a public performance of this sort, though pantomime's roots go back at least to the fifth century B.C. (it is mentioned by Xenophon), and other sources suggest that in the intervening centuries it had become very popular in two great Hellenistic capitols: Antioch and Alexandria.[39] Pantomimes appear to have burst on the Roman scene in the reign of Augustus through performances by a Cilician named Pylades and became wildly popular immediately after that.[40] It was here that a major change was introduced in the style of performance, and it was as a result of imperial patronage that pantomime moved from the fringes of Greek entertainment to the center. This is just one of many cases where the tastes of the capitol transformed a provincial institution and returned it to the provinces with fresh importance.

Pantomime was a form of dance. Inscriptions praise the greatest pantomime of the second century A.D., Tiberius Julius Apolaustus, as the "performer of rhythmic tragic movement," a description that reflects the mythological content of the dance (the description of something as "tragic" indicates that it derived its theme from the epic tradition).[41] The setting of the performance is described as follows.

> The appearance of the dancer is attractive and appropriate . . . that much is clear to anyone who is not blind. The mask is attractive and appropriate to the theme of the drama: the mouth is not wide open as in tragedy and comedy, but closed: the dancer has a lot of people to do the shouting for him. They used to sing themselves, but afterwards, as the panting that accompanied their movement disturbed the song, it seemed better for others to do the singing for them. (Lucian *On Dancing* 29–30)

39. Robert 1930, 109= *OMS* 1:657.

40. Lucian *On Dancing* 34; Athenaeus *Doctors at Dinner* 1.20; Jory 1996, 23–24, 26–27.

41. *F. Delphi* 3. 1. 551.

The dancer himself carried some props and wore a mask and an elaborate cloak that he used to suggest various features of the story that he performed. He was accompanied by music and a chorus that sang the story to which his dance and the gestures of his hands (an evidently critical feature) gave meaning (Jory 1996, 3–4). All manner of stories were attempted; audiences and other pantomimes appear to have rated performances in terms of the degree of difficulty involved in the mimesis. Portraying the blind Oedipus, for instance, appears to have been rated comparatively easy, while portraying the mad Hercules was very difficult (not least because it involved shooting arrows while dancing). Other routines—of indeterminate difficulty though great popularity—were erotic in nature: Leda and the swan appears to have been a favorite (Macrobius *Saturnalia* 2.17 ff.).

It is clear that the best performers in the imperial period could achieve considerable influence in the imperial palace. A mime named Mnester was the lover of the empress Messalina, and a Jewish mime named Halityrus was able to obtain an interview with the emperor for an embassy from Judaea. Three pantomimes named Apolaustus are known from the second century, two of them imperial freedmen. The fact that three Apolausti are known from one half century reflects another feature of the profession: the assumption of the name of one famous performer by another. The greatest pantomime of all was probably the Pylades who reformed the art in the reign of Augustus, and his renown is reflected by the fact that we know of no fewer than five other pantomimes who called themselves Pylades, or "the Pylades," in the course of the next two centuries.[42]

The training of pantomimes was similar to that of other actors, in that aspiring performers apprenticed with their elders, sometimes even acquiring enough fame to challenge their mentors. Such challenges could arise out of crowd response to performances or out of the contests of pantomimes that were admitted to the traditional Greek *agones* by the middle of the second century A.D. (a reflection of the importance of the art at Rome). Indeed, it appears that pantomimes would show up

42. For Mnester see Seneca *The Pumpkinification of Claudius* 13.4; Tacitus *Annals* 11.4.1, 28.1–2, 36.1; Dio *History of Rome* 60.28.3–5, 60.31.5; Suetonius *Life of Caligula* 36.1, 55.1, 57.4; Leppin 1992, 261–62. For Halityrus see Josephus, *Life* 16; Leppin 1992, 247. For the Apolausti see Leppin 1992, 205–11 (two others are known from the first century). For Pylades see Leppin 1992, 284–88. See also the various pantomimes named Paris discussed in Leppin 1992, 270–76.

to heckle each others' performances and acquired claques to protect themselves or silence their rivals. These confrontations could become violent.

As the history of pantomime suggests, the tale of scenic performance was anything but static under the emperors. Even after the reign of Constantine, new styles of performance were coming into vogue, and old ones were continuing in new venues. One of the most curious appears to be a festival known as Maiouma. Originally, it seems, of Syrian origin (*mai* means "water"), it appears to have been a carnival that was celebrated around springs of water. Some of these activities may have become rather risqué, leading to imperial strictures against "lewdness" in its celebration. But even the emperors had to concede that there was nothing wrong with it if the activities were kept within the bounds of decency, and we have evidence for the spread of this festival into Asia Minor during the sixth century A.D. Maiouma and other survivals of the ancient traditions of entertainment appear to cease in the wake of the Arab conquests of the seventh century A.D.[43]

Maiouma was not the only sort of entertainment that involved water. The more spectacular events, naumachiae, or sea battles, have been treated by Hazel Dodge, and the evidence need not be rehearsed here (or in the context of subgladiatorial spectacles involving condemned prisoners, where it would be more appropriate). On the less violent side we have clear evidence for a display that appears to have been offered in the context of the dedication of the Colosseum and to have involved women who cavorted as sea nymphs (Neriads), probably with minimal clothing for the delight of the crowd.[44] No clothing is said to have been worn by the women whose aquatic displays allegedly prevented people from going to listen to the sermons of John Chrysostom in late fourth-century Antioch (Coleman 1993, 64–65).

With the naked swimmers of Antioch may be numbered a very large class of performer of the sort referred to in one decree as those who were hired to put on various shows without competing for a prize. Mimes were members of this group, as were pantomimes before the exaltation of their art under Augustus. So, too, were the *homeristae,* who

43. See Rouché 1993, n. 65 with discussion and the correction in Jones 1994, 286. For an excellent summary of the issues connected with theatrical performance of all sorts in the post-Constantinian period see Barnes 1996.

44. See Coleman 1993, 63–65. For the event involving a Leander in Mart. *Concerning Spectacles* 25, 25b as an execution see Coleman 1993, 62–63.

put on performances of scenes from Homer with props and music, and the "singing ropedancers" attested in fifth-century Oxyrhyncus.[45] The "singing ropedancers" may in fact be a variety of *embolariae,* or specialists in entr'acte entertainment. We know of such people from the lifetime of Cicero (he says the sister of an enemy was versed in *embolaria*) and from inscriptions. One of these suggests that the women, at least, could be quite young: Phoebe Vocontia, *embolaria,* was twelve when she died.[46] At times these performers could be more exciting than the main event. Terence complains that he lost an audience to the initial performance of one of his comedies to tightrope walkers, and we hear of a famous *embolaria* who reappeared on the stage as a special treat at the age of 104.[47]

Tightrope walkers might be accompanied by *petauristes,* acrobats who leapt off of springing platforms, or by *grallatores,* who walked on stilts (Blümner 1918, 10–16). There were jugglers, clowns, and animal trainers of all sorts. Then there were miracle workers, performing various acts of magic for the fascination of the crowd (Blümner 1918, 20–21). It is impossible to write a history of these people, because beyond the fact of their existence, we know very little about them. Most are rarely attested on inscriptions, and the bulk of the evidence for them comes from literary texts where they appear, as in real life, on the fringes of the main events. The concentration on the higher levels of the profession enforced by the evidence can only allow us brief glimpses of the extraordinary range of entertainment that was available when the athletes rested, when the chariots were not running, or between the acts of a play. One thing that is clear is that here there was room for women as well as men, and while the opportunities for great reward were not as obvious as with the "higher" forms of performance, they were still there. The daughter of a bear keeper for a chariot faction in sixth-century A.D. Constantinople, who is said to have been a very good mime actress, became empress.

The emergence of the monarchy under Augustus sparked an explosion of athletic competition throughout the eastern provinces of the empire. The obsessive commemoratory activity of Augustus and his associates may be the proximate cause of ignition. Leading citizens of

45. See Blümner 1918, 5; see *P.Oxy.* 2707 for the performers on Oxyrhyncus.

46. See Cicero *On Behalf of Sestius* 116, where the context suggests that singing was part of the act. For Phoebe Vocontia see *ILS* 5262.

47. Terence *The Mother-in-Law* 34; Pliny *Natural History* 7.158.

Fig. 25. Mosaic illustrating athletic events. The mosaic presents the activity at the contest on four levels. The first and third levels represent the events of the pentathlon: footrace (top left and center), javelin (top right, almost completely lost), long jump (third row, left; the implements in the photograph are for smoothing sand), discus (third row, second from left), and wrestling (third row, right). Also depicted are boxing (third row, center), the pankration (fourth row, second from left, distinguished from boxing by the absence of gloves), and a torch race in armor (fourth row, right). There are two scenes depicting the award of prizes (second and fourth rows, center). (From Gafsa, Tunisia; photo reproduced from M. Blanchard-Lemée, *Mosaics of Roman Africa* (New York, 1996), fig. 139.)

the cities of the empire seem to have attuned themselves with remarkable speed to the ebb and flow of events connected with Augustus, and games honoring the *princeps* and his family were found to be an excellent way to attract favorable attention.[48] Imperial government was viewed by provincials as a remarkably personal phenomenon. The senate and people of Rome had failed to provide the security that he offered, and Augustus presented himself as the person responsible for

48. For the close attention paid to political developments in Rome under Augustus by provincial cities see Millar 1993.

the peace and order of the world. His subjects, for whatever reason, were eager to tell him that they agreed. The creation of a commemorative festival was both an enjoyable and an effective way to do this. Throughout the next three centuries we therefore find the festival cycles of cities changing to reflect changing dynastic realities at Rome. Control of these festivals through the granting or withholding of permission to actually institute them was likewise found to be a useful way for emperors to influence local politics. Games were established not only to honor individual emperors but also to commemorate individuals who had earned an emperor's special favor.

The tendency of the festival cycle to reflect political realities can be seen as early as the reign of Augustus. The first extant text to mention a festival instituted by the international synods of crowned victors at the sacred games lists, among more traditional events, several in honor of Augustus within a decade of the victory at Actium, which may suggest that the emperor himself inspired them; Augustus himself decided to commemorate his victory at Actium with quadrennial games in honor of the event. The rapid growth of such festivals, mirroring developments in the imperial cult, where cities founded their own temples as a way of advertising their loyalty to the new regime, is perhaps most evident in a text of c. A.D. 5 from the island of Cos that mentions no fewer than five festivals in addition to the Actian games in honor of Augustus or his family members.[49] The connection with the vagaries of imperial politics becomes even more clear when inscriptions from the later part of the first century are compared to such inscriptions as that from Cos. By the time of Domitian (A.D. 81–96) we find no reference to events in honor of Augustus' family members. Instead, there are more general festivals sponsored by provincial assemblies in honor of "the emperor" and occasional festivals honoring highly successful provincials (funded by themselves). Perhaps the most successful of these was the Balbillea, at Ephesus, honoring Tiberius Claudius Balbillus, prefect of Egypt in A.D. 55 and occasional astrologer to the emperor Nero (Moretti 1953, n. 67). Another important change that begins to be evident toward the beginning of the second century and that becomes apparent with increasing frequency over the next century and a half is the spread of these festivals away from their traditional home in the Greek mainland and coastal Asia Minor.

49. Moretti 1953, n. 60. See also Moretti 1953, n. 61 and n. 72 with discussion on p. 210; *IG* 7.1856; *Corinth* 8.1 n. 19; *Corinth* 8.3 n. 272; *MDAI*(A) 1888, p. 177, n. 22 (at Apollonia); Robert 1966a, 118; Robert 1966b, 102, 105.

One of Augustus' last acts was to attend Greek games in the heavily Greek city of Naples in Italy, an event, which, at that time, appears to have been of no more than local significance. In the reign of his grandson Claudius (A.D. 41–54), games at Naples received direct imperial recognition, with the result that they began to attract athletes from the east (Moretti 1953, n. 65). Nero (A.D. 54–68), who fancied himself a connoisseur of all things Greek, was the first Roman ruler to found games specifically for Greek competitors at Rome (and to compete in them himself with stunning, if unsurprising, success). This festival died with Nero in A.D. 68, but less than a generation later, another emperor who fancied himself a fan of Greek culture built a stadium next to his palace on the Palatine and sponsored "Capitoline" games in the Greek style (Robert 1970, 6–27).

The impact of the Italian foundations was felt quite quickly in the east. We find numerous references to the games at Naples and the Capitoline Games in texts that describe the careers of people whose primary sphere of activity was eastern. Some of the practical significance of this appears in a letter from a governor of Asia with reference to a new foundation by a wealthy gentleman of Aphrodisias in Caria at the end of the second century A.D., stating that "after] these the contest from the bequest of Callicrates son of Diotimus [will be celebrated in the coming] year, in the sixth month, before the [departure of the synod] for Rome" (Rouché 1993, n. 51; translation by Rouché).

As the number of festivals expanded in the second and third centuries, we begin to be able to glimpse at work various forces that shaped the constantly evolving cycle. Perhaps the most important of these was the shift from simple, local assertion of devotion to the imperial house and its varied members that stemmed from the desire for local self-advisement, on the one hand, to the manipulation of the festival cycle by emperors who saw its connection with the imperial cult as an important vehicle for propaganda, on the other. We can also see an extension of agonistic territory away from traditional areas of Greek settlement into the hinterlands of Anatolia and Egypt as well as North Africa, Cilicia, Syria, and Palestine (fig. 25). These are areas where we have an ever increasing number of Roman soldiers, ever more frequent visits by important imperial dignitaries, the evolution of highly organized systems of extraction of agricultural surplus, and increase in the number of Roman senators as well as, in the fullness of time, emperors. In the imperial desire for self-promotion, local elites saw an opportunity to assert their own growing importance by achieving a positive response to one of their requests from an emperor, a process that may have been fostered in the third century by the increasingly rapid turnover of emperors, many of whom had a vested interest in separating themselves somewhat from an immediate predecessor (e.g., responsibility for his death).[50] Finally to be considered is the role of the synods themselves. It is clear that they played an active role in suggesting the creation of new events for their members.

The connection between the agonistic explosion of the later second to mid–third centuries and imperial politics reflects increasing sophistication on the part of the people who became emperor with respect to communicating their ideas to their subjects. The emperors of this period all descended from families that had worked their way into the imperial hierarchy from the provinces. Even the most refined of these characters, Antoninus Pius (A.D. 138–161) and Marcus Aurelius (A.D. 161–180), were chosen by an emperor who appears to have been particularly appreciative of adulatory expressions from his subjects. This emperor was Hadrian (A.D. 117–138). Hadrian's extensive wandering around the empire—he spent more time on journeys not connected with warfare than any of his predecessors—and his taste for all things Greek had a profound impact. His taste is particularly obvious in festivals that were connected with Hadrian's homosexual lover, Antinous, after the latter's death on the Nile; and exploitation of his other tastes to the advantage of a local aristocrat in designing a festival is particularly obvious—before the death of Antinous—in a festival that was established in the Lycian city of Oenoanda in honor of Gaius Julius Demosthenes.[51]

Demosthenes himself was the moving force behind the festival. The holder of a number of equestrian offices under Trajan (A.D. 98–117), Demosthenes took advantage of Hadrian's presence in the province of Asia during 124 to arrange for a celebration of himself through scenic events. Hadrian gave his assent to Demosthenes' proposal, and Demosthenes appears to have used this assent to convince what appears to have been the somewhat reluctant town council to go along with him.[52] Once all had agreed to the form of the festival, the provincial governor needed to be involved. One feature of the festival that would attract

50. See the superior discussion in Mitchell 1993, 1:217–25.

51. See Robert 1980, 132–38 for Antinous; Wörrle 1988 publishes the text relating to the Demosthenia with extensive (and invaluable) commentary.

52. Rogers 1991, 91–100, especially 94–96.

visitors was the provision for tax-exempt trading during the whole month of the celebration. In his response, the governor was explicit about the overall financial arrangements (especially the impact on the city's tax base), but as the emperor had already agreed, there was little question that the governor would as well. Another concern is with the long-term health of the endowment. Local officials were notoriously lax in their administration of such funds once they had passed under their care, and as time passes we get more and more evidence for imperial officials *(curatores)* whose job it was to look after local finances that governors were simply too busy to look after on their own with sufficient care (Wörrle 1988, 164–72).

The variety of interests and points of potential friction revealed by this dossier are important reminders that these festivals involved a substantial investment of time and money on the part of the communities that supported them. They are also a reminder of the fact that, despite occasional complaints about the waste of money, most emperors felt that the festival cycle was a worthwhile expenditure of surplus revenue.

The link between the imperial government and the festival cycle appears to have had some collateral implications for the types of events presented—Demosthenes appears to have been aware that Hadrian was particularly fond of scenic festivals (Jones 1990, 486–88)—as well as for the nature of the participants and, occasionally, the rewards or outcome of the contest. Two inscriptions from Aphrodisias in Caria reveal the career of Titus Aelius Aurelius Menander, a pankratiast of the second century A.D. (Rouché 1993, nn. 91, 92). It is noted that he received the prize for victory at the Capitoline Games from the emperor Antoninus Pius (A.D. 138–161) in person and that some twenty years after what appears to have been the prime of his career, he took a tour of Bithynia and Syria-Palestine at precisely the time that Roman armies were mustering for a war with Persia. One can only assume that the presence of Lucius Verus (A.D. 161–168), coruler with Marcus Aurelius, had something to do with his desire to come out of retirement. In the previous generation, the pankratiast P. Aelius Aristomachus of Magnesia competed at a number of festivals in mainland Greece while Hadrian was there, winning, in addition to the ordinary prizes, Roman citizenship for himself, his father, his mother, and his brothers.[53] As the

53. Moretti 1953, n. 71 with Robert 1966b, 102 n. 1; compare Moretti 1953, n. 84 (M. Aurelius Demostratus Damas).

emperors took personal interest in the careers of athletes, it is not surprising that we also find the assertion that a particular person had never won a contest through imperial favor, with the clear implication that others did (Moretti 1953, n. 74).

The role of the imperial government is likewise evident in the tangled history of athletic, and scenic, synods. At the end of the first century B.C., two "international" associations existed alongside local associations of victors at the international games. In the first century B.C., the two "international" associations appear to have coalesced into a single "traveling international" association of athletes. In the reign of Nero (A.D. 54–68), we first find references to something that is referred to as the *katalusis.* The ordinary meaning of this Greek word is "dissolution," which led to the view that these synods (or this synod if the two groups had in fact merged) had been dissolved and that an international association was re-created with its headquarters at Rome. The view that *katalusis* refers to a dissolution has been challenged on the grounds that in some contexts the word *katalusis* means "retirement."[54] The second view appears to correspond best to the evidence, and the association that begins to be attested in the reign of Nero is new, in addition to the old one. Its members were retired athletes who were given important posts in athletic administration throughout the empire. Evidence shows that in the second century this association, whose full title appears to have been "the sacred traveling athletic synod of Hercules after retirement in the royal city of Rome," had an office near the baths of Trajan.[55]

Further evidence shows that the "sacred traveling athletic synod of Hercules after retirement in the royal city of Rome" retained a definite corporate identity at Rome into the fourth century, that it acquired corporate property and a status that was on a par with the vestal virgins. This is of particular interest as the synod retained a religious aspect resulting from the fact that it was technically devoted to the worship of the god Hercules, just as Greek scenic artists participated in a synod devoted to Dionysus, while mimes and pantomimes were members of a synod devoted to Apollo. These synods were also connected with the

54. Pleket 1973, 218–19. The word translated here as "gymnastic" is *xystos,* which technically means a portico attached to a gymnasium and thus, by extension, the gymnasium as a whole. The translation "athletic" is a liberty taken to make reasonable English.

55. The full title appears on *IG* 14.1109. See Pleket 1973, 215–16.

cult of the emperors and acquired further dynastic titles that commemorated the favor of various monarchs.

We cannot trace the relationship between the synod offices at Rome and provincial manifestations of each group with anything like the detail that we might desire. It is, for instance, extremely suggestive that the long papyrus guaranteeing the privileges of a boxer from Hermopolis in Egypt contains extracts from two letters of Claudius (A.D. 41–54) that are connected with a priest of the synod from Antioch, an edict of Vespasian, and a record of the fact that the boxer paid his association fee at a festival at Naples in A.D. 194. The selection of precedents was clearly not up to the boxer but seems rather to derive from a person at the central archive. The fact of the central archive could determine imperial responses to local requests, as appears to be the case with the orphaned descendant of famous athletes who receives all the privileges of athletes from the emperor Gallienus (A.D. 253–268). In cases such as these we are confronted with the shadowy outlines of an extensive entertainment bureaucracy. A similar bureaucracy appears to operate in the case of scenic artists, and there is a striking similarity in the way that the two institutions worked to ensure privileges for paying members. It is even more striking that this system worked under the auspices of the emperors themselves, who had turned the day-to-day management of what were, in effect, the athletic and scenic entertainment industries over to professionals from within those industries.[56] They may have had a role in selecting individual professionals, but they then appear to have been content to allow both scenic artists and athletes to retain their independent corporate structures. Those who had attained membership in these corporate bodies were clearly regarded as privileged members of society by others. The privileges associated with these groups show that the status of Greek-style entertainers violated technical Roman ideas of the *infamia* that attached to those who offered their bodies on display for the pleasure of others, and this is a case where the ideals of Greek society changed those of Rome in the second and third centuries A.D. Furthermore, the status of the athletes and scenic entertainers was very different from that of two other entertainers in whom the emperors took a direct interest: charioteers and gladiators. Attention must now be directed to these groups.

---

56. See Millar 1992, 456–63 for further discussion.

Chariot Racing

On A.D. 18 January 532 the emperor Justinian took his Bible into the imperial box at the hippodrome in Constantinople and promised to redress the grievances of his subjects. The population of Constantinople (or a substantial proportion thereof) had already been rioting for several days, an event sparked by the botched execution of some men who had been arrested in connection with earlier disturbances at the hippodrome. The emperor's appearance failed to mollify his subjects, and he retired to the palace while a mob raced through the streets to find a nobleman whom it might proclaim in his place. The acclamation of the new ruler culminated at the imperial box in the circus. Justinian contemplated flight until, as legend has it, his wife—a former prostitute and actress—urged him to fight back. He did. Soldiers entered the hippodrome in force, and some thirty-five thousand people were killed before order could be restored (Malalas *Chronicle* 18. 475).

The events of 532 illustrate the central place that circus chariot racing came to occupy in the political life of the Roman empire. A circus, the arena for chariot racing, was the largest public building in the Roman world, and under the emperors it had become the central location for communication between the emperor and his people. How and why did chariot racing become so important? How did it evolve from the sport of aristocrats to the most popular public entertainment in the Roman world, with structures under which all other forms of entertainment were subsumed?

There are no simple answers to these questions, and the metamorphoses of the sport stem from various factors. First and foremost it must be acknowledged that the preeminence of circus chariot racing was a late development, occurring from the late third century A.D. onward, and that it was, at least in part, stimulated by Christian distaste for amphitheatrical events (a distaste that may have stemmed from the fatal participation of Christians in some of those events as much as from scriptural abhorrence of bloodshed). Up until the third century we have very few circus buildings outside of Rome itself, especially when the total of circuses is compared with over three hundred amphitheaters. Circus buildings were comparatively rare (under one hundred) even in the third century.[57] A circus was the prestige building

57. For amphitheaters see Golvin 1988; for circuses see Humphrey 1986 and Dodge's contribution to the present volume (chap. 6).

par excellence, marking a city out from others as a center of power. It also needs to be acknowledged that the Roman form of circus chariot racing evolved in a purely Roman context. There were other forms of chariot racing in the Mediterranean world, and the Roman variety was determined by the shape of the racing ground at the Circus Maximus, which ultimately provided a model for other circuses; the organization of the event, with chariots fielded by four professional factions (stables), was also, as far as we know, a peculiar development at the city of Rome.

Greek Chariot Racing

People other than Romans raced chariots, and they had done so for centuries prior to the Roman conquest of the Mediterranean. These races differed in various ways from the seven laps around a long, low barrier that characterized Roman races. The earliest description of a chariot race is in the twenty-third book of Homer's *Iliad,* where it appears as the main event at the funeral games for Achilles' deceased friend Patroclus. In this narrative, which probably reflects the style of chariot racing that was current in eighth-century Greece, a group of heroes drive four-horse chariots over a flat plain to a turning post marked by two white stones and a judge. They pass around the turning post and race back to the starting line. The key features of this event are that the heroes are out for themselves, supplying their own teams and driving the teams themselves (unlike the situation in battle, where they would have a driver); the ground has not been specially prepared for the race; there are no permanent seats; and the contestants race around a turning post in a counterclockwise direction. The use of a turning post makes for a longer race and a more economical use of space that is to the advantage of spectators who would be inconvenienced if the chariots dashed off out of sight. The counterclockwise turn is characteristic of all chariot races in the Mediterranean world, where it was assumed that charioteers would be right-handed.[58] Other factors of interest are the stones, which help prevent the chariots from running into the turning post, and the judge. Even in the heroic age, steps had to be taken to prevent cheating. Finally, it is of interest that Homer's heroes drew lots to determine their starting positions. Even a slight difference in position with regard to the turning post could have an impact on the race. It was very

58. See the discussion in Humphrey 1986, 5–6.

difficult for chariots to pass each other, and the ability to force an opponent to take a slightly longer course could be a crucial factor in a race.

Chariot grounds in ancient Greece are not easy to locate. This is because permanent seating was not considered a requirement and because in the Greek system a flat plain was a sufficient condition for a race. Even starting gates were rare. The absence of permanent starting mechanisms may stem from the fact that the number of contestants was not predictable: there is evidence that as many as forty-one chariots took part in a single race at Delphi in the third century B.C. It is only at Olympia that we get evidence for a regular starting mechanism, and here there was provision for as many as forty-eight teams when in the fifth century B.C. a mechanism was finally constructed to permit a staggered start so that the teams that were furthest from the turning post left the gates before those that were closest.[59] The fifth-century date for the construction of this mechanism, which seems to have been modeled on the mechanisms used for footraces, is significant in itself. The first attested Olympic chariot race was in 680 B.C., yet the general absence of purpose-built mechanisms and dedicated race courses in most of mainland Greece suggests a certain level of amateurism.

One of the most important aspects of Greek chariot racing is that it ordinarily remained outside the structures of civic athleticism. Although there is some evidence for cities sponsoring teams, teams and drivers were usually provided by aristocrats who wanted to participate in this sport.[60] The concern of these aristocratic participants was their own glory, and as early as the sixth century B.C. we begin to get evidence that the glory that attached itself to the aristocrat who managed to finance a successful team at one of the Panhellenic festivals was a very important aspect of competition for status. In this climate of aristocratic competition, the most interesting shift in emphasis appears to have been away from the actual driver to the team of horses. We do not know when the person providing the horses ceased, de facto, to be the person who drove them, and as we do get evidence, there does not seem to have been a hard-and-fast rule as to who would be in the chariot.[61]

59. Pausanias *Description of Greece* 6.20.10–15. It is also interesting that the dimensions of the track are given in terms of the track for a footrace (see Pausanias *Description of Greece* 6.16.4) and that special footraces could be run on it.

60. Robert 1935, 461–62; 1967, 17; 1978, 279.

61. Suetonius *Life of Nero* 24 (in the chariot); *F.Delph.* 3.240 (Eumenes of Pergamon, certainly not driving); *E&J*[2] 78 (Tiberius) and *AE* 1960, n. 307 (for his running of a team at Thespiae); *SIG*[3] 792 (Germanicus, probably not in the chariot).

The key organizational features of Greek chariot racing were as follows.

1. It was an activity for the very wealthy.
2. There could be a very large number of teams in each race.
3. There was very little permanent construction associated with the racetrack.

While we can trace an interest in chariot racing at the great Panhellenic festivals of mainland Greece into the second century A.D., when Pausanias notes that chariot races were still being held, it does not have much of a context elsewhere. Chariot racing of the Greek sort cannot be traced outside of mainland Greece in the imperial period. While we have some evidence for a race in four-horse chariots at Thespiae in Boeotia, the evidence from the extensive epigraphy of Asia Minor suggests that when natives of the region raced chariots, they did so in Greece.[62] This does not mean that it did not happen, but it does mean that it was not a common event. In Egypt we have a curious concentration of evidence for Greek-style chariot racing in the late third century A.D. The Capitoline games at Oxryhyncus, founded in imitation of games that were established by the Roman emperor Gordian III (238–244), included a race for two-horse chariots, while a race in a "Dacian" chariot was run at the scenic, athletic, equestrian Antinoian . . . Philadelphian contest known as the most glorious Capitoline Games" in 272.[63] Rather than being indigenous developments, events such as these are antiquarian exercises inspired by imperial patronage.

62. See *MDAI*(A) 1919, p. 33, n. 18e; *F.Delph.* 3.482 (for Tenos' participation in the Soteria); *F.Delph.* 3.242 (for the participation of Sardis in 166). But see *Horos* 3 (1985): 99–101, 6a for a late Hellenistic list from Chios recording victories by chariots owned by Mithridates of Pontus, also discussed by Robert 1935, 461–62; the evidence against Robert's view that Mithridates did not race the chariots in person is offered by Plutarch *Life of Pompey* 37 and Suetonius *Life of Nero* 24. Other exceptions are the festival for Artemis Leucophryne (*I.Magnesia* 14), a *gymnasion hippikon* attested c. A.D. 400 at Bakseyis in Phrygia (Haspels 1971, n. 39); and the Romaia at Xanthus in the late second century A.D., on which see Robert 1978, 279.

63. See *P.Oxy.* 3116 for the race at Oxyrhyncus; *P.Oxy.* 3367 for the Dacian chariot race—which may not be a Dacian chariot race at all, but rather a Greek chariot race with a model of a Dacian chariot as a prize (see Thomas 1976, 481). See also *P.Oxy.* 3135, a contract for a charioteer in 273/4.

Chariot Racing in Italy

We know very little about chariot racing in Italy prior to the emergence of a set racecourse in the Circus Maximus at Rome. What little evidence we do have, other than that for southern Italian and Sicilian Greek participation at the Panhellenic festivals of mainland Greece, is primarily from Etruria. On the basis of Etruscan tomb paintings and some relief sculpture, we know that the Etruscans appear to have held chariot (and horse) races in the same arenas that provided the forum for some other athletic contests. We can see that they could erect temporary wooden stands for these events, and it appears that seating was stratified by class. The racecourses have posts at the end opposite the starting line, but we cannot be absolutely certain that chariots turned around these posts. They could, conceivably, mark a finish line. In either case it appears to be difficult to link the practices that appear here with the Roman custom of having the finish line in the middle of the track (Humphrey 1986, 12–17).

Interest in the differences between Etruscan and Greek practices and in the possible connection between these Etruscan habits and developments at Rome is connected with the long-standing belief that Rome was dominated by Etruria in the late sixth century, precisely the period at which Rome emerged as the major city in central Italy. This view of the relationship between Rome and Etruria has now been seriously challenged, and there is now no reason to privilege Etruscan practice over any other as a source for Roman behavior (Cornell 1995, 151–72). Indeed, there is now a tendency to allow that institutions at Rome that have no obvious parallel elsewhere are the result of indigenous developments at Rome itself. This is the proper course, and there is no reason to invent an Etruscan filiation for Roman chariot racing, which developed in a way that was very different from any other Mediterranean city that we know of. The fact that Tacitus, writing in the second century A.D., says that equestrian events came to Rome from Thurii, a Greek city of southern Italy (*Annals* 14.21), is no evidence at all. The sort of racing that was practiced at Thurii was plainly connected with that of mainland Greece and was thus very different from the activity that emerged at Rome. Tacitus' statement reflects the Roman belief that many of their own institutions went back to cultures that the Romans believed to have been older than that of Rome. As such, Tacitus' observation is a very much more interesting for the study of the Roman psyche than it is for the study of Roman chariot racing.

The merits of the literary tradition for the history of Rome have long been the object of intense debate. It is very disturbing that the surviving accounts of the period of Roman history prior to 264 B.C. were written under Augustus (or later) and that the first Roman to write history did so at the end of the third century B.C. Relying on this literary tradition is the equivalent of depending on two books written in 1995 for our whole knowledge of the history of North America from the landing of Columbus to the beginning of the twentieth century. Subsequent generations of historians would be far more interested in the footnotes of the surviving books than in their text, to see what primary sources had informed the authors of these hypothetical books. Just so, classical historians have a great deal of trouble in determining what, if anything, can be believed about Roman history prior to the middle of the third century. The Romans themselves said that they had basic records of major events for the early period, and the shape of the Roman state when we start getting contemporary accounts of Roman history confirms at least some of the outline that has come down to us from our Augustan sources. In this context, although there are scholars who would question even this, I am inclined to believe that statements about the dates when certain laws were passed and when certain buildings were constructed are likely to be correct. Without these dates we can know nothing about Roman chariot racing prior to the early second century B.C., when the poet Ennius offers a simile based on a chariot race.

The dates in question are those for construction in the Circus Maximus. These dates are important because the developed form of Roman chariot races (evident in the lines of Ennius that I just mentioned) is intimately connected with the shape of the Circus Maximus. The basic features are as follows.

1. Chariots were raced in multiples of four (but never more than twelve at a time).
2. The chariots were provided by four professional stables that were identified by color (the Blue, Green, Red, and White factions).
3. Chariots start from purpose-built gates *(carceres).*

4. There were two turning posts, around which the chariots raced seven times.
5. There was a sprint from the starting gates to the first turning post.
6. The teams ran in a counterclockwise direction around the turning posts.
7. The finish line was in the middle of the track.

The Circus Maximus, which, as far as we know, was the only location in early Rome where chariots were raced, is a flat plain between the Palatine and Aventine Hills.[64] The earliest date for building in this area is provided by the Augustan historian Livy, who says that Rome's fifth king, Tarquinius Priscus, built seats there. Dionysius of Halicarnassus (another Augustan historian) says that Tarquinius' grandson—also named Tarquinius—who was also the last king of Rome, completed the work there.[65] The traditional dates for Tarquinius Priscus, 616–575 B.C., are complete conjecture (some would say that the same is true of Tarquinius himself), but the younger Tarquinius was almost certainly a real person, and the regal period appears to have ended between 509 and 500 B.C. The tradition that the younger Tarquinius built stands in the Circus Maximus suggests that the Romans believed that a racecourse was laid out before the beginning of the Republic, and this would not be inconceivable. What is exceptional about this project as an act of urban planning is that the racecourse was placed well within the settled urban area (Humphrey 1986, 60–61).

The early date for a racetrack in the Circus Maximus appears to be confirmed by the statement that in 494 B.C. a permanent seat at the races, a seat near the shrine of Murcia, was reserved for Manius Valerius Maximus.[66] Statements about honorific monuments (in this case a special chair) are among the most reliable in the tradition about early Rome, and the traditional dates of early Roman magistrates generally appear to be accurate within a year or so. The next date of significance is 363 B.C., when we are told that a flood of the Tiber interrupted

64. Wiseman (1976, 44–47) shows, conclusively, that chariots were never raced in the Circus Flaminius, the only other site associated with chariot racing in early Rome.

65. Livy *History of Rome* 1.35.8; Dionysius of Halicarnassus, *Roman Antiquities* 4.44.1. For further discussion see Humphrey 1986, 60–67.

66. *Insc. Ital.* 13.3; Festus 464L; Livy *History of Rome* 2.31.3.

races in the circus (this is another sort of event that made its way into early records), and we are then told that in 329 permanent starting gates were built.[67] The original name of these starting gates was *oppidum,* a word that usually means "town" in Latin, suggesting that they were of quite substantial size. According to the Roman antiquarian Varro:

> The place in the circus from whence the horses are first released is now called the *carceres;* but Naevius called them the *oppidum.* They are called *carceres* because the horses are restrained *(coercentur),* so that they do not leave before the magistrate gives the signal. Because the *carceres* were once decorated with high towers like a wall, the poet wrote: when the dictator sits in his chariot, he is carried as far as *oppidum.* (*Concerning the Latin Language* 5.153)

Varro's testimony here is of particular interest because, unlike some other antiquarian statements that we will be examining, he actually has a text from the mid–third century.

The building of the *carceres* is perhaps the most important piece of evidence that we have for the evolution of Roman racing. As Varro's text makes plain, the *carceres* were substantial structures, and it is not unreasonable to believe that the first set of gates provided the model for later ones. Since there is a necessary correlation between the structure of the starting mechanism and the number of contestants, it is reasonable to assume that the basic elements of Roman chariot racing had emerged by the second half of the fourth century B.C. This would mean that the four factions had come into being, even though our first reference to them does not come until the early second century B.C., when the poet Ennius wrote:

> they waited in anticipation, just as when the consul wishes to give the signal *(mittere signum)* for the start, and they all stare with rapt attention at the mouths *(orae)* of the *carceres,* which will immediately send painted chariots out from their jaws *(fauces).* (Ennius *Annals* 1 fr. xlvii, 79–83 Skutsch)

67. Livy *History of Rome* 7.3.1–3, 8.20.2: *carceres eo anno in circum primum statuti.*

The painted chariots are those decorated with the colors of the factions, and it is interesting that Ennius here uses several terms that are also known from the later vocabulary of racing: *mittere signum* is the standard phrase for starting a race, and the *orae* are the barriers at the front of the *carceres.* We have some reason to think that the term for the area behind the *orae* was *fauces.*[68]

The one problem with the view put forward in the last paragraph is that one source tells us that there were only two circus factions in early Rome. This source is an attack on public entertainments by the third-century Christian, Tertullian.

> In the beginning there were only two: White and Red. White was sacred to the winter because of the white snow; Red was sacred to the summer because of the color of the sun. But later, inspired by pleasure or superstition, some connected Red to Mars; others dedicated White to the zephyrs (winds), Green to mother earth or spring, Blue to the sky, the sea, or autumn. (*On the Public Shows* 9.5)

Some scholars have taken this text at face value and argued that the Blue and Green factions were much later creations, only coming into existence in the first century A.D. Such a view is manifestly false (Cameron 1976, 56). Tertullian clearly has no ideas why the Blues and Greens were so called, an ignorance that would be inconceivable if they were creations of the Principate, and the only date that he gives is the reign of Romulus (this is clear from context of the whole passage) for the Whites and Reds. The fact that we have no record of the date at which the other factions were created suggests that their origin was before the beginning of Roman historiography but that Romans felt that they were later than the regal period (where later Roman historians tended to place the origins of institutions for which they had no date). A further point of interest is that while there is some, limited evidence for aristocrats winning gold crowns, possibly for chariot victories, in the fifth century, there is none later (Rawson 1991, 392–93). Under these circumstances a date in the mid–fourth century B.C. appears reasonable.

Once the factions were formed, there is no reason to imagine that their structure changed very much before the fourth century A.D. Their

68. See Skutsch's notes ad loc. (1985); Cameron 1976, 57.

primary function was to supply all the necessaries for a race: charioteers, assistants to the charioteers, horses, operators for the starting mechanisms. In doing this they needed to maintain permanent stables with their attendant staffs. Our best evidence for the structure of a faction appears on an inscription that may date from the reign of Domitian (who introduced two new factions, the Golds and the Purples, neither of which survived his reign).

> The association for four-horse chariot racing *(familia quadrigaria)* of Titus Ateius Capito of the red color,[69] for which Chrestus was treasurer, distributed oil to the decurions who are inscribed below: Marcus Vipsanius Migio, Docimus the overseer, Chrestus the *conditor,* Epaphrus the *sellarius,* Menander the charioteer, Apollonius the charioteer, Cerdo the charioteer, Liccaeus the charioteer, Helletus the assistant *conditor,* Publius Quinctius Primus, Hyllus the doctor, Anterotes the *tentor,* Antiochus the blacksmith, Panaces the *tentor,* Marcus Vipsanius Calamus, Marcus Vipsanius Dareus, Erotes the *tentor,* Marcus Vipsanius Faustus, Hilarius the charioteer, Nicander the charioteer, Epigonus the charioteer, Alexander the charioteer, Nicephorus the *sparsor,* Alexion the *morator* . . . the messenger. (*ILS* 5313)

We know that in addition to the diverse functionaries—the *conditor,* assistant *conditor, sellarius,* overseer, doctor, *tentor, morator, sparsor,* messenger, and charioteer—mentioned in this text, there were people called the *hortatores* (singular *hortator*) in all factions (figs. 19, 26). What did all these people do? The *conditor* appears to have been the person charged with the oversight of the stable, and the assistant *conditor* was his assistant. The overseer may have been responsible for the staff. We do not really know what the *sellarius* did (the word as it appeared here is a term for male prostitute), but the change of a single letter, to *cellarius* from *sellarius,* gives us the word for the person in charge of a storeroom. The roles of the *tentor,* the *morator,* and the *sparsor* (as well as the

69. The Latin is *panni chelidoni,* and Dessau records the suggestion, on the basis of Pliny *Natural History* 37.155, that this is a reference to the Purple faction instituted by Domitian (Suetonius *Life of Domitian* 7.1: *duas circensibus gregum factiones aurati purpureique panni ad quattuor pristinas addidit*). Rawson (1981 = 1991, 398 n. 36) suggests that the word may be a synonym for "red." The nomenclature of the text suggests a date earlier than Domitian.

hortator) become clear to us through works of art connected with the races. A *tentor* appears to have been the person who operated the starting mechanism. The *morator* held the horses while they were within the starting gate, the *sparsor* threw water at the horses as they raced around the track, and the *hortator* rode a horse either behind or in front of the charioteer as he drove, to shout encouragement and, it may be presumed, advice about other chariots that the driver could not see. Something else that is immediately obvious from the inscription quoted above is the mix of nationalities within the faction. The majority of the names are Greek, and the absence of Roman elements to these names (the praenomen and nomen) as well as the absence of status markers suggesting that they were slaves or freedmen shows that they were free inhabitants of the Greek east who had come to Rome to win fame and fortune in the circus. Other inscriptions reveal that this phenomenon was not limited to easterners, as Rome drew on the talents of its whole empire to entertain its population. A further point that emerges from this text is the size of the staff. The people receiving oil are described as decurions, a description that might imply that they represented a group of ten people and thus that there were at least 240 to 250 people connected with the stable.

The title of the organization that has been occupying our attention—the *familia quadrigaria* of Titus Ateius Capito of the red color—is also of significance. The reason it is so named is that it was but one of several such groups that constituted the totality of the Reds. We cannot now know if these other parts of the Red faction also fell under the leadership of Capito, but the appearance of his name in this context is enough to identify him as a member of a very influential group: the faction masters. Unlike the people who ran the stables (Chrestus, for instance, is not a Roman citizen), a faction master, a *dominus factionis,* was a Roman citizen of high status. Some faction masters are explicitly identified as equestrians, and Ateius Capito himself may very well have been related to the early first-century jurist C. Ateius Capito, a senator who played a role in drafting the imperial legislation limiting the participation of senators and equestrians in scenic and amphitheatral entertainments.[70] One of the most interesting features of this particular piece of legislation is precisely the fact that circus games are not men-

70. The possibility is canvassed by Dessau in his note on *ILS* 5313. The name is uncommon, which enhances the appeal of this suggestion.

tioned, a point that may confirm the importance of the equestrian contribution to the organization of the sport (though not earlier involvement by Capito's family in the business).

References to the activities of the faction masters suggest that they exercised unusual influence, an influence that may have stemmed from the fact that they could withhold the services of their employees if their terms were not met and make it so that a person who wanted, or was required by the terms of his office, to put on chariot races could not perform his function in an acceptable way.[71] The extraordinary popularity of their sport might have other collateral benefits. The future emperor Vitellius, whose father was the most important member of the senate in the reign of Claudius, liked to spend his time in the stables, offering the heads of those stables an informal avenue of access to the very center of power at Rome; and as the pinnacle of this iceberg of connections, we have the extraordinary career of Ofonius Tigellinus, the vicious éminence grise of the later years of Nero. Nero was obsessed with chariot racing, and Tigellinus was a breeder of excellent chariot horses that were sold to the faction stables.[72] Somehow the two met, and Tigellinus achieved the highest equestrian office, that of praetorian prefect, in A.D. 61. The story that Elagabalus, the deeply unstable individual who ruled Rome from A.D. 217 to 222, selected high officials of court from the faction stables may also be true.[73]

Factions and Races

The four factions—Blues, Greens, Reds, and Whites—are attested from the first century B.C. to the twelfth century A.D.; and there is good reason to think that they were in existence for centuries before we get our first explicit references to them (Cameron 1976, 50). This continuity occludes a problem of some interest. Although there were four factions, emperors who are said to have favored a faction are said (with one exception) to have been partisans of either the Blues or the Greens, and there is good evidence for such partisanship as early as the first century

71. For corporate action by the *domini factionum* see Suetonius *Life of Nero* 5, 22; Dio *History of Rome* 61.6. See also Historia Augusta *Life of Commodus* 16; *Lives of the Gordians* 4; Friedländer 1908–13, 2:27.

72. See Suetonius *Life of Vitellius* 4 for Vitellius; for Tigellinus see *PIR*² O 91 with Demougin 1988, 99 for the context.

73. Historia Augusta, *Life of Elagabalus* 6; Dio *History of Rome* 79.15.

A.D. What is more, when the emperor Marcus Aurelius gave thanks, in his private *Meditations*, for the absence of personal addiction to racing, he did so by saying that he was glad to be a partisan of neither the Blues nor the Greens. His contemporary, the doctor Galen, described as "partisans of the Blues and Greens" the devotees of chariot racing who sniffed the dung of chariot horses to make sure that they were eating correctly.[74] What was wrong with the Reds and Whites?

While there is not absolute consistency on this point from all parts of the empire at all periods, it appears that the Reds were regularly paired with the Greens and the Whites with the Blues. By the sixth century this pairing had become so thoroughly institutionalized that the Blues and Greens were referred to as the major factions, the Whites and Reds as the minor. The Reds and Whites produced some notable champions, and the Reds even acquired an emperor as a fan in the sixth century, but this does not change the overall picture. Moreover, it appears that this pairing of factions was used to arrange a particular type of race known as the *diversium*. In this race a charioteer who had won an earlier race traded teams with a driver from a "like-minded" opposing faction, that is, an opponent from a faction with which his was paired.[75] Similarly, we hear of another sort of race where the chariots from all four factions raced as two teams—Reds and Greens on one side, Blues and Whites on the other. Such races are attested as early as the second century A.D., when we encounter them on an inscription that preserves details of the spectacular career of Gaius Appuleius Diocles.

The text that presents the deeds of Diocles is remarkable not only for the duration and success of the career—Diocles drove chariots for twenty-four years, in 4,257 races, winning no fewer than 1,462 times—but also for the vast amount of information that it conveys about the structure of a charioteer's life and the wider variety of races that were run.[76] When the text is examined in light of other documents, it proves to be fundamental for our understanding of the sport.

Diocles, who was born in modern Portugal, drove in his first race as a charioteer for the Whites when he was eighteen years old. This was, if

74. Marcus Aurelius *Meditations* 1.5; Galen *On the Therapeutic Method* 10.478 (Kuhn with Cameron 1976, 54).

75. Sidonius Apollinaris *Poems* 23.307–427; *Palatine Anthology* 15.47. 5–6 with Cameron 1973, 209; Cameron 1976, 51–52.

76. *ILS* 5287; the basic study of this text remains that in Friedländer 1908–13, 4:148–63 (appendix 24).

Fig. 26. Relief from Foligno, Italy, dating from around the middle of the third century A.D., illustrating significant aspects of a chariot race. Particularly notable are the representation of the *tentor,* who operated the mechanism of the starting gate; of the figures of the *sparsor* and *hortator* (far left), who assisted the charioteers as they were driving; and of the charioteers straining to keep their teams under control as they approach a turn. (DAI Rome neg. 37-1338.)

anything, a bit old for a first race, and he did not win one until he was twenty. Four years after his first victory as a White, we find Diocles driving as a Green, and three years after that for the Reds. This movement from faction to faction is not without parallel in other texts, showing that free agency is anything but a modern concept, and the movement of charioteers will offer a parallel to some features of gladiatorial life that will be examined later in this chapter.[77]

In the tale of his victories, Diocles first notes that he won sixty times after the procession. A procession around the track in which statues of the gods were paraded along with the participants in the games was the first event of any day at the circus (or, for that matter, the amphitheater and athletic contests). The stress on a victory immediately after the procession suggests that the first race was regarded as a main event.

77. Compare *ILS* 5281, 5286, 5288.

Second, Diocles reveals that of his victories, 1,064 came in races where only one team from each faction was entered. In races where there were two teams from each faction, he won 347 times, while in races where there were the maximum of three teams from each faction, he won only 51 times. These numbers are fascinating in and of themselves as they suggest that the chances of victory for even the most skilled of charioteers were greatly diminished in a large race, which may well be testimony to the general level of excellence among the competitors. Furthermore, the fact that Diocles won in more races after the procession (sixty times) than he won in races with twelve teams (fifty-one times) suggests that races with the largest possible field were not the premium events. People seem to have wanted to see champions racing against each other, and it may also be that it took only a relatively few outright victories in these larger races to establish a person as a charioteer to watch. The view that races with a field of four were the most important is supported by the fact that all the most substantial monetary prizes that Diocles won were in races of four teams, and in the case of the races with eight teams, the biggest prizes came in races held on training grounds—presumably for a select audience of imperial favorites. Finally, Diocles lists prizes for victories in chariots drawn by six or seven horses—again all in the context of these races of champions.

Diocles can also tell us a good deal about what happened in a race. He says, for example, that he led from the start in 815 of his victories, while he came from behind only sixty-seven times and won after being passed (if this is what the rather obscure Latin of this passage means) only thirty-six times. He won in other ways (after his opponents had crashed into each other?) forty-two times. Despite the image conveyed by reconstructions such as that in the movie *Ben Hur*, it is clear that victory in this sport usually went to the good front-runner and rarely to a charioteer who was behind when the chariots reached the white line at the end of the *spina* (where the contestants would break from their lanes).

The account of Diocles' deeds has already shown us that the number of contestants could vary, as could the number of horses—Diocles tells us that he was the first person to win a race of chariots drawn by seven horses and that he also raced in two-horse and six-horse chariots. There could be other varieties of chariot race as well. The most obvious of these, the *diversium*, where drivers drove teams from their paired faction, has already been mentioned. Diocles mentions other races where he drove a team provided from his own faction and new to him or with one new horse. The existence of such races points to another issue that plainly concerned racing fans: the relative responsibility of the charioteers and the horses to the victory that they won.

The monumental record of Roman chariot racing is not devoid of commemoration of horses independently of charioteers or of monuments where the charioteer shares the credit for his victories with a favored team or teams. Likewise, the literary record contains references to concern for the acquisition of the best possible horses. It was the ability to provide superior horses that brought Tigellinus to the attention of Nero, and in more general terms, we learn that Spain, Sicily, North Africa, and the region of Hirpinum in Italy were regarded as prime sources of horseflesh in the early empire. Cappadocia, in central Anatolia, can be added to the list in the later empire. The training of chariot horses was obviously intense, so intense that on at least one occasion a team that had thrown its driver at the beginning of the race went on to finish first and, even more remarkably, to stop at the finish line.[78] The role of the animal as a star is one to which we will return when we turn to combats between human and beast, and it may also be reflected in the fact that the imperial government involved itself in the supply of prime animals.

The issue of the imperial government's intervention in the operation of chariot racing has also been raised in connection with a change in the social background of the *domini* of the factions in the late third century. At this time we find *domini* of the factions who were former charioteers rather than members of the equestrian order.[79] One view of this change is that it reflects a continuing effort to evict members of the upper classes from the management of public entertainments. This view may be correct, but there is another possibility that merits attention. The other view is that with the passing of time the imperial government became more willing to recognize the status charioteers won for themselves in the eyes of their fans and that victory in the circus permitted charioteers to attain positions that had once been reserved for members of the upper classes.

---

78. Pliny *Natural History* 8.160. On the sources of horses see Friedländer 1908–13, 2:25; Cameron 1976, 8.

79. *ILS* 5296, 5297. Cameron (1976, 7–9) suggests that this development was part of a process of removing private businessmen from the entertainment industry. This may be a contributing factor, but the development is far too late if it is to be significant.

The crucial period for the transfer of control of the factions from equestrians to former performers is the late third century. We hear nothing of charioteers as faction *domini* earlier, and the charioteer Hierocles who rose to high office under Elagabalus appears to have gone straight from the track to the administration.[80] But in the reign of Aurelian (270–75) or shortly afterward, we have two charioteers who became *domini.* A number of factors may have contributed to their rise. One is quite simply wealth. The rewards of a successful career were enormous—Diocles acquired over 35,000,000 HS in the course of his career, an income well in excess of any but the wealthiest senators. A second factor is that the imperial government was capable of allowing public entertainers in the form of actors and athletes to run their own professional associations. It is not a great leap from having actors run a privileged association of actors to having charioteers run organizations central to their sport.

A third factor is that aristocratic society of the later third century, contrary to what is implied in many studies of the period that emphasize the increasingly autocratic nature of the Roman state, was far more permeable than that of the first or second centuries. The emperor Aurelian was not a man of senatorial family any more than his predecessor, Claudius II (268–70), had been or than the emperor Diocletian (284–305) would be. From the middle of the third century onward, there ceased to be an automatic connection between senatorial status and high command in the Roman state. This change was observed in the fourth century when it was asserted that it was the result of an edict issued by the unpopular emperor Gallienus (253–270). But the edict is a fabrication that masks a broader process of social development.[81] The story of the edict reflects the fact that it was possible for people whose backgrounds would never have permitted them to rise to the highest position in the state in the second century to do so in the later third. There are signs of change even in the second century: the emperor Pertinax (acclaimed and murdered in 193)—a freedman's son—owed his membership in the senate to his extraordinary military ability, but he was the exception rather than the rule.[82] His career serves only to remind us that social change is a process of gradual evolution.

---

80. See n. 73.
81. Potter 1990, 57 with bibliography.
82. *PIR*² H 73.

A final point that may be relevant to the rise in the status of charioteers is that the ideology of victory that accompanied triumph in the arena accorded well with the ideology of victory that underpinned the imperial office. The circus was the locus for the celebration of imperial success, and it may have been that charioteers tinged with the color of imperial victory thereby became acceptable in positions of responsibility (Cameron 1973, 250–52).

Conclusion: Charioteers and Their Fans in the Late Empire

The rise of charioteers to positions of leadership in their profession is only part of the story of the extension of the social and political role of the drivers and their sport. As early as the reign of Augustus, it is clear that the successful charioteer occupied a prominent position within the entertainment hierarchy of the capitol. The only comparable figures were successful pantomimes. Augustus granted pantomimes exemption from corporal punishment, a significant concession as they had a tendency to appear as the agents provocateurs of public disorder, and it is said that Nero forbade the amusement of charioteers who, as our source for this information puts it, "had the right" of beating people up with impunity. As no Roman law gave private citizens the right *(ius)* to beat people up, this statement must refer to some immunity from the usual penalty for disorderly conduct.[83] We also know that charioteers excited enormous passion. A partisan is said to have thrown himself on the funeral pyre of a deceased charioteer in 70 B.C. (Pliny *Natural History* 7.186). But, for all this, the phenomenon was plainly one of life in the capitol until the vast expansion of circus building into the provinces that began in the mid–second century A.D.

The consequence of the extension of circus chariot racing to the provinces was entirely predictable: it made charioteers into people of great influence in most of the major cities of the empire, transforming what had once been a local phenomenon into one that encompassed the major urban areas of the Roman world. Chariot racing had by this time become intimately associated with the imperial ideology of victory, and as the circus had become the focal point for popular expression at

83. Suetonius *Life of Augustus* 45; Tacitus *Annals* 1.77 (exemption for pantomimes); Suetonius *Life of Nero* 16. For a different view see Cameron 1973, 246 n. 4.

the capitol, so it now became the focal point for popular expression elsewhere.

The comparative flood of information about the sport from the fourth to sixth centuries reveals organizations of ever increasing power and significance: charioteers could not be depicted in their "rough clothing" in paintings placed in front of portraits of the emperor in porticoes, but statues of charioteers stood inside the hippodrome at Constantinople (*Theodosian Code* 15.7.12). One charioteer honored in this way, with two monuments, was the great Porphyrius, whose appearance in the hippodrome at Antioch had once been sufficient to cause a riot.[84] One text suggests that professional associations within cities identified themselves with specific factions and that civic politics could be defined in terms of conflict between the supporters of the Blues and Greens. So could displays of civic unity. Governors could be found trying to move chariot teams from city to city in efforts to enhance their popularity, and emperors could be found telling them to stop, to stay out of the circus on any but imperial holidays, and even then to leave before noon (*Theodosian Code* 15.5.1, 2, 3). The ability of circus performers to mix with members of the highest aristocracy resulted in the daughter of a bear keeper of the Green faction becoming the empress Theodora. The marriage of Theodora and Justinian, unthinkable in the Rome of Augustus, symbolizes above all else the marriage between court and circus in the late Roman world.

A lot had changed to make this possible. The legislative record of the fourth century suggests that various forms of scenic entertainment remained very popular and lucrative. But the Christian church had an official position against activities of the stage, all of which were felt, in some way, to promote indecent thought. The church also appears to have taken a very negative view of gladiatorial combat, and the imperial system of management that had dominated the sports of the amphitheater in the second and third centuries, a subject of the final part of this chapter, appears to have withered after the conversion of Constantine. It is perhaps not surprising that the church had not evolved an official detestation of the circus to the same degree as it did of other entertainments. In the formative period of Christianity, it had been a local rather than universal phenomenon; and the conversion of

84. For the monuments see Cameron 1973, 121–26; for his role in the Antiochene riots of 507 see Cameron 1976, 151.

government coincided to some degree with the spread of the circus, where the premier event had never been the shedding of blood and the occasional manufacture of a martyr or the putative invitation to unrestrained fornication.

The future of circus chariot racing was coincidental with the future of the classical city-state. We still find circus races in the high period of medieval Byzantium, but only where the imperial government held sway. It died with the classical city in the rest of the Mediterranean world in the course of the sixth and seventh centuries A.D., possibly a victim of its own extravagance. As the audience demanded more and more, the state, faced with barbarian invasion and crisis on the frontiers, could offer fewer and fewer races (Cameron 1973, 252–58).

Gladiators, Beast Hunts, and Executions

Few images are as evocative of Roman culture as those of the gladiator standing amid a pile of bodies, waiting for a crowd to pass a death sentence on his defeated foe (fig. 27), or of a lion approaching an assemblage of decorously attired Christians praying in the arena. The sports of the amphitheater seem to typify the Roman in the modern imagination in the same way that football, baseball, or basketball symbolize American culture in the world at large.

The student of American history will know that the spread of baseball to Asia and Latin America is essentially a post–World War II phenomenon and that the spread of basketball and American football around the globe is of even more recent date. This student will, hopefully, be aware that an effort to describe the historical development of American culture through one period in the history of American sports would be foolish. So, too, the student of Roman history must be aware that the sports of the amphitheater achieved unparalleled prominence in the period from the first century B.C. to the third century A.D. This same student should also be aware that the images of amphitheatral carnage exemplified by the paintings of Gérôme or such Hollywood spectacles as *Spartacus* or *Demetrius and the Gladiators* are essentially false. Gladiators were not, primarily, executioners, and the ideology of the execution was quite separate from that of their conflicts. The amphitheater was the venue for a wide variety of public combats—between beast and beast, man and beast, man and man (and, on rare occasions, woman and woman), or society and its enemies. As far as we

Fig. 27. *Pollice verso* by Jean-Léon Gérôme, first exhibited in 1872, capturing what was then, and in some quarters still is, the image of barbaric slaughter in the amphitheater. The gladiator, standing alone on an arena littered with other bodies and broken weapons, looks up at a crowd straining to demand death of his defeated rival. Particularly poignant is the stress on the decisive gestures of the vestal virgins in the front row as they reject the appeal of the defeated fighter. (Photo courtesy of the Phoenix Art Museum.)

know, the only "public combatant" (a useful term to characterize amphitheatral performers as a class) to engage in both beast hunts and gladiatorial duels was the emperor Commodus—and he may well have been insane.

The fact that amphitheatral conflict was not simply about death does not mean that a great deal of blood was not shed on the sands of the arena. The quantity of blood revolts most modern sensibilities, and it even revolted the sensibilities of some Romans.[85] To suggest otherwise would be nonsense. But it would be equally incorrect to concentrate on bloodshed alone. An understanding of the reason why people from

85. The approach taken in this discussion is manifestly influenced by Ville 1981 and Robert 1940. Stress on bloodshed is a constant in Barton 1993, with much confusion of fact; A more sophisticated approach appears in Plass 1995; Hopkins 1983; Wiedemann 1992.

Britain to Syria filled the venues of ritualized conflict for centuries is not aided by moralizing judgments. Public combat was a fact of life in the Roman world, just as were scenic performances, athletic competitions, and chariot racing: the same people went to events of all sorts.

Origins

The first recorded display of gladiators at Rome took place at the funeral of Junius Brutus Pera in 264 B.C.[86] The exhibition, offered by Brutus' sons, consisted of three pairs that fought in the Forum Boarium. The sons of Brutus did not invent the sport. Evidence dating to the fourth century B.C. from southern Italy, evidence provided by pottery and tomb paintings, suggests that gladiatorial combat originated there and was a feature of funerary celebrations (Ville 1981, 19–35). Even if the two Bruti were not the first Romans to exhibit gladiators (the first recorded occurrence in sources as poor as those for the early third century B.C. can scarcely be recorded as definitive), the fact that Rome had only recently come to control the homeland of the gladiators makes it reasonable to think that there were no gladiatorial exhibitions much earlier. The Romans themselves believed that gladiatorial combat was introduced to the city from elsewhere in Italy, and even if their later version of how it happened is not correct (they claimed an Etruscan origin), their understanding stands in stark contrast with their view of circus chariot racing, which they saw as indigenous or south-Italian Greek.[87] Tending to confirm the Roman tradition that gladiatorial games were a relatively late development at their city is the fact that gladiatorial games were originally parts of *munera,* or obligatory gifts given to a community by an individual, rather than *ludi,* which were state ceremonies (Wiedemann 1993, 1–3).

What does it mean that the earliest evidence for gladiatorial combat occurs in the context of funeral games? Were they viewed as human sacrifices to the deceased—was a death to be commemorated by death? If so, these were rather unusual sacrifices. We know how Romans and Greeks sacrificed human beings. They tied them up and slit their

86. Livy *Summaries* 16; Valerius Maximus *Memorable Deeds and Sayings* 2.4.7 with Ville 1981, 42 n. 100.

87. For the claim of Etruscan origins see Athemaeus *Wise Men at Dinner* 4.153. The myth of Etruscan origins is demolished by Ville (1981, 1–8); for an explanation of the attribution to the Etruscans see Wiedemann 1992, 30–33.

throats on the funeral pyre of a dead hero or before an altar, or they buried them alive. Neither Greeks nor Romans invited the sacrificial object to wave a sword or spear at someone else. The fact that gladiatorial combat did not resemble any other form of human sacrifice should be enough to show that it was not viewed as a sacrifice.[88] Furthermore, funeral games were not about death. In both the Greek and Roman worlds they were held as celebrations of the life of the deceased, where his (almost invariably his) contributions to society were recalled. Gladiatorial combats were held along with a wide range of other events, including athletics and scenic performances that were intended to illustrate the virtues of the society and of the prominent person who had died. Beyond the context of the aristocratic funeral, the best Italian evidence for the meaning of gladiatorial combat comes in the context of the development of the amphitheater. Permanent amphitheaters first appear in the first century B.C. in Campania, in the context of colonies populated by veterans of the Roman army, as a way of demonstrating a connection with Rome. They were popular with soldiers, for it was in the amphitheater that they could witness displays of precisely those virtues that they espoused: strength, courage, and quickness. Far from being substitutes for war, gladiatorial combat signified the virtues of the warrior for those who had once engaged in hand-to-hand combat themselves (Welch 1994, 79–80).

If gladiatorial events were not sacrifices or about death, what were they about? Here the best evidence is provided by the Seleucid king Antiochus IV, who spent several years in Rome as a hostage. In 167 B.C. he offered to the world an enormous procession in which gladiators paraded with his soldiers and fought for thirty days in conjunction with athletic contests.[89] The reason that gladiators were included, we are told, was to provide a display of courage that would inspire the young men in the audience. We are also told that some of the youth of

88. For a thorough demolition of the notion of gladiatorial combat as a sacrifice see Ville 1981, 9–19. For a different perspective see Barton 1993, especially 13–15, 23–24, 40–46, etc., without consideration of technical aspects. Plass (1995, 59–60) offers a more nuanced variation by concentrating on violence as a form of social inoculation, though he, too, reverts in passing to the notion of a sacrificial origin (29).

89. Polybius *History* 30.25.5. He says that there were 250 pairs and that the performances lasted for thirty days (30.26.1).

Syria were sufficiently impressed that they decided to fight as gladiators themselves.[90] The idea here is not death but courage in life. This is also the implication of the Greek word meaning "gladiator," *monomachos,* which refers to a person who fights in single combat.

The terms under which the gladiators fought for Antiochus, as given by the Roman historian Livy, are interesting. Livy says that "sometimes they fought until there were wounds; at other times, *sine missione.*" A fight until there were wounds was a fight that ended when one gladiator wounded another, even if the person who was wounded was capable of continuing the fight. The meaning of the other sort of fight that Livy mentions, of a combat *sine missione,* is less obvious.[91] The technical term for the end of a gladiatorial fight was *missio,* which means release—in this context, release from the authority of the person who was offering the combat to the public (the *munerarius*) and who had set the rules for the combat and prescribed the choice of weapons. *Missio* does not mean victory. A clear victory was not a requirement of all combats. If two fighters fought long and hard without either being able to obtain the conditions for a victory, the fight would be a draw, and the fighters would be *stantes missi,* "released standing." A combat *sine missione* was one where *missio* without a clear victory was not permitted, except under the most extraordinary circumstances. The phrase does not mean, as it has unfortunately been taken to mean in many studies of gladiators, a fight to the death. There was no such thing as a mandatory fight to the death between gladiators.

Man and Beast

Failure to separate the different aspects of amphitheatral combat and to translate the terms associated with it correctly has often led to confusion. A passage of the younger Seneca that refers specifically to condemned prisoners being forced to fight to the death has often been quoted as if it referred to gladiators; a law of Constantine that, after some rhetorical sputtering, seeks to eliminate the condemnation of

90. Livy *History of Rome* 41.20 with Ville 1981, 50–51.

91. Robert 1940, 258–61; Ville 1981, 403–5. Key texts are Seneca *Letters* 92.26 *(stans non potest mitti, aut vincatur oportet, aut vincat)* and Martial *Concerning Spectacles* 39.5 *(lex erat, ad digitum posita concurrere parma),* in the context of a *munus sine missione.*

prisoners to the same activity observed by Seneca has, at times, been taken as a ban on gladiatorial combat.[92]

Those condemned to serve in a gladiatorial *ludus* were servants to the gladiators, not gladiators in their own right. A picture of a gladiatorial troop offered by the second-century A.D. novelist Apuleius shows clearly that the condemned, or *noxii,* are a class apart, acting as servants to the others (*Metamorphoses* 4.13). But they were the lucky ones. If they fought well, they might survive either to fight another day or even to obtain freedom. Those who were condemned to more spectacular punishments—exposure to the beasts or some other horrific penalty—appear to have been kept under close confinement until the moment of their death. Forms of execution involved dressing up the condemned as a famous criminal from the past or as a beast. Another well-attested form of execution was assimilated to the style of the beast hunt—combat between two sorts of animal bound together, the hunting of herbivores (both by humans and animals), and single combat between human and animal. Such were the models for the execution of the condemned. The status of the condemned prisoner was assimilated to that of the beast, and an execution represented society's revenge on those who had offended against it.[93] Like the animals, the condemned prisoners were handled by *bestiarii,* and it was expected that they would display terror and contrition. Nothing could be further from the ethos of the gladiator. The beast hunt itself suggested a rather different idea: it demonstrated the Roman emperor's control over the entire world, for the whole world provided beasts for his shows (and for the shows of those whom he particularly favored). As humans cheered the slaughter of animals, often in naturalized settings, they may also have felt a momentary twinge of satisfaction at seeing nature under human control, for a change.

The hunting of wild animals as a public spectacle appears to have originated in neither Italy nor Greece. The source of the Roman tradition appears to have been Carthage, which also set an example for the use of animals to execute humans.[94] The first attested combat involving animals occurred during the first war between the Carthaginians and

92. Seneca, *Letter* 7.4; *Theodosian Code* 9.18.1 with Potter 1994, 230.

93. Potter 1993. See Potter 1996 on public involvement; Coleman 1990 on mythological punishments.

94. Ville 1981, 52–54.

Romans (264–241 B.C.) and featured beasts captured from the latter. The next beast hunts that we hear of postdated the humiliation of Carthage at the end of the second war between the two great powers (218–201 B.C.) and specifically featured African animals.[95] We know very little else about these events and cannot even know if professional beast handlers *(bestiarii)* and hunters *(venatores)* were a permanent feature on the Roman scene at this period; if not, they may have been imported from abroad, with the animals. The only possibly relevant piece of information about the nature of these combats is the statement that at a beast hunt *(venatio)* around 93 B.C., a hundred lions fought at once for the first time.[96] From the end of the second century onward, the *venatio* was well established on the Roman scene, and the acquisition of suitable animals was a major concern for those about to put one on. The emphasis was on unusual or fierce animals.

The separate history of the *venationes* is reflected by the quite different context in which they were offered to the people. The gladiatorial *munus* remained in the notional context of funerary celebration until very late in the Republican period, when their use to influence the outcome of elections led to a spate of legislation attempting to prevent close proximity between a *munus* and an election involving the *munerarius* and, after a particularly remarkable display by Julius Caesar, to limit the number of participants.[97] *Venationes* never seem to have had a funerary context, and by the end of the second century B.C., they are attested as a regular component of the *ludi* that aediles were expected to offer during their year in office. In the Republic, a *venatio* was never held at the same time as a *munus,* although a *venatio* could be held in the context of a battle between prisoners of war who were condemned to fight to the death. Caesar offered one of these combinations, in 46 B.C., and so did Augustus, seventeen years later. At some point prior to 6 A.D., someone, possibly not Augustus, began to combine the two events; the *venatio* came in the morning and the *munus* in the afternoon,

---

95. Pliny *Natural History* 8.6, 17 (252 B.C.); Plautus *Persian Girls* 199 (c. 197 B.C.); Livy *History of Rome* 39.22.2 (186 B.C.); Livy 44.18.8 (169 B.C.) with Ville 1981, 51; Palmer 1997, 42–43. For the execution of the condemned see Potter 1993; Coleman 1990.

96. Pliny *Natural History* 8.54 with Ville 1981, 88. See also Coleman 1996, 60–63 on the ideological aspects of beast displays.

97. Ville 1981, 81–87; Suetonius *Life of Caesar* 10.3.

Fig. 28. Mosaic evidently commissioned to celebrate the *venatio* offered by one Mageirius, depicting the deeds of a *familia* of *venatores*, the Telegenii. The acclamations of the crowd, saluting the generosity of Mageirius, are recorded around the figure of the herald who is bringing bags of prize money into the arena. It is particularly interesting that names of both the hunters and the leopards they hunt are recorded. (From Smirat, Tunisia; photo reproduced from M. Blanchard-Lemée, *Mosaics of Roman Africa* (New York, 1996), fig. 162.)

an organization that appears to have become standard almost immediately.[98]

Stemming as they did from a tradition different from that of gladiatorial combat, beast hunts always remained notionally independent. So did the participants. *Bestiarii* and *venatores* could be no more confused with each other (the *venator* was regarded as a far superior character) than with gladiators. Although, like gladiators, *bestiarii* and *venatores* were organized into *familiae* administered by *lanistae*, they were never members of the same *familiae* as gladiators, and they trained in different areas (fig. 28). It is also the case that *venatores*, at least, were able to form

98. See Ville 1981, 94–99 (for differing contexts), 93–94, 99–100, 116–17 (for the events of Caesar and Augustus), 126 (on the date of the introduction of combined *venationes* and *munera*).

independent associations and sell their services to *munerarii* on their own, both in the east and in the west.[99] The independence of the *venatio* ensured the survival of this form of entertainment well after gladiatorial combat ceased to be a serious entertainment option in the late fourth and early fifth centuries A.D.[100]

A Gladiatorial Duel

The evidence for what actually happened when two gladiators met in the arena derives from numerous sources—not one of them offering a clear account of a typical fight from beginning to end. The literary accounts offer some insight into aristocratic perceptions of what happened, numerous inscriptions offer pieces of information that suggest something of the perception of the professional fighter, and mosaics and other works of art illustrate events, both ordinary and spectacular, that the audience might expect.

Before the fight started, a gladiator had to place himself (or herself) under the authority of the *munerarius*. This could happen in three ways. First, the gladiator could be a member of a troop *(familia)* owned by the prospective *munerarius*. Prior to Augustus, all gladiatorial troops were the property of private individuals, who maintained them both for the provision of *munera* and, on some occasions, to provide a nucleus of trained force that could be called out in the violent world of late Republican politics. After Augustus, we still find troops of gladiators belonging to private individuals, but they appear to be considerably less common. The imperial manipulation of the personnel for gladiatorial exhibitions will be the subject of the next section of this chapter.

The second way that a gladiator could come under the authority of a *munerarius* was through an agreement with the *lanista* who oversaw the *familia* of which the gladiator was a member. *Lanistae* were all people of low social status (rating with pimps on the Roman scale of personal value), and they were ordinarily managers for members of the aristocracy. Some appear to have been independent contractors, but with the exception of a spectacular disaster associated with one of them in the reign of Tiberius, their activities are ordinarily lost to our view in the

99. For the east see Robert 1940, n. 175, an inscription of Augustan date from Mylasa; and see the bibliography in Roueché 1993, 74–75.

100. Ville 1960, 273–335 remains the classic study of the end of gladiatorial combat; for the continuation of *venationes* see Roueché 1993, 76–79

imperial period.[101] The *lanista* would agree on a fee with the *munerarius* (negotiated separately for each gladiator).[102] Needless to say, they had an interest in getting their gladiators back in one piece or receiving sufficiently great compensation if they did not.

Both of the systems already outlined presuppose that the gladiators in question were slaves. A third system applied to free people. Some of these people might have been born free; others might be ex-slaves who had won their freedom in the arena. It appears that even slave gladiators kept all or portions of the monetary prizes that they won in the arena. It also appears that free people were regarded as superior gladiators, possibly because there was a general expectation that they would be more experienced.[103] The free person who intended to fight would first make a declaration of the intent to fight before a magistrate. The next step would be to negotiate a contract, specifying the fee and the terms of the combat with the *munerarius.* Once the terms of the contract had been negotiated, the gladiator swore an oath, for which the following terms are attested by numerous sources: "to be burned with fire, chained, beaten with rods, killed with steel." We do not have a record of the conditions that would lead to this treatment—did the gladiator swear to win or else suffer these fates, or did he or she swear to be liable to these fates for failure to perform up to standard? Having sworn the oath, the gladiator would receive the money for which he or she had agreed to fight. Finally there was a symbolic initiation in which the gladiator was struck with a rod, demonstrating submission to the rules of combat (Ville 1981, 246–49).

---

101. On private troops see Ville 1981, 242–44; Robert 1940, 25–27, 196–97. For the nature of gladiatorial training see [Caesar] *African War* 71, where a remarkable simile compares Caesar, who is showing his men precisely how to move into combat, with a *lanista.*

102. Prices appear to have been set by market forces until the first century A.D., when Tiberius imposed limitations on the number of pairs of gladiators. Actual price-fixing may date from the reign of Antoninus Pius; see Ville 1981, 274 n. 104.

103. Petronius *Satyricon* 45 is the locus classicus, but see, more significantly, *ILS* 5163, 62–62: *liberatus si discrimen instauraverit, aestimatio eius post hac HS $\overline{XII}$ non excedat* [if, having been freed, he should take up this occupation again, his valuation shall not exceed 12,000 HS]. The point here is clearly to limit the amount that could be demanded by private individuals for their services, but the amount selected is that of the second class of imperial gladiator and thus comparatively high. The theory did not always match the practice; see *CIL* 4.1421, 1422, 1474, 2387 for defeats of free gladiators.

The night before the combat, all the human combatants dined at a public banquet, the *cena libera,* to which the public was admitted. Some have seen this banquet as a symbolic gift from the *munerarius* to those who were going to fight for him on the next day. This suggestion is not impossible, but the fact that condemned prisoners were included suggests a slightly less-elevated explanation: simple advertisement. In many cases the gladiators would have put on some sort of preliminary parade through a public area of the city so that people would be able to recognize them. I suspect that the same purpose lay behind the *cena libera* and that this is why the condemned were included: the public needed to be reminded who the condemned were; in some cases it might have been months since the trial, and those responsible for their condemnation may well have thought that a prior public display might help inflame the crowd.[104]

On the day of the great event (assuming a post-Augustan date), the festivities would begin with a parade through the amphitheater. If multiple events were on offer, they would follow a strict course: beast hunts (both those engaging beasts against beasts and those engaging beasts against humans) up until lunchtime, the execution of the condemned around lunch (roughly 10:45–1:15 in the summer, 11:15–12:45 in the winter), and gladiatorial displays for the rest of the day. The time allotted (the Roman day ended around 7:30 in the evening) and the number of pairs that would ordinarily perform offers the most important clue as to what was expected of a fight. It appears that at a festival where gladiators would take up the whole afternoon (this was not true in all places) there would be between ten and thirteen pairs. In some cases arrangements were made for combats that included a *suppositicius* or *tertiarius*—a person who would fight the winner of the initial bout—thus giving a total of from twenty to twenty-six fights in about six hours.[105] It is there-

---

104. For the parades see Robert 1940, n. 171 with the correction of Ville 1981, 365; for the *cena libera* see Ville 1981, 363–64; for publicity and executions see Potter 1996, 152–55. See especially *The Passion of Saints Perpetua and Felicity* 17 for the atmosphere when the Christians discussed their faith with those who had come to see who was at the dinner; the suggestion is that people came to see who the condemned were.

105. Ville 1981, 395–99 is crucial on this point. See especially *CIL* 4.7994 (forty-nine pairs at Puteoli over four days), 1179, 1200, 1185, 3384, 7992, 7995 (thirty pairs over three days at Pompeii; but see 2508 [fifteen pairs over two days, six on one day, nine on the other]), 1193, 1201 (twenty pairs with no dates), 1204 (thirty pairs over more than one day), 3881 (20 pairs over three

fore reasonable to assume that the average fight lasted from ten to fifteen minutes, if gladiators fought one pair at a time, as the bulk of the evidence suggests that they did.

Before the actual fighting began there was an official inspection of the weapons, a display of the instruments of encouragement mentioned in the gladiatorial oath, and a general showing off by the contestants. Then, at a signal from the *munerarius,* a trumpet sounded and the first pair of gladiators were matched against each other under the supervision of two referees.[106] A variety of different encounters was then to be expected: between gladiators on foot, armed with different sorts of weapons; between mounted gladiators; and between gladiators driving chariots. In a festival that went on for several days, a conscious effort seems to have been made to save the best for the last (Ville 1981, 395).

A duel was a contest of skill and endurance.[107] By the first century A.D. the equipment of gladiators had evolved so as to afford the maximum protection for different styles of fighting, while also being as light as possible. The *retiarius,* who entered the arena with a trident and net, wore a sleeve of armor that extended from wrist to shoulder on his left arm, some armor around his waist, and greaves. His opponent, who would be armed with a sword and carry a shield, would be expected to slash the exposed left arm or legs. It would be most unlikely that he would land a blow on the right arm, so there was no need to protect it, but a slashing blow at the waist could be permanently disabling (as could one to the left arm). A blow to the chest was much less likely to be extremely dangerous. The various sorts of swordsmen were distinguished by different types of shield and helmet, but they all wore armor around the waist, an armor sleeve reaching to the shoulder on the sword arm, and greaves. Representations of duels between swordsmen and *retiarii* reveal that a standard blow with the trident would be

---

days), 3882 (twenty pairs over four days). For other discussion of the length of time that it was feasible to expect human beings to engage in close combat (between fifteen and twenty minutes) see Goldsworthy 1996, 224.

106. Ville 1981, 407–8. Note especially Cicero *Concerning Oratory* 2.325 and Ovid *Ibis* 45–50 on gladiatorial self-display.

107. It was rare—though not unheard of—for a gladiator to lose his nerve and run or to perform so badly that someone burned his flesh with a heated metal plate or ordered a flogging. The stigma of flight was likely to stick: see *CIL* 4.2351, 5214; Petronius *Satyricon* 45.

aimed at the legs—which might throw the swordsman off balance and end the fight, but which would not be likely to draw blood, with the legs protected as they were. Other depictions of defeated gladiators often show a wound where the armor sleeve ended at the shoulder—not much of a target. A mosaic reveals a spectacular move where one gladiator disarmed the other with a blow from his shield.

The average fight ended either with a wound to one of the contestants or when one fighter's endurance gave out. The standard way of describing the end of a fight was with the phrase *ad digitum,* which referred to the point at which one fighter raised a finger to indicate that he had had enough or simply threw down his shield. It was then up to the referee to make sure that the fight ended: they are often depicted as standing between the victor and vanquished or even grabbing the hand of the victor to prevent his dealing a fatal blow. It is only natural in such a sport that the combatants could lose control of themselves, and it was equally dangerous for a fighter to lay off an opponent in the expectation that he would resign. The latter seems to have happened to Victor the "lefty" whom a demon rather than the "forsworn Pinnas" killed, and likewise Diodorus of Amisos in northern Turkey died because he "did not kill Demetrius immediately."[108] There is perhaps no more poignant expression of the emotions of combat than that of a gladiator who speaks from beyond the grave to tell the viewer of his epitaph that his strength did not desert him before he killed the "guardian of his soul" by his own hand. He died while killing an opponent filled with "unreasoning hate" (Robert 1940, n. 124). In other texts we find some gladiators who claim that they never killed anyone, others who claim that they killed everyone, and the occasional grudge match.[109] The key point here is that the gladiators say that the responsibility for life and death lay with them, not with the crowd.

Death at the hands of one's colleagues was rarely attributed to lack of skill, or so the epitaphs of gladiators tell us. In Latin we often find that the defeated combatants were tricked *(deceptus),* and the word *deceptus* alone is enough to indicate death as a result of combat. Gladiators who died in the Greek east could likewise be victims of treachery or fate. One tells us that he was "victorious throughout the province,

108. Robert 1940, nn. 34 (Victor), 79 (Diodorus).

109. Robert 1940, nn. 54, 55, 20 (sparing opponents), 84, 106, 214; Gregori 1989, n. 50 (killing); Robert 1940, n. 124 (grudge match). See in general Robert 1940, 302–7.

unbeaten in twenty fights," and not killed by any failure of skill but that he fell victim to the youth of his final foe.[110]

Whatever the gladiators may say—and the stress on personal control is significant—it is nonetheless true that the *munerarius* had the final say. But he had to listen to the crowd, which could call for the defeated gladiator to be either released or killed. Two fingers extended straight out were the sign for mercy; *pollice verso,* probably thumbs-down (though it could be thumbs-up), was the signal that the *munerarius* gave the chief referee if he decided that death was appropriate. If death was chosen, the final blow was struck away from the floor of the arena, with a dagger driven through the spinal column in an area known as the *spolearium* (Ville 1981, 419–20).

The victor received a variety of prizes. The basic prize was a palm leaf, as in chariot races and most athletic events. If a victory was considered especially brilliant, a gladiator might receive a crown, if the *munerarius* agreed with the crowd that it was deserved (Ville 1981, 313–14, 426–27). Through a process of "prize inflation" it appears to have become customary to award both a crown and a palm by the end of the first century A.D. Once he had received his prizes, the victor took a celebratory lap around the arena. Then he might receive some rather more substantial awards: Claudius is said to have handed out pieces of gold according to the demands of the crowd as he held up his fingers to indicate various amounts; other prizes were spears (with tips of gold and silver) or torques. The combination of prizes is unique to the gladiatorial arena, for while the palm and crown were rewards for which athletes contended, the lance and torque were rewards of valor given to soldiers.[111] As such they are symbolic of the ideals of the gladiatorial sport.

Another sort of reward was intimately related to the status of the performers: manumission. The symbol of freedom was a staff of wood, or *rudis,* resembling the staff of a referee. The crowd might demand that the *munerarius* grant this reward on the sands of the arena, though here

---

110. Robert 1940, n. 169. See also Gregori 1989, nn. 47 *(in Nemese ne fidem habeatis sic sum deceptus),* 52; *ILS* 5111 *(fato deceptus non ab homine),* 5112; Buonocore 1992, n. 69, l. 5 (*adversario occisus* is unusual); Robert 1940, 304.

111. Suetonius *Life of Claudius* 21.9; Mart. *Concerning Spectacles* 1.29.6. For military honors see Maxfield 1981, 84–88. The gladiatorial crown was sometimes of gold (also a military decoration). For other rewards—including, in one case, a country estate and, in another, a palace—see Wiedemann 1992, 122.

there could be technical problems. The *munerarius* had no business freeing someone else's slave. The law was explicit on this point, and it is of some interest that pronouncements on this subject date from the later second century A.D. onward, when the emperors appear to have held a virtual monopoly on gladiators used at major civic performances. Whatever else a distinguished citizen of the empire might do, he had absolutely no business making decisions that had an impact on his imperial majesty's property.[112] If a gladiator was to be released in the arena, a prior arrangement (and, no doubt, payment) had to be made. The dramatic effect may well have been worth the price.

Gladiatorial Organization

A great deal of organization lay behind a successful afternoon in the arena. Gladiators did not grow on trees, nor did suitable beasts. Suitable candidates (human and animal) had to be located, recruited, trained, fed, and, on occasion, repaired. The tip of this administrative iceberg has reared its head from time to time in the course of the preceding pages. It is time now to look more closely at what lay below the surface.

It was preferable that gladiators be well matched. Only an evil *lanista* sent unevenly matched pairs off to the *munus;* he might do this out of favoritism toward or dislike of one of his charges or simply to cheat the *munerarius.* By the later first century A.D. an official ranking system had developed within gladiatorial *ludi* to make mismatching more difficult. A gladiator was ranked as a novice *(novicius),* a recruit *(tiro),* a veteran *(veteranus)* or a member of a *palus.* A *novicius* was a new arrival at the *ludus;* a *tiro* was a gladiator who was felt to be ready to engage in his first fight; the title *veteranus* was awarded to a gladiator who had emerged alive from his first fight.[113] Four grades of *palus* are regularly

112. *Digest* 4.9.17; *Code of Justinian* 7.11.3. Both refer to enactments of Marcus Aurelius.

113. For *novicius* and *tiro* see Sabbatini Tumolesi 1988, n. 45 (dating to the reign of Commodus). The term *novicius* is attested as early as Cicero *On Behalf of Sestius* 78. See also Ville 1981, 311 n. 196—a gladiator who did not survive the first fight is described as a *tiro* in death; see, for instance, Sabbatini Tumolesi 1988, n. 97. A *tiro* was not necessarily matched with another *tiro* in his first encounter: see Robert 1940, n. 54 and Sabbatini Tumolesi 1988, n. 92, with discussions in both places. See also *CIL* 4.1474, where a *tiro* kills a free gladiator in his first fight.

attested; admission to these grades must have depended on victory, and the first *palus (primus palus)* was the highest grade to which a person could aspire.[114] The word *palus* derived from the stake in the *ludus* against which gladiators practiced, and its usage in the sense of a grade is paralleled in the language of the amphitheater by the term *rudis*, referring to the referee's wand, which could be used to designate either the referee or a gladiator who had won his freedom in the arena.

By the late second century a more elaborate system of ranking appears to have developed, and it is explicitly connected with the costs of shows. Our evidence here derives from one of the most remarkable epigraphic discoveries of the last century, the record of a debate in the senate on the expenditures for shows.[115] The debate probably took place in A.D. 177 or 178, and it was stimulated by the emperor Marcus Aurelius' decision to rescind a 25–33 percent surcharge on gladiators that may have been imposed to help finance wars on the northern frontier. In the course of this discussion a member of the senate proposed a ranking of gladiators by price and experience, matching them with the quality of the *munus* that a local magistrate was required to fund. The substance of his suggestion may be tabulated as follows.

Price per Gladiator	**Rank of Gladiator**	**Price of *Munus***
Not given	Not given	*Munus assiforanus* (not more than 30,000 HS)
3,000 HS	Third class	30,000–40,000 HS
4,000 HS	Second class	30,000–40,000 HS
5,000 HS	First class	30,000–40,000 HS
5,000 HS	Third class	40,000–100,000 HS
6,000 HS	Second class	40,000–100,000 HS
8,000 HS	First class	40,000–100,000 HS
5,000 HS	Fifth class	100,000–150,00 HS
6,000 HS	Fourth class	100,000–150,00 HS
8,000 HS	Third class	100,000–150,00 HS
10,000 HS	Second class	100,000–150,00 HS
12,000 HS	First class	100,000–150,00 HS

114. For discussion of the meaning of *palus* see Robert 1940, 28–31.
115. Oliver and Palmer 1955, 320–49 remains the standard publication.

6,000 HS	Fifth class	150,000–200,000 HS
7,000 HS	Fourth class	150,000–200,000 HS
9,000 HS	Third class	150,000–200,000 HS
12,000 HS	Second class	150,000–200,000 HS
15,000 HS	First class	150,000–200,000 HS

One oddity is immediately obvious: while there are classes of 8,000 and 10,000 HS for entertainments that cost between 100,000 and 150,000 HS, there are classes rated at 7,000 and 9,000 HS in the most expensive entertainments. The difference should be explained as a discounting scheme and should not compel us to think that there were ten, rather than eight, separate classifications. The decree also specifies that gladiators will be furnished in equal numbers from each category. This does not mean that—with the probable exception of the lowest class (which must be the equivalent of the *tiro*)—members of the same class would necessarily fight each other. Other texts clearly show members of different *pali* fighting against each other, and it is not unreasonable to suppose that one criterion for promotion from a lower *palus* to a higher one was victory in such a fight.[116]

Gladiators are not the only people being ranked in the decree. Locations and *munerarii* are being ranked according to their ability to support entertainments of different sizes. The system of ranking reinforces two hierarchies. One is the hierarchy of communities within the empire—the bigger the place, the better the games, and there was no point in a lesser city trying to compete. The other hierarchy is that within the individual communities. *Munera assiforana*, games for which admission was charged, were not the ordinary venue of aristocratic display. People who lacked the inherited or appointed social status of the regular givers of *munera* had to be prevented from offering better shows, restricted to a level below the lowest level of official *munera* required of officeholders as gifts to the people of their community as notional repayment for the honor of holding office.[117] Furthermore,

116. See Sabbatini Tumolesi 1988, n. 92, where a gladiator who had fought to a draw as a *tiro* wins his second fight against a free gladiator with nine fights under his belt.

117. There are cases, however, where members of municipal aristocracies can be detected offering such *munera* and then dedicating statues from the profits: see *ILS* 411 (Cirta), 3316, 3589; *AE* 1969/70, n. 134 (Canusium); *ILS* 6208 (Tusculum).

members of the ruling class had to be prevented from doing actual harm to each other.

It was a basic tenet of ancient political theory that political influence could be gained or asserted by the provision of spectacles.[118] If all the players on the stage of local political power had started on a level playing field, this would have been a problem if one person started an upward spiral of entertainments, forcing his rivals to do one better. But all the players were not equal, and not all those who found themselves in a position where they would be expected to offer a *munus* wanted the post. Office holding was often compulsory; we have record of some officeholders who had to take out loans from their cities in order to provide the requisite games, and in this decree it is explicitly stated that officeholders designate would form associations with their friends so that they would be able to offer the entertainments required of them.[119] In a society where most wealth was held in land and where the expected annual return on an investment in land was around 6 percent, an estate valued at the vast sum of 500,000 HS was the minimum required to finance the least expensive games listed here (and that would obviously leave the prospective officeholder with no other income that year).[120] The implicit social contract of the classical city was based on the assumption that the wealthy would retain control of the political apparatus if they guaranteed entertainments and economic stability for the less well-off. Those who attended the games determined whether or not a *munerarius* had fulfilled his part of the bargain. As the average officeholder would appear to have had insufficient or barely sufficient means to accomplish this task, the Roman state imposed limits on expenditure so that an extremely wealthy person could not effectively price his neighbors out of the market by putting on games that few, if any, other members of the local aristocracy could hope to match. The state could also waive these limits as a way of demonstrating particular favor to an individual who was rich enough, and was deemed important enough, to merit such a boost in local poli-

118. See Ste. Croix 1981, 305–6.

119. On loans see Duncan-Jones 1982, 153–54.

120. On rates of return for Roman investments see Duncan-Jones 1982, 33–59; most of the entertainments for which we have prices fall into the lowest category of expenditure.

tics.[121] Thus here, as elsewhere, public entertainment is a focal point for the exercise of power on many different levels—both within the city and between the city and Roman imperial authorities.

The Trade in Gladiators

Gladiatorial schools are first attested at Capua in the late second century, and in the last years of the Roman Republic there appears to have been a lively trade in gladiators and other amphitheatral entertainers (Welch 1994, 69). Lentulus Battiatus, in whose *ludus* the famous Spartacus resided, appears to have been a speculator who provided gladiators for the personal *familiae* of members of the Roman aristocracy. Cicero and his friend Atticus appear to have gotten into the gladiator business in the fifties B.C.—plainly renting gladiators to *munerarii* who needed them.[122] Julius Caesar, whose manpower needs were extraordinary, clearly decided that it was more efficient (and cheaper?) to establish his own *ludi.* Augustus inherited Julius' gladiators along with much else. Originally based at Capua and Ravenna, imperial troops are attested in Gaul and Spain under Augustus, gradually accruing a substantial administrative mechanism within the imperial *fiscus,* the vast economic empire that was the private property of the emperor (Ville 1981, 277–79). Under Caligula is the first clear attestation of a *ludus* (gladiatorial training ground) at Rome for the emperor's gladiators—though it was probably created by Augustus—and evidence for the formation of a parallel structure for *bestiarii* and *venatores,* the Ludus Matutinus, deriving its name from the part of the day (early morning) in which its occupants performed. Domitian built a new *ludus* in the capitol, in close proximity to the recently opened Coliseum. He then built two more *ludi,* the Ludus Dacicus, originally housing prisoners from his Dacian war, and the Ludus Gallicus, built to house gladiators recruited from Gaul (Ville 1981, 277–79, 280–83).

As early as the reign of Claudius, the general administration of imperial *familiae* was felt to be a position of such importance that it

121. For limits (as early as the reign of Nero, and the context suggests an even earlier date) see Tacitus *Annals* 13.49.1; Pliny *Panygeric* 54.4. Note also *CIL* 5.7637 (saying that events should not violate existing statutes). For dispensations see Robert 1940, n. 63, n. 152 with p. 281.

122. Ville 1981, 270–76; for Cicero see *Letters to Atticus* 4.8.2, 4.4a.2.

rated a procurator of equestrian rank.[123] The job of the procurator was to oversee the activities of the *lanistae* who were charged with the day-to-day administration of the individual *familiae.* With Domitian we get the first evidence for an imperial procurator in charge of the *ludus* at Alexandria, and we have reason to think that Domitian may have been responsible for the creation of the imperial procurator in charge of the Ludus Matutinus.[124] The procurator in charge of the Ludus Matutinus may also have been in charge of the imperial zoos, three of which are attested by the middle of the first century A.D. One was an elephant park at Laurentinum; another was reserved for "fierce animals" (carnivores), the third for herbivores (Sabbatini Tumolesi 1988, nn. 8–10). In the eastern provinces, imperial procurators in charge of the emperor's *familiae* begin to appear in the second century.[125]

Evidence for private troops, both those belonging to individuals and those under the control of provincial high priests (who passed the gladiators along to their successors), continues well into the third century. In a text of the second century A.D. we are given a picture of an ambitious *munerarius* recruiting the best gladiators that he could find, and it is in this context that we receive some information from the great doctor Galen about gladiatorial lifestyle as represented in the *ludus* of the high priests of the imperial cult at Pergamon.[126]

Galen did not care much for a particular gladiatorial food, a special barley porridge. He thought that it made the gladiators too muscular. Gladiatorial diet garners a few negative reviews from other sources as well, much of it connected with physiognomic discussions that devalued physical types that the average aristocrat could not hope to obtain. The barley porridge—quintessential high-fiber stuff—was surely not the only item on the gladiatorial menu, especially as gladiators were plainly free to wander about town, but it does represent a rather interesting effort to match diet to physical activity.

The fact that Galen was in a *ludus* to comment on the diet is an important point in and of itself. He was a child of the aristocracy and

123. Tacitus *Annals* 11.35, 13.22 (listed as a major office in both places); Pflaum 1950, 42. And it remained so (see Pflaum 1950, 281).

124. *ILS* 1397; Ville 1981, 286; Sabbatini Tumolesi 1988, n. 22.

125. Robert 1940, n. 70, 258, 267 n. 1.

126. On private troops see especially the decree of A.D. 177 (?); Robert 1940, 283–85. For the ambitious *munerarius* see Apuleius *Metamorphoses* 10.18; for Galen see *Compound Drugs Arranged by Kind* 3.2 (Kuhn 19: 599–600).

proved to be a person who combined remarkable intellectual energy, technical skill, and diplomatic prowess. The *ludus* was not a place where people of his sort ordinarily spent time—but in his case we may suspect that it served as a sort of equivalent to a residency at an inner-city hospital for a person interested in trauma, offering the best possible hands-on training. Practical convenience could break down barriers: the *ludi* could use good doctors, and aspiring doctors could use the experience. Galen ultimately ministered to the emperor Marcus Aurelius and never had to apologize for having healed a gladiator. This was an anomaly born of economic necessity.

The Ambiguity of the Amphitheater

Nowhere is aristocratic fear of the entertainer as obvious as with the entertainments of the amphitheater. The gladiator may have been the quintessential representative of the virtues of Roman aristocratic society; but while gladiators suggested that they obtained the status commensurate with those virtues, aristocratic society seems to have closed ranks against public combatants more forcefully than against any other type of entertainer. In his brilliant studies of gladiatorial epitaphs from the Greek east, the French epigraphist Louis Robert showed how public combatants appropriated the language connected with Greek athletics in their self-presentation (Robert 1940, 22–23). This sort of self-presentation may have influenced Christian appropriation of the same language to describe martyrdom—another activity explicitly connected with the amphitheater.

Critics of public combat were explicit in their statements that the champions of the arena were not culture heroes. They were engaged in mindless bloodshed.[127] Both sides overstated their case. A person who chose or was drafted into the amphitheater entered a world that was explicitly Italian, where the entertainers were the servants of, rather than participants in, aristocratic society. It is notable that gladiatorial self-presentation in the Greek part of the empire differs markedly from that in the Latin in seeking an alternative model—that of the athlete. No such parallel was available in the west, for even as athletes became more socially acceptable in the west, they did so because of a Greek cultural heritage. The heritage of the public combatant was always Italian.

127. Wiedemann 1992, 128–46 is excellent on critics.

The voices critical of the amphitheater come precisely from the class that supported it with its money. Cicero might refer to people whom he did not like as gladiators, but he tried to make money out of real gladiators—and other voices speaking against the amphitheater are those of people whose status removed them from the necessity of putting on games for their homeland, because they were important enough to resist such demands. Before the spread of circus chariot racing to the provinces, amphitheatrical entertainment was the focal point for expressing the ideology of Rome.

Conclusions

"Bread and circuses"—these things were all that the Roman people cared about according to Juvenal, the great Roman satirist of the second century A.D., and others. The second century A.D., when the Roman state achieved unparalleled security, was the great age of the actor, athlete, and gladiator, the period in which it appears that the Mediterranean world reached a historical pinnacle in the allocation of social resources to its own entertainment.

"Bread and circuses" were a substitute, in Juvenal's terms, for an interest in higher politics. That may be unfair. The entertainment industry consisted of a group of institutions that achieved a great deal of influence in the Roman world, offering a form of common cultural expression that had never existed before in a region of the world that was never again to be united to the degree that it was in the first three centuries A.D.

Entertainment is not only a reflection of a society's view of itself; it also reflects the degree of security that a society feels. The chief forms of entertainment in the Roman world share a number of features. There is great emphasis on the individual star. Team sports were not venues for leading performers (in the amphitheater they were the venue for those condemned to death). On the stage, soloists overshadowed the efforts of troops. This was the world of the great individual who could achieve great feats of technical virtuosity or display extraordinary physical endurance. The stress on technical virtuosity and physical endurance descends from the earliest periods of classical entertainment and remains constant until the end of the urban society that supported these activities.

More than any other enterprise, the diverse entertainment structures created a cultural vocabulary to unite the diverse peoples of the Roman world. This vocabulary and the activity of entertainers challenged the aristocratic hierarchy of the classical city by offering slaves and other socially disadvantaged individuals avenues of advancement. Hence come the disparaging remarks that emanate from the very members of the aristocratic power structure that was forced to fund these entertainments.

Disruption of the social hierarchy may be the least serious consequence of the extension of the influence of public entertainment. By the beginning of the third century A.D., the Roman empire had already entered a period of relative decline with respect to its neighbors. The cultural self-congratulation represented by the entertainment establishments of the Roman empire may be taken as a symptom of an excessive and false sense of security in a society that had lured itself into complacency. The great age of public entertainment was not the great age of social improvement, nor was it only the age in which Rome's neighbors began to acquire greater force. It was also the period of Roman history where alternative ideological systems began to spread and gain adherents—the most important of these being the Christian church and Judaism. Human institutions are, by their very nature, unstable and persistently evoke diverse responses to themselves. As the Roman world changed, so did its entertainments, until both ceased to exist.

Bibliography

Chapters 1–3

Alter, G. 1992. "Theories of Fertility Decline: A Non-specialist's Guide to the Current Debate." In J.R. Gillis, L.A. Tilly, and D. Levine, eds., *The European Experience of Declining Fertility, 1850–1970*, 13–27. Cambridge, Mass.

Bagnall, R.S., and Frier, B.W. 1994. *The Demography of Roman Egypt*. Cambridge.

Bauman, R.A. 1992. *Women and Politics in Ancient Rome*. New York.

Bernstein, P.L. 1996. *Against the Gods: The Remarkable Story of Risk*. New York.

Boatwright, M.T. 1987. *Hadrian and the City of Rome*. Princeton.

Bonner, S.F. 1977. *Education in Ancient Rome*. Berkeley and Los Angeles.

Boserup, E. 1981. *Population and Technological Change*. Chicago.

Bradley, K.R. 1987. "On the Roman Slave Supply and Slavebreeding." In M.I. Finley, ed., *Classical Slavery*, 42–64. London.

———. 1991. *Discovering the Roman Family*. Oxford.

———. 1994. *Slavery and Society at Rome*. Cambridge.

Champlin, E. 1991. *Final Judgments: Duty and Emotion in Roman Wills, 200 B.C.–A.D. 250*. Princeton.

Chesnais, J.-Cl. 1992. *The Demographic Transition: States, Patterns, and Economic Implications*. Trans. E. Kreager and P. Kreager. Oxford.

Clarke, J.R. 1991. *The Houses of Roman Italy, 100 B.C.–A.D. 250: Ritual, Space, and Decoration*. Berkeley and Los Angeles.

Coale, A.J., and Watkins, S.C. 1986. *The Decline of Fertility*. Princeton.

Coarelli, F. 1975. *Guida archeologica di Roma*. Rome.

Cohen, J.E. 1995. *How Many People Can the Earth Support?* New York.

Corbier, Mirelle. 1991. "Family Behavior of the Roman Aristocracy, Second Century B.C.–Third Century A.D." In S.B. Pomeroy, ed., *Women's History and Ancient History*, 173–96. Chapel Hill.

———. 1995. "Male Power and Legitimacy through Women: The *Domus Augusta* under the Julio-Claudians." In R. Hawley and B. Levick, eds., *Women in Antiquity: New Assessments*, 178–93. New York.

Cribiore, R. 1996. *Writing, Teachers, and Students in Graeco-Roman Egypt*. ASP 36. Atlanta.

D'Arms, J. 1970. *Romans on the Bay of Naples: A Social and Cultural Study of the Villas and Their Owners from 150 B.C. to A.D. 400*. Cambridge, Mass.

de Franciscis, A. 1975. *Die pompejanischen Wandmalereien in der Villa von Oplontis.* Recklinghausen.

Deiss, J.J. 1985. *Herculaneum: Italy's Buried Treasure.* New York.

Dionisotti, A.C. 1982. "From Ausonius' Schooldays? A Schoolbook and Its Relatives." *JRS* 72:83–125.

Dixon, S. 1988. *The Roman Mother.* London.

———. 1992. *The Roman Family.* Baltimore.

Dover, J.K. 1978. *Greek Homosexuality.* Cambridge, Mass.

Doxiadis, E. 1995. *The Mysterious Fayum Portraits: Faces from Ancient Egypt.* London.

Duncan-Jones, R.P. 1990. *Structure and Scale in the Roman Economy.* Cambridge.

———. 1996. "The Impact of the Antonine Plague." *JRA* 9:108–36.

Edwards, C. 1993. *The Politics of Immorality in Ancient Rome.* Cambridge.

Egbert, J.C. 1896. *Introduction to the Study of Latin Inscriptions.* New York, Cincinnati, and Chicago.

Fantham, E., Foley, H.P., Kampen, N.B., Pomeroy, S.B. and Shapiro, H.A., eds. 1994. *Women in the Classical World.* Oxford.

Fayer, C. 1994. *La familia romana.* Problemi e ricerche di storia antica 16. Rome.

Foucault, M. 1986. *The Care of the Self.* Vol. 3 of *The History Sexuality.* New York.

Frier, B.W. 1982. "Roman Life Expectancy: Ulpian's Evidence." *HSCP* 86:213–51.

———. 1983. "Roman Life Expectancy: The Pannonian Evidence." *Phoenix* 37:328–44.

———. 1994. "Natural Fertility and Family Limitations." *CPh* 89:318–23.

Galinsky, K. 1996. *Augustan Culture.* Princeton.

Gardner, J.F. 1984. "A Family and an Inheritance: The Problems of the Widow Petronilla." *Liverpool Classical Monthly* 9, no. 9:132–33.

———. 1986. *Women in Roman Law and Society.* London.

———. 1993. *Being a Roman Citizen.* London.

Gardner, J.F., and Wiedemann, Th., eds. 1991. *The Roman Household: A Sourcebook.* London.

Garnsey, P., and Saller, R. 1987. *The Roman Empire: Economy, Society, and Culture.* Berkeley and Los Angeles.

Gleason, M.W. 1995. *Making Men: Sophists and Self-Presentation in Ancient Rome.* Princeton.

Gourevitch, D. 1984. *La mal d'être femme.* Paris.

———. 1995. "Comment rendre à sa véritable nature le petit monstre humain?" In Ph.J. van der Eijk, H.F.J. Horstmanshoff, and P.H. Schrijvers, eds., *Ancient Medicine in Its Socio-cultural Context,* 1:239–60. Amsterdam and Atlanta.

Hallett, J.P. 1984. *Fathers and Daughters in Roman Society: Women and the Elite Family.* Princeton.

Halperin, D.M. 1990. "One Hundred Years of Homosexuality." In D.M. Halperin, ed., *One Hundred Years of Homosexuality and Other Essays on Greek Love.* London.

Hands, A.R. 1968. *Charities and Social Aid in Greece and Rome.* Ithaca.

Hanson, A.E. 1990. "The Medical Writers' Woman." In D. M. Halperin, J. J.

Winkler, and F. I. Zeitlin, eds., *Before Sexuality: The Construction of Erotic Experience in the Ancient Greek World*, 309–37. Princeton.

———. 1991. "Ancient Illiteracy." In J. Humphrey, ed., *Literacy in the Roman World, Journal of Roman Archaeology* supp. 3, 159–98. Ann Arbor.

———. 1994a. "A Division of Labor: Roles for Men in Greek and Roman Births." *Thamyris* 1, no. 2:157–202.

———. 1994b. "Obstetrics in the *Hippocratic Corpus* and Soranus." *Forum* 4, no. 1:93–110.

Hanson, A.E., and Green, M.H. 1994. "Soranus, *Methodicorum princeps*." *Aufstieg und Niedergang der Römischen Welt* 2.37.2:968–1075.

Harris, W.V. 1989. *Ancient Literacy*. Cambridge, Mass.

———. 1994. "Child-Exposure in the Roman Empire." *JRS* 84:1–22.

Hopkins, K. 1983. *Death and Renewal*. Cambridge.

———. 1993. "Novel Evidence for Roman Slavery." *Past and Present* 138:3–27.

Joshel, S.R. 1992. *Work, Identity, and Legal Status at Rome: A Study of Occupational Inscriptions*. Norman.

Kaster, R.A. 1988. *Guardians of Language: The Grammarian and Society in Late Antiquity*. Berkeley and Los Angeles.

Kehoe, D. 1988. *The Economics of Agriculture on Roman Imperial Estates in North Africa*. Göttingen.

———. 1992. *Management and Investment on Estates in Roman Egypt during the Early Empire*. Bonn.

King, H. 1991. "Using the Past: Nursing and the Medical Profession in Ancient Greece." In P. Holden and J. Littlewood, eds., *Anthropology and Nursing*, 7–22. London and New York.

Krause, J.-U. 1994. *Witwen und Waisen im Römischen Reich*. Vol. 1. Stuttgart.

Laqueur, Th. 1992. *Making Sex: Body and Gender from the Greeks to Freud*. Cambridge, Mass.

Lefkowitz, M.R., and Fant, M.B., eds. 1992. *Women's Life in Greece and Rome*. 2d ed. Baltimore.

Littman, R.J., and Littman, M.L. 1973. "Galen and the Antonine Plague." *AJP* 94:243–55.

Livi-Bacci, M. 1991. *Population and Nutrition: An Essay on European Demographic History*. Trans. T. Croft-Murray. Cambridge.

Lo Cascio, E. 1994. "The Size of the Roman Population: Beloch and the Meaning of the Augustan Census Figures." *JRS* 84:23–40.

MacDonald, W.L. 1982. *The Architecture of the Roman Empire*. Vol. 1. New Haven and London.

———. 1986. *The Architecture of the Roman Empire*. Vol. 2. New Haven and London.

MacMullen, R. 1980. "Roman Attitudes to Greek Love." *Historia* 31:484–502.

Marrou, H.I. 1982. *A History of Education in Antiquity*. Trans. George Lamb. Reprint, Madison.

McNeill, W.H. 1970. *Plagues and Peoples*. Garden City, N.J.

Meiggs, R. 1973. *Roman Ostia*. 2d ed. Oxford.

Morley, N. 1996. *Metropolis and Hinterland: The City of Rome and the Italian Economy, 200 B.C.–A.D. 200.* Cambridge.

Murray, O., and Tecusan, M., eds. 1995. *In Vino Veritas.* Rome.

Newell, C. 1988. *Methods and Models in Demography.* New York.

Parkin, T.G. 1992. *Demography and Roman Society.* Baltimore and London.

Perring, D. 1991. "Spatial Organisation and Social Change in Roman Towns." In J. Rich and A. Wallace-Hadrill, eds., *City and Country in the Ancient World,* 273–93. London.

Pomeroy, S.B. 1988. "Women in Roman Egypt." *Aufstieg und Niedergang der Römischen Welt* 2.10.1:708–23.

Price, S.R.F. 1987. "The Future of Dreams: From Freud to Artemidorus." *Past and Present* 28:9–31.

Rathbone, D. 1991. *Economic Rationalism and Rural Society in Third-Century A.D. Egypt.* Cambridge.

Rawson, B. 1986. "Children in the Roman Familia." In B. Rawson, ed., *The Family in Ancient Rome,* 170–200. London.

Richardson, L. 1992. *A New Topographical Dictionary of Ancient Rome.* Baltimore.

Richlin, A. 1992. *The Garden of Priapus.* Rev. ed. Oxford.

Riddle, J.M. 1992. *Contraception and Abortion from the Ancient World to the Renaissance.* Cambridge, Mass.

Rowlandson, J., ed. Forthcoming. *Women in Greek and Roman Society.* Cambridge.

Saller, R.P. 1987. "Men's Age at Marriage and Its Consequences in the Roman Family." *Classical Philology* 82:21–34.

———. 1991. "Roman Heirship Strategies in Principle and in Practice." In D.I. Kertzer and R.P. Saller, eds., *The Family in Italy from Antiquity to the Present,* 26–47. New Haven and London.

———. 1994. *Patriarchy, Property, and Death in the Roman Family.* Cambridge.

Salway, B. 1994. "What's in a Name? A Survey of Roman Onomastic Practice from c. 700 B.C. to A.D. 700." *JRS* 84:124–45.

Scheid, J. 1992. "The Religious Roles of Roman Women." In P. Schmitt Pantel, ed., *A History of Women,* vol. 1, *From Ancient Goddesses to Christian Saints,* 377–408. Cambridge.

Scobie, A. 1986. "Slums, Sanitation, and Mortality in the Roman World." *Klio* 68:399–433.

Sebesta, J.L., and Bonfante, L., eds. 1994. *The World of Roman Costume.* Madison.

Segal, E. 1968. *Roman Laughter: The Comedy of Plautus.* Cambridge, Mass.

Shaw, B.D. 1987. "The Age of Roman Girls at Marriage: Some Reconsiderations," *JRS* 77:30–46.

Slater, N.W. 1985. *Plautus in Performance: The Theatre of the Mind.* Princeton.

Stambaugh, J. 1988. *The Ancient Roman City.* Baltimore.

Syme, R. 1939. *The Roman Revolution.* Oxford.

Taylor, R. 1997. "Two Pathic Subcultures in Ancient Rome." *Journal of the History of Sexuality* 7:319–71.

Treggiari, S. 1991. *Roman Marriage:* Iusti Coniuges *from the Time of Cicero to the Time of Ulpian.* Oxford.

United Nations Development Programme. 1996. *Human Development Report, 1996.* New York and Oxford.
Veyne, Paul. 1987. "The Roman Empire." In Ph. Ariès and G. Duby, eds., *A History of Private Life,* vol. 1, *From Pagan Rome to Byzantium,* 6–233. Cambridge, Mass.
Wallace-Hadrill, A. 1994. *Houses and Society in Pompeii and Herculaneum.* Princeton.
Weaver, P.R.C. 1991. "Children of Freedmen (and Freedwomen)." In B. Rawson, ed., *Marriage, Divorce, and Children in Ancient Rome,* 166–90. Oxford.
Weiss, K.M. 1973. *Demographic Models for Anthropology.* Memoirs of the Society for American Archaeology 27. Menasha, Wisc.
White, J.L. 1986. *Light from Ancient Letters.* Philadelphia.
Wiedemann, T. 1989. *Adults and Children in the Roman Empire.* New Haven.
Wilkins, J., Harvey, D., and Dobson, M., eds. 1996. *Food in Antiquity.* Exeter.
Williams, C.A. 1995. "Greek Love at Rome." *CR* 45:517–39.
Winkler, J.J. 1990. *The Constraints of Desire.* New York and London.
Wrigley, E.A. 1987. *People, Cities, and Wealth.* Oxford and New York.

Chapter 4

Bauman, R.A. 1974. *Impietas in Principem: A Study of Treason against the Roman Emperor with Special Reference to the First Century A.D.* Munich.
Beard, M. 1990. "Priesthood in the Roman Republic." In M. Beard and J. North, eds., *Pagan Priests: Religion and Power in the Ancient World,* 19–48. Ithaca.
———. 1994. "Religion." In J.A. Crook, A. Lintott, and E. Rawson, eds. *The Cambridge Ancient History,* 2d ed., 729–68. Cambridge.
Bowersock, G.W. 1969. *Greek Sophists in the Roman Empire.* Oxford.
Fishwick, D. 1987. *The Imperial Cult in the Latin West.* Vol. 1. Leiden.
Gauthier, Ph. 1985. *Les cités grecques et leurs bienfaiteurs ive-ier siècle avant J.-C.* Paris.
Gordon, R. 1990. "The Veil of Power: Emperors, Sacrificers, and Benefactors." In M. Beard and J. North, eds., *Pagan Priests,* 201–31. Ithaca.
Habicht, C. 1970. *Gottmenschentum und griechische Stadte.* 2d ed. Munich.
———. 1985. *Pausanias' Guide to Ancient Greece.* Berkeley and Los Angeles.
Koskenniemi, E. 1994. *Apollonios von Tyana in der neutestementlichen Exegese.* Tübingen.
Liebeschuetz, J.H.W.G. 1979. *Continuity and Change in Roman Religion.* Oxford.
Linderski, J. 1982. "Cicero and Divination." *La Paraola del Passato* 202:12–38.
———. 1986. "The Augural Law." *Aufstieg und Niedergang der Römischen Welt* 2.16.3:2146–2312.
Mackie, J.L. 1981. *The Miracle of Theism.* Oxford.
Matthews, J.F. 1973. "Symmachus and the Oriental Cults." *JRS* 63:175–95.
Merkelbach, R. 1981. "Das Epigram auf Veleda." *ZPE* 43:241.
Nock, A.D. 1947. "The Emperor's Divine *Comes.*" *JRS* 37:102–16. = Z. Stewart, ed., *Essays on Religion in the Ancient World* (Oxford, 1972), 653–75.

North, J. 1989. "Religion in Republican Rome." In A.E. Astin and F. Walbank, ed., *The Cambridge Ancient History*, 2d ed., 7.2, 573–624. Cambridge.

Orr, D.G. 1986. "Roman Domestic Religion." *Aufstieg und Niedergang der Römischen Welt* 2.16.2:1557–91.

Potter, D.S. 1990. *Prophecy and History in the Crisis of the Roman Empire: A Historical Commentary on the Thirteenth Sibylline Oracle.* Oxford.

———. 1993. "Martyrdom as Spectacle." In R. Scodel, ed., *Theatre and Society in the Classical World*, 53–88. Ann Arbor.

———. 1994. *Prophets and Emperors: Human and Divine Authority from Augustus to Theodosius.* Cambridge, Mass.

Price, H.H. 1969. *Belief.* London.

Price, S.R.F. 1984. *Rituals and Power: The Roman Imperial Cult in Asia Minor.* Cambridge.

———. 1987. "From Noble Funerals to Divine Cult: The Consecration of Roman Emperors." In D. Cannadine and S.R.F. Price, *Rituals of Royalty: Power and Ceremonial in Traditional Societies.* Cambridge.

Rawson, E. 1978. "Caesar, Etruria, and the *Disciplina Etrusca.*" *JRS* 68:132–52. = *Roman Culture and Society: Collected Papers* (Oxford, 1991), 289–323.

Rives, J.B. 1995. *Religion and Authority in Roman Carthage from Augustus to Constantine.* Oxford.

Robert, J., and Robert, L. 1989. *Claros.* Vol. 1, *Décrets hellénistiques.* Fasc. 1. Paris.

Robert, L. 1980. *A travers l'Asie Mineure: Poètes et prosateurs, monnaies grecques, voyageurs et géographie.* Paris.

Rosenstein, N.S. 1990. *Imperatores Victi: Military Defeat and Aristocratic Competition in the Middle and Late Republic.* Berkeley and Los Angeles.

Salzman, R. 1990. *On Roman Time: The Codex Calendar of 354.* Berkeley and Los Angeles.

Scheid, J. 1985. *Religion et piété à Rome.* Paris.

———. 1990. *Romulus et ses frères: Le collège des frères Arvales, modèle du culte public dans la Rome des empereurs.* Rome.

Schilling, R. 1962. "A propos des *exta:* L'estispicine Étrusque et la *litatio* romaine." In *Hommages à A. Grenier*, 1371–78. Brussels. = *Rites, cultes dieux de Rome* (Paris, 1979), 183–90.

Scullard, H.H. 1981. *Festivals and Ceremonies of the Late Republic.* London.

Syme, R. 1986. *The Augustan Aristocracy.* Oxford.

Szemler, G.J. 1972. *The Priests of the Roman Republic: A Study of Interactions Between Priesthoods and Magistracies.* Brussels.

Taylor, L.R. 1971. *Party Politics in the Age of Caesar.* Berkeley and Los Angeles.

Torelli, M. 1975. *Elogia Tarquiniensia.* Florence.

Van der Meer, L.B. 1987. *The Bronze Liver of Piacenza: Analysis of a Polytheistic Structure.* Amsterdam.

Walbank, F.W. 1972. *Polybius.* Berkeley and Los Angeles.

Watson, A. 1993. *International Law in Archaic Rome: War and Religion.* Baltimore.

Wiseman, T.P. 1992. "Lucretius, Catiline, and the Survival of Prophecy." *Ostraka* 1, no. 2:7–18.

———. 1995. "The God of the Lupercal." *JRS* 85:1–22.
Wissowa, G. 1912. *Religion und Kultus der Römer.* 2d ed. Munich.

Chapter 5

Allbaugh, L.G. 1953. *Crete: A Case Study of an Underdeveloped Area.* Princeton.
Amouretti, M.-C. 1986. *Le pain et l'huile dans la Grèce antique.* Paris.
Balsdon, J.P.V.D. 1969. "Panem et Circenses." In J. Bibauw *Homages a Marcel Renard II,* 2:57–60. Brussels.
Basile, B. 1988. "A Roman Wreck with a Cargo of Marble in the Bay of Giardini Naxos (Sicily)." *JNA* 17, no. 2:133–42
Bertrandy, F. 1987. "Remarques sur le Commerce des bêtes sauvages entre l'Afrique du Nord et l'Italie." *MEFRA* 99:211–41.
Blasquez-Martinez, J.M., and Remesal Rodriguez, J. 1980. *Produccion y Comercio del Aceite en la Antigüedad.* Vol. 1. Madrid.
———. 1983. *Produccion y Comercio del Aceite en la Antigüedad.* Vol. 2. Madrid.
Bloch, H. 1953. "Ostia: Iscrizioni rinvenute tra il 1930 e il 1939." *Notizie degli Scavi di Antichita* 7:239–306.
Braund, D. 1985. *Augustus to Nero: A Sourcebook.* London.
Brunt, P.A. 1980. "Free Labor and Public Works at Rome." *JRS* 70:81–100.
Carandini, A., Ricci, A., and de Vos, M. 1982. *Filosofiana, la villa de Piazza Armerina, Imagine di un Aristocratico Romano al Tempo di Constantino.* Palermo.
Carcopino, J. 1941. *Daily Life in Ancient Rome.* Trans. E.O. Lorimer. London.
Casson, L. 1965. "Harbor and River Boats of Ancient Rome." *JRS* 55:31–39.
———. 1971. *Ships and Seamanship in the Ancient World.* Princeton.
———. 1978. "Unemployment, the Building Trade, and Suetonius, *Vesp.* 18." *BASP* 15:43–51.
———. 1980. "The Role of the State in Rome's Grain Trade." *MAAR* 36:21–33.
Castagnoli, F. 1980. "Installazioni Portuali a Roma." *MAAR* 36:35–42.
Chevallier, R. 1976. *Roman Roads.* London.
Colls, D., et al. 1977. "L'Epave Port Vendres II." *Archaeonautica* 1.
Corcoran, T.H. 1963. "Roman Fish Sauces." *Classical Journal* 58:204–10.
Cozzo, G. 1970. *Ingegneria Romano.* Rome.
Curtis, R.I. 1991. "Salt Food Products around the Strait of Gibralter." *JRA* 4:299–305.
D'Arms, J. 1970. *Romans on the Bay of Naples.* Cambridge, Mass.
———. 1981. *Commerce and Social Standing in Ancient Rome.* Cambridge, Mass.
d'Escurac, H.P. 1976. *La Préfecture de l'annone Service administratif imperial d'Auguste à Constantin.* Paris.
———. 1977. "Aristocratie senatoriale et profits commerciaux." *Ktema* 2:339–55.
Dodge, H. 1988. "Decorative Stones for Architecture in the Roman Empire." *Oxford Journal of Archaeology* 7, no. 1:65–80.
Duncan-Jones, R.R. 1982. *The Economy of the Roman Empire: Quantitative Studies.* 2d ed. Cambridge.
———. 1990. *Structure and Scale in the Roman Economy.* Cambridge.

Evans, J.K. 1981. "Wheat Production and Its Social Consequences in the Roman World." *Classical Quarterly* 31:428–42.

Finley, M.I. 1985. *The Ancient Economy.* Rev. ed. London.

Foxhall, L., and Forbes, H.A. 1982. " *Sitometreia:* The Role of Grain as a Staple Food in Classical Antiquity." *Chiron* 12:41–90.

Frank, T. 1940. *An Economic Survey of Ancient Rome.* Vol. 5. Paterson, N.J.

Frederiksen, M. 1984. *Campania.* Ed. N. Purcell. London.

Garnsey, P. 1983. "Grain for Rome." In P. Garnsey, K. Hopkins, and C.R. Whittaker, eds., *Trade in the Ancient Economy,* 118–30. London.

———. 1988. *Famine and Food Supply in the Graeco-Roman World.* Cambridge.

Garnsey, P., and Rathbone, D. 1985. "The Background to the Grain Law of Gaius Gracchus." *JRS* 75:20–25.

Garnsey, P., Gallant, T., and Rathbone, D. 1986. "Thessaly and the Grain Supply of Rome during the Second Century B.C." *JRS* 76:30–44.

Greene, K. 1986. The *Archaeology of the Roman Economy.* London.

Hopkins, K. 1978. *Conquerors and Slaves.* Cambridge.

———. 1983a. *Death and Renewal.* Cambridge.

———. 1983b. "Models, Ships, and Staples." In P. Garnsey, K. Hopkins, and C.R. Whittaker, eds., *Trade in the Ancient Economy,* 84–109. London.

Jennisson, G. 1937. *Animals for Show and Pleasure in Ancient Rome.* Manchester.

Jones, A.H.M. 1964. *The Later Roman Empire.* Oxford.

Le Gall, J. 1953. *Le Tibre: Fleuve de Rome dans l'antiquité.* Paris.

MacDonald, W.A., and Rapp, G.R., eds. 1972. *The Minnesota Messenia Expedition.* Minneapolis.

MacMullen, R. 1974. *Roman Social Relations, 50 B.C.–A.D. 284.* New Haven.

Mattingly, D.J. 1988a. "Oil for Export? A Comparison of Libyan, Spanish, and Tunisian Olive Oil Production in the Roman Empire." *JRA* 1:33–56.

———. 1988b. "Olea Mediterranea?" *JRA* 1:153–61.

———. 1988c. "The Olive Boom: Oil Surpluses, Wealth, and Power in Roman Tripolitania." *Libyan Studies* 19:21–41.

———. 1996. "First Fruit? The Olive in the Roman World." In G. Shipley and J. Salmon, eds., *Human Landscape in the Ancient World,* 213–53. London.

Meiggs, R. 1973. *Roman Ostia.* Oxford.

———. 1982. *Trees and Timber in the Ancient Mediterranean World.* Oxford.

Moritz, L. 1958. *Grain Mills and Flour in Classical Antiquity.* Oxford.

Panella, C. 1983. "I contenitori oleari presentati ad Ostia in età antonina: Analisi tipologica, epigraphica, quantitativa." In J.M. Blasquez-Martinez and J. Remesal Rodriguez, eds., *Produccion y Comercio del Aciete en la Antigüedad,* 2:225–61. Madrid.

———. 1985. "I commerci di Roma e di Ostia in età Imperiale (Secoli I–III): Le derrate alimentari." In *Misurare la Terra,* 180–88. Modena.

Parker, A.J. 1984. "Shipwrecks and Ancient Trade in the Mediterranean." *Archaeological Review from Cambridge* 3, no. 2:99–113.

———. 1992. *Ancient Shipwrecks of the Mediterranean and Roman Provinces.* BAR International Series 580. Oxford.

Peacock, D.P.S., and Williams, D.F. 1986. *Amphorae and the Roman Economy.* London.

Pensabene, P. 1978. "A Cargo of Marble Shipwrecked at Punta Scifo near Crotone (Italy)." *JNA* 7, no. 2:105–18.

Pflaum, H.-G. 1960–61. *Les carrières procuratoriennes équestres sous le haut-empire romain.* 3 vols. Paris.

———. 1982. *Les carrières procuratoriennes équestres sous le haut-empire romain. Supplément. Paris.*

Ponsich, M. 1988. *Aceite de Oliva y Salazones de Pescado: Factores Geo-Economicos de Betica y Tingitania.* Madrid.

Remesal Rodriguez, J. 1986. *La annona militaris y la exportacion de aceite Betico a Germania.* Madrid.

Rickman, G. 1971. *Roman Granaries and Store Buildings.* Oxford.

———. 1980. *The Corn Supply of Ancient Rome.* Oxford.

Rodriguez-Almeida, E. 1980. "El Monte Testaccio, Hoy: Nuevos Testimonios Epigraphicos." In J.M. Blasquez Martinez and J. Remesal Rodriguez, eds., *Produccion y Comercio del Aceite en la Antigüedad,* 1:57–103. Madrid.

———. 1984. *Il Monte Testaccio: Ambiente, Storia, Materiali.* Rome.

Rossiter, J. 1981. "Wine and Oil Processing at Roman Farms in Italy." *Phoenix* 35:345–61.

Rouge, J. 1981. *Ships and Fleets of the Ancient Mediterranean.* Middletown.

Scobie, A. 1986. "Slums, Sanitation, and Mortality in the Roman World." *Klio* 68:399–433.

Sirks, B. 1991. *Food for Rome: The Legal Structure of the Transportation and Processing of Supplies for Rome and Constantinople.* Amsterdam.

Spurr, M.S. 1986. *Arable Cultivation in Roman Italy.* London.

Tchernia, A. 1980. "D. Caecilius Hospitalis et M. Iulius Hermesianus." In J.M. Blasquez Martinez and J. Remesal Rodriguez, eds., *Produccion y Comercio del Aceite en la Antigüedad,* 1:155–61. Madrid.

———. 1986. *Le Vin de l'Italie Romaine.* Rome.

Van Berchem, D. 1939. *Les distributions de blé et d'argent à la plèbe romaine sous l'Empire.* Geneva.

Veyne, P. 1990. *Bread and Circuses: Historical Sociology and Political Pluralism.* Trans. B. Pearce. London.

Virlouvet, C. 1985. *Famines et Emeutes a Rome des Origines de la Republique a la Mort de Neron.* Rome.

Ward-Perkins, J.B. 1971. "Quarrying in Antiquity: Technology, Tradition, and Social Change." *PBA* 57:3–24.

———. 1980. "The Marble Trade and Its Organization: Evidence from Nicomedia." *MAAR* 36:325–38.

White, K.D. 1970. *Roman Farming.* London.

Whittaker, C.R. 1985. "Trade and the Aristocracy in the Roman Empire." *Opus* 4:49–75.

Yavetz, Z. 1962. "The Policy of C. Flaminius and the Plebiscitum Claudianum." *Athenaeum* 40:325–44.

———. 1988. *Plebs and Princeps.* 2d ed. Oxford.

Chapters 6 and 7

Akurgal, E. 1993. *Ancient Civilizations and Ruins of Turkey.* 8th ed. Istanbul.
Barnes, T.D. 1996. "Christians and the Theater." In W.J. Slater, ed., *Roman Theater and Society,* 161–80. Ann Arbor.
Barton, C. 1993. *The Sorrows of the Ancient Romans: The Gladiator and the Monster.* Princeton.
Bernard, P. 1976. "Campagne de fouilles 1975 à Aï Khanum (Afghanistan)." *CRAI,* 287–322.
Bieber, M. 1961. *The History of the Greek and Roman Theatre.* London.
Blümner, H. 1918. *Fahrendes Volk im Alterum. Sitzungsberichte der Königlich Bayerischen Akademie der Wissenschaften: Philosophisch-philologische und historische Klasse* 6. Munich.
Boethius, A. 1978. *Etruscan and Early Roman Architecture.* 2d ed. Harmondsworth.
Brodribb, G. 1987. *Roman Brick and Tile.* Gloucester.
Browning, I. 1982. *Jerash and the Decapolis.* London.
Buonocore, M. 1992. *Epigrafia anfiteatreale dell' occidente romano.* Vol. 3. Rome.
Cameron, A. 1973. *Porphyrius the Charioteer.* Oxford.
———. 1976. *Circus Factions: Blues and Greens at Rome and Byzantium.* Oxford.
Camp, J. 1986. *The Athenian Agora.* London.
Caputo, G. 1987. *Il Teatro Augusteo di Leptis Magna: Scavo e Restauro (1937–1951).* Rome.
Carettoni, G. 1956–58. "Le gallerie ipogée del Foro Romano e i ludi gladiatori forensi." *Bollettino Communale* 76:23–44.
Cavalieri Manasse, G., Massari, G., and Rossinari, M.P. 1992 *Piemonte, Valdaosta, Liguria, Lombardia.* Guide archeologiche Laterza. Rome.
Coarelli, F. 1976. *Guida archeologica di Pompeii.* Rome.
———. 1987. *I Santuari del Lazio in éta repubblicana.* Rome.
Coleman, K.M. 1990. "Fatal Charades: Roman Executions Staged as Mythological Enactments." *JRS* 80:44–73.
———. 1993. "Launching into History: Aquatic Displays in the Early Empire." *JRS* 83:48–74.
———. 1996. "Ptolemy Philadelphus and the Roman Amphitheater." In W.J. Slater, ed., *Roman Theater and Society,* 49–68. Ann Arbor.
Conforto, M.L., et al. 1988. *Anfiteatro Flavio: Immagine, testimonianze, spettacoli.* Rome.
Connolly, P., and Dodge, H., 1998. *The Ancient City.* Oxford.
Cornell, T.J. 1995. *The Beginnings of Rome: Italy and Rome from the Bronze Age to the Punic Wars (c. 1000–264 B.C.).* London.
Cozzo, G. 1971. *The Colosseum, the Flavian Amphitheatre.* Rome.
Crowther, N.B. 1983. "Greek Games in Republican Rome." *AntCl* 52:268–73.
Csapo, E., and Slater, W. 1995. *The Context of Ancient Drama.* Ann Arbor.
De Bernardi-Ferrero, D. 1966–74. *Teatri classici in Asia Minore.* 4 vols. Rome.
De Caro, S., and Greco, A. 1981. *Campania* Guide archeologiche Laterza, Rome.
Delaine, J. 1988. "Recent Research on Roman Baths." *JRA* 1:11–32.

———. 1989. "Some Suggestions on the Transition from Greek to Roman Baths in Hellenistic Italy." *Mediterranean Archaeology* 2:111–25.

———. 1997. *The Baths of Caracalla. A Study in the Design, Construction and Economics of Large-Scale Building Projects in Imperial Rome. JRA* Suppl. 25. Portsmouth, R.I.

Demougin, S. 1988. *L'ordre équestre sous les Julio-Claudiens.* Rome.

Drinkwater, J. 1983. *Roman Gaul.* London.

Duncan-Jones, R. 1982. *The Economy of the Roman Empire.* 2d ed. Cambridge.

Dupont, F. 1993. "Ludions, *Lydioi:* Les danseurs de la *pompa circensis.*" In J.P. Thuillier, ed., *Spectacles sportifs et scéniques dans le monde étrusco-italique,* 206–8. Rome.

Edmondson, J.C. 1996. "Dynamic Arenas: Gladiatorial Presentations in the City of Rome and the Construction of Roman Society during the Early Empire." In W.J. Slater, ed., *Roman Theatre and Society,* 69–112. Ann Arbor.

Erim, K.T. 1986. *Aphrodisias.* London.

Frézouls, E. 1990. "Les monuments des spectacles dans la ville: Théâtre et amphithéâtre." In Cl. Domergue, Chr. Landes, and J.-M. Pailler, eds., *Spectacula,* vol. 1, *Gladiateurs et Amphithéâtres,* 77–92. Lattes.

Friedländer, L. 1908–13. *Roman Life and Manners under the Early Empire.* Trans. J.H. Freese, A.B. Gough, and L.A. Magnus. 4 vols. New York.

Fulford, M. 1989. *The Silchester Amphitheatre Excavations of 1979–85.* London.

Gauthier, Ph., and Hatzopoulos, M.B. 1993. *La loi gymnasiarchique de Beroia.* Athens.

Ginestet, P. 1991. *Les organisations de la jeunesse dans l'occident Romain.* Brussels.

Ginouvès, R. 1962. *Balaneutikè: Recherches sur le bain dans l'antiquité grecque.* Paris.

Goldsworthy, A. 1996. *The Roman Army at War, 100 B.C.–A.D. 200.* Oxford.

Golvin, J.C. 1988. *L'amphithéâtre romain: Essai sur la théorisation de sa forme et de ses fonctions.* Paris.

Golvin, J.C., and Landes, C. 1990. *Amphithéâtres et Gladiateurs.* Paris.

Golvin, J.-C., and Reddé, M. 1990. "Naumachies, jeux nautiques et amphithéâtres." In Cl. Domergue, Chr. Landes, and J.-M. Pailler, eds., *Spectacula,* vol. 1, *Gladiateurs et Amphithéâtres,* 165–77. Lattes.

Gregori, G.L. 1989. *Epigrafia anfiteatreale dell' occidente romano.* Vol. 2. Rome.

Grenier, A. 1958. *Manuel d'archéologie gallo-romaine.* Vol. 3. Paris.

Hammond, N.G.L. 1982. "The Peloponnese." In Boardman, J., and Hammond, N.G.L., *The Cambridge Ancient History* 3.3, Cambridge. 321–59.

Hanson, J.A. 1959. *Roman Theatre-Temples.* Princeton.

Haspels, C.H.E. 1971. *The Highlands of Phrygia: Sites and Monuments.* Princeton.

Holum, K.G., et al. 1988. *King Herod's Dream Caesarea on the Sea.* New York.

Hopkins, K. 1983. "Murderous Games." In *Death and Renewal: Sociological Studies in Roman History,* 2:1–30. Cambridge.

Hornum, M. 1993. *Nemesis, the Roman State, and the Games.* Leiden.

Humphrey, J.H. 1986. *Roman Circuses: Arenas for Chariot Racing.* Berkeley and Los Angeles.

———. 1988. "Roman Games." In M. Grant and R. Kitzinger, eds., *Civilization of the Ancient Mediterranean,* 2:1153–65. New York.

Humphrey, J.H., Sear, F.B., and Vickers, M. 1972–73. "Aspects of the Circus at Lepcis Magna." *Libya Antiqua* 9–10:25–97.

Jones, C.P. 1990. Review of *Stadt und Fest in Kaiserzeitlichen Kleinasien,* by M. Wörrle. *JRA* 3:484–88.

———. 1991. "Dinner Theater." In W.J. Slater, ed., *Dining in a Classical Context,* 185–98. Ann Arbor.

———. 1994. Review of *Performers and Partisans at Aphrodisias,* by Ch. Rouché. *JRS* 84:285–86.

Jory, E.J. 1970. "Associations of Actors in Rome." *Hermes* 98:224–53.

———. 1995. "*Ars Ludicra* and the *Ludus Talarius.*" In A. Griffiths, ed., *Stage Directions: Essays in Honour of E.W. Handley,* BICS supp. 66, 139–52. London.

———. 1996. "The Drama of Dance: Prolegomena to an Iconography of Imperial Pantomime." In W.J. Slater, ed., *Roman Theater and Society,* 1–27. Ann Arbor.

Keay, S., 1988. *Roman Spain,* London.

Keil, J. 1964. *Führer durch Ephesos.* 5th ed. Vienna.

Kraeling, C.H. 1962. *Ptolemais: City of the Libyan Pentapolis.* University of Chicago Oriental Institute Publications 90. Chicago.

Krauss, F. 1973. *Das Theater von Milet.* Berlin.

Lachaux., J.-Cl. 1979. *Théâtres et Amphithéâtres d'Afrique Proconsulaire.* Aix-en-Provence.

Lawrence, A.W. 1983. *Greek Architecture.* 2d ed. London.

Lebek, W.D. 1996. "Moneymaking on the Roman Stage." In W.J. Slater, ed., *Roman Theater and Society,* 29–48. Ann Arbor.

Leppin, H. 1992. *Histrionen.* Bonn.

Lewis, N. 1983. *Life in Egypt under Roman Rule.* Oxford.

Lézine, A. 1969. *Les thermes d'Antonin à Carthage.* Tunis.

Magie, D. 1950. *Roman Rule in Asia Minor.* Princeton.

Massa-Pairault, F.-H. 1993. "Aspects idéologiques des *Ludi.*" In J.P. Thuillier, ed., *Spectacles sportifs et scéniques dans le monde étrusco-italique,* 248–79. Rome.

Maxfield, V. 1981. *The Roman Military Decorations of the Roman Army.* London.

McDonnell, M. 1991. "The Introduction of Athletic Nudity: Thucydides, Plato, and the Vases." *JHS* 101:182–92.

———. 1993. "Athletic Nudity among the Greeks and Etruscans: The Evidence of the 'Perizoma Vases.'" In J.P. Thuillier, ed., *Spectacles sportifs et scéniques dans le monde étrusco-italique,* 395–407. Rome.

Meiggs, R. 1973. *Roman Ostia.* 2d ed. Oxford.

Millar, F.G. 1992. The Emperor in the Roman World. Rev. ed. London.

———. 1993. "Ovid and the *Domus Augusta:* Rome seen from Tomoi." *JRS* 83:1–17.

Mitchell, S. 1993. *Anatolia: Land, Men, and Gods in Asia Minor.* 2 vols. Oxford.

Mitens, K. 1988. *Teatri greci e teatri inspirati all'architettura greca in Sicilia e nell'Italia meridionale. AnalRom* supp. 13. Rome.

———. 1993. "Theatre architecture in Central Italy: Reception and Resistance."

In P.G. Bilde, I. Nielsen, and M. Nielsen, eds., *Aspects of Hellenism in Italy*, Acta Hyperborea 5, 91–106. Copenhagen.

Moretti, J.C. 1992. "L'adaptation des théâtres de Gréce aux spectacles impèriaux." In C. Landes and V. Kramerérovskis, eds., *Spectacula*, vol. 2, *Le théâtre antique et ses spectacles*, 179–86. Lattes.

Moretti, L. 1953. *Iscrizioni agonistiche greche.* Rome.

Nielsen, I. 1990. *Thermae et Balnea.* Århus.

Nippel, W. 1995. *Public Order in Ancient Rome.* Cambridge.

Oliver, J.H., and Palmer, R.E.A. 1955. "Minutes of an Act of the Roman Senate." *Hesperia* 24:320–49.

Olivova, V. 1984. *Sports and Games in the Ancient World.* London.

Palmer, R.E.A. 1997. *Rome and Carthage at Peace.* Historia Einzelschriften 113. Stuttgart.

Pflaum, H.-G. 1950. *Les procurateurs équestres sous le haut-empire romain.* Paris.

Picard, G. Ch. 1976. "La date du théâtre du Cherchel." *CRAI* 386–97.

Pickard-Cambridge, A.W. 1946. *The Theatre of Dionysos in Athens.* Oxford.

———. 1988. *The Dramatic Festivals of Athens.* Rev. ed. Oxford.

Plass, P. 1995. *The Game of Death in Ancient Rome.* Madison.

Pleket, H.W. 1973. "Some Aspects of the History of the Athletic Guilds." *ZPE* 10:197–227.

Plommer, H. 1983. "Scythopolis, Caesarea, and Vitruvius: Sounding Vessels in Ancient Theatres." *Levant* 15:132–40.

Poliakoff, M. 1987. *Combat Sports in the Ancient World: Competition, Violence, and Culture.* New Haven.

Potter, D.S. 1990. *Prophecy and History in the Crisis of the Roman Empire: A Historical Commentary on the Thirteenth Sibylline Oracle.* Oxford.

———. 1993. "Martyrdom as Spectacle." In R. Scodel, ed., *Theatre and Society in the Classical World*, 53–88. Ann Arbor.

———. 1994. Review of *Emperors and Gladiators*, by T. Weidemann. *JRS* 84:229–31.

Rawson, E. 1981. "Chariot-Racing in the Roman Republic." *PBSR* 49:1–16. = *Roman Culture and Society: Collected Papers* (Oxford, 1991), 389–407.

———. 1985. "Theatrical Life in Republican Rome and Italy." PBSR 53:97–113. = *Roman Culture and Society: Collected Papers* (Oxford, 1991), 468–87.

———. 1987. "*Discrimina Ordinum:* The *Lex Iulia Theatralis.*" *PBSR* 55:83–114. = *Roman Culture and Society: Collected Papers* (Oxford, 1991), 508–45.

Rea, R. 1988. "Le antiche raffigurazioni dell'anfiteatro." In M.L. Conforto et al., eds., *Anfiteatro Flavio: Immagine, testimonianze, spettacoli*, 23–46. Rome.

Robert, J., and Robert, L. 1989. *Claros.* Vol. 1, Décrets *hellénistiques.* Fasc. 1 Paris.

Robert, L. 1930. "Pantomimen im griechischen Orient." *Hermes* 65:106–22. = *Opera Minora Selecta*, vol. 1 (Amsterdam, 1969), 654–70.

———. 1935. "Sur des inscriptions de Chios," *BCH* 59:453–70. = *Opera Minora Selecta*, vol. 1 (Amsterdam, 1969), 512–29.

———. 1936. "ΑΡΧΑΙΟΛΟΓΟΣ." *REG* 49:235–54. = *Opera Minora Selecta*, vol. 1 (Amsterdam, 1969), 671–90.

———. 1940. *Les gladiateurs dans l'orient grec.* Paris.

———. 1966a. "Deux inscriptions agonistiques de Rhodes." *AE* 108–18.
———. 1966b. *Documents de l'Asie Mineure méridionale.* Paris.
———. 1967. "Sur les inscriptions d'Éphèse: Fêtes, athlètes, empereurs, épigrammes." *Rev. Phil.* 41:7–84. = *Opera Minora Selecta,* vol. 5 (Amsterdam, 1989), 347–424.
———. 1970. "Deux concours grecs à Rome." *CRAI,* 6–27. = *Opera Minora Selecta,* vol. 5 (Amsterdam, 1989), 647–68.
———. 1978. "Catalogue agonistique des Romaia de Xanthos." *Rev. Arch.,* 277–90. = *Opera Minora Selecta,* vol. 7 (Amsterdam, 1990), 681–94.
———. 1980. *A travers l'Asie Mineure: Poètes et prosateurs, monnaies grecques, voyageurs et géographie.* Paris.
Rogers, G. 1991. "Demosthenes of Oenoanda and the Models of Euergetism." *JRS* 81:91–100.
Roueché, Ch. 1993. *Performers and Partisans at Aphrodisias in the Roman and Late Roman Periods.* London.
Sabbatini Tumolesi, P. 1988. *Epigrafia anfiteatreale dell' occidente romano.* Vol. 1. Rome.
Scnurr, C. 1992. "The *lex Julia theatralis* of Augustus." *Liverpool Classical Monthly* 17, no. 10:155–60.
Scullard, H.H. 1981. *Festivals and Ceremonies of the Late Republic.* London.
Skutsch, O. 1985. *The Annals of Quintus Ennius.* Oxford.
Sear, F.B. 1990. "The Theatre at Leptis Magna and the Development of Roman Theatre Design." *JRA* 3:376–83.
———. 1993. "The *Scaenae Frons* of the Theater of Pompey." *AJA* 97:687–701.
Shoe, L.T. 1936. *Profiles of Greek Mouldings.* Cambridge, Mass.
Spawforth, A.J., and Walker, S. 1985. "The World of the Panhellenion." Part 1, "Athens and Eleusis." *JRS* 85:78–104.
———. 1986. "The World of the Panhellenion." Part 2, "Three Dorian Cities." *JRS* 86:88–105.
Stambaugh, John. 1988. *The Ancient Roman City.* Baltimore.
Ste. Croix, G.E.M. de. 1981. *The Class Struggle in the Ancient Greek World.* London.
Swaddling, J. 1980. *The Ancient Olympic Games.* London.
Thomas, J.D. 1976. "Notification of a Victory at the Games." In H.E. Hanson ed., *Collectanea Papyrologica: Texts Published in Honor of H.C. Youtie,* 2:471–83. Bonn.
Thuillier, J.P. 1985. *Les jeux athletiques dans la civilization étrusque.* Rome.
———. 1993. "Les representations sportives dans l'oevre du peintre de Micali." In J.P. Thuillier, ed., *Spectacles sportifs et scéniques dans le monde étrusco-italique,* 21–44. Rome.
Traversari, G. 1960. *Gli spettacoli in Aqua nel Teatro tardo-antico.* Rome.
Travlos, J. 1971. *A Pictorial Dictionary of Ancient Athens.* London.
Vann, R.L. 1989. *The Unexcavated Buildings of Sardis.* Oxford.
Ville, G. 1960. "Les jeaux de gladiateurs dans l'empire chrétien." *MEFRA* 72:273–335.
———. 1981. *La gladiature en occident des origenes à la mort de Domitien.* Rome.

Ward-Perkins, J.B. 1981. *Roman Imperial Architecture.* Harmondsworth.
Ward-Perkins, J.B., and Toynbee, J.M.C. 1949. "The Hunting Baths in Lepcis Magna." *Archaeologia* 93:165–95.
Welch, K. 1991. "Roman Amphitheatres Revived." *JRA* 4:272–81.
———. 1994. "The Roman Arena in Late-Republican Italy: A New Interpretation." *JRA* 7:59–80.
Wensch-Klein, G. 1990. *Liberalitas in rem publicam.* Bonn.
Wiedemann, T. 1992. *Emperors and Gladiators.* London.
Wightman, E. 1970. *Roman Trier and the Treveri.* London.
Williams II, C.K., and Russell, P. 1981. "Corinth: Excavations of 1980." *Hesperia* 50:1–44.
Wilson, R.J. 1990. *Sicily under the Roman Empire.* Warminster.
Wiseman, T.P. 1976. "Two Questions on the Circus Flaminius." *PBSR* 44:44–47. = *Roman Studies: Literary and Historical* (Liverpool, 1987), 157–60.
———. 1995. *Remus: A Roman Myth.* Cambridge.
Wörrle, M. 1988. *Stadt und Fest in Kaiserzeitlichen Kleinasien.* Munich.
Yegül, F. 1979. "The Small City Bath in Classical Antiquity and a Reconstruction Study of Lucian's Bath of Hippias." *ArchCl* 31:108–31.
———. 1986. *The Bath-Gymnasium Complex at Sardis.* Archaeological Exploration of Sardis Report 3. Cambridge, Mass.
———. 1992. *Baths and Bathing in Classical Antiquity.* New York.

Index